TRENDS IN BANKING STRUCTURE AND REGULATION IN OECD COUNTRIES

COMPETITION IN BANKING

BY

G. BRÖKER

ORGANISATION FOR ECONOMIC CO-OPERATION AND DEVELOPMENT

Pursuant to article 1 of the Convention signed in Paris on 14th December 1960, and which came into force on 30th September 1961, the Organisation for Economic Co-operation and Development (OECD) shall promote policies designed:

- to achieve the highest sustainable economic growth and employment and a rising standard of living in Member countries, while maintaining financial stability, and thus to contribute to the development of the world economy;
- to contribute to sound economic expansion in Member as well as non-member countries in the process of economic development; and
- to contribute to the expansion of world trade on a multilateral, non-discriminatory basis in accordance with international obligations.

The original Member countries of the OECD are Austria, Belgium, Canada, Denmark, France, the Federal Republic of Germany, Greece, Iceland, Ireland, Italy, Luxembourg, the Netherlands, Norway, Portugal, Spain, Sweden, Switzerland, Turkey, the United Kingdom and the United States. The following countries became Members subsequently through accession at the dates indicated hereafter: Japan (28th April 1964), Finland (28th January 1969), Australia (7th June 1971) and New Zealand (29th May 1973).

The Socialist Federal Republic of Yugoslavia takes part in some of the work of the OECD (agreement of 28th October 1961).

Publié en français sous le titre :

LA CONCURRENCE
DANS LE SECTEUR BANCAIRE

The business of banking has been, and is still, going through a period of rapid and profound changes, of which the major ingredients are the development of new technological capabilities for processing and transmitting data, the growing interdependence of economies and interpenetration of financial markets, and the breaking down of barriers between financial institutions previously engaged in different lines of business. Against this background, changes in banking legislation and regulation have sometimes encouraged these trends and sometimes adapted to them.

In order to shed more light on these developments and their implications for policy, the Committee on Financial Markets decided to carry out an extensive enquiry into banking structures and regulations in OECD countries. An objective is to identify and assess the most significant changes that have taken place in recent years seen from the angle of the interaction between market forces, on the one hand, and official regulation, on the other.

The enquiry covers six areas, viz:

— The internationalisation of banking;
— Banking and electronic fund transfers;
— Banking and monetary policy;
— Prudential supervision in banking;
— Asset and liability management;
— Competition in banking.

A special group of government and central bank experts, under the chairmanship of Mr. D.K.R. Klein, Bundesbankdirektor at the Deutsche Bundesbank, Federal Republic of Germany, has been set up by the Committee on Financial Markets to carry out the study.

The report on competition in banking has been prepared by Mr. G. Bröker, Head of the Financial Markets Division of the OECD, with the active assistance of national experts[1]. The opinions and views expressed in the report are those of the author and do not necessarily represent the views of the Committee on Financial Markets or of the national experts who have assisted in its preparation. The report is published under the responsibility of the Secretary–General.

1. A list of members of the Expert Group on Banking is found on page 8.

Also available

« Trends in Banking Structure & Regulation in OECD Countries » Series

PRUDENTIAL SUPERVISION IN BANKING by R.M. Pecchioli (May 1987)
(21 87 03 1) ISBN 92-64-12916-2 298 pages   £13.00   US$26.00   F130.00   DM58.00

TRENDS IN BANKING IN OECD COUNTRIES. Committee on Financial Markets – Expert Group on Banking (October 1985)
(21 85 04 1) ISBN 92-64-12762-3 72 pages   £60.00   US$12.00   F60.00   DM27.00

BANKING AND MONETARY POLICY by T.R.G. Bingham (July 1985)
(21 85 03 1) ISBN 92-64-12693-7 254 pages   £13.50   US$27.00   F135.00   DM60.00

BANKING AND ELECTRONIC FUND TRANSFERS by Professor J.R.S. Revell (November 1983)
(21 83 05 1) ISBN 92-64-12505-1 202 pages   £11.00   US$22.00   F110.00   DM49.00

THE INTERNATIONALISATION OF BANKING. The Policy Issues by R.M. Pecchioli (November 1983)
(21 83 04 1) ISBN 92-64-12488-8 222 pages   £11.00   US$22.00   F110.00   DM49.00

* * *

INTERNATIONAL TRADE IN SERVICES: BANKING. Identification and Analysis of Obstacles (August 1984)
(21 84 03 1) ISBN 92-64-12586-8 86 pages   £6.00   US$12.00   F60.00   DM27.00

INTERNATIONAL TRADE IN SERVICES: INSURANCE. Identification and Analysis of Obstacles (February 1984)
(21 84 01 1) ISBN 92-64-12552-3 78 pages   £5.00   US$10.00   F50.00   DM25.00

COSTS AND MARGINS IN BANKING: STATISTICAL SUPPLEMENT 1978-1982 by Professor J.R.S. Revell, Director of the Institute of European Finance, University College of North Wales, Bangor (February 1985) bilingual
(21 85 02 3) ISBN 92-64-02667-3 112 pages   £12.50   US$25.00   F125.00   DM55.00

COSTS AND MARGINS IN BANKING. An International Survey by Professor J.R.S. Revell (December 1980)
(21 80 03 1) ISBN 92-64-12064-5 318 pages   £10.80   US$24.50   F98.00   DM49.00

GOVERNMENT DEBT MANAGEMENT:

Volume 1. Objectives and Techniques (March 1982)
(21 82 05 1) ISBN 92-64-12299-0 60 pages   £2.90   US$6.50   F29.00   DM15.00

Volume 2. Debt Instruments and Selling Techniques (May 1983)
(21 83 03 1) ISBN 92-64-12447-0 134 pages   £8.50   US$17.00   F85.00   DM38.00

Prices charged at the OECD Bookshop.

*THE OECD CATALOGUE OF PUBLICATIONS and supplements will be sent free of charge
on request addressed either to OECD Publications Service,
2, rue André-Pascal, 75775 PARIS CEDEX 16, or to the OECD Distributor in your country.*

TABLE OF CONTENTS

Annex I

CONCEPTS AND DEFINITIONS

Annex II

STATISTICAL TABLES ON GROWTH OF FINANCIAL INSTITUTIONS AND MARKETS AND STRUCTURAL CHANGES IN FINANCIAL SYSTEMS

Annex III

DOCUMENTATION ON MEASURES AFFECTING COMPETITION IN BANKING AND ON DIVERSIFICATION OF FINANCIAL SERVICE ACTIVITIES

Annex IV

THE APPLICATION OF COMPETITION LAWS AND POLICIES TO THE BANKING SECTOR

Annex V

CONFLICTS OF INTEREST IN BANKING AND FINANCE AND THEIR CONTROL AND MANAGEMENT

Annex VI

LIST OF TABLES

LIST OF CHARTS

MEMBERS OF THE EXPERT GROUP ON BANKING

Spring 1986

CHAIRMAN: Mr. D.K.R. KLEIN,
Deutsche Bundesbank, Germany

Australia
L. Phelps, Reserve Bank of Australia

Austria
A. Gancz, Ministry of Finance
J. Pingitzer, Oesterreichische Nationalbank

Belgium
C. Dauw, Commission Bancaire
B. Falys, Commission Bancaire

Canada
E.P. Fine, Bank of Canada

Denmark
B. Andersen, Danmarks Nationalbank
F.N. Rasmussen, Tilsynet Meg Banker og Sparekasser

Finland
V. Saarinen, Bank of Finland

France
H. Colmant, Commission Bancaire

Germany
J. Henke, Ministry of Finance
W. Nimmerrichter, Deutsche Bundesbank

Greece
C. Thanopoulos, Bank of Greece

Ireland
F. O'Sullivan, Central Bank of Ireland

Italy
G. Godano, Banca d'Italia
C. Nanni, Banca d'Italia
F. Passacantando, Banca d'Italia

Japan
K. Fujiwara, Ministry of Finance
I. Kuroda, Bank of Japan
K. Tatebe, OECD Delegation

Luxembourg
J.P. Schoder, Institut Monétaire Luxembourgeois

Netherlands
F.C. Musch, Nederlandsche Bank
A.P. Ranner, Ministry of Finance
J.W. van der Vossen, Nederlandsche Bank

Norway
E. Bjorland, Norges Bank
I. Hyggen, Banking, Insurance and Securities Commission

Portugal
S. Ferreira, Banco de Portugal
M. Remedio, Banco de Portugal

Spain
R. Poveda, Banco de Espana

Sweden
W. van der Hoeven, Sveriges Riksbank

Switzerland
U.W. Birchler, Swiss National Bank
A. Cornu, Commission Fédérale des Banques

Turkey
C. Akbay, Central Bank of Turkey
A. Berber, Undersecretariat of Treasury and Foreign Trade
A.V. Celik, Central Bank of Turkey

United Kingdom
J.B.C. Atkinson, Bank of England

United States
R.R. Bench, Comptroller of the Currency
F.R. Dahl, Federal Reserve Board
E. Ettin, Federal Reserve Board

B.I.S.
J. Alworth
T.R.G. Bingham

E.E.C.
P. Clarotti

Chapter 1

INTRODUCTION AND SUMMARY

1.1 INTRODUCTION

Financial institutions and markets in the OECD area have undergone a profound transformation process over the last decades, in particular since the late seventies. Competition in the vast and complex markets for financial services has considerably intensified; banks, securities firms and other providers of financial services have often changed from administration–like institutions to highly competitive enterprises applying modern management techniques and marketing strategies. Market forces have thus come to play a decisive role in the functioning of financial systems, which, in many countries, have had a long history of protection and restrictive regulation. Important demand and supply changes in the markets for financial services, new communication and information technologies, ever increasing internationalisation and interpenetration of national financial systems and, last but not least, public policy have all contributed to an intensification of competition in the financial services industry and have ultimately resulted in a considerable improvement in the efficiency of financial systems.

The purpose of the present study is threefold:

1. To provide an overview of demand and supply changes, since the early sixties or so, in major sectors of the vast and complex markets for financial services such as the markets for retail banking services, corporate financial services, securities–related financial services, interbank financial services and international financial services (Chapter 2);
2. To review public policy towards national financial systems in OECD countries since the early sixties, with particular focus on the role played by competition policy as an instrument for improving the efficiency and

the functioning of financial systems (Chapter 3);
3. Finally, to identify and discuss common problems and issues which the authorities in OECD countries have been faced with in pursuing policies towards efficient financial systems; and to focus, in particular, on problems raised by efforts to reconcile such policies with the policy objectives of ensuring the stability of the financial system and maintaining an adequate level of investor protection (Chapter 4).

In accordance with the purpose of the study, banking has been defined in a broad sense to comprise securities–related and other financial services which fall within the scope of banking activities, at least in some countries, such as, for example, the marketing of insurance contracts, leasing, factoring etc. Only the business of insurance underwriting i.e. the provision of protection against particular forms of risk based on the law of large numbers is excluded from the scope of the study.

The concept of "efficiency" used in the study refers to "functional efficiency". It is a broad concept that relates to the role and the functions of the financial system. In the light of this concept, an efficient financial system is seen as one which adequately satisfies the financial service needs of an economy and its participants. The concept of "functional efficiency" covers different "aspects" of efficiency such as the allocation aspect; the availability, quality and convenience aspect; the cost aspect; the aspect of competitiveness of financial institutions; and the dynamic, or flexibility and adaptability, aspect. The concept of "functional efficiency" as used in the context of this study has been derived from various government, or government–assigned, commission reports dealing with policies towards improving the functioning of national financial systems. It is not a concept which as yet has found wide acceptance in the academic literature.

The term "competition policy" is used in a wide sense. It does not only relate to policies dealing with restrictive business practices resulting from concentration, dominant market positions or anti-competitive co-operation agreements, but covers also all measures which encourage, or provide more scope for, competition in the financial sector. Thus, a wide range of domestic financial deregulation as well as international liberalisation measures such as the abolition of interest rate controls, and the removal, or easing of, restrictions on specific domestic financial service transactions or on international capital and other financial service operations are considered as being covered by the term "competition policy". A generally supportive policy attitude towards strengthening market elements and intensifying competition in the financial sector is considered as falling within the scope of this term as well. Indeed, market developments have in recent years had a major impact on policy, and the authorities have often reacted to market forces rather than taking a lead, notwithstanding any differences of degree in policy attitudes towards financial systems in different countries.

1.2 SUMMARY

The competitive structure of the markets for financial services has undergone profound changes since the early sixties. The pace and scope of structural changes affecting competition in these markets, notably as regards institutional features of the supply side, have considerably increased since the mid-seventies or so, under the impact of an accelerating and self-reinforcing process of domestic financial deregulation and international liberalisation, a much more volatile national and international economic environment, and rapid advances in telecommunication and computer technologies. All main sectors of the financial services markets have been affected by these changes: the markets for retail banking services, corporate financial services, securities-related financial services, interbank financial services and international financial services. Chapter 2, which is more in the nature of a background chapter setting the stage for the discussion of policy and of related issues in Chapters 3 and 4, provides a broad picture of demand and supply trends in these various financial service market areas and attempts to assess related changes in the competitive situation and the impact of these changes on efficiency.

Retail banking — comprising services such as the supply of savings instruments and the intermediation of financial savings and related securities business, the supply of consumer loans and housing finance, payment services and a wide range of advisory services — has become a most important sector within the financial services industry in OECD countries. The proportion of "banked" people has substantially increased since the sixties and has been approaching the saturation point in many countries. Today, new banking clients can often be gained only by bidding them away from other institutions. This feature has no doubt generated considerable competitive pressures in the markets for retail banking services, fostering the efficiency of these markets, notably as regards the availability and quality of services and the range of borrowing and savings instruments and financial services offered. While innovative product competition, and to a lesser extent price competition, have gained in importance, geographical competition through "brick and mortar" branching has generally been losing momentum since the late seventies while the growth of automated teller machine (ATM) networks and "home banking" facilities has accelerated.

Product competition has become particularly sharp in the markets for household savings as this large and ever increasing pool of investible funds has attracted an increasing number and a widening range of competitors from inside and outside the banking system — commercial banks, savings banks, building societies, credit co-operatives and credit unions, trust and mortgage companies, finance companies, life insurance companies and pension funds, collective investment funds and a wide range of issuers of securities generally including governments. In the distribution of retail banking services and products, department stores and other retailers have become serious competitors of banks and other retail banking institutions, and internationally operating credit card companies compete fiercely with local or regional issuers of payment and credit cards from the banking as well as the non-banking sector. In more recent years, banks and specialised credit companies as well as department stores and other retailers have made particular efforts to promote the consumer credit business, which offers comfortable profit margins. As these markets as well as many other sub-markets for retail banking services tend to lack visibility, the question for policy arises whether sole reliance on the working of market forces should be the only way of dealing with the problem of efficiency, in particular cost efficiency, in retail banking.

In the markets for corporate financial services, which are highly competitive markets as corporations are generally more flexible than private households in choosing their banking connections, three major trends deserve attention. First, there has been increasing demand for, and supply of, sophisticated asset and liability management services making increasing use of computer technology, on the one hand, and of a greater variety of asset and liability instruments, including the newly developed financial options and futures, on the other. Banks have been challenged by treasurers of large corporations setting up their own financial management departments. Second, there has been a general trend towards greater bank involvement in corporate affairs and growing demand for merchant banking services involving the financial and organisational restructuring of firms, mergers and acquisitions, management buy-outs, and general advisory and computer services for enterprise management. Banks, competing with specialised non-banking firms, have made increasing efforts in recent years to meet these new demands. Third, particular efforts have been made towards developing markets for risk capital for small- and medium-sized enterprises involving both the creation of special venture capital firms and funds and the introduction of new segments in the organised securities markets — so-called "second markets" or "unlisted securities markets" — which make it possible for smaller firms of good standing to raise risk capital in the equity market without having to meet full listing requirements.

The markets for securities-related financial services — comprising activities such as the new-issuing business, brokerage services, securities trading, portfolio management, investment advisory and information services and related market research, and new product development — have become the most dynamic growth sector within the financial services markets since the early eighties. A general trend towards greater "securitisation" of financial market activity involving, inter alia, an increasing integration of financial institutions and money and securities markets, has played a major role in this development. In addition, institutional investors and professional as well as private portfolio managers, benefiting from generally increased freedom in international capital operations and from spectacular improvements in information and communication technology, have made increasing efforts towards a greater international diversification of their portfolios. In response, a growing number of banks including subsidiaries of banks which in their home countries are not allowed to conduct the full range of securities-related activities, have expanded their securities departments at a rapid pace and have, in sharp competition with specialised securities firms, strengthened their presence in domestic and foreign securities markets, notably in the major international financial centres. Product competition

in money and securities markets has been particularly strong as is evidenced by the proliferation of innovative market instruments designed to meet special borrower and investor needs including growing needs for hedging increased foreign currency, interest rate and other price risks.

The markets for interbank financial services — or "intra-system" financial services — which are essential for the functioning and the interaction of national financial systems, have often grown overproportionally, notably in connection with the internationalisation of banking and finance. They comprise activities such as interbank deposit and other money-market transactions, payment services, foreign exchange and securities trading and brokerage services, the development and operation of the technological infrastructure of these markets such as clearing and settlement systems, as well as a wide range of information services. In money and securities markets, including newly developed markets for options and futures, banks and other financial institutions are the main operators, whether for own or client account; and "intra-system" operations in these markets are often more important than business with non-financial clients. "Correspondent banking" continues to play an important role in interlinkages of national financial systems, notwithstanding the build-up of extended international networks by large banks, as well as in geographically fragmented national financial systems. The efficiency of these interbank financial service markets has been considerably improved owing to increasing use of modern computer technology and under pressure from increased international competition, on the one hand, and co-operative efforts in the development of the technological infrastructure of the financial service markets and the formulation of "rules of the game", which are important for the management of markets, on the other hand.

The growing internationalisation of banking and securities-related activities has led to spectacular growth of the markets for international financial services. From the sixties to the early eighties, in addition to traditional and mostly trade-related business and new-style eurobond transactions, the main emphasis was on euromoney-market business and direct eurolending by large, financially strong and internationally competitive banking institutions. Since about 1982, as the major banks' balance sheets and capital bases became increasingly exposed to country and liquidity risks as a result of direct lending to a number of countries in payment difficulties, there has been a noticeable shift to securities-related activities, in particular the underwriting of international bond issues and brokerage services in connection with cross-border transactions in domestic securities. Furthermore, there has been an unprecedented growth of new forms of off–balance–sheet business in the OECD area, especially as regards the international issue of money–market paper with or without the backing of underwriting banks. New instruments for interest rate and foreign currency hedging, which, however, opened up also new possibilities for speculation, have been developed. As a result, price as well as product competition amongst international banks has become extremely fierce. However, geographical competition at international level has also assumed a new dimension owing to the ongoing expansion of international banking networks and competition between major financial centres. Foreign bank entry has now been largely liberalised in most OECD countries in line with the generally accepted principle of the right of establishment.

Financial policy in OECD countries has, since the early sixties, increasingly focused on the objective of improving the efficiency of the financial system, without, however, neglecting the two other main objectives, namely to ensure the stability and soundness of the financial system and to maintain an adequate level of investor protection (Chapter 3). Efforts towards modernising national financial systems have gathered considerable momentum since the late seventies, under the impact of increasing internationalisation of the financial service markets and intensifying competition within and between national financial systems. Competition policies have become a major, although not the only, policy tool for improving the efficiency of national financial systems.

In implementing policies towards improving the efficiency of national financial systems, the authorities in OECD countries have taken a wide range of measures designed to stimulate competition and strengthen the role of market forces, such as the following:

— Widening the scope for price competition through deregulation of interest rates and fees and commissions for financial services, and prohibiting cartel agreements in this field;
— Increasing the number of competitors in various sectors of the financial service markets through providing more scope for despecialisation and diversification and by removing obstacles to the domestic and cross–border expansion of banking networks;
— Increasing investor and borrower choices through encouraging the creation of a wide range of new financial asset and debt instruments;
— Removing obstacles to free lending and investment decisions of banks and other financial institutions by abolishing, or easing, direct lending controls and mandatory investment regulations;
— Improving the visibility of financial service markets through better information; and
— Forestalling anti–competitive concentration movements in banking and finance by merger and ownership control.

The process of domestic financial deregulation and international liberalisation has become self–reinforcing and thus has gathered further momentum since the late seventies. Faced with the increasing eventuality of losing international business to foreign financial centres, the authorities of a growing number of countries have opted in recent years for a policy of opening their countries to foreign competition even further and have intensified their efforts towards strengthening the international competitiveness of their national financial systems.

This worldwide move towards greater financial deregulation and liberalisation is an ongoing process. There are still a number of restrictions, often rooted in historical country differences in financial system structures, which affect the nature and degree of competition in national financial service markets and pose problems for the international financial integration process. From a competition policy point of view, such restrictions may no longer be justified. However, considerations relating to the stability objective or to monetary policy as well as to investor or consumer protection policies make it desirable for some countries to maintain some restrictions on competition. In view of the complexity of the competition question and of the scope for conflicts with other financial policy objectives it was to be expected that the authorities in OECD countries would be faced with a wide range of issues and problems in formulating competition policies in the financial field. A number of main issues and problems are discussed in the concluding Chapter 4 of the study and in the following paragraphs.

It is widely accepted in OECD countries that free price competition in the financial service markets has a favourable impact on the functioning of the financial system and on the allocation of financial and real resources in national economies and enables financial institutions — in the absence of direct lending controls, mandatory investment regulations and other major asset and liability restrictions — to react flexibly and dynamically to demand and supply changes in the markets for financial services. In a number of countries, the authorities see, however, under present circumstances an advantage in maintaining some interest rate controls, mainly in the retail banking area. While in some of these countries it may be only a matter of time until remaining price restrictions are lifted, controls on interest rates in retail banking, notably on deposit rates, are sometimes maintained for more general reasons relating to the competitive features of the retail banking market. As this market notoriously lacks visibility and as retail banking clients are fairly insensitive to price differences, it is sometimes difficult for the authorities to achieve an adequate level of competition between two extreme situations: destructive competition amongst major banks or banking groups for market shares on the one hand, and too little competition resulting in inefficiencies and excessive bank profits on the other. For overall stability reasons as well as with a view to enhancing visibility in retail banking, some countries, indeed, prefer — at least for the time being — to maintain some price controls in this area. The view that free price competition in retail banking is not necessarily beneficial for the customer is also, to some extent, supported by the fact that, in some instances, the freeing of commissions on securities brokerage services has resulted in a noticeable increase in commissions paid by individuals.

Supporting the general trend towards despecialisation by widening the range of permissible activities and products of financial institutions has been increasingly accepted as a policy approach towards promoting competition and, hence, improving the efficiency of the financial sector. Formerly highly specialised financial institutions have thus been enabled to seize more flexibly and dynamically new business opportunities under changing demand and supply conditions in the financial service markets without being prevented from deciding themselves whether and how to specialise in particular product and service areas. However, in a number of countries the authorities see an advantage under present circumstances in limiting the despecialisation process. The separation of some securities-related activities from commercial banking is still maintained in a few countries for perceived conflict of interest reasons and concerns relating to the concentration of power in the financial sector. However, it may be only a matter of time until a reorganisation of supervision on the one hand, and sufficient evidence of intensified international competition on the other, renders any such concerns redundant.

Some types of savings institutions and the financial services of post office systems continue to be prevented from becoming fully-fledged banks in a number of countries for fear of overbanking and for related stability as well as efficiency and fair competition reasons.

Conflicts of interest considerations which have an efficiency aspect, an investor protection aspect and a safety and stability aspect, have an important weight in the debate about the desirability of the separation of commercial banking and securities-related activities or the separation of some securities-related activities such as, for example, the underwriting business and portfolio management or brokerage, dealing and investment advice. Although it is widely recognised that conflicts of interest do arise in a universal bank and a financial conglomerate as well as a securities firm, there are considerable country differences as regards the degree of concern about abuses of conflict of interest situations. The approaches towards dealing with this problem range from reliance on market forces and market discipline to a strict institutional separation of functions. A compromise between these two extreme solutions is the so-called "Chinese Wall" principle, i.e. the strict separation of functions within an institution or the requirement that some securities-related activities have to be conducted through specialised and separately capitalised subsidiaries. More generally, it appears that in working out solutions towards dealing with the conflicts of interest issue, priority is increasingly given to efficiency considerations which no longer point to a need for an institutional separation of functions in the financial sector. At the same time, investor protection aspects and stability aspects of the conflicts of interest problem are increasingly handled via an adaptation of supervisory practices and the application of detailed codes of conduct.

It is widely accepted in OECD countries that a liberal competition policy in the financial sector should not be confused with a "laisser-faire, laisser-aller" policy and that — in addition to free price, product and territorial competition — a number of conditions need to be fulfilled to ensure that market forces work properly and that competition is maintained at an appropriate level. The following conditions and principles deserve special attention in this regard:

— Competition should take place on a "level playing field" i.e. market participants should compete on equal terms and conditions so that there is equality of competitive opportunity;
— Competition should be subject to agreed "rules of the game" such as codes of conduct, rules of market practices and principles of market organisation;
— "Club arrangements" — which often play a useful role in the formulation of "rules of the game" and for an appropriate market

organisation — should not give rise to anti-competitive practices and co-operation agreements;
— Anti-competitive effects of concentration and dominant positions of market participants should be prevented.

Although there is general agreement on these broad principles, there are considerable country differences as regards the degree of importance attached to these issues, the ways in which these principles are implemented, and the respective roles that self-regulation and official regulation play in this latter regard.

In an effort to improve the efficiency of national financial systems through more reliance on market forces, the authorities have often supported the deregulation process by the creation of markets for new instruments, in particular money-market instruments, or by widening and deepening existing securities markets. Policy action in this direction has essentially been guided by the conviction that the allocation of financial resources through markets for negotiable instruments is in many respects superior to institutional allocation, in particular as regards cost efficiency. Policies towards strengthening the market element in the financial system have also been used in support of measures designed to promote the despecialisation and decompartmentalisation process as open markets tend to have a forceful integration impact in the financial system. In pursuing such policies, the authorities, or self-regulatory bodies operating under their general supervision, have increasingly been occupied with the question of market organisation and have generally paid greater attention to conditions for the functioning of markets such as standardisation, liquidity, depth, visibility, orderly markets, and safety and soundness of markets.

There is general agreement that reliance on competition and on the working of market forces does not solve all efficiency problems in the financial sector. In a certain number of areas, a good deal of co-operation is needed for improving efficiency or for ensuring that market forces work properly. According to experiences in OECD countries, co-operation as an approach towards improving efficiency plays an important role in essentially four broad areas:

— Development of the technological infrastructure of the financial systems, notably in areas such as payment systems, and information, trading, clearing, settlement and depository systems in the securities markets;
— Organisation and management of markets, notably stock exchanges and regulated over-the-counter markets;
— Financing large projects, and development of financial products;
— Co-operation between "producers" and "distributors" of financial products and services.

An increasing need for co-operation between "producers" and "distributors" of financial products and services arises because a growing number of "producers" — such as credit card companies, mutual fund managers, "producers" of insurance products etc. — are lacking an appropriate network for the distribution of their products and services. Thus, "selling" products to other "distributors" is often preferred to building up a new, and costly, distribution network. From an efficiency point of view, such co-operative arrangements have considerable cost advantages for the system as a whole although adequate supervision should be in place in order to avoid anti-competitive practices.

A policy move from a highly regulated and protected financial system to a more market-oriented system may give rise to a number of problems during the period of transition depending on the scope of financial deregulation and external liberalisation measures and the speed with which such measures are implemented. Countries which start from a position in which banking institutions have been protected against competition for many years, may need a longer period for adapting the financial system to the new competitive environment than countries in which market elements have already played a considerable role for quite some time. Before engaging in a process of deregulation and liberalisation the authorities have often felt a need to consider the following kinds of questions: first, whether measures designed to stimulate competition need not be accompanied by flanking safety measures designed to prevent competition from becoming excessive; second, how to deal effectively with any banking failures so that chain reactions and crises of confidence can be avoided; third, how to handle any concentration movements which might result from increased competition; fourth, how to implement financial deregulation and liberalisation measures over time and co-ordinate different types of such measures in a balanced manner. An effective handling of the "exit problem" has been considered as particularly important in this context. While, from an efficiency point of view, it has been highly desirable that inefficient and non-competitive institutions should discontinue their operations it has been feared that a series of banking failures, if not well handled, could trigger a confidence crisis and could thus provide a threat to the stability of the financial system as a whole.

In the process of internationalisation of financial markets and increasing interpenetration of national financial systems, international competition in financial services has considerably intensified, and the strengthening of the international competitiveness of national financial institutions and markets has become a major objective of financial policy, not only in international financial centre countries but also in countries which aim at reducing their dependence on "imports" of financial services from such centres. Policies designed to strengthen the international competitiveness of national financial systems comprise a long list of more general measures aimed at increasing the efficiency of the system as well as of more specific measures aimed at promoting international financial service activities in the national marketplace. The measures that countries have taken to varying degrees and in different combinations, depending on countries' positions in the international financial services markets, may be grouped under the following headings which indicate broad policy strategies in this field:

— Improving the efficiency of the national financial system through general deregulation measures aimed at stimulating competition;
— Attracting foreign market participants: borrowers, investors, financial intermediaries;
— Increasing the range of products and services in response to the changing needs of internationally–operating market participants;
— Developing an efficient technological infrastructure (telecommunication systems; payment systems; information, trading, clearing, settlement and depository systems in securities markets etc.);
— Strengthening linkages with other international financial centres at the level of market organisation and supervision, and of telecommunication technology as well as at the level of institutions on both an establishment and a cross–border transaction basis;
— Ensuring the safety and soundness of the marketplace through adequate financial regulation and supervision;
— Removal of taxes which unnecessarily impair the functioning of financial markets.

These measures have affected international competition in the financial service markets both at the level of international financial markets which operate across the jurisdictions of several countries, and at the level of national financial systems where typically relatively few foreign institutions compete in the domestic financial services markets with host country institutions.

Although the broad issues for policies towards international competition in the financial service markets are essentially the same as those met with in a national policy context, there are substantial differences as regards the weight some of these issues have — for example the question of competitive equality and the closely related question of market access — in the international context. Moreover, policy approaches towards dealing with these issues are at international level much more complicated than at national level. Considerable progress has been made towards "levelling the playing field" for international competition in the financial service markets in essentially two areas: first, obstacles to market access have been largely removed, or are in the process of being removed, thanks to the liberalisation efforts under co–operation within the OECD and the EC; second, capital adequacy standards are in the process of being harmonized thanks to the work of the Basle Committee on Banking Regulations and Practices. However, as these competitive inequalities are being reduced or removed altogether, other regulatory differences are gaining more weight as factors resulting in competitive inequalities. Amongst such other factors affecting competition within the global financial system the following may be mentioned in particular: differences in taxation regimes; investor protection regulations including rules on insider trading and arrangements for dealing with conflicts of interest; bank secrecy legislation; and last, but not least, differences in the quality and efficiency of the technological infrastructure of national marketplaces. However, in all these areas co–operative efforts towards convergence of systems are under way.

Ever since the authorities have felt a need to regulate and supervise the financial sector — essentially since the twenties and thirties — financial policy has been directed towards three major objectives: to ensure the efficiency of the financial system; to ensure its stability and soundness; and to maintain an adequate level of investor protection. However, the priorities that have been attached to these objectives have varied between countries and, within countries, over time. In the early period of bank regulation, the efficiency objective, apart from ensuring that basic functions of the financial system such as the operation of the payment system and an adequate credit and liquidity supply are reasonably well performed, received relatively low priority as stability was mainly sought to be achieved by a global protection of the financial sector and by corresponding arrangements for limiting competition. This approach to financial policy was substantially revised after World War II as, with a general policy move towards more market–oriented economies, the efficiency objective received higher priority and more attention in practically all countries, although at different times and to varying degrees. Thus, the whole post–World War II history of financial regulation may be seen as a major attempt to reset priorities amongst the three main objectives of financial policy and to strengthen the efficiency of the financial sector — largely through reliance on competition and the working of market forces — without, however, neglecting the stability and soundness objective and the objective of adequate investor protection.

The lessons to be learned from this history suggest that, basically, the three objectives of financial policy — efficiency, stability, and investor protection — are complementary and mutually reinforcing and can, under certain conditions, be reconciled in a balanced way. Indeed, it is now widely accepted that adequate regulation and efficiency are not necessarily conflicting objectives, and that a well–functioning financial system, in fact, needs to be based on adequate prudential regulation/supervision and investor protection. Conversely, it is also widely agreed that the stability and soundness of the financial systems rests largely on the financial strength and the efficient management of financial institutions which are able to compete effectively and flexibly in the financial service markets both domestically and internationally. Thus, setting the conditions for the proper working of market forces and strengthening the competitiveness of financial institutions are often seen as appropriate approaches not only towards improving the efficiency of the financial system but also towards ensuring the stability and soundness of the system as well as maintaining an adequate level of investor protection.

As countries proceeded to modernise their financial systems, it was inevitable that financial policy and monetary policy influenced each other, given the financial system's role as a channel through which monetary policy measures are transmitted to the economy. However, the degree and the direction of these influences have varied from country to country and, within countries, over time depending on the attitude of the monetary authorities towards the deregulation process and on their role in the related decision–making process. In an impressive number of countries, the monetary authorities supported deregulation policies designed to stimulate competition and to improve efficiency by removing direct lending controls. It was recognised that credit ceilings not only impair competition and innovation in the financial sector but are also ineffective as an instrument of monetary policy because rapidly developing unregulated markets increasingly tend to escape monetary control. In some other countries, the monetary authorities adopted a more neutral position towards deregulation and, as they never relied on credit ceilings, confined their action to some minor adaptation of their monetary policy techniques to the new market environment. In a third group of countries, the monetary authorities attempted, with varying success, to resist the general trend towards the broadening of money markets and the spreading of variable interest rate instruments as this was seen as impairing the effectiveness of monetary policy. Nevertheless, there has been a fairly general trend towards making increasing use of market–based intervention techniques, and money–market rates have generally become the preferred operating objective of monetary policy permitting flexible policy reactions to rapid changes in market conditions. As far as monetary targeting techniques are concerned, there is no doubt that in a number of countries using these techniques the process of financial deregulation has "disturbed" the relationship between monetary aggregates, notably "narrow money" definitions, and income and expenditure variables. In several countries, this led to redefinitions of aggregates and revisions of intermediate targets while in other countries a multi–indicator approach has been increasingly adopted. On the whole, it may be said that it has been possible to reconcile policies towards improving the efficiency of financial systems with the development of effective monetary policy techniques that are compatible with the new market environment.

A review of worldwide trends in the financial service markets and of policies towards modernising national financial systems and interlinking them to an efficient global system suggests that there is an increasing need for taking a global view of financial system developments and financial regulation; and it has become evident that the authorities in OECD countries, indeed, increasingly do feel this need. The need for a global view and a global financial policy approach has a dual aspect and actually concerns both policies towards the development and adequate regulation of national financial systems and co–operation for developing a coherent approach towards financial system integration and regulation at international level.

At national level, developments in the financial services markets over the last twenty years or so have clearly been characterised by a general trend towards integration resulting from both market developments and policies designed to break down barriers between previously specialised financial institutions and market segments. On the market side, strategies of financial institutions towards diversifying their activities and a general development towards broadening the markets for negotiable instruments — the trend towards "securitisation" — have strongly favoured this integration process. From a regulatory and supervisory point of view, a most important aspect of this process is the integration of financial institutions and the money and securities markets. On the regulatory side, the consequences of this integration process in national financial systems have in many countries not yet been fully drawn although the awareness that there is a need for a more integrated approach towards regulation and supervision has steadily increased and has gathered further momentum in the aftermath of the October 1987 stock market crash.

Internationally, the trend towards greater financial integration manifests itself both through the expansion of the international financial markets such as the euromoney, eurobond and euro–equity markets, and through the increasing interpenetration of national financial systems. Thus, the need for adopting a global view and approach in financial policy and regulation relates increasingly to international aspects of the financial integration process as well. Countries which are in the process of modernising their national financial systems and of reforming their regulatory frameworks, cannot avoid influencing other countries, and, hence, increasingly take into account financial system developments abroad in order to make sure that the various aspects of market organisation, regulation and functioning are internationally compatible and permit effective linkages between national financial systems. Thus, there is considerable need, and pressure, for convergence as regards the development of markets, techniques and instruments, and related codes of conduct and rules of market practices; and, at a more technical level, as regards payment systems and information, clearing, settlement and depository systems in securities markets. However, convergence is in particular needed in areas such as prudential regulation and investor protection rules including insider trading rules and disclosure requirements in order to achieve a "level playing field" for fair international competition in world financial service markets. There can be little doubt that a co–ordinated approach towards integrating national financial systems to an efficient and safe global system requires substantial international co–operation efforts, both bilaterally and multilaterally.

Chapter 2

DEMAND AND SUPPLY TRENDS IN THE MARKETS FOR FINANCIAL SERVICES

2.1 INTRODUCTION

The markets for financial services, which provide a not negligible potential for general economic growth and employment (Chart 2.1)[1], consist of a large number of sub–markets with different product characteristics, types of customers, institutional supply features and territorial boundaries. Accordingly, there are considerable differences between sub–markets for financial services as regards the demand and supply constellation, the competitive structure which is determined by the number of participants on either side of the market, and the degree of market visibility and related information that is readily available. The competitive situation in sub–markets for financial services is also affected by the choices regarding substitutes for specific services or financial instruments that are available to demanders for financial services. Finally, there are differences between sub–markets for financial services with regard to the types and combination of competitive weapons and strategies that providers of financial services are willing, or able, to use, depending inter alia, on the regulatory frameworks within which they operate[2].

In order to provide an overview of demand and supply trends in the markets for financial services, which is the purpose of the present chapter, it is necessary to combine various closely interrelated

Chart 2.1
EMPLOYMENT IN FINANCIAL SERVICES
(Per cent of total employment)

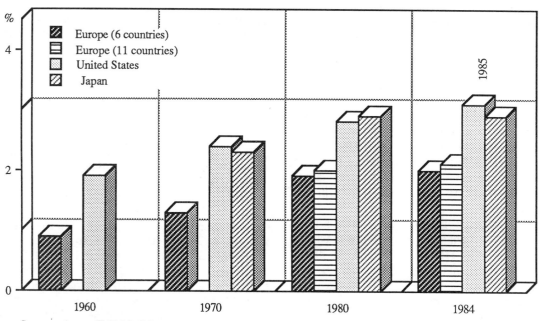

Source: Annex II, Table 2.2.

sub–markets for financial services to broader market areas which may be dominated by particular types of financial institutions, depending, inter alia, on the institutional characteristics of a national financial system. As the present chapter is essentially aimed at setting the background for a discussion of the role of competition policy as an instrument for improving the efficiency of national financial systems (Chapter 3) and a subsequent discussion of related issues for policy (Chapter 4), it has been found useful to distinguish between, and to review demand and supply trends in, the following broad market areas:

— Retail banking services;
— Corporate financial services;
— Securities–related financial services;
— Interbank (or intra–system) financial services; and
— International financial services.

The competitive structure and characteristics of these market areas have undergone profound changes since the early sixties. The pace and scope of structural change affecting competition in these market areas, notably as regards the institutional features of the supply side, have considerably increased since the mid–seventies, under the impact of an accelerating and self–reinforcing process of domestic financial deregulation and international liberalisation, a much more volatile national and international economic environment, rapid advances in telecommunication and computer technology, and last, but not least, policies designed to improve the efficiency and the functioning of national financial systems. As all the various factors have interacted in a complex process it is generally not possible to identify clear cause/effect relationships. This is particularly true for the relationship between market developments reviewed in the present chapter and policy action dealt with in the next chapter. Although policy has played a major role in modernising national financial systems it is not always clear whether and to what extent the authorities or market participants have taken a lead. There are certainly considerable country differences in this regard. While in some countries the authorities have taken action on the basis of a "blueprint" for a comprehensive financial system reform, there are others in which public policy has more or less reacted to pressures for change coming from market participants. While the trends identified in the present chapter are seen as being typical of all, or most, OECD countries it is obvious that there are considerable country differences as regards the amplitude and the time path of the various developments described.

2.2 THE MARKETS FOR RETAIL BANKING SERVICES

The markets for retail banking services — comprising activities such as the collection and intermediation of household savings, the issue of corresponding savings instruments, the granting of consumer and mortgage loans, the provision of a variety of payment services and instruments and related account management services as well as a host of brokerage and advisory services, notably in the securities area — have been one of the most important growth areas in the financial service markets since the early sixties. It has been mainly in this particular field of banking where changes in the banking landscape have become most visible for the man in the street. In the fifties, only a relatively small part of the population of many OECD countries had bank accounts and used cheque books or giro transfers for effecting payments. Relationships with the banking system were mostly confined to the possession of a savings–pass book issued by a savings bank, a building society or a similar type of institution including the postal savings system. These institutions often operated under a public policy mandate to promote the savings habit and to collect and safeguard small savings. In return, they often enjoyed corresponding tax privileges. Only a relatively small number of wealthy people and owners of businesses maintained relationships with private bankers or commercial banks.

Today, most people or families in most OECD countries have bank accounts and many use cheque books and other convenient payment instruments such as plastic cards for effecting payments or using automated cash dispensers; and buying on credit has become a widespread feature in retail banking as well.

Main Trends in the Demand for Retail Banking Services

Since the late fifties, demand for financial services by private persons and households has been strongly affected by two closely interrelated developments: first, a strong expansion of personal income and wealth has resulted in a substantial accumulation of financial wealth in the hands of persons, so that household sector financial assets have generally become the most important pool of investible funds (Table 2.1). This development, by itself, generated considerable demand for financial services and corresponding business opportunities in retail banking, notably in the field of financial asset management and related advisory services.

20

Table 2.1 **Household sector financial assets**
Per cent of financial assets of all domestic
non–financial sectors

	End–1960	End–1984
Australia	66.9	76.1
Canada	60.8[1]	62.6
Germany	44.8	62.9
Italy	57.3[2]	61.1
Japan	45.8	54.0
United States	78.6	79.6

1. 1961.
2. 1963.
Source: See Annex II, Table 5.1.

Second, the spreading of the "banking habit", which has been encouraged by enterprises and other employers with a view to rationalising wage and salary payments, has manifested itself in a strongly increasing demand for banking services, notably in the field of payment services. This trend has been very much promoted by the banks and other providers of retail banking services themselves as bank managers increasingly realised that a solid private customer base offered unique growth and profit opportunities in a wide range of financial services including profitable consumer loan activities.

The spreading of the "banking habit" and a corresponding increase in the number of bank customers, which largely set the stage for the "retail banking revolution"[3], did not only result in an extraordinary growth in cashless payments by means of cheques, giro transfers, cheque guarantee cards and credit cards and other more recent forms of cashless payments; it also assisted private persons in familiarising themselves with other financial products and services offered by banks and other providers of financial services and with financial and investment matters more generally. The spreading of the banking habit coupled with an extraordinary expansion of tourism and travelling at home and abroad generated demand for convenient means of payment such as travellers' cheques and credit cards and for foreign exchange at retail banking level. In a number of countries, banks have sometimes supplemented these travel–related financial services with more general travel agency services.

The massive accumulation of financial assets in the hands of private households had a number of further consequences for developments in the financial services markets. As individual financial asset holdings of households rose, there was increasing demand for the diversification of these assets into higher–yielding and more sophisticated investment outlets such as various types of non–marketable or marketable fixed–interest securities, mutual funds and equities. The search for higher–yielding assets providing protection against inflation was much enhanced during the early seventies as private savers increasingly realised that returns on traditional savings instruments such as ordinary pass book savings offered negative "real" rates of interest. Middle– and high–income savers, in particular, turned to more sophisticated portfolio management in order to earn positive "real" rates of return and increasingly solicited high–quality advisory and brokerage services including advice on taxation and on opportunities for investing in non–financial assets such as precious metals, art objects or real estate, or for investing abroad.

In the process of diversification of households' financial assets, increasing amounts of savings were channelled into contractual forms such as savings with insurance companies and pension funds. In a number of countries, this form of savings has been encouraged by tax incentives designed to bring the tax treatment of voluntary savings for old age in line with that of mandatory retirement contributions to social insurance. In some countries, the promotion of this type of saving has given rise to an extraordinary growth of insurance companies and pension funds. This, in turn, has had considerable implications for the structure of these countries' financial systems, notably as regards the growth of securities markets, and for competition for household savings within the financial system.

The rise in income and wealth during the last two decades or so also meant a considerable improvement in the household sector's debt service capacity, which increased the scope for household sector borrowing (Table 2.2). Thus, the sixties and the

Table 2.2 **Household sector debt**
Per cent of liabilities
of all domestic non–financial sectors

	End–1960	End–1984
Australia	22.3	32.1
Canada	14.3[1]	16.8
Germany	3.0[2]	5.7
Italy	4.2[2] [3]	3.3
Japan	15.9	22.5
United States	29.1	33.7

1. 1961.
2. Excluding mortgage debt for housing purposes.
3. 1963.
Source: See Annex II, Table 5.1.

seventies saw a considerable surge in demand for consumer finance in its two major forms: first, demand for housing loans for the construction and acquisition of owner–occupied houses and dwellings including secondary residences; and second, demand for consumer loans needed for the acquisition of consumer durables such as household equipment and cars and for other consumption purposes. Not all countries were affected by the boom in consumer loan and housing loan activity in the same way. Differences in the level of income and wealth played a considerable role in explaining country differences in this field. In some countries, demand for housing loans was particularly strengthened in connection with public policy designed to promote private home–ownership. In other countries, housing loans were restricted in the context of structural economic policy designed to promote industrial development and the growth of export industries as a matter of high priority. Consumer loans were sometimes also restrictively controlled in the context of monetary policy aimed at restraining consumption.

Finally, there has been a more general change in the attitudes of consumers towards their banks. Private customers have become more demanding as regards the quality and scope of service, the supply of information and advice on financial matters, and the general nature of the relationship with their local bank. Convenience, speediness and promptness of service have become important considerations for the private banking client in building up and maintaining a banking relationship of a more lasting nature. These changes in consumer attitudes towards convenience in banking and the quality of service have become an important factor strengthening the competitive climate within the financial services industry. Sometimes this development has been described in terms of a shift from a "sellers'" to a "buyers'" market. This latter feature is all the more important as the markets for private banking clients have become largely saturated in many countries so that the reservoir of "unbanked" people, apart from young newcomers to the banking market, has more or less been exhausted. As a result, individual banks can generally increase the number of their private banking clients only by attracting them away from other institutions. This situation has no doubt had implications for the banks' competitive strategies in retail banking in the sense that banks and their competitors have generally sharpened their competitive weapons.

The Response of Banks and other Providers of Financial Services to Demand Trends in the Markets for Retail Banking Services

The way in which demand trends in the markets for retail banking services have affected OECD countries' financial systems and the way in which banks and other providers of financial services have responded to these trends, has been determined by a number of factors: a country's starting situation in the early sixties as regards the structure of the financial system and the relationships that existed at that time between various types of financial institutions and the personal sector; the scope provided by regulatory frameworks for various types of institutions to engage in retail banking; subsequent changes in relevant regulatory frameworks; and the strategies of financial institutions towards their participation in these newly emerging markets.

Initially, those types of financial institutions which traditionally had close links with small savers i.e. savings banks, building societies, credit co-operatives, smaller local and regional banks benefited most from the expansion of private income and financial wealth. Larger commercial banks often reacted at a later stage to the business opportunities offered by a strong retail banking clientele and thus, initially, lost market shares in the financial services markets. In some countries, commercial banks were prevented from moving massively into the retail banking market through both branching restrictions and controls on interest rates applying to retail deposits. However, in other countries, commercial banks have energetically developed their retail banking business at a relatively early stage and have since well maintained solid positions in this market (Table 2.3).

Structural Pressures for more Competition in Retail Banking

The accumulation of financial wealth in the household sector led to considerable financial imbalances between sectors which, in turn, created structural pressures within the financial system for more competition in both retail banking and corporate banking and for a diversification of activities of formerly more specialised groups of institutions.

As already mentioned, the traditional collectors of small savings initially benefited most from the increased fund accumulation in the household sector and largely invested these funds, according to tradition or under special legal arrangements, in housing loans and/or fixed–interest securities. In addition, large liquidity surpluses were invested in the money market or deposited in accounts held at special central institutions, the treasury department of the government, or with commercial banks, depending on the institutional structure of the national financial system. Thus, the traditional collectors of small savings were structurally large suppliers of surplus funds as they did not have sufficient outlets for direct lending to their traditional customers i.e. households, retailers, artisans and other small businesses and sometimes also local authorities. Under

Table 2.3 Growth of commercial banks and other deposit-taking institutions
Compound Annual Rates of Growth of Balance Sheet Totals

		1960–1970	1970–1980	1980–1984
a)	*Countries in which commercial banks (CBs) generally expanded more rapidly than other deposit-taking institutions (ODTIs)*			
Austria	CBs	14.2	18.1	7.5
	ODTIs	13.9	16.8	11.6
Belgium	CBs	16.9	18.1	19.3
	ODTIs	..	15.0	10.8
Netherlands	CBs	10.1	14.8	15.1
	ODTIs	13.3	12.8	6.6
Sweden	CBs	10.1	14.8	15.1
	ODTIs	9.0	12.1	8.9
b)	*Countries in which commercial banks (CBs) generally expanded less rapidly than other deposit-taking institutions (ODTIs)*			
Australia	CBs	7.2	14.5	22.6
	ODTIs	10.3	16.9	13.5
Canada	CBs	10.9	17.9	7.1
	ODTIs	13.1	19.1	6.2
Germany	CBs	12.4	10.7	5.3
	ODTIs	13.0	13.6	7.0
Japan	CBs	17.0	14.1	10.4
	ODTIs	22.0	16.1	8.2
Spain	CBs	18.4	22.1	18.3
	ODTIs	22.9	22.9	21.1
United States	CBs	8.3	10.7	9.8
	ODTIs	8.7	12.3	10.9

Source: Annex II, Table 3.1.

these conditions, increasing pressures built up for these institutions to widen the range of activities towards offering full banking services including consumer loan business and to seek new customers in the field of business lending. In the process, savings banks and credit co-operatives in many countries, have gradually moved into the area of corporate financial services and have thus increasingly become competitors of commercial banks and have often been able to conquer important market shares in this field. The authorities have often confirmed, or supported, this trend by amalgamating or harmonizing the legal frameworks applying to savings institutions of different kinds with the law applicable to commercial banks (Chapter 3).

Commercial banks, on the other hand, were faced with increasing borrowing demands from the corporate sector which could be funded from traditional deposit resources only at a declining rate as these sources — essentially liquidity reserves of enterprises and deposits from wealthy individuals — were growing at relatively modest rates. Thus, commercial banks found themselves under increasing pressures to move into the markets for relatively cheap household savings as other funding alternatives such as recourse to the money market, to the bond market, or to central bank credit were more costly or subject to restrictions. It was broadly in this way that "banks discovered people"[4].

These broad structural imbalances in the financial system resulting from traditional customer relationships — increasing funding needs on the part of the commercial banks and increasing surpluses on the part of savings collectors — resulted, on the one hand, in increased competition for private customers and in efforts on the part of commercial banks to spread the banking habit of people and to move into the small savings and retail banking business; on the other hand, savings institutions moved increasingly into the markets for corporate financial services.

The Struggle for New Private Customers and the Spreading of the Banking Habit

Banks, in competing for new private customers, have used weapons in combinations which have differed from country to country and over time. Initially, in the years of highly unsaturated markets characterised by a high proportion of unbanked people, banks made energetic efforts to extend their branch networks — provided that this was legally possible — as geographical nearness to the prospective client was a prime consideration in strategies towards gaining new retail banking clients. Thus, practically all countries have seen a spectacular extension of the banking network in the sixties

and seventies either through branching by existing banks or, in some countries, also by the setting up of new banks (Chart 2.2)[5]. In a number of countries, banks supported this process of the geographical extension of their presence in local markets by active promotion of the concept of salary accounts which required corresponding advisory action at employer level, essentially in companies but also in administrations. In some countries, the process of spreading the banking habit was also facilitated by the authorities in that they granted limited or unlimited payment account powers to savings institutions which previously were not allowed to offer payment services. In countries in which standard–of–living considerations ranked high in public opinion, banks and their competitors have often attracted new customers by referring to convenient consumer loan facilities; in other countries, reference to full banking facilities covering services such as current account management with overdraft and other consumer loan facilities, cheque, credit card and other efficient payment facilities and investment advice, was used more generally as a sales argument for attracting new customers. In this way, banks gradually changed their attitudes and increasingly adopted marketing concepts that had been used in other product and service industries for some time[6].

Chart 2.2
EXPANSION OF DOMESTIC BANKING NETWORKS
(Number of bank offices per 100 000 inhabitants)

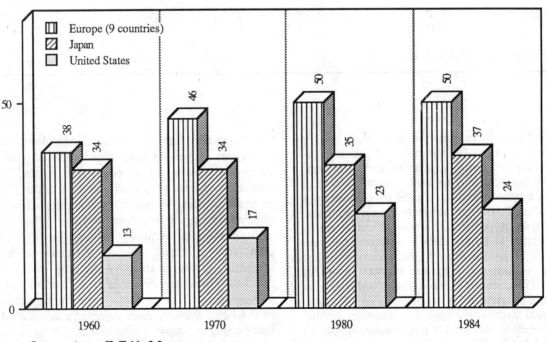

Source: Annex II, Table 2.2.

Chart 2.3
EXPANSION OF AUTOMATED TELLER MACHINE NETWORKS
(Number of ATMs per 1 million inhabitants)

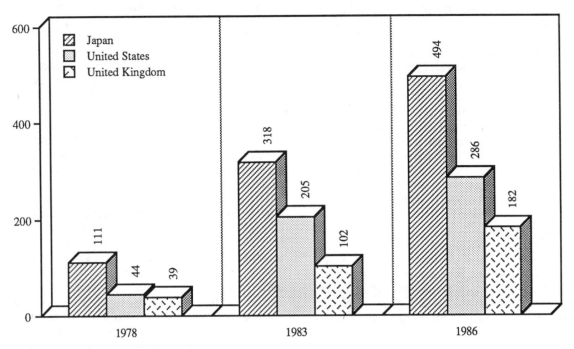

Source: Annex II, Table 3.5.

A striking feature of this early phase of private customer acquisition was that price competition was hardly used as this was considered by the banks as too costly and inefficient and was moreover in conflict with current banking practice and official restrictions on deposit rates applying at that time in most countries. In more recent years, however, banks and their competitors have increasingly introduced either direct interest incentives on current accounts or indirect techniques of efficient current account management providing remuneration of cash–like deposit facilities in order to attract new customers. This more aggressive and also more costly competitive behaviour of providers of financial services has largely to be viewed against the background of the changing nature of the retail banking market, which, in the meantime, had become largely saturated as far as the number of "banked" people is concerned. Thus, new customers often could only be acquired by attracting them away from other institutions.

The struggle for new customers has thus clearly resulted in an intensification of competitive pressures within the financial service industry forcing the banks and their competitors to make increasing use of their whole arsenal of competitive weapons such as price competition, product innovation, extending their local presence, and competition as regards the quality and convenience of service. Marketing activities and advertising including efforts to provide better information and to educate clients in financial matters more generally have also been intensified.

The trend towards approaching the saturation point in retail banking as far as the acquisition of previously "unbanked" people is concerned, also had consequences for the banks' branching strategies. Since the late seventies, the expansion of the branch network has, in most countries, slowed down considerably, or has even given way to some reduction in the number of branches[7]. This development has also to be seen in the light of the expansion of automated teller machines (ATMs) (Chart 2.3)[8] which, although not generally replacing brick and mortar branches, have to some extent the effect of a further extension of the branch network insofar as they increasingly become interlinked with different institutions, or groups of institutions, as far as cash dispenser facilities are concerned. In addition, there is slow but steady progress in the spreading of computerised "home banking" which in some countries is sponsored by the authorities[9].

25

Improved Efficiency through more Competition

The competitive process in retail banking just described has no doubt resulted in considerable efficiency gains as regards the range and the quality of the financial services and products that have become available to private households. In most OECD countries, the private customer's freedom of choice as regards his preferred banking connection has increased considerably thanks to increased geographical competition amongst different banks and groups of banking institutions and the extension of banking service powers to those institutions which previously acted exclusively as collectors and administrators of savings. The management of private customer's financial affairs, though becoming more complex over time, has been much facilitated by the increasing use of modern technology and by corresponding innovations in the services offered by banks and other providers of financial services. Current account management services nowadays provide a wide range of payment techniques and facilities such as the use of cheques, giro transfers, pre–authorised debiting, cheque and credit cards, travellers' cheques, easy access to foreign exchange, and in many countries also increasing use of automated facilities for cash withdrawal and other account handling and information. In most cases, these payment facilities are combined with overdraft facilities, and, increasingly, banks offer additional facilities for an efficient cash management such as "sweep accounts" designed to minimise the client's opportunity costs of holding cash.

Competition for market shares in the vast pool of household savings, in which governments as important issuers of savings instruments have actively participated since the early seventies, has resulted in a considerable widening of the range of products and instruments amongst which the private saver can choose according to his preferences. The distribution network through which these instruments and products can be acquired has been extended considerably. Today, the small saver often has a choice between the traditional pass book with easy, and often immediate, withdrawal facilities and a wide range of higher–yielding non–marketable and marketable savings instruments with a wide maturity spectrum, such as time deposits, non–marketable savings–bond types of instruments, marketable medium– and long–term paper, and investment certificates of various types offering risk–spreading facilities for customers seeking to invest in equity instruments or bond and money markets. Insurance–linked savings products, notably life–insured savings plans, have in recent years been increasingly offered by banks in competition with insurance companies in several countries. Middle– and high-income private investors have at their disposal, in addition to the products just mentioned, a wide range of investment outlets in domestic and foreign bond and equity markets, which have become increasingly accessible to them through the much developed investment services offered by banks and/or special securities firms. This group of more sophisticated private investors has greatly benefited from the improvement of investment advisory and information services which banks and securities firms have strongly developed in recent years. Savers in search of higher–yielding financial assets providing protection against inflation losses, have generally benefited very much from interest rate liberalisation measures taken in many countries in recent years (Chapter 3), whereas countries in which price indexed–savings instruments have been allowed in recent years, have remained relatively small in number[10].

The availability of consumer credit facilities has also been greatly improved under the impact of competition between banks and other more specialised providers of such facilities. Choices as regards suppliers and instruments have increased. Today, consumers in many countries may choose between overdraft facilities, credit facilities offered by the use of credit cards, highly standardised and easily accessible term loans offered by banks, hire-purchase loans offered by special finance companies and supplier loan facilities offered by department stores. However, despite the substantial increase in the number of players in this market and in the choice of facilities now available, a typical weakness of this particular market, the lack of visibility as far as conditions are concerned, has remained. Although the costs of consumer loans offered by banks have sometimes become comparable to those of small–business loans, there are still a number of lenders in this market charging rates which, compared with funding costs, must be considered as excessive[11].

Housing finance is an area which in many countries has been subject to considerable government intervention designed to promote social housing, to facilitate access of families to private home–ownership, or to improve the mechanisms for channelling more savings into the housing sector generally. Moreover, the scope for competition in this segment of retail banking has been subdued in many countries. Nevertheless, in those segments of the housing finance markets in which market forces have been allowed to play a role, increased competition, often stemming from commercial bank entry into the housing loan market, has resulted in wider choices available to private customers as regards suppliers, financing techniques and instruments and has led in some countries also to a conspicuous reduction in borrowing costs. Particularly noteworthy is the proliferation of innovations in housing finance that was experienced in countries in which high and volatile rates of inflation and interest rates created considerable problems for the debt service capacity of private households. Loan characteristics designed to bring the time path of debt service payments more in line with the expected time profile of private household income received special attention[12]. Another area of noteworthy improvement concerns the administrative procedures connected with housing finance operations and with changes in house-ownership and a related transfer of debt to the buyer. Banks have increasingly offered special services which simplify such procedures for the customer, notably if various sources of housing finance such as employer loans, and first and second mortgage loans are involved. Thus, a policy of more reliance on market forces, i.e. on private institutions' initiatives and innovative skills, has, on the whole, led to an increase in the availability of funds for housing finance purposes and an improvement in the quality and convenience of related services.

2.3 THE MARKETS FOR CORPORATE FINANCIAL SERVICES

The markets for corporate financial services at large — comprising financial services for small- and medium-sized enterprises as well as for multinational corporations — have also undergone considerable changes since the early sixties, although these changes, on the whole, have been less visible to the man in the street than developments in retail banking. In comparing these two large areas of financial services markets, it should be taken into account that the borderline between the two is blurred in the sense that many of the changes that have taken place in retail banking have also affected small businesses, artisans, shopkeepers and other self-employed persons. Competition between providers of financial services in local markets has intensified considerably as a result of the spectacular expansion of the banking network during the sixties and seventies. Payment services have become more sophisticated, convenient and efficient. Choices for liquidity and financial asset management of small businesses and for the financing of business expansion have widened considerably, as has already been mentioned in the section on retail banking services.

Similar to demand developments in retail banking, there have been considerable changes in enterprise demand for financial services. Special demands and needs have arisen in connection with the development of an entirely new category of enterprises, the multinational companies operating worldwide. Demand trends in the markets for corporate financial services have been affected by a number of developments: the ever-intensifying internationalisation of trade and commerce and the interpenetration of national economies generating increased demand for related international financial services; increased competition in industry and commerce at domestic and international level contributing to increased demand for more sophisticated financial management and related rationalisation measures; a shortening of the reinvestment and equipment-renewal cycles requiring corresponding changes in financing techniques; and the advent of electronic data processing and information technology providing increased scope for more sophisticated asset and liability management techniques generally. A more recent development, a sharp increase in the number of business failures and difficulties resulting from the worldwide recession of the early eighties, has been a noticeable increase in the demand by enterpreneurs and corporate managers for general management assistance from banks and other providers of financial and related advisory services. Parallel to this development, there has been increasing demand for risk capital, in particular for small- and medium-sized firms including new ventures in high-technology and other industries.

Financial Services for Multinational and Large National Corporations

The emergence of multinational corporations has generated demand for complex, rather specialised and sometimes entirely new services. These include, first of all, advisory services on market conditions, foreign exchange market trends, tax laws, investment conditions, financing conditions and socio-economic conditions in foreign countries in which multinational companies operate and invest or intend to do so. Such services have, of course, also been made available to corporate clients maintaining only trade, and no investment, relationships with foreign countries. In addition, there has been increasing demand by multinational corporations for adequate financing facilities in support of their worldwide investment and trading activities. Such special financing needs have often required special solutions, notably the recourse to the international financial markets offering a wide range of choices and a readily available pool of funds for large project financing. In many cases, the recourse to the international financial markets, in fact, offered the only viable solution in this regard as the domestic markets of both the host country and the home country of the corporation were not accessible because of exchange controls or for other reasons. Recourse to the rapidly developing international financial markets was also increasingly sought by large national corporations.

A third type of demand for entirely new financial services has been generated by the multinational companies' increasing needs for an active and often centralised management of their worldwide cash balances and liquidity reserves, which included also the need for active management of the foreign exchange risks involved in international investment and trade operations and related billing and payment procedures. Demand for foreign exchange risk management has become particularly strong since the generalised floating of foreign exchange rates in 1973.

A need for a more active and sophisticated cash and liquidity management and the related management of payables and receivables has, of course, also been increasingly felt in other large and medium-sized corporations whose activities were less multinationalised. This problem has been much enhanced in more recent years, when in the face of subdued business and investment activity, many corporations accumulated unusually large liquidity reserves.

The complex financial service demands of the newly-emerging multinational corporations have generally been taken care of by a relatively small number of large internationally-operating banks which often have had to co-operate in areas such as the syndication of large credits or the flotation of corporate bonds in the international markets while at the same time competing very strongly in areas such as the lead management for syndicated loans and bond flotations and a whole range of other financial and related advisory services. With a view to maintaining business relationships with multinational corporations headquartered in their home countries, banks have often supported their corporate clients' international operations by setting up branches, subsidiaries or representative offices in the main foreign countries in which these corporations operate, thereby attempting to facilitate access by their corporate clients to the financial services and products available in the host country[13].

As most internationally-operating banks have pursued the same strategies in servicing multinational corporations and large national companies so that there was practically no scope for "niche playing", competition in this market has become very intensive, as is evidenced by the compression of fees and margins charged for international borrowing operations that has taken place in the seventies and eighties and by the proliferation of new borrowing instruments and techniques which the internationally-operating banks offer to their multinational corporate clientele. Competitive advantages gained by innovation were usually short-lived as new instruments and techniques in finance can generally be imitated very easily. Competitive pressures in this market arose also from the behaviour of the corporations themselves, as they were in constant search for best-quality and lowest-cost services and products and tended to entertain multiple banking relationships for this purpose. Competition was further enhanced by the fact that corporations tended to become competitors of the banks in areas such as global financial management and centralised cash management for the worldwide corporate group as a whole. Some corporations have in fact set up their own specialised finance subsidiaries which are in charge of these functions[14]. Banks responded to these pressures by making energetic efforts towards developing efficient computerised cash management systems which they made available on a licence basis not only to their international corporate clients but also to their bank competitors. Such systems were, of course, also made available to large national corporations. Competition in this field has been further strengthened by the entry into this market of specialised computer-service firms which sometimes have the competitive advantage vis-à-vis banks that corporations are often more inclined to entrust such outside firms with the collection and processing of relevant data which provide considerable insight into the corporations' worldwide banking relationships. Demand by large national and multinational corporations for facilities for efficient asset and liability management has increasingly been met, with support from the authorities, by the creation of markets for a variety of short-term debt instruments (commercial paper, bankers' acceptances and similar short-term promissory notes). In a similar way, the ever-increasing demand for facilities enabling corporations to cover foreign exchange risks and interest rate risks has been met by strongly expanding markets for financial futures and options (Chart 2.8)[15], on the one hand, and markets for foreign currency and interest rate swaps, on the other hand. These markets have, of course, also been increasingly used by banks and institutional investors. (See also section on International Financial Services.)

Some General Trends in Enterprise Financing

In the field of enterprise financing at national level, a number of changes which have generated new demands for funds are noteworthy. On the whole, there has been a trend towards a decline in equity-to-debt ratios, which may in part be explained by the fact that tax systems have often favoured borrowing rather than the raising of risk capital. This trend has apparently been reversed to some extent in more recent years. Although relatively high positive real rates of interest have prevailed since the early eighties, the rate of return on real investments has improved in recent years even more strongly. Thus, the attractiveness of investment in risk capital was restored again in particular after the massive stock price correction of October 1987. The development of markets for risk capital for medium–sized enterprises has also been much encouraged by government taxation policies providing incentives for the formation of venture capital firms and venture capital funds or designed to widen private shareholdership generally. The creation of new segments in the stock markets for firms unable to meet the full listing requirements has also been a factor favouring the raising of risk capital by medium–sized firms in a number of countries.

As far as enterprise borrowing is concerned, the most noticeable development since the late fifties has been a sharply rising demand for medium–term loans. Two factors have had a major influence in this regard. First, with rapid progress and change in technology, industrial equipment has tended to become obsolete within shorter periods than in the past so that equipment renewal or entire changes in production techniques had to take place at shorter intervals; second, with the emergence of high and volatile interest rates in the early seventies, enterprises have, on the whole, become more flexible in their liability management and have tended to shorten the maturity of their debt, partly for interest rate risk reasons and partly reflecting an effort to adapt financing demands to changes in investor preferences and bank lending attitudes.

In many countries, the banks have made major efforts towards meeting these new medium–term financing demands of enterprises and have strongly developed their medium–term lending business at fixed or variable rates and have introduced new financing facilities such as leasing and factoring. The latter two forms of financing were particularly welcome to the firms as they helped to relieve pressures on capital ratios insofar as they do not involve an increase in outstanding debt.

Competition in these markets for medium–term enterprise financing has considerably increased in most countries. In a number of countries, where this has been possible under existing regulatory frameworks, retail banking institutions such as savings banks and credit co–operatives, have gradually moved into the commercial loan market (see section on The Markets for Retail Banking Services). In some countries, new competitors in the form of finance companies specialised in industrial hire purchase finance, leasing or factoring, have entered this market. Sometimes, the banks themselves have set up such finance companies in order to be able to compete more effectively for medium–term funds needed for funding the medium–term lending business. This has been the case particularly in countries in which banks had been subject to interest rate controls, interest rate cartel agreements or direct lending controls and in which the setting up of finance companies was thus seen by

banks as an appropriate way of by–passing such regulatory constraints. In some other countries with more scope for competition within the banking sector, the expansion of the medium–term lending business has provided a major impetus for the banks to move into, or energetically expand, the savings business in order to broaden the funding base for lending at medium term.

Sometimes, regulatory frameworks made it possible for insurance companies and pension funds to become powerful competitors in the business term loan market. Finally, the development of the international term loan market — notably the market for syndicated loans — has added to the competitive pressure in the medium–term loan market, although the international sector of this market tends to be accessible only by enterprises of a certain size and standing. The development of competitive markets for term loans has in some countries such as Germany, the Netherlands and the United Kingdom resulted in a more or less complete disappearance of the corporate bond market, although the biggest corporations in these countries continue to tap the international money, note and bond markets from time to time in connection with worldwide financing and investment operations.

As far as term lending to small– and medium–sized enterprises is concerned, it is less clear whether banks and their competitors have been able to satisfy the financing needs of this part of the business sector. What has sometimes been considered as constituting a financing gap in national financial systems in this field, often proved to be a problem of a lack of adequate security and collateral or a lack of own capital. The setting up of special credit guarantee associations, or schemes, has sometimes remedied the situation to some extent as far as term lending to small businesses is concerned. However, more recent efforts on the part of both market participants and the authorities directed towards promoting the markets for risk capital for these firms appear to be a more promising approach towards dealing with financing problems in this field.

Risk Capital for Small– and Medium–Sized Enterprises

While there is a large measure of agreement on the part of both market participants and governments that there has been a considerable increase, in recent years, in the underlying demand for risk capital for small– and medium–sized enterprises both in connection with the creation of new businesses and the expansion of existing businesses, there is little knowledge about the "size of the problem". The question of risk capital for such enterprises is complicated by the fact that enterpreneurs in need of risk funds are generally not prepared to

Table 2.4 **Emergence of the venture capital industry**[1]

	Number of Venture Capital Firms		Venture Capital Pool (US$ million)	
	1986	1988	1986	1988
North America	594	698	21 000	30 850
OECD–Europe (8 countries)	310	454	7 130	14 310
OECD–Asia	81	90	900	3 550
	985	1 242	29 030	48 710

1. Venture capital firms were virtually non–existent in the early 1980s except for the United States where the capital pool amounted to about US$5 billion.
Source: Venture Economics Limited, London.

see the control over their business affairs diluted by accepting outside providers of risk capital who have an influence on the management.

Banks and other deposit–taking institutions with relatively low capital ratios have generally done very little in terms of directly providing risk capital for small– and medium–sized enterprises as this would have been in conflict with their own, and the authorities', prudential concerns. However, within the scope provided by capital ratio requirements, financial institutions have sometimes combined forces amongst themselves, or with large commercial and industrial enterprises, to set up special venture capital firms and/or funds designed to provide participations in small– and medium–sized firms with a good performance and profit outlook. While venture capital funds organised in the form of closed–end investment funds are designed to raise risk capital in the open market and to channel these funds into eligible firms without being involved in their management, venture capital firms with usually a small number of shareholders see their role more in providing management advice to the firms in which they hold participations as well. Such venture capital firms have often been set up outside the banking sector, in particular in countries without a strong merchant bank tradition (Table 2.4).

In a number of countries, banks and/or securities firms and the stock exchanges of which they are members, have taken special steps to promote access to the organised market for risk capital by medium–sized enterprises which cannot meet full–listing requirements. Thus, new segments of the stock exchange, which are sometimes referred to as "second" markets or "unlisted securities markets", have been created in Australia, Canada, Denmark,

France, Germany, Italy and the United Kingdom and have seen a strong development in some of these countries in recent years[16]. Shares of smaller unlisted companies which are not eligible for listing in the "first" or "second" segment of a stock exchange are usually traded in unregulated over–the–counter m arkets.

The authorities have often been concerned with the problem of ensuring an adequate supply of risk capital for small– and medium–sized enterprises because of the employment and technological progress potential that is offered by such firms and have, therefore, often supported developments in this field by providing fiscal incentives or by encouraging the banks more generally to assist smaller companies in "going public".

Increasing Needs for Merchant Banking Facilities

Apart from these developments in the markets for risk capital for small– and medium–sized enterprises, which are an area of typical merchant banking activities, there has been a more general trend in recent years, since the late seventies, towards greater bank involvement in company affairs. Unprecedented numbers of firms in difficulty have generated considerable demand for outside management advice, notably as regards enterprise restructuring, the organisation of rescue operations, mergers and acquisitions, management buy–outs (Charts 2.5 and 2.6), and general financial management. Banks or qualified non–banking firms specialised in these types of merchant banking activities, faced with an explosive demand situation in this area, have seen a spectacular expansion of their activities, and commercial banks as well as consultancy firms have made major efforts to move forcefully into this rather promising line of business as well. In the process, banks which traditionally abstained from being closely involved in corporate affairs, have considerably strengthened their corporate advisory services or have set up entirely new departments or subsidiaries for such services[17]. For the clearing banks in the United Kingdom and most commercial banks in the United States such a move into business management advisory services meant an almost revolutionary departure from the banks' traditional relationship with business customers. In other countries such as Germany and Japan, where banks traditionally had close management relations with their business customers, the response of the banks to the newly arising financial and other service needs of these customers has been a more gradual process. Nevertheless, a strong upward trend in such activities has also been noticeable in these countries.In some other countries, both market participants and the authorities have felt in recent years an increasing need for the development of merchant banking facilities as these were not offered by the existing banking system because of regulatory constraints or the lack of knowledge, ex-

perience and initiative. Thus, the authorities in Italy have taken legislative measures aimed at facilitating the creation of merchant banks[18]. Other countries have allowed foreign merchant banks to enter the domestic market with a view to promoting competition and efficiency in this particular field.

2.4 THE MARKETS FOR SECURITIES–RELATED SERVICES

The markets for securities–related services are a vast area covering a wide range of sub–markets for different and heterogeneous services and activities with different demand and supply characteristics and competitive structures. The following broader market areas may be distinguished:

— The new–issuing business which comprises both advisory services on instruments of various types to be issued and the activity of selling such instruments to investors through a variety of techniques;
— Secondary market activities comprising the handling of client orders i.e. brokerage business, and trading on own account i.e. jobbing and market–making activities, which

Chart 2.4
GROWTH OF "SECOND" EQUITY MARKETS
(Number of quoted companies)

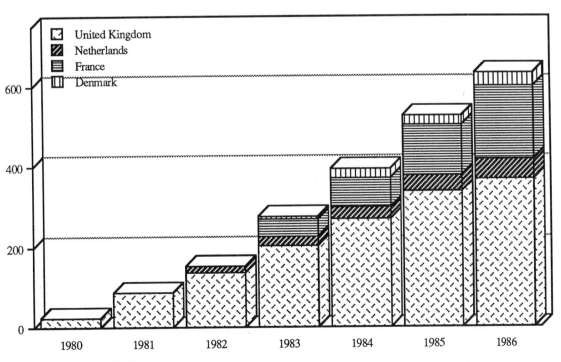

Source: Annex II, Table 4.6.

Chart 2.5
DEVELOPMENTS IN "BUY-OUT" ACTIVITIES

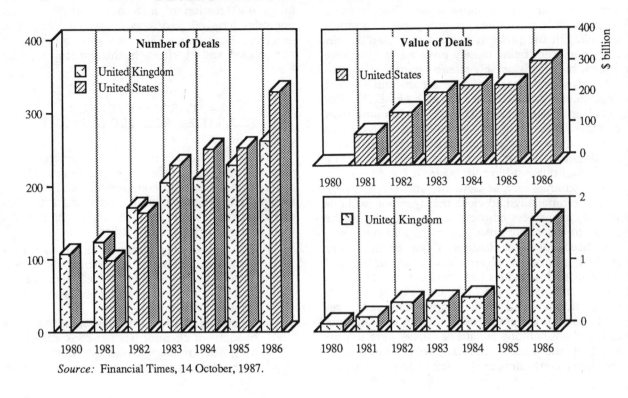

Source: Financial Times, 14 October, 1987.

Chart 2.6
DEVELOPMENTS IN ACQUISITIONS AND MERGERS
IN THE UNITED KINGDOM

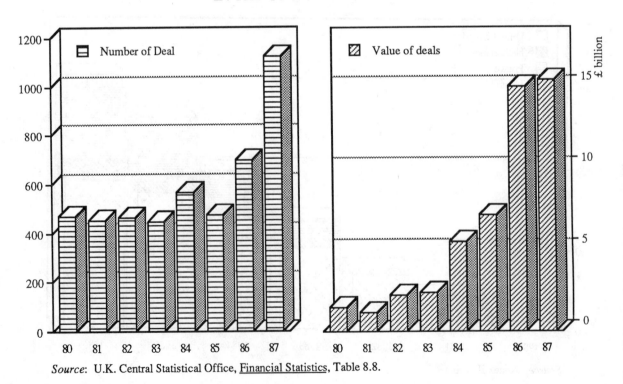

Source: U.K. Central Statistical Office, Financial Statistics, Table 8.8.

Chart 2.7
REVENUES AND EXPENSES OF NEW YORK
STOCK EXCHANGE MEMBER FIRMS

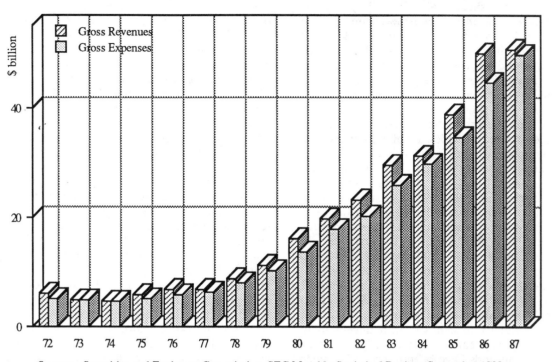

Source: Securities and Exchange Commission, SEC Monthly Statistical Review, September 1988.

may take place within or outside stock exchanges depending on regulatory frameworks and market practices;

— Portfolio management of various types and related administrative services: the management of own portfolios, portfolios of mutual funds, insurance companies or pension funds, discretionary portfolio management for clients with different degrees of client involvement, and portfolio administration which includes safe–custody services for clients and the handling of debt service operations such as interest rate and redemption payments and, as far as shares are concerned, the handling of company information to be transmitted to shareholders and dividend payments etc.;

— Investment advisory services comprising market analysis and financial analysis of individual companies and other issuers.

The markets for all these activities have considerably expanded since the early sixties, subject to certain cycles relating to alternating phases of monetary ease and restraint and accelerating and decelerating economic activity. The importance of most of these activities cannot be assessed with any

precision. While it is easy to follow trends in the new issue markets and secondary market activity on stock exchanges, it is almost impossible to measure the growth of secondary market activity outside the stock exchanges and of financial service markets in areas such as portfolio management and investment advisory services. It can, however, be concluded from the growth of the portfolios of institutional investors such as pension funds, insurance companies and mutual funds that portfolio management activities and related advisory services must have expanded considerably over the years. This is also evidenced by the rapidly increasing flood of related financial investment and market literature produced by the banks' and securities firms' advisory services and the specialised press. As far as the United States is concerned, developments in revenues and expenses of New York Stock Exchange (NYSE) member firms indicate a sharp expansion in securities–related activities since the late seventies (Chart 2.7).

Since the late seventies or early eighties, there has been a pronounced acceleration or even something like a quantum jump in all or most of these activities. One indication is that bond markets measured in terms of volume of bonds in circula-

33

tion, have, in the eighties, expanded more rapidly than national banking systems while in the preceding twenty years, both in the sixties and in the seventies, bond markets generally grew more slowly than bank balance sheet totals (Table 2.5). As far as the sharp expansion of new issue volumes in the early eighties is concerned, there can be little doubt that the decline in interest rates after 1981 or so has strongly favoured this trend. In addition, industrial corporations lacking profitable plant and equipment outlets, became important buyers of securities in the first years of the eighties. Another relatively recent trend has been the pronounced internationalisation of securities–related activities, notably in areas such as portfolio management, securities trading activities and investment advisory services. In the late seventies, large institutional investors in Japan, the United Kingdom and the United States began to concentrate their interests on foreign securities markets and have since intensified their efforts towards international diversification of their portfolios. In the United Kingdom, this development has been much favoured by the abolition of exchange controls in 1979. In other countries such as France, Germany, the Netherlands, and Switzerland, the international diversification of securities portfolios, notably of mutual funds, has been a development which started much earlier, in the early seventies. In Italy, mutual funds have been in operation since the end of 1984.

Main Features of Competition in the New Issuing Business

Since the late seventies, banks and securities houses have considerably expanded their new-issuing business (Table 2.6) in line with demand trends and have, on the whole, been rather efficient in broadening their placing power. Considerable skills have been developed as regards the design of new instruments reconciling as best as possible the often diverging preferences of borrowers and investors. The proliferation of new products appears to have been strongest in the international new issue markets reflecting the intensity of product competition which is characteristic of these markets[19]. Thus, the history of the international issue markets, which hesitantly started to operate on a rather small scale in the mid–sixties, has seen the development of a whole range of new instruments such as floating rate notes, bonds with warrants of various kinds, dual currency bonds, bonds denominated in various kinds of composite currencies, zero coupon bonds and new issues endowed with interest rate or currency swap features making it possible to reduce interest rate or currency risks or accessing particular currency sections of the international market at lower costs than otherwise. While some of these features have been copied from some national bond markets[20], the reverse has also occurred, namely that product innovation spread from the international bond market to some national markets. Most of these innovative features have been a fairly recent development starting in the late seventies and gaining, as far as volume is concerned, greater momentum in the early eighties. However, not all innovative instruments have remained a lasting success as the need for creating efficient secondary markets in such instruments has not always been sufficiently respected[21]. It appears to be a general feature of the new issuing business that competition in this important financial service market tends to take mainly the form of product differentiation and

Table 2.5 Growth of secondary bond markets

Compound Annual Rates of Growth of Outstanding Amounts in Constant US Dollars

		1964–1970	1870–1980	1980–1985
North America	BMs	6.9	10.9	15.3
	BSs	8.6	11.8	9.7
OECD–Europe	BMs	10.8	14.8	16.8
	BSs	14.5	17.3	13.7
Japan	BMs	18.2	22.3	12.9
	BSs	16.5	15.0	9.3
Total (14 OECD Countries)	BMs	8.6	13.6	15.1
	BSs	11.8	14.7	11.7

BSs = Banking Systems
BMs = Bond Markets
Source: Annex II, Table 4.4

Table 2.6 Growth of bond issue markets
Average Annual Amount of Gross New Issues in Current US$ Billion

	1962–1970	1971–1975	1976–1980	1981–1985	1986
I. *National Bond Markets*					
1. North America	48.4	112.1	233.4	466.7	750.5
2. OECD Europe	24.6	83.4	191.8	283.7	430.8
3. Japan	9.8	44.5	134.5	212.6	428.4
4. OECD Total	82.8	240.0	559.7	963.0	1 609.7
Of which: Traditional foreign bond issues	(3.0)	(5.5)	(16.8)	(26.0)	(38.6)
II. *International Bond Markets*	2.0	6.7	19.7	71.8	187.0
GRAND TOTAL	84.8	246.7	579.4	1 034.8	1 796.7

sharp pricing of an issue rather than resulting in commission cutting. Even in the otherwise highly competitive international issue market, in which the free choice of lead managers is an important competitive feature, banks and securities houses have resisted pressures from issuers for lower commission rates very well. Banks and securities houses have only slightly reduced nominal commission rates on shorter–term instruments and on some issues of the most prestigious borrowers in the international market. Nevertheless, the overall profitability of the new–issuing business, notably in the wholesale area, has come under considerable competitive pressure as institutional investors were increasingly able to obtain "rebates" on the posted issue price which applies to retail sales.In many domestic bond markets, the new–issuing business has pronounced monopolistic features. This is notably the case in countries in which the consortium technique is used, which provides, against a special fee, a guarantee that the issue will be firmly placed. In the absence of flexible issue–consortium arrangements, which is characteristic of small markets, the issue costs may indeed be seen as being fixed in a monopolistic fashion.

Governments, which have been directly affected by this situation insofar as they have become important issuers in the bond market since the early seventies, have made considerable efforts in some countries to inject more competition into the new–issuing business. This has essentially been attempted by introducing auction techniques, which have more competitive features than the consortium technique. In the United States this technique has been used for some time while in other OECD countries the use of auction techniques has been a more recent feature[22].

As far as the selling of new issues of borrowers other than the government is concerned, which usually raise much smaller amounts than the government, an attempt has been made by the authorities to increase competition in the new issue market by giving the issuer free choice of the lead manager, thus adopting the practice of the international issue market. In some other countries, governments have negotiated with the consortium a reduction in issue commissions on their own issues.

Competitive Changes in the Securities Trading and Brokerage Business

The securities trading and brokerage business, which has also expanded considerably since the early eighties (Chart 2.8), has traditionally been the domain of the stock exchanges and their members although non–member institutions have usually been allowed to accept buy and sell orders from clients and pass them on to stock exchange members for execution. The procedures and related commissions involved have been set by the stock exchange members in a rather rigid way so that stock exchanges, in fact, had traditionally many features of a closed "club" dominating the business of secondary market activities in securities.

This broad general picture does not apply in the same way to all countries, however. In a number of countries, where stock exchanges were not established as monopolies, market pressures have gradually led to the development of securities trading markets outside the stock exchange. For the trading of unquoted securities this was a necessity although officially–quoted securities also increasingly found their way into such unregulated markets in which professionals trade on the basis of net ask

Chart 2.8

STOCK EXCHANGE EQUITY TRADING
(Trading volume in U.S. dollar billion)

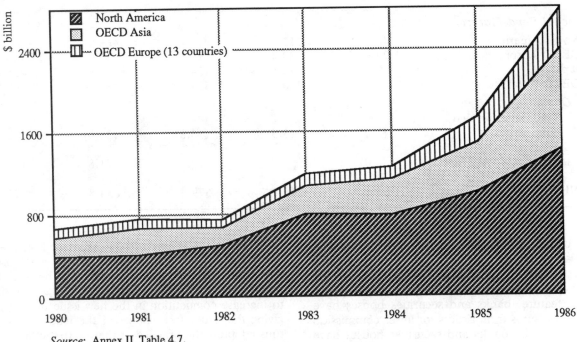

Source: Annex II, Table 4.7.

and bid prices, thus adopting the practice of foreign exchange markets. The banks' and securities dealers' clients other than large institutional investors — which in some countries have tended to trade amongst themselves — for a long time benefited little from these new, more competitive, trading practices as their orders, irrespective of the way in which they were executed, were subject to fixed commissions.

Since the abolition of the system of fixed minimum commissions at the New York Stock Exchange in 1975, market pressures in favour of abandoning the previous "club arrangements" in the securities trading and brokerage business gradually gathered momentum and encouraged the stock exchanges in some other countries such as Australia, Canada, France and the United Kingdom to follow the US example and abandon the system of fixed minimum commissions. In other countries such as the Netherlands and Switzerland, stock exchange members revised commission structures downward, notably as regards commissions on large transactions.

The abolition of the system of fixed minimum commissions led to a considerable intensification of competition in the securities brokerage business, which, on the whole, resulted in a sizeable reduction in transaction costs[23]. In the United States and Canada, the new entry of a considerable number of discount–brokers, which are highly specialised in the handling of large numbers of buy and sell orders without, however, providing related investment advisory services, has contributed to the improvement of cost efficiency of this particular service market.

As far as securities trading is concerned, there is evidence that the advent of modern computer technology and electronic data processing and information systems provides a major impetus to a profound transformation of dealing techniques. Judging from the spreading of the techniques developed in the United States by the National Association of Securities Dealers, it seems that securities markets — as far as the price determination process is concerned — will gradually change to a situation in which the traditional auction markets, which generally do not provide much scope for an active market making, will co–exist with dealer markets in which market makers compete with each other in the price–setting process. This latter trading technique is, moreover, based on price information which, thanks to modern communication techniques, is available on a nationwide or even worldwide basis. A number of securities, for example, the shares of the world's biggest companies, are already traded on a worldwide basis; and their number is rapidly increasing[24].

Internationally–operating banks and securities houses have responded to these new developements in the securities trading and related portfolio-management business and to the opportunities offered by these activities in future, by making major efforts towards extending their presence to all major financial market centres in the world. In countries in which domestically the business of commercial banking is legally separated from some securities–related activities, the authorities have adapted regulatory frameworks with a view to enabling domestic banks to benefit from these developments and to move abroad also into securities–related activities[25].

Portfolio Management and Investment Advisory and Information Services

The growth of securities portfolios of insurance companies, pension funds, and open–end or closed–end funds, on the one hand, and of wealthy private individuals, on the other, not only contributed to a pronounced increase in turnover in the brokerage and trading business, but has also gene-

rated ever–increasing demand for portfolio management services and related advisory and information services. The need for high–quality services in this field — information on financial market trends in different countries and on individual securities and related financial analysis of companies and other issuers of securities — has become even more pressing as institutional as well as wealthy private investors made increasing efforts towards diversifying their portfolios on a worldwide basis. This trend has been much enhanced by a generalised move towards liberalisation of international capital movements.Floating exchange rates since 1973, increased volatility in interest rates and a sharp increase in related investment risks have strongly contributed to a more active and more sophisticated portfolio management resulting in much higher turnover as well as generating increasing demand for facilities for hedging foreign exchange, price and interest rate risks. These new needs for risk management facilities, which were increasingly felt not only by securities portfolio managers but also by internationally–operating banks and industrial and commercial corporations, have no doubt been a major driving force behind the development of markets for financial futures and options (Chart 2.9)

Chart 2.9
GROWTH OF FINANCIAL FUTURES AND OPTIONS MARKETS (1)
(Number of traded contracts in 1000s)

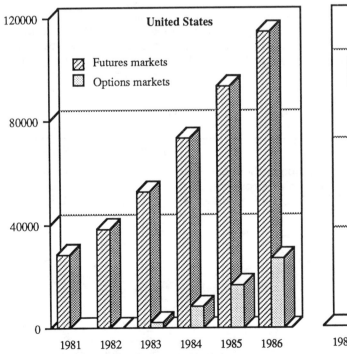

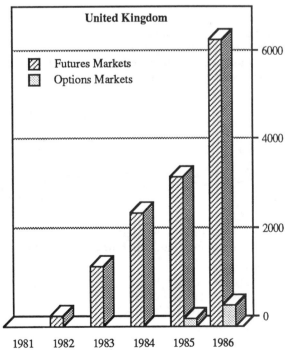

1. Excluding options on individual shares.
Source: Annex II, Tables 4.8 and 4.9.

and currency and interest rate swaps which have seen an explosive expansion in recent years[26].

In response to these demand trends, competition in the provision of these special services has considerably intensified as banks with securities departments and securities firms as well as newcomers from the non–banking sector have made considerable efforts to seize business and profit opportunities offered by these fast–growing special service markets. Competitive strategies were mainly directed towards product differentiation in the form of offering high–quality information and advisory services and efforts to produce high returns on discretionary portfolios. Price competition has been less important in these special markets. Competition amongst providers of these services has often taken the form of "head hunting" as well, with corresponding effects on salaries offered to specialists in this field.

While a relatively small number of large and financially strong securities service conglomerates have adopted a strategy of offering the whole range of securities–related services on a worldwide basis, which requires their presence in all major international financial centres, there is considerable scope for smaller firms to carve out market niches for themselves by specialising in relatively small sub–markets of this vast and complex service market area. Thus, many national securities markets have specialists for certain areas such as the relatively small, but often dynamic, markets for unlisted securities and for securities traded in unregulated markets. Other firms have become specialists for globally–traded shares of the biggest companies in the world. The large universal banks with nationwide branch networks and important retail banking interests have made considerable efforts towards expanding their investment advisory services to their middle–income clientele also. Such services, if efficiently managed, are perceived as having potential for considerable fee income.

As in a number of countries portfolio management, advisory and information services do not require a special licence under banking or securities laws, there has been considerable scope for outsiders to enter this special service market. As a result, pressures on banks and securities firms to offer high–quality services have increased. The tendency amongst institutional investors to become more active in the self–management of their portfolios has worked in the same direction.

2.5 THE MARKETS FOR INTERBANK FINANCIAL SERVICES

A review of demand and supply trends in the financial service markets would be incomplete if no reference were made to the markets for interbank financial services, or services needed and offered within the financial sector. Although this market area is difficult to measure statistically, it is obvious that the functioning of national financial systems and linkages between national financial systems generate substantial demand for financial services on the part of banks and other financial institutions themselves. The most obvious case is the growth of interbank money markets which the banks have created themselves for an efficient asset and liability management. These markets, and related operations and services, have grown substantially both at national and international level (Table 2.7)[27]. The working of the foreign exchange markets and of securities markets outside the stock exchanges — and the "making" of these markets — is also largely based on interbank or interdealer transactions

Table 2.7 **Growth of international interbank markets**

	1966–1974	1974–1980	1980–1987	End–1987
	Compound Annual Rates of Growth of Outstanding Amounts			Outstanding Amounts $US Billion
1. Cross–border Interbank Claims	32.5	22.8	20.2	2 780
2. Cross–border Interbank Liabilities	39.0	21.3	15.6	3 009
For comparison:				
3. Total Cross–border Claims of Reporting Banks	34.7	24.1	17.8	4 157
4. Total Cross–border Liabilities of Reporting Banks	36.5	22.6	17.8	4 201

Source: Bank for International Settlements.

which even out regional or international price differences by arbitrage operations and which may attain large volumes[28]. In order that these intra–system operations, whether related to customer transactions or not, may be conducted effectively, banks and dealers have made major co–operative efforts to develop efficient communication and information networks and related data banks[29], partly in co–operation with computer firms and information vendors. These efforts have also covered areas such as the operation of computerised and automated settlement and clearing systems for payments and for securities transactions. Book–entry systems for securities may also be mentioned in this context. In a number of countries, such developments have been actively encouraged and monitored by the authorities (Chapter 3).

Demand for interbank financial services has become particularly strong in connection with cross–border financial transactions and services. As only a relatively small number of banks and securities firms are in a position to maintain subsidiaries and/or branches in other countries, it is clear that financial service links between countries have largely to be based on correspondent–banking relations and related intersystem financial services. In a similar way, international securities buy and sell orders have to be passed mostly through a chain of several financial institutions, which sometimes creates problems as regards costs, time, safety and reliability of such operations. The international banking and securities dealer community is at present making considerable efforts towards streamlining these linkages through developing an efficient and reliable technological infrastructure.

2.6 THE MARKETS FOR INTERNATIONAL FINANCIAL SERVICES

The markets for international financial services cover a wide range of different, though often closely interrelated, activities such as the traditional activities of import and export financing and related advisory services, foreign exchange and brokerage services; and the more recently developed activities such as international money–market operations, notably amongst the banks themselves (see section on The Markets for Interbank Financial Services); special financial and advisory services of various kinds for multinational companies which developed entirely new financial service needs (see section on Financial Services for Multinational and Large National Corporations); international loan operations with a wide range of borrowers in– and outside the OECD area including operations serving the finan-

cing of balance–of–payment deficits; the international securities issuing business; and cross–border securities trading and brokerage activities as well as portfolio management and related advisory services (see section on The Markets for Securities–related Services). Finally, operations in national financial markets of other countries form an important part of the international business of banks[30].

Demand for international financial services originates from practically all sectors of the economy (Table 2.8, Charts 2.10, 2.11). In the retail banking area, there has been increasing demand from private households for convenient payment and retail foreign exchange brokerage services in connection with the dynamic expansion of international tourism and business travelling. With the internationalisation of trade and commerce and the development of multinational companies, the company sector, including smaller companies with international trade activities, has become an important demander for international financial services. Governments and other public–sector entities have generated important demand for capital imports for budget deficit and/or balance–of–payment deficit financing purposes. Demand from this sector for services relating to the management of external debt has also increased substantially in recent years. Finally, there are the banks and other financial institutions themselves which have generated considerable demand for international financial services in connection with international asset and liability management[31], international payment services, foreign exchange risk management and international securities–related activities.

As most of these activities have already been dealt with elsewhere in this chapter, it seems sufficient to provide in this section a broad overview of trends in these various sub–markets of the international financial services markets and to point to some special developments which deserve stressing in this context. At a time when financial innovations in the international financial markets (including innovations which are relatively short–lived and more in the nature of gimmicks) make the headlines of the financial press, it seems indicated to recall that the creation of the international money, credit and bond markets has been the first, and most important, innovation which the banking community introduced after World War II. The creation of this vast and rapidly growing pool of internationally available funds has no doubt facilitated the expansion of international trade and investment at a time when extensive use of capital movement controls limited the scope for cross–border financing operations quite drastically.

From a national financial policy point of view, it is remarkable that these international financial markets have come into being largely as a result of free interplay of market forces and with a minimum of

Table 2.8 **Growth of external financial assets and liabilities of selected OECD countries**
Compound Annual Rate of Growth

		1960–1970	1970–1980	1980–1984
I. *Financial Assets*				
Eight OECD	EA	..	11.8	12.2
Countries (1)	ADA	..	11.1	9.4
Of which:				
United States	EA	7.1	9.2	5.5
	ADA	6.9	9.1	9.3
Japan	EA	..	19.2	20.9
	ADA	..	15.1	9.1
II. *Liabilities*				
Eight OECD	EL	..	15.6	14.2
Countries (1)	ADL	..	12.2	10.4
Of which:				
United States	EL	9.3	15.0	11.6
	ADL	7.0	10.7	10.9
Japan	EL	..	23.0	15.9
	ADL	..	14.7	8.5

1. Australia, Belgium, Canada, Germany, Japan, Spain, Sweden, United States.
EA = External financial assets.
EL = External liabilities.
ADA = All domestic non–financial sectors' financial assets.
ADL = All domestic non–financial sectors' liabilities.
Source: Annex II, Table 6.1.

Table 2.9 **Internationalisation of bank lending**
Compound Annual Rates of Growth

	1960–1970	1970–1980	1980–1985	End–85 Outstanding Amounts US$ Billion
North America				
EA	10.6	26.6	1.1	232
TA	8.5	11.8	9.7	2 528
OECD Europe				
EA	27.1	23.0	17.6	1 394
TA	14.3	17.4	13.7	4 049
OECD Asia				
EA	22.1	16.5	18.2	127
TA	16.7	14.9	9.6	2 087
OECD Total				
EA	21.7	23.4	15.3	1 753
TA	11.8	15.0	11.9	8 666

EA = External assets of banks.
TA = Total assets of banks.
Source: Annex II, Table 6.2.

Chart 2.10
INTERNATIONALISATION OF BOND ISSUE MARKETS
a) Average annual amount of gross   b)Per cent of total gross bond issues
issues in dollar billion   in the OECD area

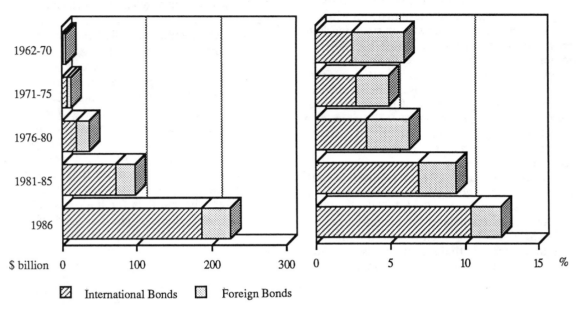

International Bonds   Foreign Bonds

Source: Annex II, Table 4.2.

Chart 2.11
CROSS BORDER SECURITIES TRANSACTIONS (1)
a) Resident Transactions   b) Non-resident Transactions
in Foreign Securities   in Domestic Securities

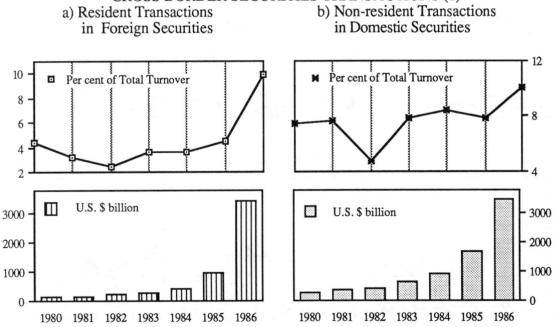

1. Four Countries: France, Germany, Japan, United States.
Source: Annex II, Table 6.6.

government intervention and sometimes against the intentions of the authorities of a number of countries. It needs recalling, however, that in some important countries, the authorities have set regulatory frameworks, including exchange controls affecting international banking operations, with a view to facilitating the development of these markets while in some other countries the growth of such markets was prevented by restrictive measures.

Another area in which private financial institutions, not necessarily banks, have created international service facilities in response to newly developing needs, is the development of financial futures and options markets and markets for interest rate and foreign currency swaps, which all provide hedging facilities for operators in the international financial markets seeking to protect themselves against losses that could arise in connection with unexpected foreign exchange rate, interest rate and securities price movements. Such hedging facilities are, of course, also available for operators on national financial markets. However, the international significance of these markets is probably much more important insofar as these facilities may help maintain international trade and investment relations at sustained levels under conditions of considerable uncertainty as regards foreign exchange rate and interest rate movements. In the absence of efficient hedging facilities these uncertainties would probably exert a restraining effect on the international exchange of goods, services and capital. Competition in all these international financial services has been strong as these markets are generally open to newcomers.

International competition in national financial systems has also increased as most countries have gradually opened their frontiers to foreign banks, often with the intention of increasing competition in areas such as foreign exchange trading, international trade financing, and other international financial services and thus improving the efficiency of these particular financial service markets.

Although the markets for international financial services are generally characterised by intense, sometimes even excessive, competition, there has been a noticeable change in recent years, in the competitive climate in particular sub-markets for

Chart 2.12
INTERNATIONALISATION OF BANKING NETWORKS

a) Foreign Banking Presence

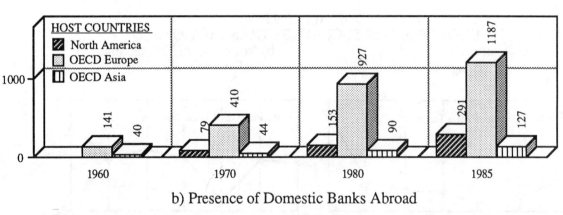

b) Presence of Domestic Banks Abroad

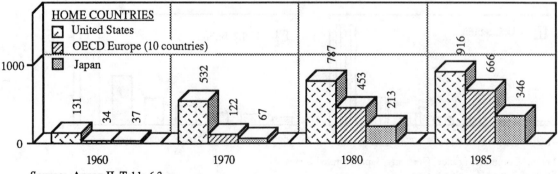

Source: Annex II, Table 6.3.

42

such services. Thus, in view of the increased risks involved, loan operations with developing countries have lost most of their previous attraction. Interbank operations with countries in difficulty have also been affected by the international debt crisis. While in the international loan and interbank business banks have largely concentrated on operations with first–class borrowers from developed countries, they have also made considerable efforts, since the early eighties or so, towards expanding off–balance–sheet operations of various kinds such as the new–issuing business in the traditional bond markets and the new markets for euronotes and eurocommercial paper as well as securities–related operations in general. Capital adequacy considerations have played a major role in this regard. As has already been mentioned in the preceding section, banks with securities departments and securities firms have most recently concentrated their efforts particularly on the expansion of their international issuing, trading and brokerage activities in securities combined with portfolio management services and related advisory services. A substantial increase in the establishment of foreign banks and securities firms in major financial centres in most recent years — 1985–1988 — has been the most visible sign of these efforts (Chart 2.12).

NOTES AND REFERENCES

1. Annex II, Tables 2.1 and 2.2.

2. Annex I, Section 1.

3. P. Frazer, D. Vittas, *The Retail Banking Revolution, An International Perspective*, London, 1982. The book provides a detailed international survey of trends in retail banking.

4. T.W. Thompson, L.L. Berry, P.H. Davidson, *Banking Tomorrow*, New York, 1978.

5. Annex II, Table 3.4. Annex III, Section XII.

6. C. McIver, G. Naylor, *Marketing Financial Services*, The Institute of Bankers, London, 1980.

7. Annex II, Table 3.4.

8. Annex II, Table 3.5. See also: OECD, J.R.S. Revell, *Banking and Electronic Fund Transfers*, Paris, 1983.

9. In France, electronic "home banking" has been much encouraged by official policy designed to promote the expansion of the Telecom screen-based information transmission and dissemination system "Minitel". Thus, "Minitel" screens increasingly serve as vehicles for offering and using "home banking" facilities.

10. Annex III, Section V.

11. The French Bankers Association has conducted an inquiry on margins in consumer loans/personal loans according to which the margins between money-market refinancing costs and interest rates charged on personal loans are as follows: France: 4–10 per cent; Germany: 7–11 per cent; Switzerland: 8–11 per cent; United Kingdom: 13–14 per cent; Italy: 18–23 per cent; Spain: 7–12 per cent; United States: 7–18 per cent. The margins are, in fact, much wider if it is assumed that personal loans are largely extended on the basis of customer current account, time and savings deposits, which, on average, earn considerably less than money-market rates. See: Association Française des Banques, *La concurrence bancaire en France et en Europe*, Paris, 1987.

12. OECD, *Housing Finance, Present Problems*, Paris, 1974; and OECD, J.R.S. Revell, *Flexibility in Housing Finance*, Paris, 1975.

13. For more detail see OECD, R.M. Pecchioli, *The Internationalisation of Banking*, Paris, 1983.

14. While many multinational companies have their in-house treasury and finance departments, which sometimes have become forceful competitors of banks, notably in areas such as foreign exchange dealing and the raising of, or trading in, short-term funds, there are other companies which have set up their own special banks. Examples of such corporate banks are: ASEA Finance and ASEA Kapitalforvaltning, Sweden; British Petroleum Financing International, London; GEC Finance, London (the bank of General Electric Company); Renault Finance, Lausanne and New York; Fortos, Sweden (the bank of Volvo). For more detail see: R.A. Melcher, "Do-it-yourself financing hits lenders where it hurts", in Business Week, 25th November 1985.

15. Annex II, Tables 4.8 and 4.9.

16. Annex II, Table 4.6.

17. French, German and United Kingdom commercial banks have in recent years reportedly expanded their business advisory services quite noticeably. The Midland Bank Group, for example, introduced at the end of 1983 a special Business Advisory Service which was staffed by a number of carefully selected and fully trained Regional Business Advisers (see Annual Accounts and Report 1983). Deutsche Bank acquired in the autumn of 1987 a participation in the biggest German Consultancy firm — Roland Berger Verwaltungsgesellschaft mBH — in order to accelerate the expansion of its business advisory services.

18. In February 1987, the Interministerial Commission on Credit and Savings (Comitato Interministeriale per il Credito ed il Risparmio — CICR) issued a decree according to which commercial banks in Italy are allowed to set up, or take participations in, so-called Financial Intermediation Companies (Società di Intermediazione Finanziaria — SIF). These new financial intermediaries are authorised to carry out the following activities: advisory services in the field of enterprise financing; assisting companies in capital raising operations i.e. issuing debt or equity instruments; temporary holdings of any such debt or equity instruments until final placement. For more detail see: Pückler, Graf von, "Italien erlaubt Merchant Banken", *Die Bank* No. 11, Köln, 1987.

    Denmark may be mentioned also as an example of a country which envisages facilitating the involvement of banks in corporate financial affairs. In September 1988, the Government announced legislative measures designed to provide scope for bank participations, at least on a temporary basis, in industrial and commercial enterprises with a view to strengthening the capital base of the productive sector.

19. Annex III, Section V, "International Money and Securities Markets".

20. Annex III, Section V, "United States".

21. Chapter 4, section on "Organisation of Markets" and "Notes and References" (28).

22. Annex III, Section III.

23. Chapter 3, Table 3.5.

24. For example, the number of companies whose shares are traded on the "SEAQ International" system of the International Stock Exchange in London amounted to 653 end-November 1988.

25. Annex III, Section IV, D.

26. Annex II, Tables 4.8 and 4.9.

27. In some European countries such as Luxembourg, Belgium and France, interbank claims and liabilities, both domestic and cross-border, reach very high proportions. At the end of 1986, for example, interbank liabilities in these three countries accounted for 63 per cent, 62 per cent and 45 per cent, respectively. At the same time, the corresponding ratios for the Netherlands, Germany and Switzerland were 26 per cent, 23 per cent and 20 per cent, respectively. By contrast, in the United States, the share of interbank liabilities in total liabilities of commercial banks dropped sharply from about 12 per cent end-1980 to less than 6 per cent end-1986. For more detail on related data see: OECD, *Bank Profitability — Financial Statements of Banks, Statistical Supplement, 1982-1986*, Paris, 1988.

28. According to surveys conducted in March 1986, the share of interbank operations in total foreign exchange turnover was as follows: Canada: 69.0 per cent; Japan: 66.6 per cent; United Kingdom: 88.9 per cent; United States: 86.6 per cent. See: Bank of Canada Review, November 1986, page 8.

In securities markets data for intra-system trading have recently become available in the London market which show that for the period March to June 1988 intra-system trading in government securities accounted for 44.8 per cent of total turnover; in equity trading the corresponding ratio was 32.7 per cent. Source: *Financial Statistics*, August 1988, Central Statistical Office, London.

29. The Swiss company Telekurs AG is an example of such a joint venture which was set up by a large group of banks, essentially for solving common problems relating to the technological infrastructure of the financial sector. The Telekurs AG, which at present is owned by 350 Swiss banks, provides its shareholders as well as outside customers with a wide range of services in the field of data processing and collection and dissemination of market information. It also provides advisory services in the field of technology developments relating to payment services on the one hand and the securities business on the other. For example, the computerisation of the Zürich Stock Exchange was carried out by the Telekurs AG. Telekurs AG stressed in one of its brochures that in some areas of financial services competition is neither economically nor organisationally an adequate approach and may, in fact, produce disadvantages for the consumer (see Telekurs AG, "Know-how und Technik im Dienste der Banken und Börsen", Ein Unternehmensportraet, Zürich, no year).

30. For more detail, see OECD, R.M. Pecchioli, *The Internationalisation of Banking*, Paris, 1983.

31. See also, OECD, R. Harrington, *Asset and Liability Management in Banking*, Paris, 1987.

Chapter 3

POLICIES TOWARDS EFFICIENT FINANCIAL SYSTEMS: THE ROLE OF COMPETITION POLICY

3.1 INTRODUCTION

The purpose of the present chapter is to provide an overview of public policy towards the financial system and to identify in particular to what extent and how the authorities in OECD countries have implemented competition policies since the early sixties with a view to improving the efficiency and the functioning of financial institutions and markets in their countries. It is recalled that in the context of this study competition is not considered as an end in itself. Rather, competition policies are seen as a major, but not the only, instrument for improving the efficiency of the financial system. The chapter will at the same time point to the limits of the market–oriented approach towards dealing with the efficiency issue.

The term "competition policy" is used in a wide sense. It does not only relate to policies dealing with restrictive business practices, concentration and dominant market positions and co–operation agreements but covers all measures that are designed to encourage and to provide more scope for the working of market forces and competition in banking and finance. Thus, a wide range of domestic deregulation as well as external liberalisation measures — the abolition of interest rate and other price controls, of restrictions on the range of operations which financial institutions are allowed to conduct in the domestic markets and on a transborder basis, the removal of new entry restrictions and other obstacles to the functioning of financial markets — are considered as falling within the scope of competition policies. A generally supportive attitude of the authorities towards the development of markets and intensifying competition is seen as forming part of such policies as well.

The concept of efficiency used in this study refers to "functional efficiency". It is a broad concept that relates to the role and the functions of financial systems, mainly in a macro–economic context, such as the following:

— To ensure the proper functioning of a country's payment system;
— To channel funds from surplus units to deficit units in amounts and forms which correspond to the needs and preferences of borrowers and lenders;
— To safeguard the nation's financial wealth;
— To serve as a vehicle for implementing monetary policy.

An efficient financial system is seen as one which fulfils these functions adequately and which generally satisfies the sometimes rapidly changing financial service needs of an economy and its participants at reasonable cost. The concept of "functional efficiency" covers different aspects of efficiency such as the allocation aspect, the availability, quality and convenience aspect, the cost aspect, the aspect of competitiveness of financial institutions and the dynamic, or flexibility and adaptability, aspect. The latter aspect has received particular attention in many countries in recent years while at other times the allocation aspect, the credit cost aspect and the availability aspect played a major role[1].

In line with the main purpose of the study — which is to explore the role and the limits of competition policy as an instrument for improving the efficiency and the functioning of financial systems — the present chapter deals with the wide range of measures which the authorities in OECD countries have used in the period under review in order to stimulate competition and to ensure a proper working of market forces in banking and finance. In discussing policies in this field a distinction has been made between the following types of measures:

— Interest rate and other price deregulation measures;
— Removal of direct credit controls and of mandatory investment regulations;
— Measures designed to promote the trend towards despecialisation and diversification of financial service activities and products;
— Application of the principle of competitive equality and neutrality;
— Measures designed to provide more scope for the entry of new competitors from both inside and outside the country;
— Measures designed to improve market visibility and information;
— Supportive merger and ownership policy;
— Measures designed to strengthen the international competitiveness of financial institutions and markets.

These latter measures deserve special attention as public policy towards the strengthening of the international competitiveness of national financial systems has considerably gained in importance since the early eighties and has, in fact, been a major driving force in the worldwide financial deregulation and external liberalisation process.

The chapter ends with two sections which point to the limits of the use of competition policies for promoting an efficient functioning of financial systems. The first deals with specific objectives regarding the allocation of financial resources in line with some broader social policy objectives which cannot be achieved by simple reliance on market forces. Practically all OECD countries see a need for channelling funds to some extent at costs below market level into specific and socially desirable uses. There are different methods by which such financial assistance programmes can be implemented not all of which are compatible with a proper functioning of financial markets. As countries have moved towards more competitive systems they have increasingly felt a need for reviewing the methods of financial assistance to specific sectors and, if necessary, fitting them better into the market system.

The final section deals with policies towards streamlining national payment systems. This is an important area of financial policy in which, in many OECD countries, sole reliance on competition and market forces is not considered as an appropriate means of approaching the problems involved. Co-operation amongst market participants or between market participants and the authorities has often been seen as a preferred approach towards promoting efficiency in this particular field. These considerations apply also to the development of other areas of the technological infrastructure of the financial system such as trading, clearing, settlement, book entry and depository systems in securities markets.

While the present chapter is confined to providing a record of policy action towards improving the efficiency and the functioning of national financial systems with particular emphasis on competition policy, it is the role of Chapter 4 to discuss problems and issues with which the authorities in OECD countries have been faced in implementing such policies and to report on the present state of the discussion of such issues.

Although the present study is intended to focus on policy developments since the early sixties it has been thought useful for an understanding of the evolution of competition policies in banking and finance during the last two decades to introduce the analysis by taking a brief look backwards towards the twenties and thirties and review the history of the relationship between policies designed to preserve stability and soundness of national financial systems and policies directed towards ensuring their efficient functioning. The line taken in this study is that a proper functioning of financial institutions and markets has been an important policy objective ever since the authorities have had an interest in the management of their national economies and that banking regulation introduced in the twenties and thirties has ultimately served the purpose of ensuring an adequate functioning of financial systems. Looking back to the twenties and thirties seemed also indicated because many of the measures that have been taken in the period under review, have often meant a revision of the regulations and the protectionist policies that were adopted in the twenties and thirties.

3.2 FINANCIAL POLICY IN RETROSPECT

Since the first major move in many countries towards regulating and supervising the business of banking, which occurred in the twenties and thirties in the aftermath of major and sometimes massive banking failures in connection with the world depression, it has become apparent that national authorities have a vital interest both in an adequate functioning and in the stability and soundness of their countries' financial systems[2]. Although these early banking regulations were primarily aimed at maintaining the stability and soundness of individual financial institutions thereby strengthening or restoring the general public's confidence in the stability of the financial system, these measures may be seen as ultimately serving the purpose of ensuring an adequate functioning of the financial system. Given the basic functions of the financial system mentioned above, it seems natural that with increasing involvement in the management of their countries' economies, national authorities have also paid increasing attention to the issue of how to ensure the functioning of their national financial systems.

The experiences with banking failures in the twenties and thirties made it clear that the functioning of national financial systems is essentially based on the stability and soundness of financial systems as a whole and on the general public's confidence in the effectiveness of the authorities' supervision of individual institutions operating in the system. A financial system can work properly only if market participants have confidence in the authorities' ability, first, to deal satisfactorily with individual banking failures so that domino effects on the system as a whole can be avoided; and, second, to protect the participants in the financial system, notably the banks' and other financial institutions' clients, against losses from fraud, malpractices, abuses of power, an adverse impact of conflicts of interest inside financial institutions and against losses arising from failures of individual institutions. In other words, the achievement of the basic objectives of preserving stability and soundness of individual financial institutions and of the financial system as a whole and of ensuring adequate investor protection, which requires adequate supervision, is an indispensable condition for achieving the objective of efficiency and of ensuring an adequate functioning of the financial system. Without stability and soundness the financial system cannot properly fulfil its basic functions: the smooth functioning of the payment system is endangered; the process of efficient allocation of financial resources in the economy is disturbed; with lack of confidence in the stability and soundness of financial institutions the financial system cannot properly fulfil its role as the guardian of the nation's financial wealth; with instability in the financial system the effectiveness of monetary policy is impaired. In more recent years, with the rapid internationalisation of financial systems, the stability and soundness aspect has gained another dimension insofar as a national marketplace is not internationally competitive if market participants have no confidence in the stability and soundness of the system concerned.

Although the achievement of the objective of stability and soundness of individual financial institutions and of the financial system as a whole is of prime importance for policies aimed at improving the functioning and increasing the efficiency of national financial systems, it is important to note that the two objectives are not identical. The history of banking and financial policy shows that policies towards pursuing the two objectives are not necessarily, but can be, conflicting and indeed have become increasingly conflicting since the late fifties when the authorities in many countries began to pay more attention to the efficiency question, often in connection with the increasing internationalisation of banking. The whole post–World War II history of financial regulation may, in a way, be seen as a policy effort towards establishing a new balance between the stability objective and the efficiency objective.

In the twenties and thirties, considerable efforts were made by the authorities in many countries to deal with the stability and soundness problem. The approach generally chosen was one of protecting the banking and financial sector as a whole against the dangers of instability and failures largely by reducing the scope for competitive pressures on profits and capital through tight interest rate regulation and a pronounced policy of compartmentalisation of financial institutions, sectors and markets. At the same time, public interest in the functioning of national financial systems manifested itself in concerns as well as measures regarding an adequate supply of the economy with means of payment, liquidity and credit, adequate credit allocation to small- and medium-sized enterprises and avoidance of overbanking and of concentration of power in banking and finance[3]. Public intervention in the process of allocating financial resources to priority sectors through newly-created financial institutions played a considerable role in a number of countries as well.

In the earlier post–World War II period, public concern about the functioning of national financial systems was mainly directed towards the generation and mobilisation of savings and ensuring an adequate allocation of funds to investment projects serving the reconstruction and the industrial development of national economies. The promotion of priority sectors which often included basic industries, export industries and the housing sector, and a corresponding allocation of scarce financial resources to such sectors, received special attention in many countries for many post-war years. During this period, regulatory frameworks designed to protect the financial service industry as a whole remained largely intact. Interest rates were generally kept stable at below market levels. In a number of countries this was motivated inter alia by cost considerations relating to the huge amounts of government debt inherited from the war period. The dirigiste environment of that period left generally little scope for the working of market forces.In subsequent years, however — at different times in different countries — the authorities began to change their views and attitudes towards the question of efficiency in banking and finance. With the rise in income and wealth, the diversification in industrial and commercial activities and the intensification of international trade and investment relations, when market elements in the functioning of national economies were generally being strengthened, the authorities in an increasing number of countries began to realise that more reliance on market forces in banking and finance could have positive effects on the functioning of national financial systems and on the increasingly complex process of allocation of financial and real resources within national economies. Thus, there has been increasing recognition that the approach to bank regulation and supervision adopted in the twenties and thirties, which largely consisted of global protection of the financial system against the potentially destabilising impact of excessive competition, was becoming counterproductive as regards the ultimate objective of ensuring the functioning of the financial system. National authorities increasingly adopted the view that the highly diversified and complex and rapidly changing financial service needs of modern economies could no longer be adequately met by over-protected and over-regulated financial systems, particularly in an environment of increased internationalisation.

This change in national authorities' attitudes towards the efficiency question set in train a long process of domestic deregulation and external liberalisation in the financial sector. Beginning in the early sixties, if not in the late fifties, and accelerating considerably in the late seventies and early eighties, there has been a pronounced public policy move towards strengthening market forces in the functioning of OECD countries' financial systems through stimulation of competition. The new approach manifested itself in many ways and through different types of action. Interest rate controls were largely, or entirely, dismantled in many countries. Cartel agreements on interest rates, fees and commissions were prohibited. Controls on the expansion of banking networks and on the setting up of new banks were lifted or eased. Regulations limiting the range of permissible activities of banks and other financial institutions were relaxed. This supported the process of decompartmentalisation of financial systems as originally more specialised financial institutions were enabled to penetrate into each others' territories; and previously closed market segments were opened to new participants. Competition in banking and finance was also intensified as many countries opened their financial systems to foreign banks and other financial institutions and to cross-border transactions. Another closely-related line of public policy action designed to stimulate competition within the financial system has been directed towards implementing the principle of

equality of competitive opportunity, or "levelling the playing field". The abolition of tax privileges for certain types of financial institutions or for the government itself are examples of such action.

While this has been a rather broad and global approach to improving efficiency in the functioning of financial systems, namely through stimulating competition generally, the authorities in many OECD countries have also taken more specific action designed to improve certain aspects of the functioning of financial systems. Measures to increase the supply of funds and institutional arrangements for housing finance, the introduction of incentive schemes for the accumulation of risk capital, efforts to reduce the cost of intermediation and to increase productivity in banking and finance, measures to introduce new facilities for hedging foreign exchange risks and interest rate risks and a host of measures designed to broaden the range of available financial services or to improve the functioning of specific financial mechanisms may all be seen as falling under the broad heading of improving the efficiency of the financial system. To provide more detail on such specific policy measures would clearly go beyond the scope of the present study.

3.3 WIDENING THE SCOPE FOR PRICE COMPETITION

3.3.1 *Interest Rate Deregulation and the Strengthening of Market Elements in the Financial System*[4]

Looking back over the last quarter of a century or so, there has been a general trend in OECD countries and elsewhere towards the deregulation of interest rates intended to provide more scope for the working of the market mechanism in financial systems. As has already been mentioned, this trend has to be seen in the wider context of broad economic developments and changes in the overall management of national economies. Most OECD countries have gradually changed from highly regulated and largely closed economies, which in the aftermath of World War II were largely occupied with reconstruction, industrial restructuring and general economic development problems, to more market-oriented and internationally interrelated economies, which, moreover, pursued ambitious growth policies during the sixties by relying increasingly on market forces and the competitive performance of market participants. This change in policy attitudes regarding the management of national economies has also influenced financial policies in the direction of a more market–oriented approach.

The move towards greater interest rate deregulation, which was by no means uniform from country to country as regards the timing and the scope of deregulation measures, received strong impulses from the external side as considerable efforts were made within the OECD area to liberalise international capital movements, initially in the field of trade financing, but later also in areas such as bank lending and borrowing, new issues of securities, mainly bonds, and other portfolio capital movements. The introduction by major countries, towards the end of the fifties, of external convertibility of their national currencies was a decisive step in this development. It was around this time that the international financial markets whose functioning is based on the free interplay of market forces and interest rate competition, started to develop. Increasing use of these markets by countries' financial institutions, industrial and commercial enterprises and public sector entities no doubt contributed to the spreading of market forces also into national financial systems. To the extent that countries with tight domestic interest rate controls relied on borrowing in the international markets at free rates, the original purpose of interest rate controls to provide low–cost finance for the economy was necessarily frustrated.

In reviewing the interest rate deregulation process in national financial systems it needs to be realised that practically no single country with highly regulated financial systems has ever managed to control all interest rates. There have always been segments within the system in which interest rates were freely negotiated so that in practically all countries there has been co–existence of regulated and unregulated sectors in the financial system. The latter sectors have often been referred to as unofficial or "grey" markets which reached considerable dimensions in some countries in which the authorities pursued policies towards artificially low interest rates. Thus, the interest rate deregulation process should generally be seen as a gradual extension of market elements within national financial systems rather than as a sudden switch from full control to full deregulation.

A first step towards the extension of the free market areas in banking and finance has often been the creation of money markets in which banks and/or large non–bank corporations could adjust their liquidity positions at freely determined rates. In some countries, a second, or sometimes parallel, step in the deregulation process, has been the development of genuine secondary markets for fixed–interest securities while conditions in the primary issue markets have often remained under close control. The deregulation of bank lending and deposit interest rates has mostly been the last step in the decontrol process, partly for monetary policy reasons as central banks often used the tying of bank lending and deposit rates to their discount rates as an instrument of monetary policy, partly because such controls, notably on the deposit side, met with the banks' own interests in avoiding too intensive price competition in this area and reflected the authorities' concerns that any such competition could provide a threat to the stability of financial institutions.

The process of deregulating bank lending and deposit rates applying to bank customers, as opposed to interbank rates and other market borrowing rates, started around the middle of the sixties in Germany, France and Canada. In February 1965, the German authorities took the first step to deregulate bank deposit rates with maturities between two and a half and less than four years. In July 1966 all large deposits in amounts of one million Deutschemarks and over with maturities between three months and less than two and a half years were freed. The deregulation of interest rates on all remaining deposits followed in April 1967. Interest rates for DM lending to domestic non–banks with maturities of less than four years, which had been officially set at a fixed margin above the official lombard and discount rates, were also freed in April 1967 in a single step. Since then, banks have been entirely free to set their lending and deposit rates on competitive terms. The authorities in France introduced a full deregulation of all bank lending rates (with the exception of interest rates on special government lending schemes) in 1966 and a partial deregulation of deposit rates applying essentially to larger business deposits with longer maturities in 1967. Canada abandoned, with the Bank Act of 1967, the statutory ceiling on bank lending rates of 6 per cent and thus enabled the banks to compete more effectively also on the deposit side, following the recommendations of the Porter Commission[5].

In the United Kingdom, the London clearing banks and the Scottish banks dismantled their interest rate cartel at official request in connection with the introduction, in 1971, of "Competition and Credit Control"[6]. The climate for this move had already been prepared through the 1967 report by the National Board on Prices and Incomes on Bank Charges which contained the recommendation that banks should abolish their agreements on interest rates and tariffs[7].

In the United States, following the removal in 1970 of the interest rate ceiling on large certificates of deposit (with denominations of $100 000 and over and with maturities of less than three months), the 1971 Report by the President's Commission on Financial Structure and Regulation ("Hunt–Commission")[8] recommended a decisive move towards deregulating bank deposit rates which were subject to Regulation Q. When rising market interest rates and the development of money–market mutual funds induced and facilitated withdrawal by the public from regulated deposits ("disintermediation") for investment in market instruments, the authorities were forced to react with the introduction, in mid–1978, of six–month money–market certificates of deposit with a floating deposit rate ceiling tied to the rate on six–month Treasury bills. With further increases in market rates and innovation in private market instruments, disintermediation increasingly made Regulation Q untenable, and the Congress enacted "The. Depository Institutions Deregulation and Monetary Control Act of 1980"[9] which provided for interest rate ceilings on time and savings deposits at depository institutions to be phased out over a period of six years. This and subsequent legislation in the United States enacted in 1982 also expanded the asset powers of non–bank deposit–taking institutions. In the seventies and early eighties, quite a number of other countries took deregulation measures in the field of bank lending and deposit rates mostly in connection with some broader measures designed to stimulate competition and the working of market forces in the financial sector[10].

The number of countries in which the authorities no longer control interest rates by way of regulation or by tolerating interest rate cartel agreements or conventions increased considerably in the period 1960–1987 (Table 3.1). The interest rate deregulation process has gathered considerable momentum since the late seventies both as regards the number of measures taken and the number of countries moving towards more competitive and market–oriented financial systems and policies. At the same time, market elements in financial systems have been strengthened considerably through the creation of negotiable money–market instruments such as certificates of deposit, Treasury bills, commercial paper and bankers acceptances (Table 3.2). In fact, the interest rate deregulation process at the level of bank lending and deposit rates has in several instances been preceded, and thus prepared, by the introduction of markets for money–market paper.

The objectives which the authorities have pursued by deregulating interest rates thereby providing more scope for the working of market forces in national financial systems have been manifold and have often differed from country to country as regards their combination and the range of priorities. The complexity of the issue is also indicated by the fact that interest rate deregulation measures have often affected wide areas of the financial system. The more important objectives that have been identified in various countries, ranging from objectives relating to the functioning of specific markets to broader macro–economic objectives regarding the process of allocation of financial and real resources in national economies, are briefly listed as follows:

— Improvement of the functioning of money markets, notably the interbank money markets, thereby aiming at facilitating the banks' liquidity adjustment operations and/or central bank management of bank liquidity;
— Improving the functioning of secondary markets for bonds in favour of better allocation of financial resources in the economy or increasing the supply of longer–term funds for investment;
— Facilitating the placing of large amounts of government debt;
— Eliminating the distorsion in the pattern of flow of funds that have been created by a policy of artificially low interest rates, thereby contributing to more efficient management of the financial intermediation

Table 3.1 **Countries with interest rate controls or agreements**

	End–1960	End–1980	End–1987
Australia	X	X	–
Austria	X	X	X
Belgium	X	X	X
Canada	X	–	–
Denmark	X	X	–
Finland	X	X	–
France	X	X	X
Germany	X	–	–
Greece	X	X	X
Ireland	X	X	–
Italy	X	–	–
Japan	X	X	X
Netherlands	X	–	–
New Zealand	X	X	–
Norway	X	X	–
Portugal	X	X	X
Spain	X	X	–
Sweden	X	X	–
Switzerland	X	X	X
Turkey	X	X	X
United Kingdom	X	X	–
United States	X	X	X

X = Official controls or private agreements.
– = No official controls or private agreements.
Source: Annex III, Section I.

ERRATUM

COMPETITION IN BANKING

Table 3.2 on page 53 contains a printing error. It should be disregarded and readers should consult the table below.

Table 3.2 Introduction of negotiable money market instruments in selected OECD countries

	Before 1960	1960–1970	Period of Introduction 1971–1980	1981–1987
Australia		TB (1962)	CD, CP (1973)	
Canada	TB, CD, CP			
Denmark			TB (1976)[1]	
Finland				CD, TB, CP
France				CD, CP (1985), TB (1986)
Greece			CD (1975)	TB (1985)
Italy			TB (1975)	CD (1983)
Japan			CD (1979)	
Netherlands				CD, CP (1986)
New Zealand			CD (1977)	
Norway				TB, CD, CP (1985)
Portugal				TB (1985), CD (1987)
Spain		CD (1960)		TB (1981), CP (1982)
Sweden			CD (1980)	TB (1982), CP (1983)
United Kingdom	TB	$CD (1966) $CD (1970)		$CP (1986)
United States	TB, CP	CD (1970)		

TB = Treasury Bills; CD = Certificates of Deposit; CP = Commercial Paper.
1. Reintroduction after 20 years.
Source: Annex III, Section II.

Table 3.2 **Introduction of negotiable money market instruments in selected OECD countries**

	Before 1960	1960–1970	Period of Introduction 1971–1980	1981–1987
Australia		TB (1962)	CD, CP (1973)	
Canada	TB, CD, CP			
Denmark			TB (1976)[1]	
Finland				CD, TB, CP (1985), TB (1986)
France			CD, CP	
Greece			CD (1975)	TB (1985)
Italy			TB (1975)	CD (1983)
Japan			CD (1979)	
Netherlands				CD, CP (1986)
New Zealand			CD (1977)	
Norway				TB, CD, CP (1985)
Portugal				TB (1985), CD (1987)
Spain		CD (1960)		TB (1981), CP (1982)
Sweden			CD (1980)	TB (1982), CP (1983)
United Kingdom	TB	$CD (1966) $CD (1970)		$CP (1986)
United States	TB, CP	CD (1970)		

TB = Treasury Bills; CD = Certificates of Deposit; CP = Commercial Paper.
1. Reintroduction after 20 years.
Source: Annex III, Section II.

process and/or improving the scope for more effective central bank control on the credit supply process;
— Strengthening the competitiveness and viability of financial institutions which had been prevented by interest rate controls from responding vigorously to competitive pressures from unregulated sectors within the financial system or from non–financial firms moving into the financial service business; the purpose of interest rate deregulation was to enable these institutions to take defensive action against the danger of withdrawals of low–interest rate funds or against the dangers of inadequate interest–rate risk management;
— Strengthening the vitality, the competitiveness and the competitive and innovative spirit of financial institutions, thereby generally contributing to better allocation of financial resources in the economy;
— Reducing the cost of intermediation in the financial system through intensified competition;
— Increasing the flexibility and adaptability of financial institutions to meet new demands in the economy for financial services in a rapidly changing environment;

— Strengthening the international competitiveness of national financial institutions.

While most of the objectives mentioned are self–explanatory, one objective, the elimination of distorsions in the pattern of flow of funds created by a policy of artificially low interest rates, deserves further comment and explanation because of its importance and relevance for macro–economic policies.

Countries which have systematically and consistently pursued a policy of artificially low and stable interest rates over a prolonged period of time such as Australia, Finland, New Zealand, Norway and Sweden for example, have had the experience that such policies tend to produce distorsions in the flow of funds which become more important the greater the discrepancy between controlled interest rates and free market rates (i.e. rates which would have prevailed in the absence of controls) and the longer the period over which controls are maintained. Savings from more sophisticated personal investors and funds from corporations and institutional investors tend to by–pass the regulated sector, mainly the banking system and, depending on the circumstances, may tend to flow abroad, or into newly–emerging financial institutions operating outside the regulated sector. In many countries such institutions, notably finance companies, have been set up by the commercial banks themselves so that they could compete more effectively for funds from unregulated markets. Corporate treasurers have also tended to short–circuit the banking system by creating intercompany money markets and operating with assistance from money brokers or the banks themselves.The disadvantages of these distortions in the flow of funds have frequently been recognised as follows: first, the effectiveness of monetary policy measures and monetary control is impaired as considerable amounts of credit flows escape the central bank's control and may not be identified, depending on the circumstance. Second, funds by–passing the banking system are increasingly managed by agents who may be less qualified than banks so that there is a danger that the quality and the efficiency of fund management and intermediation is reduced. Third, interest rates in the unregulated sectors tend to be higher than the market level which would prevail in the absence of controls so that borrowers using the unregulated markets are penalised. Thus, the interest rate control system has often been viewed as becoming increasingly counter–productive as far as its original objective of supplying the economy with low–cost funds is concerned.

In some other countries mentioned, distortions in the flow of funds produced by regulated interest rates were greatly aggravated under the impact of high rates of inflation which resulted in high negative real rates of interest. Apart from the United States where nominal market rates on other assets above the nominal deposit–ceiling rate were much more relevant than negative real rates, such situations, while generating excessive demand for credit, have tended to result in a shortage of funds as savers were seeking inflation–proof outlets including real estate investment. In some countries this has seriously endangered the viability of some types of financial institutions. Depending on the country situation, the authorities have responded to such developments by different counteracting measures such as ad hoc rescue measures, measures to reduce the scope of controlled interest rates or a drastic upward adjustment of such rates, or authorising financial institutions to offer instruments with variable or price index–linked interest rates.

Although the interest rate deregulation process within the OECD area in recent years has been quite spectacular, it should be noted that the authorities in some countries have not, or not yet, gone as far as deregulating all interest rates. In some EC countries — because of the 1992 internal market objective — and in Japan it is probably a matter of time until full deregulation is achieved. The authorities of these countries pursue a policy of caution or gradualism in order to give the smaller

and less competitive institutions sufficient time to adjust to a more competitive situation in financial markets. Japan provides a typical example of a policy of small steps in this area. The deregulation of interest rates on deposits started in 1979 with the introduction of negotiable certificates of deposit. Interest rates on non–negotiable large–denomination time deposits were decontrolled in steps from October 1985 onwards by reducing gradually the minimum amount and minimum maturity of individual deposits which are subject to free interest rates. At the end of 1987, remaining controls applied to interest rates on deposits in amounts of Yen 100 million or less and with maturities of one month or less and on postal savings accounts.

The maintenance of some interest rate controls (Table 3.3) in the retail banking area including the prohibition of remunerating current account balances reflects sometimes more fundamental concerns. It is feared that complete freedom in the determination of bank lending or deposit rates will lead to excessive interest rate competition amongst banks, with subsequent undue pressures on interest rate margins, bank profits and capital ratios, and this at a time when generally increased risks in banking call for improved bank profitability and more comfortable capital cushions. A closely related concern is that aggressive pricing strategies under conditions of free competition could unduly favour concentration in banking and finance. The maintenance of the prohibition of interest rate payments on current account deposits in France and the United States and interest rate controls on small deposits in the former country may be seen as reflecting such concerns. For similar reasons and for maintaining orderly conditions in the banking markets, the Austrian authorities encouraged the banks in 1985, after a relatively short–lived period of complete interest rate freedom, to conclude a new agreement designed to limit price competition and competition in the field of advertising. In Switzerland, a number of local or regional interest rate agreements mainly concerning bank lending rates have so far been tolerated with a view to maintaining visibility and relative interest rate stability in these markets and to forestalling undesirable concentration movements in the banking sector.

In Belgium, certain interest rate controls — the toleration of bank cartel agreements regarding the remuneration, at 0.5 per cent, of current account balances and bank agreements with the Belgian National Bank on interest rates payable on the whole range of non–marketable savings instruments including time deposits — are, for the time being, maintained with a view to moderating interest rate competition thereby avoiding undue resistance to a

Table 3.3 Interest rate restrictions in OECD countries
Situation at the end of 1987

Austria	Interbank agreement on bank lending and deposit rates (introduced in March 1985 in order to maintain orderly market conditions).
Belgium	Interest rates on small time deposits (below BF 20 million) subject to Gentlemen's Agreement between financial institutions, the Belgian National Bank and the Ministry of Finance.
	Interest rate on current accounts (0.5 per cent) fixed by interbank agreement.
France	Prohibition of interest payment on current account.
	Official control on interest rates on time deposits below specified amounts and maturities and on savings accounts.
Greece	Official control on the majority of bank lending and deposit rates (exceptions: interest rates on certain mortgage loans and on certain loans and deposits denominated in foreign currency).
Japan	Official control on interest rates on time deposits below specified amounts and maturities and on postal savings accounts.
Portugal	Official control on maximum rates on bank lending and minimum rates on time deposits with maturities of over 180 days to one year.
Switzerland	Regional and local interbank agreements mainly on bank lending rates including mortgage rates.
Turkey	Interest rates on bank deposits set by the central bank in line with market conditions.
United States	Prohibition of interest payment on time deposits with maturities of up to 7 days.

Source: Annex III, Section I.

desirable decline on the whole interest rate level for general economic policy reasons.

The French experience with a mixed system of regulated short–term bank deposit rates and free long–term interest rates is of interest insofar as the authorities have used this system with great success for channelling increasing amounts of household savings, which traditionally tended to be held in liquid form, into the markets for long–term capital, notably the bond market. Additional incentives in favour of long–term investments in bonds have also been provided in the form of a differential tax treatment of interest income on bank deposits and bonds, respectively. This policy has, moreover, helped to contain the growth of monetary aggregates and has thus had positive monetary policy implications.

The impact of the interest rate deregulation process and the general strengthening of market elements in financial systems on the cost of intermediation of the banking system are difficult to judge on the basis of available broad data on financial statements of banks. It is true, interest margins, which measure the difference between interest income and interest expenditure as a percentage of the average balance sheet total in a given year, have come down quite strikingly between 1980 and 1986 in a number of countries (Table 3.4). It is, however, difficult to say without further evidence whether and to what extent this margin squeeze reflects increased competitive pressures in the banking market, or whether some other factors — the general decline in interest rates during the period, some shift into low–margin business or increased direct pricing of services — have played a role in this regard. Notwithstanding these qualifications it is worth noting that in some of the countries concerned — Spain, Norway, Finland, Japan — further interest rate deregulation measures were taken in the period under review

Table 3.4 Countries with declining interest margins of commercial banks

Net Interest Income as Per Cent of Average Balance Sheet Totals

	1980	1986	Percentage Change (%)
Spain	4.23	3.73	−12
United Kingdom	4.00	3.16	−21
Norway	3.50	2.84	−19
France	2.84	2.72	−4
Finland	2.28	1.27	−44
Belgium	2.03	1.62	−20
Japan	1.61	1.27	−21

Source: OECD, Bank Profitability, Financial Statements of Banks, Paris, 1987

and that in the United Kingdom and Belgium competition for deposits has become relatively intense[11].

3.3.2 Deregulation of Fees and Commissions in Financial Services

The situation as regards efforts towards widening the scope for price competition in the field of fees and commissions on financial services is somewhat different from interest rate deregulation measures insofar as fees and commissions (other than those which are closely related to interest rates) have hardly been subject to direct government regulation. Rather, restrictions on competition in fees and commissions, where they were allowed under restrictive business practice legislation, mainly took the form of cartel agreements amongst banks, members of stock exchanges, dealers associations and other groupings of providers of financial services.

As the authorities of OECD countries increasingly adopted policies towards promoting and providing more scope for competition in the financial services markets they increasingly used the instrument of competition rules for dismantling all sorts of cartel agreements in the financial services industry. In Canada and the United States any agreement amongst banks, even between two banks, is prohibited under anti–trust legislation. In the United Kingdom, the National Board for Prices and Income recommended in its 1967 report on "Bank Charges" that collective agreements on charges be abolished. The Price Commission recommended in its 1978 report on "Banks: Charges for Money Transmission Services" that "all agreements relating to jointly negotiated tariffs and joint working arrangements should be brought before the

Restrictive Practices Court as soon as possible in order that the public interest may be tested"[12].

As far as EC countries are concerned it has been clarified on several occasions that the competition rules laid down in Articles 85 and 86 of the Treaty of Rome apply also to banks and other providers of financial services as in any other industry, which means that agreements or concerted practices on interest rates, charges, commissions, terms of business, territorial restrictions etc. are prohibited if their effects extend beyond national borders.

In general, there is little information on the way in which the vast area of fees and commissions has been affected by increased competition in financial markets. A notable exception is stock exchange commissions for securities buy and sell orders which in the past were generally fixed by the stock exchange members in terms of minimum conditions. Under combined pressure from market forces — markets moving increasingly away from the stock exchanges notably as regards large transactions of institutional investors — and from the authorities — competition policies being increasingly extended to the financial sector — a number of stock exchanges in OECD countries have introduced, or will introduce in the near future, freely negotiable commissions thereby increasing the scope for price competition in this area of financial services. The movement started with the abolition of fixed minimum commissions on the New York Stock Exchange in 1975. In Australia, fixed commissions were abolished in 1984. In Europe, these events were followed by developments in the United Kingdom which led, in October 1986, to the withdrawal of minimum commission rules applied by the London Stock Exchange and which were initiated by a case brought against these rules under the Restrictive Trade Practices Act, the United Kingdom equivalent of anti–trust law. The compromise that was found by the Government's decision, in July 1983, to exempt the Stock Exchange from the Restrictive Trade Practices Act subject to their agreement to introduce freely negotiable commission rates, set in train the development in the London securities and banking industry which has been referred to as the "City revolution" and which has already led to a considerable strengthening of the international competitiveness of London as an international financial centre. The change–over to negotiable commission rates in New York and London resulted in noticeable reductions in commissions actually paid (Table 3.5)[13].

In the meantime, stock exchanges in some other countries such as Canada and France have followed the examples of the United States, Australia and the United Kingdom and have deregulated commissions on stock exchange transactions while the stock exchange members in some other countries such as the Netherlands and Switzerland have reduced commissions notably for large transactions by institutional investors in order not to lose business to London or New York or other competitive financial centres. In Germany, where banks have always been free to determine the level of commissions they charge their customers for the execution of securities buy and sell orders, the officially fixed stock exchange brokerage fee ("Maklercourtage") was reduced by 20 per cent as from 1st January 1986 (for shares) and 1st January 1987 (for bonds), respectively.

Although it is difficult to obtain hard and fast statistical information, it is well known that the overall profitability of the international bond–issuing business has come under considerable competitive pressure as institutional investors were able to obtain increasing shares in the reallowance of underwriting and selling commissions. On the domestic bond markets governments have in a number of cases negotiated lower commission rates or have reduced issue costs through an increasing use of auction techniques[14].

Table 3.5 Effect of absence of fixed rates of stock exchange commissions
Average Commissions as Percentage of Purchase Value

1. *New York Stock Exchange* (negotiable commissions introduced on 1st May 1975)

	Apr. 1975	Feb. 1977	Percent Change (%)
a) All trades			
— Institutions	0.84	0.47	−44
— Individuals	1.73	1.54	−11
b) Small trades (less than 200 shares)			
— Institutions	1.50	1.04	−31
— Individuals	2.02	1.99	−2
c) Large trades (trades of 10 000 or more shares)			
— Institutions	0.57	0.32	−44
— Individuals	0.76	0.40	−47

2. *The International Stock Exchange in London* (negotiable commissions introduced on 27th October 1986)

	Before	After	Percent Change
	27th October 1986		
Trades in liquid alpha stocks			
a) Small trades (£1 000)	1.7	1.5	−12
b) Large trades (£500 000)	0.4	0–0.2[1]	−50–100

1.Large trades may take place on a net (no commission) basis.
Source: United States: SEC.
           United Kingdom: Bank of England.

As far as overall intermediation costs in financial systems are concerned — these are no doubt difficult to measure — it can be broadly concluded that the deepening of securities markets and the relative reduction in the role of institutional intermediation should have had a favourable impact on overall intermediation costs insofar as the banking system generally operates at cost margins which are considerably higher than margins in securities market transactions (measured in terms of the difference between cost to the borrower per annum and yield to the investor per annum).

3.4 REMOVAL OF DIRECT LENDING CONTROLS AND MANDATORY INVESTMENT REGULATIONS

Efforts to increase the scope for competition and the working of market forces in financial markets through interest rate and other price deregulation measures have in many OECD countries been accompanied by the removal of direct lending controls and/or mandatory investment regulations[15]. Such quantitative controls have often had to be applied in order to implement a policy of artifically low interest rates and to channel desired amounts of funds into low–yielding assets, notably government paper or loans and bonds serving the financing of priority sectors such as social housing, for example. Direct lending controls combined with controls on capital imports have also been used as an instrument of monetary policy.

As quantitative controls on credit or capital flows provide a powerful obstacle to the functioning of the market mechanism it was to be expected that the authorities of countries applying such controls would remove them in accordance with a more market–oriented approach to financial as well as monetary policy. Such policy action was all the more indicated as mandatory investment regulations and direct lending controls, though often serving different purposes, tend to produce distortions in the pattern of flow of funds in the same way as interest rate controls. Non–priority borrowers who are adversely affected by compulsory investment regulations and the rationing of bank credit tend to turn to unregulated financing channels which demand relatively high interest rates in order to attract funds from private savers or corporate treasurers. In this way, the growth of unregulated financial channels and markets has been favoured by quantitative restrictions on financial asset holdings in the same way as by interest rate controls. Accordingly, the removal of such restrictions, apart from the broad objective of

strengthening the working of market forces in banking and finance, has often been aimed at eliminating distortions in the flow of funds thereby re–establishing the central role of the banking system and the official financial markets, which was desirable from the point of view of both monetary policy as well as financial system management.

An additional motivation for the removal of lending ceilings has been the consideration that such controls provide an important obstacle to the competitive behaviour of banks insofar as the more dynamic and efficiently operating institutions are prevented from increasing their market shares while less efficient institutions are unduly favoured and supported. Thus, the removal of any direct lending controls has often been seen as an important step in the implementation of liberal competition policies in banking and finance. Another motivation for removing ceilings on bank lending has been the authorities' intention to encourage the banks to channel increasing amounts of credit into small– and medium–sized enterprises including new ventures which tend to be neglected under a regime of bank lending controls as banks prefer to lend to prime borrowers. Thus, the abolition of direct bank lending controls may also be seen as improving the functioning of the financial system in the sense of filling gaps in the supply of funds to some sectors of the economy.

3.5 STRENGTHENING THE COMPETITIVE STRUCTURE OF THE FINANCIAL SYSTEM AND THE COMPETITIVENESS OF FINANCIAL INSTITUTIONS

3.5.1 An Overview

While the two types of measures dealt with in the previous sections — interest and other price deregulation measures and the removal of direct credit controls and mandatory investment regulations — represent a more global approach to providing more scope for the working of market forces in banking and finance, the authorities of many OECD countries have taken a host of more specific measures aimed at strengthening the competitive structure of the financial system and the competitiveness of financial institutions. Some of these measures have consisted of banking reforms involving substantial changes in existing banking laws which had to pass through parliamentary procedures while many other measures were less visible to the public but had nevertheless important implications for the functioning of the financial system.

In an appraisal of public policy designed to improve the functioning of a country's financial system through a strengthening of the competitive structure of the system and the competitiveness of financial institutions, account needs to be taken of what is commonly called the financial system or the market for financial services which consists in reality of numerous sub-markets for different products and services for different types of customers and of a large number of local and territorial sub-markets with different demand and supply structures. Furthermore, these markets have a production side which develops new products, services, instruments, techniques and technologies, and a distribution side — the delivery system — which makes all these products and services available to the demanders for financial services in local markets or on a wider territorial, nationwide or worldwide basis. Accordingly, there can be, and usually are, considerable differences between all these sub-markets on the production side as well as the delivery side as regards the competitive situation and the efficiency of their functioning.

As a general rule, it may be said that the competitive situation in a specific sub-market and its efficiency and the quality of the service or product offered in it, will be improved by increasing the number of actual and potential competitors on the supply side of the market. The reference to potential competitors is important in this context because in financial markets, which often tend to develop oligopolistic supply characteristics, the mere threat of market entry by new powerful competitors is often sufficient to ensure adequate competitive behaviour of existing suppliers of financial services and products. For this reason, the question of market access and its various aspects — access by existing institutions to particular service and product markets, access by existing institutions to the delivery system in particular local or regional markets, and access by new institutions of domestic or foreign origin to the various sub-markets with particular product/customer/area characteristics — requires particular attention in any review of the competitive situation in banking and finance and related policy action designed to strengthen competition in this field.

The present review of policies towards strengthening the competitive structure of the financial system and the competitiveness of financial institutions starts with a record of measures designed to widen the range of permissible activities of financial institutions of various types. These efforts have often been concentrated on savings banks and other institutions operating in the retail banking field such as postal chequing and savings systems and co-operative banks which traditionally were more or less specialised and constrained in their activities. While such measures increase the number of "players" in markets for financial services, there have often been accompanying measures aimed at "levelling the playing field" by making the conditions under which the institutions compete with each other more homogeneous and thus reducing, or removing altogether, competitive inequalities. Such measures have no doubt increased the scope for financial institutions to compete flexibly with each other in various sub-markets with particular product and customer characteristics thereby strengthening these institutions' competitiveness while at the same time widening the choice available to demanders of financial services and products, which is also an important factor enhancing competition. It will be noted that governments themselves have often strongly contributed to widening the choice available to demanders of savings and investment products insofar as government debt managers have generally pursued a strategy of diversifying their borrowing instruments in an effort to finance increased public sector borrowing requirements.

Another line of policy action which will be reviewed in this section and which also aims at increasing the number of players on the supply side of the financial services markets, relates to the removal of controls on branching and other limitations on the territorial expansion of the banking network including controls on the entry of foreign banks or on the creation of new domestic financial institutions. Deregulation measures of the latter kind have also served to counteract undesirable concentration movements in national financial systems.

Fears about undue concentration in the financial sector have a long history in most OECD countries, which explains why merger policies in this field have traditionally received considerable attention in the context of financial policy. In the present section, merger policies are looked at from the point of view of policies designed to strengthen the competitiveness of financial institutions. It will be seen that merger policies can play a useful role in competition policies aimed at improving the functioning of financial markets. More generally, it can be said that with increasing interpenetration of national financial systems and with intensified competition, concerns about concentration questions have lost much of their former weight.

The section ends with a review of measures that have specifically been designed to strengthen the international competitiveness of a country's financial system. This policy objective has gained considerably in importance in recent years. While the types of measures and policies mentioned so far generally support policies towards strengthening the international competitiveness of these institutions, there are a number of other more specific measures which, viewed in isolation, may appear as insignificant but which may have a considerable impact on shifts in international flows of funds and related choices of internationally–operating demanders of financial services. The removal of stamp duties on securities transactions is a case in point.

3.5.2 *Diversification of Financial Activities and Products and the "Levelling of the Playing Field"*

A most striking feature of developments on the supply side of the markets for financial services has been the trend towards diversification and decompartmentalisation, or blurring of demarcation lines between formerly separated sectors of the financial system. The driving forces behind this trend have originated both from the market side and from the authorities' side. While financial institutions have used diversification strategies as a major weapon for competing vigorously in the rapidly growing and increasingly widening markets for financial services and products, the authorities have generally supported this trend, often in connection with broader financial reforms designed to improve the efficiency and the functioning of their countries' financial systems. The diversification and despecialisation process has no doubt been one of the major factors contributing to intensified competition in the vast markets for financial services and products although the speed and intensity of this development has varied from country to country depending, inter alia, on differences in historical legal frameworks and tradition and on regulatory changes. In the process of regulatory reform designed to build more integrated financial systems, the authorities have often paid considerable attention to the question of competitive equality and have often taken measures to ensure that the "players" in the market compete with equal weapons on a "level playing field"[16].

Policies towards despecialisation and diversification of financial services and products which banks and other financial institutions are allowed to offer, were generally more important in countries with historically more segmented financial systems than in countries with more open and homogeneous systems. This applies in particular to savings institutions which in a number of countries traditionally acted as collectors and guardians of small savings that were to be channelled into narrowly defined uses such as housing finance or government securities. In most of these countries such savings institutions have gradually been allowed to become full–scale retail banking institutions and have thus been integrated with the banking system. In a similar way, the financial service powers of post office systems have sometimes been enhanced by the authorities with a view to making more efficient use in the distribution of financial services and products of the wide branch network that postal systems usually have at their disposal. A third trend within the broader development towards diversification and the blurring of demarcation lines within financial systems has been the process of integration of the banking sector with the securities markets and the specialised institutions operating in them. This process has in particular affected those countries in which the two sectors have historically been separated by law or tradition. In the following paragraphs these various trends in financial policy aimed at more integrated financial systems are illustrated by a number of country examples.

Savings Institutions

Since the early sixties, the Belgian authorities have implemented policies designed to encourage the despecialisation of financial intermediaries with a view to encouraging the financing of economic expansion. This policy corresponded largely with the intentions of the financial institutions themselves which were directed towards expanding their activities beyond the traditional limits imposed by legal frameworks. In 1967, a first series of measures increased considerably the range of permissible activities of public–sector credit institutions, including the Caisse Générale d'Epargne et de Retraite (CGER). The institutions were authorised in particular to use the whole range of savings instruments and to diversify their lending activities. The system of control applying to private savings banks was also profoundly revised and the range of the savings banks' asset activities was widened.

A second phase of despecialisation was implemented by the Law of 30th June 1975 which harmonized the regulation of banks and private savings banks and authorised a further expansion of the range of activities of the CGER. The constraints on the activities of private savings banks were progressively lifted. In 1980, the CGER was transformed into a public–sector bank and thus came under the supervision of the Banking Commission. Since then this institution may engage in all banking activities.

The private savings banks were assimilated with the banks by Royal Decree of 14th October 1984 as regards the placing of eurobonds inside Belgium. However, they are still prohibited, according to the provisions of the Stock Exchange Law, to accept securities buy and sell orders from the general public.

France is another country in which the authorities have made considerable efforts towards integrating originally highly specialised financial institutions such as the private savings institutions (caisses d'épargne privées) and the system of agricultural credit co-operatives with the banking system. The process started with the banking reform of 1969 when the private savings banks as well as the Postal Savings System were authorised to offer special money transfer facilities on the basis of savings passbooks. In 1978, private savings banks were authorised to offer chequing accounts and corresponding payment services. The Savings Bank Law of 1983 was designed to modernise the private savings bank sector by reforming and strengthening the management of these institutions and promoting their productivity and profitability. The Banking Law of 1984 has gone a step further in the direction of harmonizing the rules and regulations under which different types of financial institutions operate. However, a full integration of the savings banks with the banking system would still require further legal changes. The savings banks still enjoy the "privilege" of issuing the "livret A", a passbook for tax-exempt savings which are subject to specific individual limits. On the other hand, these institutions are not yet authorised to offer all banking services and are, in particular, constrained as far as the utilisation of their savings deposit resources is concerned. However, the process of harmonization is still under way. Certain financial institutions such as the financial services of the Post Office System and the very important Caisse des Dépôts et Consignations (CDC) are not covered by the Law of 1984 although they are held to apply the same rules of operation as other financial institutions.

The role and functions of the agricultural credit system have also been modified in the sense that the range of permissible activities has been widened. However, the system still enjoys the monopoly of distributing subsidised credits to the agricultural sector while, on the other hand, there are still some limitations as regards lending to non-agricultural sectors. It may be noted in this context that in the international financial markets the central institution of the French agricultural credit system has become a most powerful competitor, as is the case with similar institutions in other countries.

The United Kingdom is a third example of a country in which the savings banks and similar institutions, the building societies, have been subject to marked changes in regulatory frameworks. As far as the savings banks are concerned, this process was initiated by the Page Committee (the Committee to Review National Savings) which recommended in its 1973 report that trustee savings banks which were highly specialised in the collection of National Savings become full banks[17]. This process was brought to a conclusion under the 1985 Trustee Savings Bank Act as a result of which the whole trustee savings bank system has been reorganised and modernised. In the meantime the Trustee Savings Bank has become a public limited company under wide public ownership and has thus become a full member of the banking community. The range of permissible activities of the building societies in the United Kingdom has also been widened progressively to cover services such as a limited range of payment facilities and limited powers in the field of commercial lending. Under the 1986 Building Society Act building societies may opt for conversion from mutual to corporate status and thus may become commercial banks.

In a number of other countries the integration of savings banks with the banking system has required less important legal action than in the three country cases just mentioned insofar as the differences between these two types of institutions — the banks and the savings banks — had traditionally been much smaller both legally speaking as well as in operational terms. In Germany, savings banks have been considered as universal banks for many decades. Nevertheless, several of these countries have merged or homogenised the legal frameworks within which these institutions operate: Finland and Sweden in 1969, Denmark in 1975, Spain in 1977, Austria in 1979, Australia and New Zealand in 1988.

In the United States, savings banks, savings and loan associations, and credit unions are each regulated by a separate Federal agency. All of them offer transaction, savings and time deposits; while all tend to deal mainly on the deposit side with consumers, the larger savings banks and savings and loan associations offer institutional and corporate non-transaction deposits. On the asset side, credit unions deal almost solely with consumers, but the other two types of institutions are beginning to use their new powers to offer credit services to businesses, non-mortgage loans to consumers, and — through subsidiaries — to make real estate investments.

Post Office Systems

In a number of countries the authorities' efforts towards strengthening the competitive structure and the efficiency of the financial system have also included measures aimed at a further integration of the post office system with the banking system. It was hoped that by using the post office network, the local availability of retail banking products and services could be considerably improved. Several countries such as Finland, Norway, the

Netherlands, New Zealand, Sweden and the United Kingdom have gone as far as transforming the post office financial services system, which offered for a long time chequing account and small savings facilities, into a commercial bank thereby establishing an additional competitive force in the otherwise oligopolistic structure of the banking system, or, alternatively, forcing the post office financial service system to become more efficient and competitive.

The Postal Savings Bank in Austria has also been granted considerable additional powers in recent years in part including functions which in other countries are fulfilled by the central bank, such as operating as the fiscal agent of the Federal Government and other public bodies. The Austrian Postal Savings Bank together with its fully–owned banking subsidiary has become a powerful competitor in the market for household savings, current account deposits and chequing facilities as well as in other financial service and product markets.

In the United Kingdom, the post office system which, as far as financial services are concerned, has acted for a long time as a collector of small savings within the framework of the National Savings Movement, was some time ago integrated with the country's market for payment facilities. In 1968, the National Giro was set up within the institutional framework of the post office system for providing money transmission services. Its activities were later expanded to include a wider range of services, following enabling legislation in 1976. In 1978, National Giro adopted the name of National Girobank, which in 1987 was changed once again into Girobank. In 1988 the government announced its privatisation.

In some other countries in which the post office system traditionally offered payment services in addition to small savings facilities, the range of authorised activities has gradually been increased to include modern payment facilities such as the use of credit cards, cash dispensers, travellers' cheques and retail services for buying and selling foreign exchange. The authorisation to provide some limited overdraft facilities in connection with the use of credit cards and cash dispensers has often been a corollary to these measures.

In some other countries the question of the extent to which and the way in which the post office system should be integrated with the financial system is still under intense discussion. Given the fact that the financial services of the post office system in many countries represent a powerful source of investible funds, this question is no doubt an important issue for financial policy, in particular, as regards competition in banking and finance. The aspects of competitive equality, on the one hand, and of the utilisation of these resources, on the other, are of particular importance in this regard.

Commercial Banks and Securities Firms

Commercial banks have also pursued strategies towards the widening of the range of their activities in response to demand changes or promising business opportunities. Major trends in this regard have been: the diversification of liability and savings instruments, the expansion of the range of international lending, borrowing and service activities, the development of term loan facilities, the entry into, or the expansion of, mortgage lending activities as well as the development of leasing and factoring business. However, in many cases the diversification into these new business areas has not required special legal action by the authorities. To the extent that banking legislation has been amended to include these new activities in the list of authorised banking transactions, legislators have mostly confirmed market developments.

As regards the separation of commercial banking activities from securities–related activities, which is still legally imposed in Japan and the United States and which, until recently, applied also in Canada, considerable market pressures have been building up towards blurring the demarcation lines between these two large areas of the financial service markets, and this trend has to some extent been supported, or at least tolerated, by the authorities. Some banks from the three countries mentioned have become major competitors in the eurobond business and other securities–related activities via subsidiaries set up outside the home country.

In Japan, the authorities have taken a number of steps towards improving the functioning of financial markets which had the effect of partially reducing the separation of functions between banks and securities firms, largely under the impact of heavy government borrowing which made it desirable to ensure a greater bank involvement in the operation of the markets for government securities. A first step was taken in 1977 when the banks in their function as members of the syndicate for the underwriting of government issues were authorised to sell government bonds in the over–the–counter (OTC) market if held for more than one year. A second step was the authorisation given to the banks within the framework of the Bank Act of 1981 to engage in the distribution of newly–issued government bonds; and in 1984 banks were authorised to act as dealers in the secondary OTC market for government bonds but only in their own name and for their own account and not on behalf of clients. Other securities–related activities which the banks have been allowed to carry out are as follows:

— Access to the facilities offered by the government bond brokers' broker (Japan Mutual Securities Company) originally established by securities firms;
— Direct participation in government bond futures markets established by the Tokyo Stock Exchange;
— Issuance of convertible bonds denominated in foreign currencies;
— Establishment of investment advisory subsidiaries.

Securities firms in Japan, in return, have been authorised to embark on some of the activities which traditionally had been the commercial banks' domain. Thus, they have been allowed to act as dealers in the newly–established secondary markets for certificates of deposit since June 1985 and for bankers' acceptances as from April 1986. The still remaining separation of functions between banks and securities firms applies only to Japanese territory; abroad, notably in the international market, banks and securities houses can act as universal banks either directly through branches or through separate subsidiaries.

In the United States, commercial banks have in recent years generally made greater use of the scope for conducting securities–related activities provided by the Glass–Steagall Act, notably as regards the offering of investment plans and portfolio management services for individuals and institutional investors with the banks acting in a fiduciary capacity. They have also been allowed to enter the securities brokerage business via special subsidiaries acquired or set up by bank holding companies. However, they are still prohibited from underwriting and dealing for own account in corporate securities and in municipal revenue bonds. More recently, in 1987, three major banks were authorised to underwrite and deal in certain debt securities to a limited extent through a bank holding company subsidiary.

In the United Kingdom, although no legal barriers have separated commercial banking from investment and securities–related activities, there have been distinctions in this regard based on tradition and practice. Since 1985–1986 however, changes in the rules of the Stock Exchange have opened the way for banks to acquire interests in broking and jobbing firms. One effect of this has been that United Kingdom banks can compete on a more equal footing with strong foreign competitors, notably from the United States and Japan. In France, banks have also been encouraged to widen the scope of their securities–related activities insofar as they were authorised, in 1985, to form special jobbing firms through joint ventures with broker

firms. Later on, in 1987 in connection with broader stock exchange reforms, banks were authorised to become stock exchange members via taking participations up to 100 per cent in existing brokerage firms as from 1st January 1988. Moreover, from 1992 onwards access to stock exchange membership will be free.

Creation of New Financial Instruments

While it is not always easy to distinguish between financial service activities and products as each new activity may be seen as launching a new product, it is worth noting in this context that the authorities in many countries have greatly contributed to the integration of their countries' financial systems and the strengthening of their competitive structures by either encouraging other market participants to create new instruments notably in the markets for savings and investment instruments or by creating such new instruments themselves within the framework of government debt management and deficit financing operations. The catalogue of new instruments introduced in the period under review, not only in the international financial markets but also in many national financial markets is indeed quite impressive. While in many instances the process of instrument innovation consisted simply of introducing securities of various forms that were already available in other countries and markets with a longer history and tradition — just to mention certificates of deposit, Treasury bills, commercial paper, bankers acceptances — there was also genuine product innovation in response to entirely new needs on the part of both borrowers and investors. Longer–term debt instruments with variable rates or zero–coupon features, hybrid types of securities with both debt and equity features, securities offering various choices for conversion into other securities, securities serving to mobilise non–marketable claims of different sorts, and, finally, hedging instruments and facilities such as swaps, financial futures and options may be briefly mentioned in this context[18].

The process of instrument innovation has forcefully contributed to the broadening and strengthening of the market element in national financial systems and has thus enhanced competition and the working of market forces and has supported the integration of the system. On the other hand, it should be noted that central banks as well as bank and market supervisors have sometimes expressed concern about the unprecedented proliferation of new instruments both from a market efficiency point of view and a safety and soundness point of view. This was particularly the case if the creation of new instruments was not supported by the creation of corresponding efficient secondary markets[19].

A special line of government action designed to widen the range of savings and investment instruments and related investor choices and at the same time aimed at channelling more savings into securities markets has been the development of regulatory frameworks for the operation of investment companies issuing collective investment certificates of various types through the intermediary of banks and other distribution systems. In many countries the selling of such certificates and corresponding publicity has been explicitly included under the scope of banking legislation, securities laws or special laws, mainly for investor protection reasons. In a similar way, government regulation in some countries has supported the development of new types of securities both with fixed–interest features and equity features designed to assist the process of enterprise financing on competitive terms.

Finally, it is noteworthy in this context that the governments themselves via their debt managers have contributed to the process of instrument innovation by following a strategy of diversification of debt instruments in coping with the task of financing important borrowing requirements since the early seventies and rolling over large amounts of outstanding debt resulting from cumulative budget deficits. In this connection governments in quite a number of countries have found it necessary to compete with banks and other financial institutions directly in the vast market for household savings by developing and issuing new debt instruments which were specifically tailored to the needs of different types of personal investors[20]. In countries such as Japan and Sweden the need to finance large public sector borrowing requirements provided a major impulse for adopting a more market–oriented policy approach in the field of banking and finance, as under the traditional system of interest rate controls and mandatory investment requirements financial institutions and institutional investors were unable to take up such large volumes of government paper.

Although the authorities in most countries have generally tolerated or actively promoted the trend in financial systems towards despecialisation and the blurring of demarcation lines between different types of institutions and markets, they have been hesitant in many instances to carry this process to an extreme situation in which all credit and deposit–taking institutions operate under a single legal framework authorising them to offer the whole range of financial services and products individually which a country's financial system as a whole provides collectively. The authorities in a number of countries still see, at least for the time being, an advantage in maintaining a certain degree of separation of functions and specialisation in banking and finances by corresponding sets of different regulatory frameworks applying to different types of institutions separately, as can be seen from a review of despecialisation policies pursued in countries such as Belgium, Denmark, France, Japan, the United Kingdom and the United States.

3.5.3 Promoting the Entry of New Competitors

The authorities in many countries, in pursuing policies towards strengthening the competitive structure of the financial system and the competitiveness of financial institutions, have increasingly paid attention to the question of market access by potential newcomers. Providing scope for easy market access has been increasingly recognised as a powerful policy weapon for counteracting tendencies towards concentration and anti–competitive behaviour of banks and other financial institutions that may result from concentration. As has already been mentioned, the threat of new entry of competitors may often be sufficient to encourage the existing institutions to offer financial services and products on competitive terms and to ensure high quality standards in meeting the financial service needs of their customers. In addition, access by newcomers, notably from foreign countries with different experiences, can effectively help the process of financial innovation and diversification in the country and hence improve efficiency.

Decompartmentalisation

In principle, the ease of market access can be influenced by the following types of regulations:

— Regulations dealing with the range of activities which banks or other financial institutions are permitted to carry out either directly or via separate subsidiaries;
— Regulations dealing with the expansion of branch networks in banking;
— Regulations dealing with the establishment of new banks both national and foreign.

As has been seen in the preceding section, the authorities can strongly affect the access to various sub–markets in the wide area of financial service and product markets by breaking down previously existing barriers to entry that take the form of legally imposed specialisation requirements applying to different groups of financial institutions. A most conspicuous example of such entry barriers is the prohibition to enter the full range of securities business in the home market that applies to commercial banks in Japan and the United States. It has been seen in the preceding section that with a view to fostering competition and efficiency the authorities in practically all countries have engaged in despecialisation policies by widening the range of permissible activities of different types of financial institutions so that they can more easily access each other's territories. A most radical example of such policies has recently been seen in Canada where under the "New Directions for the Financial Sector" of December 1986[21] the traditional "four pillar system" — consisting of the banking sector, the trust and mortgage company sector, the insurance sector and the securities sectors — was practically replaced by a unified financial system in the widest sense. Under the new system, which is gradually being implemented, it will be possible for each institution belonging to one of the four sectors to move into each of the three other sectors either directly or via the setting up of specialised subsidiaries. The latter approach is, for example, required by law if banks decided to move into equity underwriting and trading. In order to enhance the effect of regulatory change on competition the authorities favour in general the setting up of new subsidiaries rather than the acquisition of existing firms.

In other countries, financial reform in this field has been less radical. However, it is evident from the record given in the preceding section that the trend towards unified and integrated financial systems is irreversable and rather generalised with one broad and important exception. Many countries are still quite hesitant to allow banks to move into the insurance underwriting business, for example, via ownership linkages; or to allow insurance companies to move into the business of banking. Nevertheless, the demarcation lines between these two sectors are also gradually being blurred in countries where this is legally possible[22].

Branching

As part and parcel of broader policies towards fostering competition through easier market access, several countries which previously applied controls in this area have deregulated the expansion of branch networks and related territorial restrictions. This has no doubt helped to intensify competition and improve the efficiency of local markets which often were characterised by a high degree of concentration or monopoly situations. In Germany, according to a judgement by the Federal Constitutional Court of 1958, the public–need test required hitherto for the admission of pharmacists as well as for many other economic activities was in conflict with the basic right of freedom to choose a trade, occupation or profession laid down in the German constitution. The freedom of

establishment also for banks and branches was confirmed in a judgement by the Federal Court of Administration of the same year and therefore embodied in the 1961 Banking Law which took effect from 1st January 1962. In France, bank branching was originally deregulated in 1967 in connection with interest rate deregulation measures. The authorisation procedures previously applied were replaced by simple notification procedures. A new form of control on branching was, however, introduced in 1982 in the context of regional policies. The purpose of these controls, however, has not been to limit competition in banking although some concerns regarding overbanking have also played a role. In 1986, bank branching has again been fully deregulated. In Austria, bank branching was liberalised as part of the 1979 banking reform which also lifted the territorial restrictions previously applying to the operations and the setting up of branches of savings banks. In Sweden, restrictions on bank branching which had been in force until 1981 have also been lifted.

In a number of countries, the authorities have never applied restrictions on bank branching in the belief that in line with the principle of free enterprise it was up to the banks themselves to decide on the number of branches which they felt able to run on profitable terms. Countries falling into this group are Canada, Luxembourg, the Netherlands and the United Kingdom. This does not imply, however, that in some of these countries the question of overbanking has not been a matter of concern to the authorities at some stage in history[23].

Concerns regarding overbanking are clearly part of the explanation why in some other countries the authorities maintain controls on the expansion of bank branches. Another reason may be seen in the fear that freedom in bank branching would favour the concentration process and would enable the large and powerful banking institutions to expand their institutional dominance further at the expense of smaller local and regional banks. These fears certainly play an important role in the United States and are inter alia an explanation why this country has historically favoured unit banking as opposed to branch banking. However, the trend towards an intensification of territorial competition — not mentioning examples of successful circumvention of existing restrictions — is quite evident. Between end–1960 and end–1985, the number of "unit banking states", in which branching is not allowed, was reduced from 18 to 8; the number of states in which statewide branching is allowed, increased from 17 to 24; and the number of states in which branching is allowed within limits, although not on a statewide basis, increased from 16 to 19.

Foreign Bank Entry

The liberalisation of foreign bank entry into national financial systems has been used in a number of OECD countries as a most powerful weapon for stimulating competition and mitigating any adverse impact of concentration on competition in banking and finance. The entry of large and powerful foreign banks into national financial systems in fact increases the number of large banks operating in the country and hence reduces concentration in the banking sector even if this does not show up in balance–sheet comparisons. In many cases the authorities have welcomed the entry of foreign banks not only from a competition policy point of view but also because of the immediate and direct benefits which the presence of these banks offered through the introduction of new financial products, services and know–how in financial engineering which had already been tested in other markets. This has often accelerated the process of financial innovation. On the other hand, it should be noted that in opening the national financial system to foreign banks, considerations relating to the access of the country's own financial institutions to other national financial systems have played a role as well. In Japan, in an effort to confirm that equal opportunities be accorded to foreign financial institutions desiring to engage in trust business, all of the nine foreign banks which applied for entry have been allowed to join the group of trust banks which, inter alia, engage in the management of pension funds. By comparison, only eight domestic trust banks have been authorised to operate in this area.

The process of interpenetration of national banking systems through foreign bank entry has been encouraged through international co–operation at government level both within the framework of the European Community and the OECD. The basic right of establishment, also of banks, was already enshrined in the 1957 Treaty of Rome. The First Banking Co–ordination Directive of 1977 included rules aimed at facilitating the creation of a common banking market through branching, which in fact helped the domestic deregulation process in this field to some extent as well. However, the first integration attempt had little success in the sense that branching within the Community met with a number of obstacles in connection with national authorisation requirements, notably as regards endowment capital.

A major breakthrough of EC policy towards creating a unified banking market within the Community was achieved in 1985 with the endorsement by Heads of States and Governments of the White Paper for the completion of the 1992 Internal Market which was to be based on the principles of mutual recognition and a single licence throughout the EC. The Second Banking Co–ordination Directive which was proposed at the beginning of 1988 contains the suggested regulatory framework for implementing these principles in connection with the creation of a unified market for banks by 1992. From a competition policy point of view it is interesting to note that the Second Banking Co–ordination Directive also adopts the model of a universal bank which can engage, inter alia, in all types of securities business including operations on stock exchanges. This will force countries with stock exchange member monopolies to remove restrictions on stock exchange membership. France has already taken legislative action in this direction while other countries such as Belgium, Italy and Spain are in the process of preparing similar moves[24].

As far as the encouragement of foreign bank entry through government co–operation within the OECD is concerned, several activities and instruments need to be mentioned[25]. The objective of liberalising trade in services, including financial services, and capital movements was already established in 1961 when the OECD was created as the successor of the former OEEC. Member countries agreed "to pursue their efforts to reduce or abolish obstacles to the exchange of goods and services and current payments and to maintain and extend liberalisation of capital movements". The twin codes of liberalisation of current invisible transactions and of capital movements were, and still are, the essential tools for promoting these objectives. These earlier liberalisation efforts did not specifically relate to establishment questions although, in a way, establishment was covered by reference to direct investment. However, the Code of Liberalisation of Capital Movements was amended in 1984 to the effect that the liberalisation obligation with respect to inward direct investment was expanded to include the main aspects of the right of establishment. This important change has to be seen in connection with OECD's activities in the field of liberalisation of trade in services which have received high priority in recent years. For a number of services, including financial services, establishment is essential for effective market entry.

OECD liberalisation efforts in the field of financial services including establishment–based services are supported also by the National Treatment instrument which forms part of the 1976 OECD Declaration on International Investment and Multinational Enterprises and constitutes, in a way, an obligation for an essentially non–discriminatory treatment of already established foreign–owned enterprises. The two liberalisation codes and the National Treatment instrument together provide a comprehensive set of multilateral agreements for fostering the liberalisation of both

Table 3.6 Foreign bank entry in selected OECD countries
Net Change in Number of Banks (Entry minus Exit)

	1961–1970	1971–1980	1981–1985	1961–1985
Eight European Countries[1]	81	169	86	336
Japan & Australia	4	45	27	76
United States	52	155	178	385
Total	137	369	291	797

For comparison: Net Change in Number of Domestic Banks

	1961–1970	1971–1980	1981–1985	1961–1985
Seven European Countries[2]	−497	−443	−31	−991
Japan & Australia	3	−2	3	4
United States	164	993	41	1 198
Total	−330	548	13	231

1. Belgium, Denmark, Greece, Ireland, Italy, Netherlands, Portugal, Spain and Switzerland.
2. Above countries excluding Switzerland.
Source: Annex III, Section XII.

cross–border and establishment–based trade in services. The process of foreign bank entry into national financial markets whether promoted by international co–operation efforts or reflecting essentially competitive strategies of market participants, has indeed reached impressive dimensions (Table 3.6). At the same time the number of domestic banks has been reduced in many countries.

3.5.4 *Merger and Ownership Policies*

In discussing competition policies in the present study, a distinction has been made between competition policy in a wide sense comprising all measures that encourage, or provide more scope for, competition, and competition policy in a narrow sense which deals with issues relating to concentration, dominant market positions and restrictive business practices including price cartels or other anti–competitive co–operation agreements amongst market participants. Merger and ownership policies form an essential part of competition policies dealing with the concentration question. As regards banking and finance, policy concerns about trends towards undue concentration of financial — and eventually political — power have a long history in a number of countries, notably in the United States, and, for example,

have influenced policy discussions about how to deal with conflicts of interest[26] in banking and finance. Indeed, the separation of "banking and commerce" or of "banking and securities business" or of "banking and insurance" has often been motivated by fears of concentration of power rather than by conflict of interest considerations. Such fears seem justified insofar as there has been a certain tendency in the financial sector towards the formation of large financial conglomerates or conglomerates that combine financial and non–financial activities. In many countries, the banking sector is indeed highly concentrated and consists of an oligopoly of a few large banks which co–exist with a larger number of small– or medium–sized banking units including savings banks and co–operative banks. Thus, it is understandable that most countries have arrangements in place which either formally limit participations in banks — Australia, Canada, Netherlands, Norway are examples of such countries — or which allow the monitoring in one way or another of any intentions for changes in sizeable participations in banks including takeovers and mergers. This is the case, for example, in Belgium, France, Germany, Greece, Luxembourg, the United Kingdom and the United States[27].

The authorities generally use merger and ownership policies in the financial sector in a flexible manner and integrate them with general policies towards improving the efficiency and functioning of financial systems. Two aspects of this broader policy approach seem to be discernible; first, the use of merger policies for dealing effectively with problem banks; second, the use of merger policies for strengthening the competitiveness of financial institutions, both domestically and internationally.

Merger policies are increasingly used to deal with banks that are in difficulty. With a view to avoiding panic reactions and a deterioration in public confidence which could be caused by news about imminent banking failures, the authorities have often favoured approaches according to which existing institutions would absorb problem banks through corresponding merger operations, which, moreover, might remain unnoticed by the public. Such an approach has the advantage from an overall efficiency point of view, that the product and service facilities of the failing institution which may include a not easily replaceable branch network, can be integrated with the acquiring institution so that overall there is no reduction in the supply of financial services or in the distribution network for such services[28].

It also appears that the authorities make increasing use of merger policies as an instrument for strengthening the competitiveness and financial and managerial basis of individual banking or other financial institutions. This is visible, for example, in the savings bank and co-operative bank sector of a number of countries where an important concentration movement is going on. This development is generally favoured by the authorities in view of the efficiency and productivity gains that are obtained in this way. Many of the smaller banking units in these parts of the retail banking sector are no longer viable as they cannot afford the relatively high technology input that under today's conditions is required in this field.

Other examples of merger movements in the financial sector that have been favoured by the authorities are the acquisition by banks of securities firms that have taken place in recent years in Canada, France and the United Kingdom and may be expected to occur in Belgium, Italy and Spain due to corresponding policy changes. In Canada, the new federal legislation proposed in December 1986 under "New Directions for the Financial Sector" and gradually being implemented has made it possible for commercial banks in Canada to take participations in securities firms. In France, banks were authorised in 1987 in connection with broader stock exchange reforms to take participations up to 100 per cent in brokerage firms. In the United Kingdom, the previously existing limit on capital participations in stock exchange member firms by non-member firms (including banks) was abolished and banks — as well as other firms — were allowed to acquire a 100 per cent participation in member

firms. These various measures have lead up to a considerable strengthening of the capital base and hence of the international competitiveness of the securities industry in these countries. Sometimes countries have favoured sizeable banking mergers with a view to strengthening the international competitiveness of the domestic banking community[29].

More generally it is noteworthy that with the high degree of openness of national financial systems reached as a result of ever intensifying competition and active external liberalisation policies, the traditional fear of concentration in banking and finance has lost much of its former importance. With the presence of large foreign banks in many national financial systems the concentration of financial power in the hands of a few large banks which previously may have existed has been considerably diluted even if this is statistically not easily measurable. Sometimes, the mere threat of the appearance of powerful newcomers has been sufficient to prevent the formation of banking cartels and other anti-competitive behaviour of a small group of large domestic banks. This effect is clearly visible in EC countries in the perspective of the creation by 1992 of the internal banking market which allows banks from all EC countries to move into each other's territories with a single banking licence[30].

3.5.5 Strengthening the International Competitiveness of Financial Systems

With rapidly intensifying competition between international financial market centres resulting from the ever-growing importance of the international financial markets, the strengthening of the international competitiveness of national financial markets and institutions has become a major financial policy objective in an increasing number of countries. This development has provided a major impetus to policies in OECD countries towards the improvement of the functioning of national financial systems and has accelerated and broadened the process of financial liberalisation and deregulation.

The post-World War II history of policies towards strengthening the international competitiveness of national financial systems may be seen as starting in the sixties when some countries such as the United Kingdom, France and Luxembourg began to set their regulatory frameworks in banking and finance in such a way as to favour the development and the growth of the international financial markets under their jurisdiction while at the same time protecting their domestic economies against undesirable monetary influences from these markets. Initially, these efforts were concentrated on international banking transactions which were favoured by the absence of minimum reserve requirements and other controls and by a liberal approach to foreign bank entry. In later years, efforts concentrated more on favouring the growth of international securities–related activities such as the new issuing business in the eurobond market and in the markets for traditional foreign bonds, and cross–border securities brokerage services, trading and portfolio management including mutual fund management. International securities–related activities received major impulses from liberalisation measures in the field of portfolio capital transactions and a resulting trend towards international portfolio diversification.

Policy action designed to strengthen the international competitiveness of national financial systems and attract an increasing part of the markets for international financial services and products has included a wide range of specific measures in addition to the general measures discussed in the preceding sections of this chapter. The authorities in an increasing number of countries have realised that with greater mobility in international financial transactions and operations resulting largely from much improved information and communication channels, slight cost differences in the handling of cross–border transactions could have a major impact on decisions regarding the choice of the financial centre through which international financial transactions should be channelled. Hence the importance of differences in taxation features and in commission structures including those applying to stock exchange transactions.

The abolition of withholding taxes on interest income from securities in the United States, France and Germany in 1984–1985 clearly served the purpose of increasing the international attractiveness of the financial instruments which were previously affected by these taxes. Pressures from the financial community for removing levies and taxes on stock exchange and other financial transactions in France, Germany, the Netherlands, Switzerland and the United Kingdom and the authorities' intention to review these tax arrangements also reflect concerns that the continued application of these taxes could shift a considerable proportion of international as well as domestic financial transactions into foreign financial centres. The more recent controversial plans of the German government to introduce a withholding tax on interest income are widely seen as impairing Germany's position as an international financial centre thus marking a striking set–back in German official policy in this field.

The changes in the rules and practices of the London Stock Exchange, which partly took effect as from "Big Bang Day" (27th October 1986) and resulted in freely negotiated commissions, a more competitive and technically more efficient securities dealing system, a strengthening of the capital base of the securities industry through participations from banks and other institutions, and generally greater competition amongst securities dealer firms, have considerably strengthened London's position as a leading international financial centre. This move has forced the financial communities and authorities of some other European and non–European countries to respond to the London challenge by measures designed to increase the attractiveness of their own countries' financial markets and institutions, notably as regards the functioning of stock exchanges.

Policies towards strengthening the international competitiveness of national financial systems have also included measures designed to increase the range of financial instruments, activities and facilities in national markets which are available in other major financial centres and to provide more scope for foreign participation in these various activities. The German measures taken in 1985 — allowing foreign banks domiciled in Germany in the form of a domestic subsidiary to act as lead managers for foreign DM bond issues, provided reciprocal conditions are met in the foreign bank's home country, and authorising the issue of zero–coupon DM bonds and variable interest rate notes — were clearly motivated by considerations regarding the international competitiveness of the German financial markets. Similar measures taken in the Netherlands early in 1986 served the same purpose. The actual or planned establishment of markets for currency options and financial futures in a number of countries such as Australia, France, Germany, Japan, the Netherlands, Sweden and Switzerland may also be seen as an effort towards strengthening the attractiveness of these countries as international financial centres in response to corresponding developments in the United States and the United Kingdom or, equally important, as attempts to reduce these countries' dependence on "importing" such services from foreign financial centres.

In the light of this relatively new, but increasingly important, policy objective of strengthening the international competitiveness of national financial institutions and markets, concerns about the concentration of power relating to the presence of a few large banks or securities firms in the financial system, have lost much of their traditional weight. The authorities in an increasing number of countries have, in fact, realised that national financial systems cannot remain internationally competitive without the presence of some financially and managerially strong banking and other financial service institutions. In some countries, the formation of such institutions has been actively encouraged by the authorities as has already been mentioned in the previous section on merger and ownership policies.

3.6 IMPROVING INFORMATION AND MARKET VISIBILITY

Information is an important factor affecting competition and the functioning of markets. Markets can only function properly if there is adequate visibility as regards information on the characteristics of the instruments and services offered and on related costs, prices, risks and returns. This applies not only to the highly organised and sophisticated securities and money markets in which well defined and often standardised instruments are traded within specific regulatory frameworks concerning information and disclosure requirements, it is also true for the less organised markets including "markets" for financial services such as payment services, advisory services, brokerage services, information services etc.

As far as organised markets such as the securities, money and foreign exchange markets are concerned, once the regulatory frameworks for the operation of these markets are set, the authorities see generally little need for taking specific action with a view to improving information and market visibility, all the more so as market participants and the specialised press tend to produce sufficient information and market analysis. In addition, rating agencies are increasingly seen outside the United States as fulfilling a useful information, and hence investor protection, function.

Problems often arise, however, as far as information on conditions in the unregulated markets is concerned. This applies in particular to the whole retail banking area including services for small businesses and the area of services in a narrow sense in general. Recognising the importance of information and visibility for the functioning of these "markets", the authorities have increasingly paid attention to this question as part of their overall policy designed to promote competition and the functioning of the markets for financial services. Consumer protection considerations have, however, played a role as well.

In the United Kingdom, the National Board for Prices and Incomes recommended in its 1967 report on Bank Charges[31] that banks — in addition to abolishing collective agreements — should publish a tariff of main charges including the rate of offsetting allowance given on credit balances. In Germany, the authorities introduced an Order on Price Quotations in 1973 according to which banks are held to post prices on standard services and interest rates on standardised loans and deposits. The list of services and instruments in the standardised retail banking business covered by this Order was considerably extended in 1985 to show, inter alia, effective rates of interest on consumer and mortgage loans.

In Australia, the Campbell Commission devoted a chapter of its report on the Australian Financial System[32] to the question of "Information Gaps in the Financial System". Apart from making recommendations on disclosure rules applying to banks, insurance companies, other financial institutions and corporations generally, the report takes the line that efficient and competitive markets would tend to produce adequate information themselves. However, it noted with satisfaction that the Government and the Reserve Bank were making a useful contribution to the spreading of general information on financial matters to the household and small business sector in the form of broadly available brochures. A similar information policy has been pursued by the authorities of the United Kingdom, notably as regards financial information for small businesses. It seems, indeed, that in practically all countries there is considerable scope for improving the visibility of the markets for retail financial services including services for small business and related market information although consumer organisations and product and service test organisations are making progress in producing and disseminating such information.

3.7 REVIEWING THE METHODS OF FINANCIAL ASSISTANCE TO SPECIFIC SECTORS

All countries have a history of policy action designed to facilitate the financing of specific sectors of the economy such as agriculture, export industries, the energy sector, residential construction, the small business sector including the creation of new businesses, local and regional industrialisation or general development programmes, or the public sector itself. The implementation of such financial assistance or incentive programmes is generally seen as politically acceptable and desirable also in those countries which traditionally have followed a market–oriented approach as regards the management of their national economies and financial systems. Thus, policies designed to ensure effective management of any such financial assistance or incentive programmes and to fit them into the market system may be seen as forming part of an overall policy towards efficient functioning of national financial systems.

In implementing such financial assistance programmes and incentive schemes the authorities have in principle a wide range of options available to them. Leaving aside the option of a global approach in the form of a generalised policy of low and stable interest rates combined with a policy of direct credit allocation which has already been considered in the section on interest rate deregulation, the following techniques have been applied in practice:

— Low—interest rate credits financed by the central bank through special rediscount facilities;
— The setting up of special government—owned, mixed, or private financial institutions channelling low—interest rate funds into the privileged sectors; the institutions receive favourable tax treatment, interest rate or other subsidies or simply function as an intermediary of budget funds; government—owned institutions may, moreover, be subject to relatively low capital requirements and may have no obligation to pay dividends to the public owner;
— Direct low—interest loans from the budget;
— Interest—rate subsidies payable directly to the beneficiaries;
— Mandatory investment regulations i.e. imposing on financial institutions an obligation to channel a specified proportion of available resources into the privileged sectors at low interest rates;
— Building low—interest rate circuits into the financial system with savers receiving fiscal incentives in the form of bonus payments or deductibility of invested funds from taxable income.

As the authorities in an increasing number of countries have paid more attention to the question of the functioning of their countries' financial systems and have generally adopted a market—oriented approach in this field, the question of reconciling the two financial policy objectives — ensuring an efficient and effective management of financial assistance programmes and improving the functioning of the financial system — have increasingly come under review. Attempts have been made to identify techniques of implementing such assistance programmes and incentive schemes which interfere as little as possible with the functioning of the system and the working of competitive market forces and which at the same time — given the generally strained budgetary situations — minimise the budgetary costs of these programmes.

In policies towards reforming the techniques of implementing financial assistance and incentive programmes in line with these broad policy objectives the following trends and approaches are discernible[33]:

— Low—interest rate refinancing facilities provided by central banks have increasingly been abandoned because of their inflationary nature and because such facilities have increasingly been seen as being non—compatible with the functions of a central bank;
— Government loans financed from budgetary resources whether granted directly or through the intermediary of one or several financial institutions, or through the network of the banking system, have been increasingly reduced because of the high budgetary costs;
— The subsidisation of financial institutions specialised in the financing of privileged sectors such as, for example, agriculture or housing has been increasingly replaced by more individualised subsidy schemes designed to reduce the interest rate costs of loans granted at market rates;
— Mandatory investment regulations have increasingly been abolished because of their adverse impact on the process of free interest rate determination and because of resulting distortions in the flow of funds;
— Tax incentives for savings flowing into specific types of financial institutions specialised in the financing of privileged sectors have been replaced by either generalised savings promotion schemes which do not discriminate between different forms of savings or by schemes which allow all types of savings—collecting institutions to offer those savings instruments. Arrangements of this kind have essentially been introduced for reasons of competitive equality.

3.8 STREAMLINING THE PAYMENT SYSTEM

Ensuring a safe, smooth and efficient functioning of the national payment system is in all countries a major objective of financial policy and more specifically of banking regulation and supervision and related regulation concerning the use of means of payment. Amongst the wide range of financial services it is above all the payment services which are in the nature of a public good as these services and the functioning of the mechanisms through which they are provided and effected are indispensable for the functioning of national economies as a whole.

Apart from regulations concerning the use of means of payment, the authorities in some countries have started at an early stage to encourage the development of efficient cashless payment systems which require the setting up of efficient and widely accessible clearing systems for the handling of cheque and/or money transfer (giro) orders. Thus, the Deutsche Reichsbank introduced a clearing system for interbank payments as early as 1883. The introduction of postal giro and/or chequing systems in many countries has also to be seen as an effort on the part of the authorities to improve the efficiency of the payment mechanisms and to make these facilities available both to a wide population for current payments and to the government for the collection of taxes and the payment of salaries and pensions. Sometimes, the role of providing the technical basis for efficient money transfers between the public administration and their civil servants has also been assigned to public sector-owned savings institutions or the post office system.

With the advent of new technologies in the field of money transmission services and a proliferation of different and often competing payment instruments and circuits, the authorities, notably the central banks, have become increasingly concerned about the implication of these new developments for the safety, reliability and efficiency of national payment systems and their international connections. It has increasingly been felt that these developments could not be entirely left to the working of the market forces i.e. to competitive struggles between different groups of market participants, and that a high degree of co-operation in the development of efficient payment systems was necessary. However, the ways in which co-operation in this field is organised and the role which the authorities, notably the central banks, play in such co-operative efforts, differ from country to country depending on historical developments of national payment systems and of related legal frameworks. While in some countries, for example the United Kingdom, the organisation of co-operative approaches towards dealing with the issues involved is left to the banking community and other private participants, there are other countries in which the authorities play a leading role in steering or monitoring the development of national payment systems. Australia, Canada and France are examples of this latter group of countries. The central banks' interest in issues pertaining to the development of payment systems has manifested itself, inter alia, in the setting up, under the auspices of the Bank for International Settlements, Basle, of the Group of Experts on Payments Systems of the Central Banks of the Group of Ten countries. The Group has studied and compared developments in the payment systems of the participating countries and published the results in 1980 and 1985 in the form of detailed manuals[34].

In France, the Banque de France has been heavily involved in co-operative efforts dealing with the development of national payment mechanisms and techniques. In January 1979, the then Deputy Governor of the Banque de France, M. de la Genière, was charged by the Minister of the Economy, Finance and the Budget to chair and organise a working party responsible for studying the rational and coherent development of payment media. The group included all interested parties such as representatives of the various groups of banking institutions, of the public authorities and of public-sector financial institutions, The group's mandate was:

— To determine preferred policy with regard to payment instruments;
— To define the general rules to be applied by banks to interbank exchanges of deposit money;
— To act as a forum for investigating problems relating to internetwork exchange conditions;
— To organise pilot schemes for new electronic payment systems and to monitor their development.

The group has prepared major decisions on future developments in the French national payment system including the important consensus on the interconnection of banking card and related ATM systems.

In Canada, co-operation in the field of payment systems was legally imposed by the Canadian Payments Association Act which came into effect on 1st December 1980. The Canadian Payments Association (CPA) which includes as members the Bank of Canada and credit institutions of various types (chartered banks, trust and mortgage loan companies, credit unions etc.), according to the Act of 1980, has the mandate to establish and to operate a national clearing and settlement system and to plan the evolution of the national payment system. In the meantime, the first objective has been achieved and efforts are now concentrated on the second objective of planning the evolution of the national payment system.

Australia has, in a way, followed the Canadian example. The Government accepted the Martin Group's view[35], that the development of the payment system should not be left solely to market forces and created in 1984 the Australian Payment System Council as a non-statutory body whose mandate is:

— To monitor the development of domestic payment systems;

— To promote the implementation of standards for electronic funds transfer (EFT) systems; and

— To foster interconnection between payment systems.

A priority task of the Council was to consider how best to facilitate access by other financial institutions (other than banks) to the cheque clearing system. The Council is chaired by a senior officer of the Reserve Bank and includes representatives of the major financial industry groups involved in the development of national payment systems, the Treasury, Telecom and the National Consumer Affairs Advisory Council.

In the United States, where the situation in the payment field is broadly characterised by the co-existence of competing systems and mechanisms, the Federal Reserve has, since its creation in 1913, played a major role in the development of a nationwide payment system insofar as it is involved in the clearing and collection of cheques and money transfer orders, wire transfer of funds and the clearing of payment information contained on magnetic tape. The Federal Reserve's wire funds transfer system (FedWire), which was automated in 1973 and substantially upgraded in 1982, handles essentially transfers of large dollar amounts in competition with two private systems — BankWire and the Clearing House Interbank Payments System (CHIPS). The Federal Reserve is particularly concerned about the risks involved in the operation of the networks for large fund transfers; and in 1983, it has carried out, in co-operation with the banking industry, a study of methods of controlling risks in this important field.

Italy is also a country in which the central bank has a major interest in the development of an efficient payment system. In 1984, the Banca d'Italia set up an in-house working group for studying developments in the field of payments in Italy and for co-ordinating the Bank's initiatives in this regard. The group's work resulted in the preparation of a voluminous White Paper which was published in its final version in April 1987[36].

NOTES AND REFERENCES

1. The various concepts and definitions used in Chapter 3 such as "competition policy", "functional efficiency", "financial policy", "financial regulation", "scope and characteristics of the markets for financial services" are explained in greater detail in Annex I. The Annex includes, moreover, a number of quotations from official, or government–assigned, commission reports which throw some light on the assumed relationship between competition and efficiency and related policy objectives.

2. See for example Robert Deumer, "Die Gesetzgebung des Auslandes auf dem Gebiet der Kreditbanken", in *Untersuchungsausschuss für das Bankwesen 1933*, Referat IV/1.

3. For Germany, see, for example, *Untersuchungsausschuss für das Bankwesen 1933*, several contributions, inter alia, Fritz Paersch, "Massnahmen des Staates hinsichtlich einer Beaufsichtigung und Reglementierung des Bankwesens", Referat II/3. For the United Kingdom, see *Report by the Macmillan Committee on Finance and Industry*, 1931, Cmnd. 3897.

4. For detail see Annex III, Sections I and II.

5. Porter Commission, *Report of the Royal Commission on Banking and Finance*, Ottawa, 1964.

6. Bank of England, *Competition and Credit Control*, London, 1971.

7. National Board for Prices and Incomes, Report No. 34, *Bank Charges*, Cmnd. 3292, London, May 1967.

8. Hunt Report (1971), *The Report of the President's Commission on Financial Structure and Regulation* (Washington D.C.: United States Government Printing Office).

9. *Depository Institutions Deregulation and Monetary Control Act of 1980, Public Law 96–221*. This comprehensive law contains as separate titles the Monetary Control Act of 1980, the Depository Institutions Deregulation Act of 1980, and the Consumer Checking Account Equity Act of 1980 as well as provisions relating to the powers of the thrift institutions, state usury laws, truth in lending simplification, regulatory simplification, foreign control of United States financial institutions, and other amendments to the National Bank Act.

10. Annex III, Section I.

11. The analysis of interest margins of banks is based on data on financial statements of banks compiled and published by OECD; see *Bank Profitability, Financial Statements of Banks with Methodological Country Notes, 1980-1984*, OECD, Paris, 1987 and *Bank Profitability, Statistical Supplement, Financial Statements of Banks, 1982-1986*, OECD, Paris, 1988; see also *Financial Market Trends*, No. 38, Special Feature: "Bank Profitability 1980-1985: Recent Trends and Structural Features", OECD, Paris, November 1987.

12. Price Commission, *Banks: Charges of Money Transmission Services*, 337, London, 1978; see also Note 7.

13. See Securities and Exchange Commission, Fifth Report to Congress on The Effect of the Absence of Fixed Rates of Commissions, 26th May 1977; and Bank of England, "Change in the Stock Exchange and Regulation of the City", Quarterly Bulletin, February 1987.

14. For country detail, see Annex III, Section X.

15. For country detail, see Annex III, Section III.

16. The factual background material for this section has been provided by the members of the former Expert Group on Banking and compiled in Annex III, Section IV, sub–sections a), b), c) and d).

17. *Commission to Review National Savings, Report*, Chairman Sir Harry Page, June 1973, Cmnd. 5273, London, 1973 (often referred to as "the Page Report").

18. For detail on the introduction of new financial instruments in national financial systems as well as in the international financial markets, see Annex III, Section V.

19. See, for example, Bank for International Settlements, *Recent Innovations in International Banking*, Basle, April 1986.

20. See, for example, *Government Debt Management, Volume II, Debt Instruments and Selling Techniques*, OECD, Paris, 1983.

21. The Honourable Thomas Hockin, Minister of State for Finance, *New Directions for the Financial Sector*, tabled in the House of Commons, Canada, 18th December 1986.

22. See, for example, Commission of the European Communities, Directorate–General for Financial Institutions and Company Law, *Conference on*

Financial Conglomerates, 14th–15th March 1988, Borschette Centre, Brussels, Proceedings, July 1988.

23. For further detail see Annex III, Section VIII.

24. See Georgios Zavvos, "EC Strategy for the Banking Sector: The Perspective of 1992", published in *European Affairs*, No. 1/88, Spring, Elsevier, 1988.

25. See OECD, *International Trade in Services: Banking*, Paris, 1984; OECD, *International Trade in Services: Securities*, Paris, 1987; OECD, (by R.M. Pecchioli) *The Internationalisation of Banking*, Paris, 1983.

26. See Annex V which contains further bibliographical references.

27. For more detail on bank ownership regulation, see Annex III, Section VII.

28. See, for example, Hanns C. Schroeder-Hohenwarth, "Zur Problematik insolvenzgefaehrdeter Kreditinstitute", published in: *Die Bank*, 5/84, Köln, 1984.

29. The two mergers, between the Bank of New South Wales and the Commercial Bank of Australia to form Westpac Banking Corporation; and between the National Bank of Australia and the Commercial Banking Company of Sydney to form the National Commercial Banking Corporation of Australia, essentially reflect a response of Australian banks to pressures of competition from outside following the opening of the Australian financial system as recommended by the Campbell Commission (see Note 32). See *The Banker*, September 1982, "Why the Banks Merged" (article with no author mentioned).

30. See Note 24.

31. See Note 7.

32. *Australian Financial System*, Final Report of the Committee of Inquiry, Canberra 1981.

33. *Australian Financial System*, Final Report of the Committee of Inquiry, Canberra, 1981. See in particular Section 36, "Sectoral Assistance: General Approach".

34. See Bank for International Settlements, *Payments Systems in Eleven Developed Countries*, February 1985, prepared by the Group of Experts on Payment Systems of the Central Banks of the Group of Ten Countries, Basle, 1985.

35. See *Australian Financial System*, Report of the Review Group, December 1983, Canberra, 1984 and *Reports of the Australian Payments System Council*, 1985 and 1986.

36. Banca d'Italia, *White Paper on the Payments System in Italy*, Rome, 1988.

Chapter 4

MAIN ISSUES FOR POLICIES TOWARDS EFFICIENT FINANCIAL SYSTEMS

4.1 INTRODUCTION

Policies towards efficient financial systems, which have been reviewed in Chapter 3, have gathered considerable momentum since the late seventies under the dual impact of ever intensifying competition within and between national financial systems and a rapid spreading of financial deregulation and liberalisation policies on a worldwide basis. This process, which in some countries set in as early as in the mid–sixties, has not yet come to an end, as is indicated by the debate on restructuring the financial system that is going on, for example, in the United States[1] and by the preparations for the 1992 unified banking market within the European Community[2].

There is hardly a country in the OECD area which has not been affected by international financial market developments and the worldwide financial deregulation and liberalisation process. In the early eighties, the authorities of countries with a traditionally liberal approach to financial policy such as Germany, Luxembourg, the Netherlands and Switzerland, began to take a fresh look at the functioning of their national financial systems and at related policy concepts and objectives and have found it necessary to take further measures designed to strengthen the international competitiveness of their financial centres in response to financial reforms taking place elsewhere.

Although there are considerable country differences in national financial systems and regulatory frameworks, financial policies pursued in OECD countries have many common features as regards objectives, policy approaches and the issues and problems policy makers have been confronted

with. The broad objectives of financial policy are, in fact, the same in all countries, namely:

— To ensure an efficient functioning of the financial system;
— To preserve the stability and soundness of financial institutions and the system as a whole; and
— To maintain an adequate level of investor protection.

As far as policies towards ensuring an efficient functioning of the financial system is concerned, there is also a broad consensus that such policies should essentially consist of more reliance on market forces, the promotion of competition within the financial service industry, and strengthening the competitiveness of financial institutions, as is evidenced by the host of financial deregulation measures that have been taken during the period under review.

In implementing competition policies in the financial sector, the authorities in most countries have, broadly speaking, applied the same or similar strategies such as widening the scope for price competition through interest rate deregulation measures and the freeing of fees and commissions on financial services, increasing the access to the various sub–markets of the broad financial service markets by supporting the trend towards despecialisation, and facilitating the entry of new competitors through liberal policies towards branching and the setting up of new banks, and through encouraging foreign bank entry. Policies towards strengthening the competitiveness of national financial institutions have often been supported by favouring the formation of efficient and financially strong banking units and encouraging rationalisation measures in the banking sector[3].

While these have been common features of policies designed to encourage competition in the financial system, there are considerable country differences as regards the extent to which the scope for competition and for the working of market forces has actually been widened. In a number of countries, the authorities have not gone as far as introducing full interest rate deregulation or freeing all types of commissions and fees which had traditionally been controlled or had been subject to cartel agreements.

As far as the process of despecialisation and integration of previously highly-specialised institutions with the banking system is concerned, the authorities, while often supporting this trend by appropriate measures, have in many instances not gone as far as fully harmonizing or integrating related regulatory frameworks. Many countries have, in fact, maintained different legal frameworks for different types of institutions thereby continuing to impose a certain degree of specialisation on the institutions concerned. Thus, the important policy question arises as to how far countries should go in the financial deregulation process, taking into account that such policies need to be reconciled with the stability and soundness and investor protection objectives. There is also the question for financial policy whether deregulation alone is sufficient as a policy approach or whether other conditions need to be fulfilled in order that market forces work properly.

In fact, there are a number of areas in financial systems and markets in which co-operation is a better approach to efficiency than reliance on competition and market forces. The payment system is an example of such an area, as has been seen in Chapter 3. This raises the question for financial policy to what extent co-operation should be allowed to play a role in efforts towards improving efficiency and how any such co-operation should be organised.

During the period of transition to a more market-oriented system, considerable attention needs to be paid to the ways in which individual financial institutions will, and can, adjust to intensified competition and whether weaker and less efficient institutions will be able to survive. How should the authorities cope with the increased danger of banking failures? Massive failures, if badly handled, could trigger a severe confidence crisis. There is also the closely related danger that during the transition period weaker and less efficient institutions will be taken over so that concentration will increase.

A number of difficult questions are raised by the internationalisation process in the financial service markets and by related policies designed to strengthen the international competitiveness of national financial institutions and market centres.

All countries are faced with the question of how far they should go in promoting the internationalisation process and to what extent they should rely, in this context, on the working of market forces. To what extent is there a need for international co-operation aimed at achieving at international level what countries have already largely achieved, or are in the process of achieving, at national level, namely a "level playing field" in competition and arrangements for an effective prudential supervision and adequate investor protection regulations; and how should any such international co-operation be best organised? In addition, there is the question of how to proceed in building efficient technological interlinkages between national financial systems for which there is an urgent need in areas such as payment systems and information, trading, clearing and settlement systems.

All these questions and issues just mentioned lead up to the more fundamental issue of how policies designed to improve the efficiency and the functioning of financial systems should be reconciled with policies designed to ensure the stability and soundness of the financial system and to maintain an adequate level of investor protection so that market participants can have confidence in the authorities' ability to handle any market shocks adequately and to keep the marketplace clean. There is also the question whether and how policies designed to improve the efficiency and the functioning of financial systems can be reconciled with an effective monetary policy and whether and to what extent there is scope for changing the techniques of monetary policy in the direction of a more market-oriented approach.

The various issues for financial policy addressed are increasingly seen in their combination and interrelationship, which inevitably leads to the broader issue of how to develop a policy concept of global financial system management. Indeed, under the impact of the general trend towards decompartmentalisation within national financial systems, the increasing interpenetration of these systems at international level and the ongoing process of globalisation of money and securities markets, the authorities in OECD countries are increasingly taking a broader look at their countries' financial systems as a whole, both in a national and international context, and are endeavouring to develop a more global and more coherent approach towards financial system management. The questions and problems raised by such a global approach are manifold and may require important changes, in particular from an international point of view, in areas such as the institutional organisation of the financial system and corresponding regulatory frameworks and supervisory arrangements. The present chapter is intended to discuss these various financial policy issues in more detail.

4.2 THE PROBLEM OF AN ADEQUATE LEVEL OF COMPETITION

4.2.1 *Introduction*

There is a wide measure of agreement amongst the authorities of OECD countries that policies towards improving the efficiency and the functioning of financial systems should essentially be implemented through competition policies aiming at increasing the scope for adequate price competition, product and service competition and territorial competition. Nevertheless, there are a number of problems and issues with which the authorities have been faced in practice in their efforts towards achieving adequate levels of competition in the financial service markets. Difficulties and problems arise essentially because financial service markets are a complex system of a wide range of sub–markets with different product/service, customer and territorial characteristics; and because financial institutions and other providers of financial services competing in these sub–markets apply strategies which may differ considerably from one sub–market to another. Thus in each sub–market, or larger groupings of sub–markets, the competitive situation tends to be different as regards the number of players, the degree of market visibility and related information that is available to, or actively used by, demanders of financial services, and as regards the combination of the competitive weapons which the providers of financial services are willing, or able, to use. Thus, it cannot be expected that there are simple prescriptions for policy action designed to achieve an adequate level of competition in all these different sub–markets in the same way.

4.2.2 *Free Price Competition versus Regulated Interest Rates, Fees and Commissions*

Today, there is broad agreement amongst OECD countries that a proper functioning of financial systems, notably of money and securities markets, and the determination of interest rates through the free interplay of market forces has a beneficial effect on the allocation of financial and real resources in national economies. It is widely accepted that free price competition enables financial institutions, in the absence of direct lending controls, mandatory investment regulations and other asset and liability restrictions, to react flexibly and dynamically to demand and supply changes in the markets for financial services and thus ultimately contributes to a strengthening of the competitiveness of financial institutions.

However, when it comes to the question of how far the authorities should go in encouraging, and providing scope for, free price competition in the financial system, there are considerable differences in views and policy attitudes, as is evidenced by the impressive list of interest rate restrictions that continue to remain in force[4].

It is true some restrictions on price competition in financial services which are still maintained in some countries have to be viewed as a problem of transition towards a more competitive system. Controls on interest rates on small deposits and the prohibition of interest rate payments on current accounts and/or cartel agreements on such interest rates are sometimes maintained with a view to protecting smaller institutions until they have adjusted to the changing competitive climate. Thus, it is probably only a matter of time whether remaining restrictions on interest rates will eventually be removed in Japan and some countries in the European Community.

Controls on interest rates in retail banking, notably deposit rates, are sometimes maintained for more general reasons relating to the peculiarities of the retail banking market. From the point of view of competition policy, the retail banking market is, indeed, a special market where it is difficult, via sole reliance on deregulation, to achieve an adequate level of competition between two extreme situations: destructive competition for market shares on the one hand, and too little competition, which impairs cost efficiency, on the other. The retail banking market notoriously lacks visibility and is often subject to monopoly or quasi–monopoly situations in local markets. The retail banking client has generally little bargaining power and is often less sensitive to fee and interest rate differences than the corporate customer, inter alia, because of loyalty and convenience considerations. In a deregulated environment, this can have two different consequences depending on the strategies which retail banking institutions are ready to apply in particular circumstances. If they are in search of better profit performance, as has often been the case in recent years, they may, and are able to, pursue a strategy of market segmentation which results in interest rate margins and other revenue such as, for example, spreads in retail foreign exchange transactions, which, by wholesale standards, appear excessive[5]. This — apparent — ability of banks to master the profit situation in retail banking raises difficult questions not only from the point of view of cost efficiency in retail banking, but also from a more general efficiency point of view. If banks of a universal type were using profits from retail banking on a large scale to cross–subsidise activities in more competitive markets such as markets for corporate financial services or international financial markets, this could, indeed, result in a misallocation of resources, not only within the banks but also macro–economically, not to mention the effects on income distribution[6].

The other extreme possibility is that price deregulation in retail banking leads to a situation of destructive competition. Retail banking institutions may engage in a fierce battle about market shares by attempting to attract additional retail deposits via deposit rate increases. As retail banking clients are relatively insensitive to rate and price differences, as has been mentioned, any such rate increases have to be substantial. As increased deposit rates, moreover, have to apply to the whole deposit stock, and not only to new deposits, price competition in retail banking is bound to become particularly costly. With a view to avoiding any such destructive competition in retail banking, which could provide a threat to the stability of the financial system as a whole, the authorities sometimes prefer to maintain control on retail deposit rates.

Sometimes controls on interest rates, fees and commissions in retail banking are also motivated by consumer protection considerations similar to those applying in some other retail markets such as the retail distribution of books and periodicals, or retail trade in pharmaceutical products. In these special markets, price maintenance is essentially allowed to ensure adequate market visibility and broad availability of products and services. More generally, given the special risks involved in deregulating the retail banking market, namely that the market may tend to lack visibility and competitive response or, alternatively, may become subject to destructive competition, it may, indeed, appear questionable whether price deregulation policies should be fully extended to retail banking as well. As has been mentioned, some countries are reluctant in this regard. Others make attempts at improving the visibility of the retail banking markets by strengthening disclosure requirements, for example, by requiring that the conditions for standard retail banking operations are visibly posted inside, or even outside, bank buildings. In addition, some countries rely increasingly on the activities of consumer organisations as regards the question of how to improve the visibility of retail banking markets[7]. However, whether and to what extent such approaches help to achieve an appropriate level of competition in retail banking, remains an open question.

Another area within the broad financial services markets where competition has often remained subdued and fee and commission rates tend to be sticky, is the new–issuing business, notably in countries in which the consortium technique has traditionally been the preferred way for large issuers to come to the market. As such issuers, including the government, essentially depend on the placing power of a single large underwriting syndicate, there is little scope for flexible price negotiation. Thus, commission structures in these markets have remained rather rigid. This has also been the case in the otherwise rather competitive international new issue markets although the overall profit situation of banks and securities houses in this field has suffered from increased competition in reallowances granted to institutional investors. In some countries such as Italy and Switzerland, competition in the new–issuing business has become somewhat more intense as a number of more specialised finance companies, sometimes owned by large industrial corporations, have entered this market.

Government debt managers of many countries have in recent years widened the scope for competition in the new issue markets for their own debt instruments by increasingly introducing auction techniques, which do not involve any commissions. However, it has been argued that in smaller countries in which the new issue market is dominated by a few large banks and institutional investors, the choice of the issuing technique has practically no bearing on the overall cost of a new issue, taking interest costs and commissions together[8]. Nevertheless, it is likely that this argument does not fully apply to open markets in which a number of important foreign issuing houses are allowed to participate in the primary market for government securities.

4.2.3 Freedom of Diversification for Financial Institutions and Conglomerates versus Legally Imposed Specialisation

Since the sixties, banks and other financial institutions have generally diversified their activities to a considerable extent, in response to changes in financial service needs and as part of their strategies towards strengthening their competitiveness both at national and international level. The authorities in OECD countries have largely supported this trend through an active policy of product deregulation and institutional decompartmentalisation within the financial system. Thus, widening the range of permissible financial service activities of traditionally more specialised financial institutions has generally been accepted as an effective way of increasing the scope for new entry into particular markets for financial services, thereby encouraging competition in these markets and promoting efficiency and at the same time enabling financial institutions to strengthen their competitiveness under rapidly changing demand and supply conditions.

The process of diversification and despecialisation just mentioned has often been referred to as a general trend towards universal banks, or financial conglomerates. It seems indeed that financial institutions of a certain size, notably if they operate on a nationwide as well as worldwide basis, have a "natural" tendency towards operating in the whole field of financial service activities such as commercial banking, merchant banking and securities–related activities. The management of these banks obviously feels that the wide range of financial service needs of their clientele can be best met by offering all these services through one institution and that this approach to banking also has advantages from an overall management point of view in terms of synergies or economies of scale or scope[9]. Sometimes, banks offer highly specialised services through subsidiaries thus combining the advantages offered by universal banking on the one hand and specialisation on the other. There is indeed a school of thought which explains the trend towards universal banking by synergies which are likely to be generated by a combination of a wide range of interrelated financial service activities. However this may be, the trend towards universal banking is clearly evident also in those countries in which commercial banking activities and securities–related activities, or some of these activities, have been legally separated as far as domestic operations are concerned. Foreign subsidiaries of banking institutions from the countries concerned often combine these two broad lines of activities and have generally been encouraged to do so through corresponding regulatory measures[10].

While, from an efficiency point of view, the advantages of despecialisation and diversification in banking and finance are widely recognised, there are considerable divergencies in views and policy attitudes as regards the question whether the process of despecialisation should be carried to a situation in which all financial institutions operate under identical conditions and within a uniform legal framework, or whether some degree of legally imposed specialisation should be maintained. Different views about regulatory and supervisory issues relating essentially to the stability and soundness and the investor protection objectives play a major role in explaining such divergencies. In countries in which, for efficiency reasons, the decompartmentalisation process has been carried very far, thereby increasing the scope for the formation of multi–purpose banks and financial conglomerates, the authorities have usually been confident that their regulatory and supervisory arrangements are adequate from a stability and soundness point of view as well as from an investor protection point of view, and that related conflict of interest situations can be handled satisfactorily.

Canada is an example of a country in which the authorities have — by international comparison — gone very far in the process of product deregulation and decompartmentalisation. Under the "New Directions for the Financial Sector" of December 1986, any institution belonging to one of the traditional "four pillars" of the financial system — the banking sector, the trust and mortgage company sector, the securities sector and the insurance sector — is now allowed to move into the territories of the other three pillars, either through increased direct powers or via subsidiaries[11]. Provisions regarding the form in which these various activities can, or must, be carried out, either directly or via a separately capitalised subsidiary, have been determined by prudential and supervisory considerations. Thus, banks have to conduct riskier types of securities business such as corporate equity underwriting and trading via a subsidiary while other securities transactions including operations in the government securities markets may be carried out directly.

Most other countries continue to impose some restrictions on the activities which commercial banks and other financial institutions are allowed to carry out and have thus maintained some degree of compartmentalisation in the financial system. As has been seen in Chapter 3, most countries continue to confine the financial service powers of the post office system to certain retail banking activities such as payment services and ordinary pass–book savings facilities. Building–society type of institutions also continue to be restrained as regards their lines of authorised activities. The same is true for mortgage banks or finance companies which in many countries operate within a separate legal framework. Two countries — Japan and the United States — continue to maintain domestically some separation between commercial banking and securities–related activities; and several countries continue to maintain a strict, or some degree of, separation between banking and insurance[12]. Most countries require, for investor protection reasons, that mutual funds are separately capitalised and supervised.

The reasons for maintaining these various types of regulatory separation of functions, or restrictions on permissible activities, differ according to the types of institutions involved. As far as the role of post office systems in the financial service markets is concerned, the authorities in a number of countries fear that giving retail banking status to this institution would lead to a situation of overbanking and excessive competition in the field of retail banking and that, given the otherwise special position of the post office system, the problem of competitive equality could not be solved satisfactorily. The authorities in countries in which the financial service department of the post office system has been transformed into a retail bank, have generally been guided by efficiency considerations, for example, by the objective of ensuring an adequate supply of basic financial services also in geographically remote areas which banks would tend to neglect under normal cost/benefit considerations, or to strengthen the efficiency of the financial services of the post office system through exposing them to more competition from the market system.

The maintenance of restrictions on building–society type of institutions largely reflects fears that many of the smaller institutions would not efficiently function as commercial banks and thus might become a danger for the stability of the financial system. With a view to providing, nevertheless, some more flexibility and scope for competition, the authorities sometimes allow such separately regulated institutions to acquire banking status[13].

The separation between the banking sector and the securities industry — or, to be more precise, the separation between commercial banking and some securities–related activities — has traditionally been motivated by two concerns: first, it was feared that this combination of financial activities would give rise to unmanageable conflicts of interest which would endanger the stability and soundness of the financial system as well as raise problems for protecting the investor against malpractices; second, it was feared that the combination of these activities would lead to a politically as well as economically unacceptable concentration of power. While these concerns have not been shared in many countries with universal banking systems, there are a few other countries including Canada, Germany and the United Kingdom in which the authorities have seriously considered the problems involved, but have found solutions to deal with them which do not imply a full institutional separation of these activities[14]. Nevertheless, banking and securities market regulators and supervisors are increasingly occupied with problems raised by conflicts of interest.

Objections against a combination of commercial banking and insurance are based on similar considerations. On the one hand, there is the concentration argument, which has played a considerable role, for example, in the Netherlands in the debate about the financial structure, but, in the meantime, has lost much of its previous weight in the perspective of the 1992 unified banking and insurance market within the European Community[15]. On the other hand, there is the risk argument which is, however, mainly used against insurance companies moving into banking, for example, via ownership linkages, rather than against banks acquiring participation in insurance companies. Some countries favour the idea of co–operation between banking and insurance in the sense that they allow banks to operate in the insurance brokerage business, which avoids to some extent the duplication of distribution networks for the two sectors[16].

4.2.4 Conflicts of Interest

As has been mentioned in the preceding section, conflict of interest considerations play an important role in the context of policies towards the structural organisation of countries' financial systems, notably as regards the desirability of separating certain areas of financial service activities, for example, commercial banking and securities–related activities, by legal arrangements[17]. In this sense, policies designed to handle conflict of interest problems in banking and finance have an important bearing on competition policies in this field as an institutional separation of functions introduced on conflict of interest grounds may, and often does, represent limitations on market access and hence on the scope for the working of competitive market forces.

Stated in an abstract way, a conflict of interest situation arises if a bank — or any other enterprise — which deals with a client, has a choice between two solutions, one of which is preferable from its own interest point of view while the other represents a better deal for the client. A conflict of interest situation arises also for a bank or another financial institution if it carries out activities involving two different groups of customers and if it has to strike a balance between the respective interests of the two customer groups. A practical example of the latter case is the new–issuing business which always requires a compromise between the interests of the issuer and those of the investor. As soon as a financial institution — or any other enterprise — offers two or more technically or functionally unrelated services, leaving scope for certain choice, it is faced with the problem of how forcefully it should promote either service.

As financial institutions often operate in a wide range of different financial services, they are bound to be confronted with a relatively large number of conflict of interest situations. This explains why conflicts of interests generally receive more attention in banking and finance than in other sectors of the economy.

Public policy concerns about conflicts of interest are essentially motivated by three types of basic considerations: efficiency considerations, investor protection considerations and prudential i.e.

stability and soundness considerations. In practice, discussions about conflicts of interest have often been closely related to fears about concentration of power, and measures intended to deal with conflicts of interest through an institutional separation of functions have often been motivated by such fears.

As far as the efficiency aspect of conflicts of interest is concerned, it has been argued — as has already been briefly mentioned — that a financial institution operating in different broad areas of financial services such as retail banking, corporate financial services, securities–related activities etc. cannot be expected to be equally efficient and competitive in all these services at the same time and will, hence, tend to offer less than lowest cost and highest quality services in areas of activity which are less profitable or in which the institution in question has less experience or less qualified staff. In other words, according to this argument, the financial service needs of particular customer groups, or of the economy as a whole, will be better satisfied if more specialised institutions were responsible for offering particular types of services or for dealing with particular customer groups instead of allowing multi–function institutions to operate in all these areas at the same time. Policy makers could deal with this problem either by imposing a certain degree of specialisation between financial institutions, or by setting up special institutions dealing with particular financing problems; alternatively, they could take appropriate measures designed to improve the efficiency of less developed sub–markets for financial services by increasing the scope for competition, in particular, through facilitating market access from inside or outside the country. This latter approach has generally become the preferred way of dealing with this aspect of conflicts of interest. The product deregulation and institutional decompartmentalisation process described in Chapter 3 has, in fact, been one of the ways in which access to particular sub–markets in financial services has been facilitated.

The second type of concern about conflicts of interest which is motivated by investor protection considerations, goes a step further than the efficiency concern. It is argued that in certain conflict of interest situations the quality of service offered may suffer to such an extent that investors or other market participants need special protection against intentionally bad service and malpractices. This applies mainly to securities–related activities in which a securities firm, or the securities department of a universal bank, has a fiduciary function vis-à-vis clients which, moreover, may have little experience with securities transactions. It is feared that professionals, who may have various choices for doing securities business with clients, may unduly weigh their own interests against those of their clients. In conflict of interest situations of this kind, the authorities may go beyond reliance on market discipline and may handle such cases by codes of conduct, rules of practice or conditions for doing business.

The third type of concern about conflicts of interest is motivated by stability and soundness considerations. It is argued that in extreme situations, a conflict of interest can lead to mismanagement and unacceptable risk–taking in business areas in which a given financial institution has little experience and for which it is not "fit and proper", and that in order to protect the general public against undesirable failures and losses, appropriate precautionary measures, for example, in the form of an institutional and regulatory separation of functions, need to be taken. This concern played a major role in the debate leading in the United States to the introduction of the Glass–Steagall Act of 1933, which approached the underlying conflict of interest problem by a separation of commercial banking and a wide range of securities–related activities. Today, the prudential aspect of conflicts of interest, like other risk aspects of banking and securities–related activities, is generally being dealt with by prudential regulation and supervision rather than by a separation of functions.

Conflicts of interest in banking and finance are handled in many ways, depending on their nature and the severity of concern that the authorities attach to them. An extreme solution to dealing with conflicts of interest is to seek their avoidance by a strict separation of institutions operating in conflicting financial service activities. This approach could even go as far as requiring also separate ownership of such institutions, which would not allow a financial institution to operate in conflicting business areas via separately capitalised subsidiaries. Japan is an example of a country in which not only commercial banking operations but also trust business including pension fund management is institutionally separated from most other securities–related activities. In the United States, it is essentially the corporate securities business (underwriting and trading as well as related investment advisory services coupled with brokerage services) which is separated institutionally and ownership–wise from commercial banking activities. In Canada, a similar separation of functions is obtained by the provision that banks have to conduct the corporate securities business via separately capitalised and supervised subsidiaries. A less stringent separation of functions — within one and the same institution — is obtained by so–called "Chinese Walls" which have the purpose that information which may give rise to conflicts of interest, cannot be exchanged between different departments such as the corporate finance department, the trust or fund management department and the departments for securities brokerage services, trading, investment advisory services and investment research.

A more widely adopted approach towards protecting investors and consumers against abuses of conflicts of interest by providers of financial services is based on the principles of adequate disclosure requirements. According to this approach the clients of financial institutions should be fully informed about all aspects of the business they are doing with financial institutions (nature of the transaction, capacity in which the institution is acting — as agent or principal — risks, return and costs involved etc.); and any such information should be readily available in understandable form.

A third type of a broader approach to protecting investors and other market participants against malpractices consists of implementing detailed codes of conduct, rules of practices including insider trading rules and conditions for doing business, which need to be respected by providers of financial services with a view to forestalling any abuse of conflict of interest situations. This third broad approach towards dealing with conflicts of interest receives increasing attention in OECD countries.

A fourth approach towards dealing with conflicts of interest simply consists of reliance on competition and the working of market forces. According to this approach consumers and other market participants should have sufficient scope for selecting the institutions with which they want to do business. This approach generally applies to broader conflict of interest situations in which a given financial institution may promote one line of business, for example, deposit taking, to the detriment of another line of business, for example, securities brokerage and investment advisory services. Sole reliance on this approach is increasingly considered as neglecting the seriousness of the problems that may be raised by conflicts of interest.

4.3 CONDITIONS FOR THE PROPER WORKING OF MARKET FORCES

4.3.1 Introduction

There is a broad consensus amongst OECD countries that a liberal competition policy in banking and finance should not be confused with a "laisser–faire, laisser–aller" policy and that — in addition to free price, product and territorial competition — a number of conditions need to be fulfilled to ensure that market forces work properly and that competition is maintained at an appropriate level. According to countries' experiences in this field the following conditions and principles deserve special attention in this regard:

— Competition should take place on a "level playing field", i.e. market participants should compete on equal terms and conditions so that there is equality of competitive opportunity;

— Competition should be subject to agreed "rules of the game" such as codes of conduct, rules of market practices and principles of market organisation;

— "Club arrangements" — which often play a useful role in the formulation of "rules of the game" and for a proper market organisation — should not give rise to anti–competitive practices and co–operation agreements;

— Anti–competitive effects of concentration and dominant positions of market participants should be avoided.

Although there is general agreement on these broad principles, there are considerable country differences as regards the degree of importance that is attached to these issues, the ways in which these principles are implemented, and the respective roles that self–regulation and official regulation play in this latter regard.

4.3.2 "Levelling the Playing Field"

In creating conditions for a proper working of market forces the authorities in OECD countries have paid particular attention to the issue of competitive equality, or equality of competitive opportunity. It has been increasingly realised that effective competition requires "a level playing field" on which providers of financial services of different kinds can compete on equal terms and conditions. While the basic concept of competitive equality is straightforward and· easy to accept, there is considerable difficulty in clarifying its meaning in concrete situations and in implementing it in practice. From an institutional point of view, competitive equality is generally understood to mean that institutions doing the same or similar types of business should be subject to the same or similar rules and regulations; or that institutions doing the same type of business on the liabilities side, for example, should be allowed to do the same types of business on the asset side. However, looked at from a functional point of view, the principle of competitive equality could also mean that identical types of financial service operations should be subject to identical or similar sets of rules and regulations.

From a regulatory point of view, the principle of competitive equality implies that any type of regulation — prudential regulation, taxation, the use of specific monetary policy instruments such as credit ceilings or minimum reserve requirements — should have a neutral impact on competition between financial institutions doing the same or similar types of business. The principle of competitive equality is particularly difficult to apply in countries which maintain some degree of legally imposed specialisation which allows different types of financial institution to compete in some, but not all, financial service and product markets.

With a view to clarifying the question of competitive equality from an efficiency point of view, two different types of institutions competing in the same markets on unequal terms may be considered. As one group is treated more favourably than the other, the favoured institution may be seen as enjoying a "privilege rent" which — hypothetically — can be expressed in money or profit terms. In the case of tax privileges it is relatively easy to assess the differential profit impact. In other cases such as unequal treatment under capital requirements (which may, inter alia, arise from public-sector ownership), minimum reserve requirements, mandatory investment regulations, interest rate controls, limitations on certain types of business etc., it is more difficult to assess the impact of the "privilege" on profits[18].

The basic problem that arises from an overall efficiency point of view is that the privileged group of institutions, as a result of the additional profit potential that is created by the privilege, is less under pressure to compete effectively than the unprivileged group. The "privilege rent" does not necessarily show up in higher profits. It may be passed on to the banks' customers in the form of lower interest rates on loans or higher interest rates on deposits, or a combination of both, which may be seen as an advantage from an overall economic point of view. However, it should be taken into account that any increase in market shares resulting from such a pricing policy would not reflect greater micro-economic efficiency and competitiveness of the privileged institutions.

The "privilege rent" may also be absorbed by higher operating costs insofar as there is less pressure in the privileged institutions for productivity gains than in the unprivileged institutions. In practice, it is certainly difficult, if not impossible, to identify the ways in which the "privilege rent" is actually used. There may be a combination of various uses: lower interest rates on loans, higher interest rates on deposits and higher operating costs. In extreme situations, this could lead to distortions in the flow of funds within the economy in the sense that increasing amounts of financial resources could be channelled through less efficient institutions. Whether and to what extent there is a real danger in a given country that such distortions develop, naturally depends on the size of any such "privilege rents".

In practice, problems of competitive inequalities, which have received considerable attention in financial policies of OECD countries, have been dealt with in several ways. The broadest approach towards "levelling the playing field" has been the harmonization or amalgamation of different regulatory frameworks applying to competing groups of financial institutions. The integration of savings banks with the banking sector and similar measures of decompartmentalisation (see Chapter 3) are examples of this approach. The harmonization of taxation rules has often supplemented such regulatory harmonization efforts. In Germany, the so-called tax privileges of savings banks, other public-sector owned financial institutions and of credit co-operatives have been phased out over a number of years following a Government Report on the competitive situation in the banking sector presented to Parliament in 1968. The report, which had been prepared by the Ministry of Economics, focused in particular on the question of whether and to what extent competitive inequalities had led to changes in the respective market shares of the major groups of banking institutions such as private banks, savings banks and other credit institutions owned by the public sector, and the credit co-operative sector[19].

France is also an example of a country in which the issue of competitive equality has received particular attention. Since the seventies the French authorities have pursued a systematic policy of "banalisation" i.e. of integrating formerly privileged participants in the financial markets with the rest of the system by eliminating privileges of access to particular market segments and preferential fiscal treatment of institutions such as the savings banks and the agricultural credit system. Government bond issues have also been gradually integrated with the new issue markets of the other borrowers by reducing the issue amounts to a more normal size, regularising issuing activity and exposing issue terms to the test of the market by introducing auction techniques. In addition, a number of tax-privileged savings schemes, including a special saving-for-housing scheme which was modelled on the German saving-for-housing systems, have been implemented in such a way that competitive inequalities amongst different groups of institutions were avoided. All groups of institutions engaged in the small-savings business such as commercial banks, private savings banks, the post office savings bank system, the agricultural credit bank system, and various other types of mutual institutions were authorised to offer these particular savings products. By contrast, in Germany, the promotion of the traditionally tax–privileged saving–for–housing scheme has remained the domain of the building societies (Bausparkassen). Private commercial banks can access this market only via participations or specialised subsidiaries[20].

Applying the principle of competitive equality to the financial services department of the post office systems is more difficult. Even if the postal giro services or savings bank services were managed as separate legal entities, as is the case in many countries in which these services have received banking status, the question arises how the overheads of the post office branch network should be shared between the postal services and the post office system's financial services; and how can it be ensured that the post office system, in competing in the small savings market, does not cross–subsidise its financial services from other postal services? "Levelling the playing field" at international level is a much more complicated task which raises difficult issues for international co–operation (see section on International Competition).

4.3.3 *Organisation of Markets*

Markets for a variety of negotiable instruments — foreign exchange, interbank deposits, short–, medium– and long–term debt instruments, equities, financial futures and options etc. — are naturally at the heart of the financial systems of market–oriented economies. In an effort to improve the efficiency of national financial systems through more reliance on market forces, the authorities have often supported the deregulation process by the creation of markets for new instruments, in particular, money–market paper[21], or by widening and deepening existing securities markets. Policy action in this direction has essentially been guided by the conviction that the allocation of financial resources through markets for negotiable instruments is in many respects superior to institutional allocation, in particular as regards cost efficiency. Policies towards strengthening the market element in financial systems have also been used in support of measures designed to promote the despecialisation and decompartmentalisation process as open markets tend to have a pronounced integration impact within a financial system.

In pursuing policies towards strengthening the role of markets for negotiable instruments in the financial system, the authorities have increasingly been occupied with questions concerning the organisation of markets and the conditions that should be fulfilled to ensure that markets function

well. It seems possible to draw certain lessons from these experiences as regards four important aspects of market organisation: the question of standardisation of marketable instruments; the question of depth, liquidity and visibility of markets; the question of how to maintain orderly markets; and the question of how to ensure the safety and soundness of markets.

Standardisation

Standardisation is an important aspect of market organisation. Without a minimum degree of standardisation, debt instruments or other financial instruments cannot be made marketable and markets cannot be made visible in terms of continuous and comparable price information. Standardisation in connection with marketability may relate to an individual issuer or to a particular market segment. In the first case it means that an issuer who comes to the market fairly regularly — for example, the government — uses a relatively small number of highly standardised instruments such as Treasury bills, medium–term notes, long–term bonds, the characteristics of which, except for the coupon or issue price, remain the same for consecutive issues so that each new issue can be easily sold into a broad secondary market. Sometimes the standardisation feature relates also to the issuing procedure and is then usually referred to as the "regularisation" of new issues. Examples of this are found in France and the United States; in both countries highly standardised government debt instruments are sold into the secondary market via auction techniques according to a regular issuing schedule[22].

An argument against standardisation that is sometimes heard is that special preferences of particular investor groups cannot be easily taken into account in highly standardised instruments. Thus, there is sometimes a certain trade–off between standardisation and tailoring securities to the needs of particular investor groups. However, since most of these so–called special investor needs relate to taxation, any problems of this sort should in the interest of a better functioning of markets be solved from the taxation side as marketability, liquidity and market depth and visibility no doubt are impaired if there are too many issues with special features[23].

Standardisation may also relate to market segments, for example, money markets, bond markets, equity markets etc. in which issues from different issuers are traded. In this case, standardisation means that different issuers use instruments with standard characteristics which make it easy for market operators to compare issues of different issuers and conduct arbitrage operations between them. In highly standardised and "homogenised" markets, price differences between different issues should only reflect risk or rating differences relating to the "quality" of the issuer.

Standardisation plays a major role in the "marketisation" of otherwise not, or not easily, marketable claims such as, for example, mortgage loans granted in different amounts to a large number of borrowers with different risk and project characteristics. The idea of marketising mortgage debt, which in Europe goes back to the 18th century, has in practice found two solutions. The first solution consists essentially of an exchange of a standardised security to be sold in the market, against a non-standardised mortgage deed (technique of mortgage-backed securities)[24]. In the second case, the standardisation and marketisation is achieved through a financial institution, a mortgage bank, which grants mortgage loans on the basis of standardised mortgage bonds which are issued and traded in the bond market. The first approach has a long tradition in Denmark and has, in more recent years, been strongly promoted in the United States and the United Kingdom; the technique has also been extended to the "securitisation" of other non-marketable claims such as credit card receivables or automobile loans. The second approach, putting a financial institution as a risk buffer between the ultimate debtors and the market, is the preferred way of "securitising" mortgage debt in Austria, France, Germany, Italy and Switzerland. In Germany and Switzerland, this technique of standardising and homogenising debt of a large number of individual debtors thereby securitising the debt, is also applied to local authorities and other public sector borrowers. In Switzerland, cantonal banks and regional banks which otherwise would have no, or difficult, access to the bond market, have also set up special financial intermediaries for the purpose of securitising their loan business[25].

Depth, Liquidity and Visibility

While standardisation is a major requirement for achieving market depth, liquidity and visibility, it may be necessary, because of the smallness of particular market segments, to enhance liquidity and visibility through special arrangements. Essentially two basic techniques are available in this regard, although in practice the two approaches can be combined. The first approach aims at concentrating the order flow in one marketplace, for example, a stock exchange or several stock exchanges which are technically fully integrated and interlinked. The second approach consists of applying the market-maker principle according to which market operators commit themselves to deal any time on either side of the market as may be required in situations of imbalances between buy and sell orders.

There is an impressive list of countries in which the authorities and/or self-regulatory organisations have taken action to enhance market depth, liquidity and market visibility in general through one or the other approach or a combination of the two approaches mentioned. In practically all cases, reform efforts have been strongly supported by an efficient use of modern computer technology. Efforts towards enhancing market depth and liquidity have also included measures designed to integrate over-the-counter (OTC) markets with markets concentrated in stock exchanges.

The United States was the first country in which important steps towards improving the "quality" of the OTC market in equities were taken. As early as 1971, the NASD (National Association of Securities Dealers) put into operation a highly computerised quotation-display system for the NASDAQ market[26], which is based on the market-maker principle and has become one of the fastest growing markets in the country and includes many shares that are traded also on the stock exchanges. The introduction of the NASDAQ market and its interlinkages with the stock exchanges had considerable integration effects in the US equities markets. Similar improvements in market depth and liquidity were achieved in the London equity markets through the introduction of the SEAQ system which is modelled on the NASDAQ system and started its operations on "Big Bang Day" (27th October 1986). Denmark provides another impressive example of a stock exchange and securities market reform based on modern computer technology and initiated by the 1986 Copenhagen Stock Exchange Act. The new trading system, which is linked to a new centralised securities book-entry and registration system, results in a full integration of the previously very large OTC markets and the stock exchange. In Italy, similar market integration measures are under close consideration[27]. Parallel to these stock exchange and over-the-counter market reforms just mentioned there have been considerable efforts in a number of countries towards improving the functioning of the secondary markets for government securities by introducing the primary dealer and market-maker principles, thus following the United States example. France, Italy, Spain, Sweden and the United Kingdom may be mentioned in this context.

The importance of the creation and maintenance of efficient secondary markets has also increasingly been recognised by participants in the international securities markets, which are largely self-regulated over-the-counter markets. Many of the newly created instruments in the international market have not been a lasting success because the basic requirements of an efficient market organisation — sufficient volume, liquidity, standardisation of products and trading practices — have not been respected[28].

Orderly Markets

The objective of maintaining orderly markets plays a considerable role in a number of countries in the context of policies towards the organisation of markets. Thus, several countries use issue calendars with a view to avoiding congestion and disruptions in the new issue markets. France, Germany, the Netherlands and the United Kingdom may be mentioned in this context. In France, the new issue calendar is managed by a committee of issuing houses which is chaired by the Ministry of Finance, and in the Netherlands and the United Kingdom the flow of new issues is regulated by the central bank. By contrast, in Germany, some co-ordination of new-issuing activity in the bond market is achieved by regular discussions in the Central Capital Market Committee, which is a self-regulatory body. However, in other countries, notably in the United States, such issue calendar arrangements are seen as an unnecessary interference with the working of market forces. It is argued that rigid issue schedules provide little flexibility for issuers to react promptly to changes in the market situation. To provide more flexibility in this regard, the SEC in the United States has changed its registration procedures and has introduced the so-called shelf-registration which allows corporate borrowers to sell new issues into the secondary market almost in the same way as tap issuers in other countries[29]. More flexibility in the new issue markets has also been obtained by combining auction techniques with trading practices which allow dealing in a new issue on an "if and when issued" basis i.e. before the formal date of issue. This technique is generally applied also in the international issue markets. How government debt managers should help avoid market disruptions, notably in situations in which the government is a major borrower, is controversial. In the United States and France, the government debt manager has found it useful to apply a regular issue schedule for different types of debt instruments so that the market can take these issue dates into account.

Safety and Soundness

Arrangements ensuring the safety and soundness of market systems are increasingly seen as being of utmost importance and receive particular attention in connection with the organisation of new markets such as, for example, the Financial Futures Market (MATIF) in Paris, which started operating in March 1986, the Swiss Options and Financial Futures Market (SOFFEX), which began operating early in 1988, and the German Options and Financial Futures Exchange, which is in the process of being set up. Policies towards this objective are generally based on two principles: first, the safety of the market system should rest on high professional standards and a solid capital base of market operators; hence, admission to the market should be subject to an adequate "fit and proper" test and adequate capital requirements. Second, market operators should respect generally agreed "rules of the game" such as may be laid down in a code of conduct or rules of market practices so that professional market participants as well as the general public are sufficiently protected against irregularities in market behaviour and malpractices including fraud and market manipulation.

While there is broad agreement about the objectives of market organisation, namely that markets should meet the various criteria mentioned such as standardisation, depth, liquidity and visibility, orderly conditions, and safety and soundness, it is controversial to what extent it should be the responsibility of the authorities to be concerned with the organisation of the markets. According to one school of thought, government regulation in this field should be minimised and the organisation of markets should be left to the market participants themselves. According to another view, which is increasingly gaining ground, in particular since the stock market crash of October 1987, the authorities should have the same responsibility for the safety and soundness and the functioning of markets as they have adopted in respect of the banking system[30]. In actual policy, the two views are generally mixed to varying degrees. While in most countries the authorities do accept ultimate responsibility for the safety and soundness and the functioning of national financial systems at large, there are considerable country differences as regards the degree of reliance on self-regulation in meeting these basic objectives. Moreover, it is not always clear to what extent, in a particular country, arrangements are in place for adequate supervision of self-regulatory arrangements. Thus, it appears that in many countries a variety of markets — foreign exchange markets, money markets, over-the-counter markets in various types of securities — are not subject to the same or similar safety and soundness standards as the wide range of different markets operating in London, where, for example, the Bank of England has responsibility for ensuring the safety and soundness of wholesale markets in sterling, foreign exchange and bullion and has issued corresponding regulation[31].

4.3.4 Supervising Club Arrangements

Club arrangements in the financial sector play a considerable role in all countries. Banks and other financial institutions often have multiple club relationships because of the wide range of activities they are engaged in[32]. Sometimes, club arrangements are largely social arrangements for members of the same profession, for example, Forex clubs. However, in most cases, such arrangements take the form of professional associations representing the interests of their members vis-à-vis the authorities or other professional associations. A third category of club arrangements are special groupings or associations which have a specific objective, for example, the objective of introducing new technology in areas such as payment systems, or quotation, dealing, clearing and settlement systems in the securities markets. Thus, the traditional stock exchanges have often been set up by local clubs of bankers and other business people. More recent examples of such special co-operative efforts have been the setting up of new market systems for financial futures and options, data banks for market information, or research work on new banking and stock exchange technology or internationally operating clearing systems[33].

Thus, there is no doubt that club arrangements can, and often do, play an important role in the development of markets and of the technological infrastructure of the financial sector and thus help improve efficiency. It is true that professional organisations in financial services also play an important role in the self-regulation of markets, notably in areas such as the formulation of codes of conduct and rules of market practices. However, from a competition point of view, club arrangements bear two dangers: first, that the clubs are closed to new entrants; second, that clubs are used for concluding agreements on interest rates, fees and commissions which are designed to protect the weaker members of the club or to maintain profits based on the club's monopoly position at comfortable levels. There is a long history of such price cartels in the banking and securities business. Stock exchanges typically combined the two types of anti-competitive club behaviour. It is only a fairly recent development that the stock exchange monopolies, both as regards membership and commission cartels, have come under attack from the authorities as part of broader deregulation policies[34].

The question of access to membership has also arisen for payment clearing systems that were set up by club arrangements. Thus, the ten member banks of the Bankers Clearing House in London — which includes the Bank of England — carried out in 1984 a wide-ranging review of the clearing system and formulated recommendations on a far-reaching reorganisation of the system. According to these recommendations — which have been largely implemented in the meantime — membership to the umbrella organisation as well as to the three individual clearing companies was to be open to all "appropriately regulated institutions"[35].

Canada is also an example of a country in which steps were taken to break the monopoly of the payment clearing system held by the chartered banks. As has already been mentioned in Chapter 3, one of the tasks of the Canadian Payments Association created by the CPA Act of December 1980 was to provide access by near-banks and other financial institutions to the country's payment clearing system.

The other danger raised by club arrangements, namely that clubs could serve as a basis for price cartels in financial services, has often been mitigated by competition policy in a narrow sense i.e. by including the banking sector under anti-trust legislation which prohibits anti-competitive co-operation agreements including price cartels[36]. The lessons that can be drawn from experiences with club arrangements suggest that while such arrangements can make major contributions to improving the efficiency of financial systems and to ensuring their safety and soundness as well as maintaining an adequate level of investor protection, it is necessary from a competition policy point of view that club arrangements are closely scrutinised with a view to avoiding restrictions, distortions or prevention of competition amongst the club members or from outside the club. The provisions of the Financial Services Act 1986 of the United Kingdom concerning competition may serve as an example in this regard[37].

4.3.5 Concentration

Fears of excessive concentration in the financial sector have a long history, and most countries have arrangements in place which enable the authorities to control mergers and major changes in ownership in the financial sector. Ownership controls have in recent years been strengthened to some extent as intensified competition tended to encourage concentration. There are two types of concerns: first, it is feared that concentration will have an adverse impact on competition and, hence, will ultimately impair efficiency. Second, it is feared that a few large financial institutions with dominant positions in the financial system will have an undesirable influence on political processes in the country. As has already been mentioned, the separation of the banking sector and the securities industry in the United States, or of "banking and insurance" in the Netherlands has largely been motivated by fears of concentration of power[38].

However, policy attitudes towards the concentration question have changed over the years as experience was gained with intensified competition and with an increasing interpenetration of national financial systems. Looked at from a competition policy point of view, the arguments against concentration — to be more precise, against the presence of a few large banks or other financial institutions operating side by side with a larger number of smaller institutions — have lost much of their previous weight. Several considerations play a role in this regard.

It has been increasingly recognised that the traditional indicators of concentration in financial services which measure market shares in terms of balance–sheet volume, can no longer be used for assessing the actual degree of concentration in each of the large number of sub–markets of financial services. As a result of diversification and despecialisation, financial service markets have become more integrated, and product deregulation has made it possible for different groups of previously specialised institutions to move increasingly into each others' territories. In addition, national financial systems have been opened to foreign banks so that the large internationally–operating banks from different countries compete with each other in several national markets as well as in the international markets; and this not only in operations which are reflected in balance–sheet growth such as direct lending and borrowing, but also in a wide range of services and trading and brokerage activities which are not reflected in the balance sheet as asset and liability growth.

A further consideration is that while traditional concentration indicators may show an increase in the market shares of the largest banks in the country, the expansion of branch networks, which has been important in the sixties and seventies, has actually resulted in a decline in concentration in local and regional markets; and many local banks or branches belonging to the savings bank or credit co–operative sector have lost their previous monopoly or quasi–monopoly positions in local retail banking markets as large commercial banks have moved into these markets by expanding their branch networks.

Policy attitudes towards large banks in national financial systems may be said to have changed more generally. It is increasingly recognised that the presence of large banks in a country's financial system is desirable under domestic as well as international aspects of financial policy. Large and financially strong banking institutions, notably if they have a nationwide branch network at their disposal for the distribution of their products and services, are a major driving force in financial innovation and the modernisation of the technological infrastructure of the financial sector. Large banks have generally achieved considerable productivity gains by making intensive use of modern computer technology in areas such as account maintenance, payment clearing, credit card processing, data processing relating to mass securities transactions, maintenance of securities depository accounts and the management of securities portfolios for individuals as well as for collective investment institutions.

Large banks have also considerably improved performance and quality standards in areas such as portfolio management, investment research and advice, in a wide range of other advisory and information services including management advice for companies, and in the development of new financial instruments and products such as cash management systems for corporate treasurers etc. The costs of such "production" activities, which, moreover, require highly qualified and specialised staff, can be absorbed more easily by a bank, if these new "products" can be distributed to a large number of customers via a wide "delivery" system i.e. a wide branch network, or through "sales" to other banking institutions.

It is sometimes feared that the comparative advantages of large banks in areas such as technological progress and product development will reinforce concentration in the sense that smaller local and regional institutions may be forced out of the market as their competitiveness in these areas is weakened. However, as financial service markets offer a wide choice as regards product/customer/area combinations, it will be possible for smaller institutions with an imaginative and efficient management to carve out profitable market niches in particular product/customer segments. Thus, smaller banks may be able to offer highly individualised services which, as regards quality, may be superior to the more standardised products and services offered by their larger competitors. It is increasingly realised that with a further separation in financial services between the "production" function and the "delivery" function, size is not necessarily a condition for success or survival. Smaller institutions may increasingly be able to "buy" financial services and products from "producers" and "distribute" them to their customers in the same way as larger banks. Credit card services, links with local or nationwide ATM systems, and brokerage services of different kinds are cases in point. Smaller institutions may also be able to specialise in particular activities, for example, in investment advisory services concerning local or regional "specialities". Thus, it is to be expected that, like in retail commerce and trade, universal banks and financial supermarkets will co–exist with small financial "boutiques" and "niche players", all the more so as technology has increasingly become accessible also for smaller institutions.

From an international point of view, size and financial strength of financial institutions is of vital importance. Large multinational corporations need to be serviced by large and financially strong banking institutions; and the financing of large and risky projects needs the financial support from such institutions. The international presence of large banking institutions is also important in the context of national policies designed to strengthen the international competitiveness of national financial systems. Thus, the authorities, before or while opening the national financial system to foreign banks, have sometimes strengthened the competitiveness of national financial institutions by encouraging the formation of larger units through mergers[39].

4.4 THE ROLE OF CO–OPERATION

There is general agreement that reliance on competition and on the working of market forces does not solve all efficiency problems in the financial sector. In a certain number of areas, a good deal of co–operation is needed in order to improve efficiency or to ensure that market forces work properly. Two such areas have already been mentioned in another context: co–operative efforts towards improving the efficiency of national payment systems, and the role of club arrangements for the organisation of markets[40]. In the present section, the role of co–operation as an instrument for improving efficiency is considered more broadly, thus, at the same time, highlighting the limits of competition policy in this regard.

According to experiences in OECD countries, co–operation as a means of improving efficiency plays an important role in essentially four broad areas:

— Development of the technological infrastructure of the financial system;
— Organisation and management of markets;
— Handling of large projects, and common product development;
— Co–operation between "producers" and "distributors" of financial products and services.

Some of these areas — technology development and market organisation, technology development and product/service distribution, or common product development and distribution — are often closely interlinked.

As far as the development of the technological infrastructure of financial systems is concerned, co–operation has not only played a role in the development of payment systems; considerable co–operative efforts have also been, and continue to be, concentrated on the development of screen–based quotation and trading systems in stock exchanges and on an effective linkage of these systems with the back offices of banks and securities firms, on the one hand, and with clearing and settlement systems, on the other. In countries with decentralised securities markets and several stock exchanges, efforts have also been made towards linking these various systems via telecommunication systems so that they operate as one integrated market. Stock exchange linkages at international level also receive much attention and co–operative effort. In some cases, the financial community has co–operated to develop broader market information systems with a view to strengthening the information base of the marketplace as a whole. In these latter cases, co–operation has actually resulted in intensified competition amongst information vendors[41].

As has already been mentioned in the section on Club Arrangements, co–operation as an approach to improving the efficiency of financial systems also plays an important role in the field of market organisation. Efficient markets for negotiable instruments require agreed "rules of the game" — codes of conduct and rules of market practices — which can be best worked out in co–operation with market professionals. Market participants can also play an important role in the surveillance of markets and in the control of compliance with the "rules of the game". In some countries, this task has been assigned to the associations of market professionals by law or by regulatory practice. However, from a competition policy point of view, the activities of professional organisations need official supervision in order to avoid anti–competitive practices.

It goes without saying that co–operation is also needed for the financing and development of large projects which financially cannot be managed by a single institution alone. The syndication of large credits or bond and equity issues in the international as well as in some national markets is a case in point. From an efficiency point of view, it is important that co–operation agreements in this field are allowed under competition rules. While syndication is a traditional approach to co–operation in the handling of large financing operations, banks and other financial institutions

91

have also increasingly made co-operative efforts towards the development of new products and services. Thus, there are numerous cases in which two or more banks, or banks and other types of financial institutions, have set up joint ventures for a variety of activities such as the management of mutual funds, leasing and factoring, credit insurance, venture capital, management consultancy services, data banks for market information and market research. In this way, it has been possible for some smaller regional institutions also to compete effectively in these areas with large institutions which are in a better position to develop all these products and services on an in-house basis. Co-operation in common product development thus tends to intensify competition and is, therefore, generally allowed under competition rules although corresponding co-operation agreements are scrutinised with a view to avoiding anti-competitive practices as regards the pricing and distribution of any such new common products and services.

This leads to the fourth area of co-operation mentioned, namely co-operation between "producers" of financial products and services and "distributors". Many producers of financial products or services who do not have at their disposal a wide distribution network of their own — credit card companies or mutual fund "producers" are typical examples — seek the co-operation of institutions with extensive branch networks for selling and distributing their products and services. The alternative, to build up a new distribution network which competes with the already existing branch networks, or to acquire a banking institution with a branch network via a merger, is generally too costly for such specialised product developers. Moreover, from an overall efficiency point of view, any duplication of distribution networks is often seen as impairing the cost efficiency of the financial system. Thus, in some countries, the authorities are concerned about the duplication of distribution networks for banking products and services, on the one hand, and insurance products and services, on the other, while in others problems of this kind do not arise to the same extent as banks are allowed to engage in brokerage services for insurance companies[42].

Effective access to national networks for the distribution of financial products and services is actually seen as a major problem in connection with the creation of a unified banking market in the European Community by 1992. Many banks with plans to expand their activities within the EC find it unmanageable to develop distribution networks of their own and contemplate access to the financial markets of the other EC countries via the acquisition of banks with branch networks. However, there are limits to this approach, notably

in countries with large systems of local authority-owned savings banks and co-operative institutions. Thus, co-operation agreements in the field of distribution of products and services may be a viable alternative. From an efficiency point of view, any such co-operative arrangements between "producers" and "distributors" of financial products and services are to be welcomed. However, as in other areas of co-operation, there is a certain danger that co-operation agreements give rise to anti-competitive practices, which should be avoided by adequate competition rules.

4.5 THE TRANSITION TO A MARKET-ORIENTED SYSTEM

Policies designed to improve the functioning of financial systems through stimulating competition may give rise to a number of adjustment problems during the transition period, depending on the starting position, the scope and coverage of corresponding domestic deregulation and external liberalisation policies and the speed with which such policies are implemented. Countries which start from a situation in which banks and other financial institutions have been protected against the rough winds of vigorous competition for a prolonged period of time, will need a longer time for institutions to adjust to a more competitive climate than countries in which market elements have already played a considerable role in the functioning of the financial system for many years.

A too sudden and too forceful introduction of financial deregulation and liberalisation measures bears the danger that competition becomes excessive and threatens the viability of non-competitive institutions. The painful experience of some countries[43] suggests that measures designed to stimulate competition need to be flanked by safety measures designed to ensure the stability of the system by preventing competition from becoming destructive. With a view to moderating the impact of deregulation on financial institutions, a number of countries[44] have adopted a policy of small steps and have, in the meantime, raised prudential standards, in particular capital requirements, partly with a view to strengthening the capital base of the system but also in order to reduce the institutions' ability to engage in destructive competition.

On the other hand, a deregulation policy of small steps which is stretched out over an extended period of time, bears the risk that deregulation is implemented in an unbalanced manner and that in the process new and unintended distortions and competitive inequalities develop. Foreign banks as well as specialised domestic financial institutions may not become properly integrated with the financial system and may engage in activities which from an overall efficiency point of view could be seen as an undesirable misallocation of resources. Interest rate deregulation, if not accompanied by an adequate product deregulation or a deregulation of any remaining territorial restrictions on activity, may unduly and unintendedly favour the growth of unregulated and sometimes less efficient markets and sectors. Subsequent corrective restructuring measures represent costs which the authorities need to consider in designing deregulation policies.

A policy move towards a more competitive system may entail an unforeseeable number of banking failures, which, in a way, may be desirable as the disappearance of less competitive institutions contributes to the strengthening of the competitive structure of the national financial system and may thus be seen as one of the purposes of stimulating competition in the financial service markets. However, as banking failures bear the danger of triggering a crisis of confidence, it is important that the authorities, before engaging forcefully in deregulation policies, ought to be satisfied that arrangements are in place which enable "problem banks" to be dealt with smoothly and effectively. Merger policies may receive particular attention in this regard. Rescue operations via mergers have the advantage from an overall efficiency point of view that the product and service facilities of an ailing institution can remain operational so that, overall, the supply of financial services is not impaired[45].

Undesirable tendencies towards concentration which may result from such merger activity, could be effectively mitigated by the liberalisation of foreign bank entry. The admittance of large and powerful foreign banks reduces concentration in the financial system although this may escape statistical measurement. Foreign bank entry, in addition to increasing the number of competitors in the financial system, may also have the advantage from an overall efficiency point of view that financial products and services which are new to the host country but have already been tested in other markets, become available at shorter delay than would otherwise be the case.

Any undesirable tendencies towards excessive price competition which could develop during the period of transition could be mitigated by strengthening prudential standards, notably capital requirements, and supervision. An increase in capital requirements would force institutions to give due consideration to the profitability of their activities in product and service markets in which they compete with other institutions and may thus help establish an adequate level of competition in these markets.

4.6 INTERNATIONAL COMPETITION

In the process of internationalisation of financial markets and increasing interpenetration of national financial systems, international competition in financial services has considerably intensified, and the strengthening of the international competitiveness of national financial institutions and markets has become a major objective of financial policy, not only in international financial centre countries but also in countries which aim at reducing their dependence on "imports" of financial services from such centres. Policies designed to strengthen the international competitiveness of national financial systems comprise a long list of more general measures aimed at increasing the efficiency of the system as well as more specific measures aimed at promoting international financial service activities in the national marketplace. The measures that countries have taken to varying degrees and in different combinations, depending on countries' positions in the international financial services markets, may be grouped under the following headings which indicate broad policy strategies in this field:

— Improving the efficiency of the national financial system through general deregulation measures aimed at stimulating competition (Chapter 3);
— Attracting foreign market participants: borrowers, investors, financial intermediaries[46];
— Increasing the range of products and services in response to the changing needs of internationally-operating market participants;
— Developing an efficient technological infrastructure of the financial sector (telecommunication systems; payment systems; information, trading, clearing and settlement systems in securities markets);
— Strengthening linkages with other international financial centres at the level of markets and related communication technology as well as at the level of institutions i.e. on an establishment basis;
— Ensuring the safety of the marketplace through adequate financial regulation and supervision;
— Removal of taxes which unnecessarily impair the functioning of financial markets.

These policies have affected international competition in the financial services markets both at the level of the international financial markets which operate across the jurisdictions of several countries, and at the level of national financial systems where typically relatively few foreign institutions compete in the domestic financial services markets with the banks of the host country.

Although the broad issues for policies towards international competition in the financial services markets are essentially the same as those met with in a national policy context, there are substantial differences as regards the weight some of these issues — for example the question of competitive equality and the closely related question of market access — have in the international context. In addition, policy approaches towards dealing with these issues are at international level much more complicated than at national level.

Most, if not all, problems with which international co-operative efforts or bilateral negotiations are faced in dealing with competition questions, stem from differences in regulatory frameworks within which national financial institutions and markets operate. Although practically all countries have, in recent years, engaged in policies towards financial deregulation and external liberalisation, thereby achieving some convergence of regulatory systems (Chapter 3), there still remain substantial country differences in the level of deregulation, notably product deregulation and related decompartmentalisation that has been reached, and in a host of other factors — in particular taxation — affecting international competition in the financial service markets as well as the competitiveness of the institutions operating in these markets.

International co-operation dealing with issues pertaining to international competition in the financial services markets has so far concentrated essentially on two problems which are both related to the broader issue of "levelling the playing field": first, problems of market access; and second, problems relating to the harmonization of national capital adequacy rules. The second question is, of course, also relevant in the context of policies towards ensuring the stability of the international financial system.

As far as the market access issue is concerned, — thanks to the liberalisation efforts under the aegis of both the OECD and the EC — considerable progress has already been made towards "levelling the playing field", as most countries have opened their national financial systems to foreign competition both at the level of cross-border operations and at the level of foreign bank entry. Some problems of market access relating to the establishment of foreign banks, nevertheless, remain to be solved; or the solutions so far found are not entirely satisfactory.

Problems of competitive equality in connection with foreign bank entry arise essentially in situations in which a country with a high degree of compartmentalisation in the financial system requires — in accordance with its basic policy approach to financial regulation — that any foreign financial institution seeking access via establishment has to decide in which of the various compartments of the financial system it wants to operate. This means that a bank from a country with a universal banking system does not, and cannot, have the same opportunities for doing business in the host country as it has in the home country.

In fact, the foreign bank, or any other type of foreign financial institution, is faced with entry barriers existing between different compartments of the financial system of the host country in the same way as national financial institutions and is, in this sense, subject to national treatment in the perspective of the host country ("host-country national treatment").

Considering the other case where a bank from a country with a compartmentalised financial system seeks establishment in a country with a universal banking system, host-country national treatment implies that the foreign bank has broader opportunities to do business in the host country than it has in the home country; provided that the authorities of the home country grant permission to this bank to operate abroad as a universal bank, which in practice they often do.

Thus, the application of the national treatment principle leads to a situation which, from a host country perspective, provides equality of competitive opportunity while, from a home country perspective, a case for unequal treatment can be made insofar as banks from countries with compartmentalised financial systems moving into countries with universal banking systems are in terms of business opportunities better off than universal banks moving into countries with compartmentalised financial systems.

Under these conditions, countries with universal banking systems sometimes apply the reciprocity principle to applicants from countries with compartmentalised financial systems with a view to encouraging deregulation and liberalisation in that country, and in order to obtain for their own banks "better than national treatment" in the applicant's home country. Countries sometimes include reciprocity clauses in their banking legislation also in order to be able to forestall the entry of banks from countries which do not meet satisfactory prudential standards.

While it is accepted that the use of the reciprocity principle can serve a useful purpose in special circumstances, notably if it helps the deregulation and liberalisation process, there is a broad consensus that generalised application of the national treatment principle should be the ultimate target of international co-operation in this field as it provides equality of competitive opportunity from an international perspective i.e. — so to speak — on a "consolidated basis"[47].

Financial policy within the European Community which is directed towards the completion of the unified financial services market by 1992, deals with the market access and establishment question — as well as with other regulatory problems — by applying two basic principles: first, the principle of mutual recognition of national regulatory frameworks; second, the principle of home–country responsibility and control. Although it has not yet been fully clarified what these two principles mean for establishment in EC countries with different regulatory frameworks, it is conceivable that banks from countries with high–grade universal banking systems will be able to conduct in a host country with a low–grade universal banking system all activities that are permissible under home–country regulation. This would mean, for example, that a bank which is a member of a stock exchange in its home country, would have to be given access to stock exchange membership in all other EC countries including those with traditional stock exchange monopolies. Thus, banks from countries with high–grade universal banking systems would obtain "better than national treatment" in any host country with a low–grade universal banking system, and "home–country national treatment" for all operations in the unified market. However, as those countries within the EC which, for the time being, still have stock exchange monopolies, are almost all engaged in major stock exchange reforms, which, inter alia, include deregulation of stock exchange membership, it is likely that, by 1992, no major cases of competitive inequalities will arise in this particular field.

A second area where considerable progress towards "levelling the international playing field" has been made, thanks to the work of the Basle Committee on Banking Regulations and Supervisory Practices, is prudential regulation insofar as capital requirements for banks are concerned. Although the July 1988 agreement on a framework for measuring capital adequacy and on minimum capital standards to be achieved by 1992, strictly speaking, applies only to the Group of Ten countries and Luxembourg, it is already evident that other countries will apply the same framework and standards as well. The move towards the new capital standard of 8 per cent of assets against which capital must be held, although serving in the first place the strengthening of the safety of the international financial system, will have a major impact on international competition in the financial services markets. Banks with, at present, relatively low capital ratios will have to pay particular attention to their profit performance as their scope for engaging in price competition is reduced during the transition period. After that, international competition will no longer be distorted by differences in capital requirements[48].

Although considerable progress has been made towards "levelling the playing field" for international competition in the financial service markets, important inequalities remain. In fact, as some earlier inequalities arising from differences in obstacles to market access and in capital standards have been, or are in the process of being, removed, other regulatory differences, notably differences in taxation regimes, are gaining more weight[49]. Other factors affecting competition within the global financial system are differences between financial centres as regards investor protection regulation including rules on insider trading and arrangements for dealing with conflicts of interest; bank secrecy legislation; and, last, but not least, the quality and efficiency of the technological infrastructure of national marketplaces. However, in all these areas co–operative efforts towards convergence of systems are under way.

4.7 EFFICIENCY, STABILITY AND INVESTOR PROTECTION

Ever since the authorities have felt a need to regulate and supervise the financial sector — essentially since the twenties and thirties — financial policy has been directed towards three major objectives: to ensure the efficiency of the financial systems; to ensure its stability and soundness; and to maintain an adequate level of investor protection. However, the priorities that have been given to these objectives have varied between countries and, within countries, over time. As has been seen in the section on Financial Policy in Retrospect (Chapter 3), following the experience of the 1929 crash and its repercussions on national financial systems, financial policy gave considerable priority to the stability as well as the investor protection objective. The efficiency objective, apart from ensuring that basic functions of the financial system such as the operation of the payment system and an adequate credit and liquidity supply were reasonably well performed, received low priority insofar as stability was mainly sought to be achieved by global protection of the financial sector and by corresponding arrangements for limiting competition.

This approach to financial policy was been substantially revised after World War II as, with a general policy move towards more market–oriented economies, the efficiency objective received higher priority and more attention in practically all countries, although at different times and to varying degrees. Thus, the whole post World War II history of financial regulation may be seen as a major attempt to reset priorities amongst the three main objectives of financial policy and to strengthen the efficiency of the financial sector — largely through reliance on competition and the working of market forces — without neglecting the stability and soundness objective and the objective of adequate investor protection. The efforts towards achieving a better balance between efficiency considerations and stability and investor protection considerations are evident in many instances of financial reform undertaken in OECD countries in the period under review.

A most complex issue for financial regulation requiring a well-balanced approach towards all three basic objectives simultaneously, is the working out of satisfactory arrangements for avoiding abuses of conflict of interest situations. Policies dealing with this issue are, indeed, affected by efficiency considerations as well as by safety and investor protection considerations, as has been explained in greater detail in the section on Conflicts of Interest. The separation of functions via complete institutional separation may be seen as a perfect solution from an investor protection point of view; the separation of commercial banking and some securities-related activities in Japan and the United States, or the former separation between jobbers and brokers on the London Stock Exchange, are examples of this approach. However, for reasons of efficiency and fair competition, this solution has never been adopted in countries with universal banking systems; and some other countries have recently abandoned this approach as part of their policy towards product deregulation and decompartmentalisation (Chapter 3). The objective of adequate investor protection has, in such cases, been met by other means, mainly by subjecting market professionals to detailed and binding codes of conduct.

Canadian financial policy under the "New Directions for the Financial Sector" of December 1986 provides an example of a more comprehensive trade-off between efficiency considerations and stability and investor protection considerations. The move towards a full integration of the traditional "four pillar system" was essentially motivated by efficiency considerations and by the desire to "level the playing field" in the broad Canadian financial service markets. However, as the resulting structural change in the financial system and more intense competition across the formerly separated sectors tend to increase the default risks in the system as well as the danger that customers increasingly become victims of abuse of conflict of interest situations, the reform package included far-reaching measures designed to strengthen prudential and investor protection

regulation and supervision. It cannot be excluded that the Canadian "new approach" to financial regulation will serve as an example in other countries or areas such as the European Community. As the latter is moving more closely to the 1992 target of a unified financial services market, the EC Commission is bound to deal with questions relating to the regulation and supervision of financial conglomerates and a related trade-off between efficiency considerations, on the one hand, and stability and investor protection considerations, on the other[50].

Less comprehensive situations of a trade-off between efficiency and stability considerations have, in recent years, arisen in a number of countries in connection with stock exchange reforms. As deregulation policies in this area resulted in the introduction of negotiable commissions rates and an opening of stock exchange membership, which, from an efficiency point of view appeared highly desirable, the authorities have, for stability reasons, at the same time taken action to strengthen the capital base of the securities industry by allowing banks and other financial institutions to take participations in stock exchange member firms. In several countries such as Australia, Canada, France and the United Kingdom, this resulted in the formation of financially stronger and more competitive groups which can better resist intensified competition in the markets for securities-related activities than the previously well-protected stock exchange member firms. In a similar way, the potentially destabilising effect of stronger competition in the banking sector resulting from deregulation policies — which were motivated by efficiency considerations — has been compensated for by a tightening of prudential regulations, in particular an increase in capital requirements.

Although the process of restructuring national financial systems and related regulatory reform activity is far from coming to a halt, it seems possible, on the basis of the experience gained so far, to draw some conclusions regarding the relationship between the main objectives of financial policy. It appears that many countries have been successful in seeking to reconcile policies towards improving the efficiency of national financial systems with the other two basic objectives of financial policy, namely, at the same time to ensure the stability and soundness of the financial system and to maintain an adequate level of investor protection. This suggests that, basically, the three objectives of financial policy — efficiency, stability and investor protection — are complementary and mutually reinforcing and can, under certain conditions, be reconciled in a balanced way. Indeed, it is now widely accepted that adequate regulation and efficiency do not have to be conflicting objectives, and that a well functioning financial system, in fact, needs to be based on confidence in the stability of the system and in the soundness of market practices resulting from adequate prudential regulation/supervision and investor protection rules. Conversely, it is also widely agreed that the stability and soundness of the financial system rests largely on the financial strength and the efficient management of financial institutions which are able to compete effectively and flexibly in the financial services markets. Thus, setting the conditions for a proper working of market forces and strengthening the competitiveness of financial institutions are often seen as appropriate approaches not only towards improving the efficiency of the financial system but also towards ensuring the stability and soundness of the system as well as maintaining an adequate level of investor protection.

Financial policy which attempts to pursue the three basic objectives — efficiency, stability and investor protection — simultaneously and in a balanced way, needs to be aware of the risks that are involved in approaching these objectives separately and in an unco-ordinated fashion. As far as the efficiency objective is concerned, there is a danger that the removal of anti-competitive regulation, which is largely used for achieving this objective, leads to a situation of excessive competition. This risk needs to be offset by prudential regulation, especially adequate capital requirements. On the other hand, there is a risk that a tightening of prudential regulation/supervision and of investor protection rules, which may be required by intensified competition in largely integrated and interconnected financial service markets, leads to a situation of "regulatory overkill", which impairs efficiency. It is likely that the quality and attractiveness of financial marketplaces will increasingly be determined by the extent to which financial regulation succeeds in reconciling the three objectives — efficiency, stability and investor protection — in a balanced way and that adequate regulation, in this sense, acquires increasingly the characteristics of a "quality stamp".

4.8 POLICIES TOWARDS EFFICIENT FINANCIAL SYSTEMS AND MONETARY POLICY

As countries proceeded to modernise their financial systems, it was inevitable that financial policy and monetary policy have influenced each other, given the financial system's role as a channel through which monetary policy measures are transmitted to the economy. However, the degree and the direction of these influences have varied from country to country and, within countries, over time, depending on the attitude of the monetary authorities towards the deregulation process and on their role in the related decision-making process.

In an impressive number of countries, the monetary authorities have supported deregulation policies designed to stimulate competition and improve efficiency by removing direct lending controls[51]. It was increasingly recognised that credit ceilings, notably if applied to individual institutions separately, inhibit the proper working of market forces and impair competitive strategies and innovative attitudes of banks[52]. Moreover, experience has shown that credit ceilings, if used over a prolonged period of time, become increasingly ineffective as an instrument of monetary policy as rapidly expanding unregulated markets and institutions tend to escape monetary control. Thus, a general policy move towards strengthening the market element in the financial systems has often been welcomed and actively supported by the monetary authorities as deregulation policies helped the process of reintermediation of fund flows and thus increased the scope for influencing bank liquidity through market-oriented intervention measures.

The United Kingdom was amongst the first countries where the relationship between "Competition and Credit Control" (1971) was clarified, although it was not before the early 1980s that lending guidance was no longer practised. New Zealand and Norway are other examples of countries in which the monetary authorities took a lead in encouraging a changeover to a more market-oriented approach both in the field of financial as well as monetary policy. In the former country, the monetary authorities actually went as far as establishing the principle that monetary policy should encourage the efficient functioning of the financial sector[53].

In some other countries, the monetary authorities adopted a more neutral position towards deregulation and, as they never relied on credit ceilings, confined their action to some minor adaptation of their monetary policy techniques to the new market environment. In a third group of countries, the monetary authorities attempted, with varying success, to resist the general trend towards the broadening of money markets and the spreading of variable interest rate instruments as this was seen as impairing the effectiveness of monetary policy. More recently, such monetary policy concerns were sometimes "traded off" against concerns regarding the international competitiveness and attraction of the marketplace, which largely rests on the availability of a wide range of financial instruments including variable rate and negotiable money–market instruments.

As a fairly general trend, discretionary central bank interventions in the money market have assumed a more important role in influencing bank liquidity, and recourse to conventional open–ended central bank credit facilities has been discouraged or restricted. Thus, money–market rates have increasingly become the preferred operating objective of monetary policy permitting flexible policy reactions to rapid changes in market conditions[54].

In this context, it may be noted that the effectiveness of the transmission mechanism as regards central bank intervention in the money market rests to some extent on the profit situation in the banking sector, which, in turn, depends on the intensity of competition in the financial sector. If bank profits are relatively high as a result of lack of competition there is a danger that the effects of restrictive monetary policy measures are largely absorbed by the banking sector and thus do not reach the non–financial sector to the desired extent. Unduly low profits which could result from excessive competition, on the other hand, might limit the scope for restrictive monetary policy action. In this way, policies towards efficient financial systems, insofar as they are based on liberal competition policy and help to establish an "adequate" level of bank profitability, may be seen as having a favourable impact on monetary policy as well.

Another consequence of the deregulation process and the resulting strengthening of market elements in the financial system and intensified product competition was that monetary targeting techniques became more complicated as monetary aggregates, notably "narrow money" definitions, tended to become increasingly unstable in relation to income and expenditure variables. In several countries, this led to redefinitions of aggregates and revisions of intermediate targets. In the United Kingdom, monetary targeting was eventually suspended and replaced by a multi–indicator approach. This latter approach is increasingly playing a role also in other countries in support of monetary targeting.

Leaving aside the complex and controversial question of the effectiveness of monetary policy in the new market environment as regards its impact on final spending decisions[55], it may be concluded from the experience gained so far that policies towards improving the efficiency and the functioning of national financial systems have generally not been constrained by monetary policy and that the monetary authorities have found ways of reconciling the objective of developing effective market–based intervention techniques with the efficiency objective of financial policy. It is likely that the process of adapting monetary policy techniques to the new market environment has not yet come to an end as the scope for broader market intervention techniques with reduced involvement of the banking system has not yet been fully explored.

4.9 A NEED FOR A GLOBAL VIEW

A review of worldwide trends in the financial service markets and of policies towards modernising national financial systems and interlinking them to an efficient global system suggests that there is a growing need for taking a global view at financial system developments and financial regulation; and that the authorities in OECD countries, indeed, increasingly do feel this need. The need for a global view actually concerns both financial policies towards the development and regulation of national financial systems and co–operation for developing a coherent approach towards financial system integration and regulation at international level.

At national level, developments in the financial services markets over the last twenty years or so have clearly been characterised by a general trend towards integration resulting from both market developments and policies designed to break down barriers between previously specialised financial institutions and market segments. On the market side, strategies of financial institutions towards diversifying their activities and a general development towards broadening the markets for negotiable instruments — the trend towards "securitisation" — have strongly favoured this integration process. From a regulatory and supervisory point of view, a most important aspect of this process is the integration of financial institutions, notably the banking system, and the securities markets.

On the regulatory side, the consequences of this integration process in national financial systems have not yet been fully drawn in most countries although the awareness that there is a need for a more integrated approach towards regulation and supervision has steadily increased, and some countries have taken corresponding action in this direction. The change in policy attitudes in this field that has taken place over the years, is clearly evident. Some twenty years ago, financial reform action in many countries often consisted of measures designed to cure specific symptoms of malfunctioning in the system. Regulations affecting the activities of one or the other group of financial institutions were changed on an ad–hoc, or step–by–step, basis in order to improve certain aspects of their operation. New schemes for housing finance, new institutions for industry or export finance, or new incentives to promote specific types of savings, were introduced; and many countries took reform measures aimed at improving particular aspects of the functioning of securities markets. Thus, financial reforms were essentially sector-oriented or problem-oriented. This "piecemeal" approach to financial reform was often based on commission reports concerning certain aspects of a country's financial system. It is only more recently that the authorities in OECD countries have felt a need for adopting a more global approach towards financial system reform and to mandate, accordingly, more comprehensive reviews of the financial system as a whole.

The United Kingdom was the first country to launch a comprehensive review of the functioning and regulation of the financial system as a whole. The Wilson Committee, i.e. the Committee to Review the Functioning of Financial Institutions, chaired by The Rt. Hon. Sir Harold Wilson, which was set up in January 1977 and presented its report to Parliament in June 1980, covered in its study the functioning and regulation not only of all groups of financial institutions operating in the United Kingdom but also of all major markets such as the securities markets, money markets, foreign exchange markets and insurance markets (Lloyds). As the Committee noted that "the regulation of financial institutions is conducted through a complex mixture of statutory and non-statutory arrangements, involving a wide range of government departments and other bodies of different parts", it is not surprising that it stressed "the need for an overall review body" which should have responsibility for "keeping the regulation of all parts of the financial system under regular review"[56].

Only two years later, in 1979, Australia followed the United Kingdom example and engaged in a comprehensive review of the "Australian Financial System" which was carried out by the Campbell Committee i.e. a Committee of Inquiry chaired by Mr. J.K. Campbell. An Interim Report was presented in May 1980 and the Final Report in September 1981. The Campbell Committee's review exercise was similarly comprehensive as the study by the Wilson Committee, and this Committee felt also a need for a global approach and included in the report a recommendation that the structure, regulation and operation of the financial system should be reviewed on a continuing basis with the object, from time to time, of canvassing options for change. However, in the case of Australia, it was recommended that an already existing institution, namely the Reserve Bank, should be entrusted with this task[57].

Canada may be mentioned as a third example of a country which confirmed the need for a global view by adopting under "New Directions for the Financial Sector" of December 1986 "A General Financial Sector Policy Approach". Under the new policy, all federally-regulated financial institutions were brought under the supervision of the Office of the Superintendent of Financial Institutions[58].

The call for an integrated approach towards regulation and supervision of the financial system including securities markets has gathered further momentum following the October 1987 stock market crash, although a few Nordic countries — Denmark, Norway and Sweden — had already consolidated the supervision of banks and securities markets under one authority before the crash. In the United States, the Presidential Task Force on Market Mechanisms — the "Brady Commission" — concluded in its report of January 1988 that "one agency should co-ordinate the few, but critical, regulatory issues which have an impact across the related market segments and throughout the financial system"[59]. Since then, the interdependence of all parts of the financial system has been stressed in many discussions both at national and international level, and the view has been increasingly accepted that the systemic risks involved in securities-related activities are similar to those inherent in the operation of the banking system and that a broadly-based "run" on the securities markets could have as disastrous effects on general confidence in the stability of the financial system as a "run" on the banking system. Therefore, so it is argued, prudential regulation of the securities business should be fully integrated with prudential regulation of the banking system[60].

It needs to be stressed that these various developments in financial policy and financial regulation and supervision are not only becoming "global" approaches in the sense that they relate to the financial system as a whole including securities markets; they are also increasingly "global" approaches in the sense of integrated policies aimed at pursuing the basic policy objectives — efficiency, stability and investor protection — simultaneously and in a more balanced and co-ordinated fashion than was hitherto the case.

Internationally, the trend towards greater financial integration manifests itself both through the expansion of the international financial markets such as the euromoney, eurobond and euro-equity markets, and through the increasing interpenetration of national financial systems. Thus, the need for adopting a global approach in financial policy and regulation relates increasingly to international aspects of the financial integration process as well. Countries which are in the process of modernising their national financial systems and of reforming their regulatory frameworks, cannot avoid influencing other countries and, hence, increasingly take into account financial system developments abroad in order to make sure that the various aspects of market organisation, regulation and functioning are internationally compatible and permit effective linkages between national financial systems. Thus, there is considerable need, and pressure, for convergence as regards the development of market techniques and instruments, and related codes of conduct and rules of market practices; and, at a more technical level, as regards payment systems, and clearing, settlement, book–entry and information systems in securities markets. However, convergence is needed, in particular, in areas such as prudential regulation and investor protection rules including insider trading rules and disclosure requirements in order to achieve a "level playing field" for fair international competition in the world financial services markets. A co–ordinated approach towards integrating national financial systems to an efficient and safe global financial system requires substantial international co–operation efforts, both bilaterally and multilaterally. Bilateral solutions may sometimes be useful in paving the way for broader multilateral solutions. However, there is little doubt that the solutions to be adopted in the European Community in connection with establishing the unified financial services market by 1992 will have a major impact on a worldwide basis.

NOTES AND REFERENCES

1. In the United States an increasingly urgent need is felt for restructuring the financial system and for reforming regulatory frameworks. Many of the issues discussed in this context are closely related to the issues raised in the present chapter. Amongst the vast literature dealing with restructuring questions, the following titles are mentioned for reference: Federal Reserve Bank of Kansas City, *Restructuring the Financial System*, Kansas City, 1987; for a summary of the discussion see: Federal Reserve Bank of Kansas City, "Restructuring the Financial System: Summary of the Bank's 1987 Symposium", Economic Review, January 1988. See also: E. Gerald Corrigan, President of the Federal Reserve Bank of New York, *Financial Market Structure: A Longer View*, New York, January 1987 (reprinted in the Annual Report 1987 of the Federal Reserve Bank of New York); and *Restructuring Financial Markets: The Major Policy Issues*, a Report from the Chairman of the Sub-committee on Telecommunications, Consumer Protection, and Finance of the Committee on Energy and Commerce, United States House of Representatives, July 1986, 99th Congress, 2nd Session.

2. For a discussion of the issues raised by the EC policy towards achieving a unified financial services market in the European Community by 1992, see in particular: Commission of the European Communities, *Symposium on Europe and the Future of Financial Services, Brussels, 5th, 6th and 7th November 1986, Proceedings*, Brussels, 1987; and Commission of the European Communities, *Conference on Financial Conglomerates, Brussels, 14th-15th March 1988, Proceedings*, Brussels, 1988.

3. In a number of countries, in which savings banks and credit co-operatives traditionally play a relatively important role, a pronounced concentration movement has been favoured by the authorities with a view to strengthening the competitiveness of these two sectors of the financial system. To give an example: in Germany, in the period 1966-1987, the number of credit co-operatives declined from about 9 000 to 3 500, and the number of savings banks from 862 to 586. At the same time, the "market shares" of these two sectors, measured in terms of balance-sheet volume, have noticeably increased.

   France is an example of a country, where the authorities have a strong interest in the rationalisation of the banking system through increased use of modern technology; see for example, Conseil National du Crédit, *L'Incidence des Technologies Nouvelles sur l'Activité des Intermédiaires Financiers*, Paris, April 1987.

   On the question of encouraging the formation of competitive banking units, see Chapter 3, Note 29.

4. See Chapter 3, Table 3.3; and Annex III, Sections I and XIII.

5. The French Bankers Association has conducted an inquiry on margins in consumer loans/personal loans which supports this view. According to the information collected, the margins between money-market refinancing costs and interest rates charged on personal loans are as follows: France: 4-10 per cent; Germany: 7-11 per cent; Switzerland: 8-11 per cent; United Kingdom: 13-14 per cent; Italy: 18-23 per cent; Spain: 7-12 per cent; United States: 7-18 per cent; the margins are, in fact, much wider if it is assumed that personal loans are largely extended on the basis of customer current account, time and savings deposits, which, on average, earn considerably less than money-market rates. See: Association Française des Banques, *La concurrence bancaire en France et en Europe*, Paris, 1987.

   Another example supporting the view that price deregulation does not necessarily favour the retail banking client, is found in the field of securities-related activities. In the London market for United Kingdom Government securities ("medium and long term gilts") average commission rates in per cent of trading amounts increased from 0.137 per cent in 1986 (commission rates were "freed" on 27th October 1986) to 0.318 per cent in 1987; see: The Stock Exchange, Quality of Markets Quarterly, Autumn 1987, Table 3.5. In France, following the application of competition rules to fees and commissions on financial services, some banks have set minimum fees on securities safe-custody services at relatively high levels with a view to segmenting the market in favour of large private portfolios.

6. Whether any such cross-subsidisation occurs is difficult to assess. The main problem for identifying cross-subsidisation practices in banking is the quasi-impossibility of finding a satisfactory solution to the problem of an adequate allocation of general overheads, notably if a bank operates with a large branch network.

7. In many countries, periodicals specialised in the cost and quality testing of products and services — which are often sponsored by consumer organisations — increasingly compare "prices" relating to financial services i.e. interest rates charged on consumer and mortgage loans; fees and commissions charged on payments and other services and interest rates offered on bank accounts and other savings instruments.

8. For a more detailed discussion of different issuing techniques used in the primary markets for government securities see: OECD, *Government Debt Management*, Volume II, *Debt Instruments and Selling Techniques*, Paris, 1983; for use of auction techniques in the

primary markets for government securities markets, see also Annex III, Section III.

9. There is a vast literature on the question of economies of scale and scope, or synergies, in banking. The issues involved and methods of measurement used are rather complex and controversial. For detail on the discussion and further literature see, for example: K.T. Davis, M.K. Lewis, *Economies of Scale in Financial Institutions*, Technical Paper No. 24, Australian Financial System Inquiry, Economics Department, University of Adelaide, July 1981. As these questions are closely related to issues raised by financial conglomerates, see also: Commission of the European Communities, *Conference on Financial Conglomerates, Brussels, 14th–15th March 1988, Proceedings*, Brussels, 1988.

10. See Annex III, Section IV, D.

11. See The Honourable Thomas Hockin, Minister of State for Finance, *New Directions for the Financial Sector*, tabled to the House of Commons, 18th December 1986, Ottawa; see also: B.V. Gestrin, Executive Vice President and Economic Adviser, Canadian Imperial Bank of Commerce, "Canada's Little Bang — Implications for Banks", paper given at the Annual Meeting of the International Club of Bank Economists, New York, 5th October 1987.

12. See Annex III, Section VI; see also: OECD (by R.M. Pecchioli), *Prudential Supervision in Banking*, Paris, 1987, Chapter III, The Scope of Banking Activity.

13. The 1986 Building Society Act in the United Kingdom made provision for societies to convert from mutual to corporate status as from 1988. In March 1988, a large building society announced plans to make use of this conversion option offered by the Act.

14. See Annex V and the section on Conflicts of Interest; see also: Commission of European Communities, *Conference on Financial Conglomerates, Brussels, 14th–15th March 1988, Proceedings*, Brussels, 1988.

15. See M.J.L. Jonkhart, "On Policy Instruments with Respect to the Structure of the Financial Services Industry"; in: Commission of the European Communities, *Conference on Financial Conglomerates, Brussels, 14th–15th March 1988, Proceedings*, Brussels, 1988. Professor Jonkhart's contribution refers, in particular, to the Dutch experience with the separation of banking and insurance.

16. The question of duplication of distribution networks in banking and insurance has been discussed, for example, in France in connection with general financial system reform plans; see: Commissariat Général du Plan, *Quels Intermédiaires Financiers Pour Demain ?*; La Documentation Française, Paris, 1984.

17. For a detailed list of examples of conflict of interest situations not only between commercial banks and securities–related activities but also between different types of securities–related activities, see Annex V.

18. For more detail on the concept of "privilege rent", see Wolfgang Stützel, *Bankpolitik heute und morgen*, Frankfurt, 1964, Zweiter Teil, B. Die Sonderstellung der Sparkassen im Wettbewerb der Kreditinstitute.

19. Der Bundesminister für Wirtschaft, *Wettbewerbsverschiebungen im Kreditgewerbe und Einlagensicherung*, Bericht der Bundesregierung, Drucksache des Deutschen Bundestages V/3500, Bonn, December 1969.

20. To give an example: in 1987, Deutsche Bank AG, the largest German universal bank, set up its own Bausparkasse (building society) as a separate, but wholly–owned, subsidiary which uses the wide branch network of the parent company for the sale of saving–for–housing contracts.

21. See Annex III, Section II and Chapter 3, Table 3.2.

22. See OECD, *Government Debt Management* Volume II, *Debt Instruments and Selling Techniques*, Paris, 1983, in particular Chapter 4 on "Practices Regarding the Timing and the Announcement of Government Debt Operations"; see also: Ministère de l'Economie, des Finances et de la Privatisation, *Les Valeurs du Trésor en 1988*, Paris, February 1988.

23. Mr. Simon Holberton raises this question in the Financial Times of 8th August 1988 and wonders whether there is "not a case for moving towards a situation where there are fewer but larger issues of outstanding gilts", ... "now that the market is no longer driven by considerations of taxation."

The importance of standardisation for marketability and market visibility is also stressed by J.R.S. Revell in: OECD, *Flexibility in Housing Finance*, Paris, 1975, in particular, in Section 10 (a), Theoretical Points. See also: Ministère de l'Economie, des Finances et de la Privatisation, *Les Valeurs du Trésor en 1988*, Paris, February 1988.

24. The first so–called "Landschaften", which used the technique of mortgage–backed securities, were set up in Prussia under Frederic II ("the Great") in order to provide access by the Prussian nobility to relatively cheap mortgage credit, following the damages caused by the Seven Year War. This technique was also adopted in Denmark, while in Germany the second approach to securitising mortgage debt was increasingly used, following the model of the Crédit Foncier, which was set up in France in 1852.

25. In Germany, the debt of local authorities and some other public–sector bodies has been "securitised" in the same way as mortgage debt, as mortgage banks (Hypothekenbanken) were also allowed to issue so–called communal bonds (Kommunalanleihen) for the financing of loans to local authorities (Kommunaldarlehen). This avoided too many smaller local authorities coming to the bond market directly, which would have led to considerable fragmentation of the market.

In Switzerland, three groups of borrowers have achieved similar rationalisation and marketisation effects by "bundling" their borrowing needs via a bond–issuing intermediary: cantonal banks, regional banks and local authorities. While the central institute of the cantonal banks for the issue of mortgage bonds ("Pfandbriefzentrale der schweizerischen Kantonalbanken") — with at present 29 member banks — was set up in 1931, the other central institutes were established in 1964 (regional banks' issue institute — "Emissionszentrale schweizerischer Regionalbanken") and 1972 (local authorities' issue institute — "Emissionszentrale der Schweizer Gemeinden"), respectively. The former has 22 regional banks as members, while the latter counts some 483 local authorities as members. More detail is found in the issuing prospectuses of the institutions concerned.

26. For more detail on the NASDAQ market, see various brochures distributed by the National Association of Securities Dealers (NASD) in the United States, such as *An Introduction to NASD*, 1985; NASD *Fact Book* (annual); *Annual Reports* of the NASD.

27. See Commissione Nazionale per le Società e la Borsa (CONSOB), Bolletino, Edizione Speciale, *Linee de Progretto per Una Reforma del Mercato Borsistico*, Milano, 30 April 1987 ("Blueprint for the Reform of the Securities Markets").

28. In a presentation by Mr. Christian C. Brand, Vice President and Manager of J.P. Morgan GmbH, Frankfurt, Germany, on "What are 'solid' financial innovations? — Criteria for the marketability and the risks of innovative fixed–interest securities", these points were particularly stressed.

29. So–called "shelf–registration" was introduced on a tentative basis on 3rd March 1982 under the SEC's provisional regulation 415, which was fully instituted on 17th November 1983. Under Regulation 415, registered securities are allowed to be offered and sold on a delayed or continuous basis without the filing of a new registration statement and other forms during the two years following the effective date of the original registration statement. This enables corporate issuers to sell new issues flexibly into the secondary market on a "tap issue basis". The "tap issue technique" is used in Denmark and Germany by both the Government and mortgage banks. For more detail on issuing techniques see OECD, *Government Debt Management*, Volume II, *Debt Instruments and Selling Techniques*, Paris, 1983.

30. See, for example, T. Padoa–Schioppa, "The Blurring of Financial Frontiers: In Search of an Order", in: Commission of the European Communities, *Conference on Financial Conglomerates, Brussels, 14th–15th March 1988, Proceedings*, Brussels, 1988; see also section in the present report on Efficiency, Stability and Investor Protection.

31. See Bank of England, *The Regulation of the Wholesale Markets in Sterling, Foreign Exchange and Bullion*, London, July 1987.

32. For example, in the United Kingdom, in connection with the preparation of the Report by the Wilson Committee (Committee to Review the Functioning of Financial Institutions), over 30 organisations representing the interests of particular groupings of providers of financial services submitted evidence to the Committee; see *Committee to Review the Functioning of Financial Institutions, Appendices*, London, June 1980, Cmnd. 7937.

33. The Swiss company Telekurs AG is an example of such a joint venture which was set up by a large group of banks, essentially for solving common problems relating to the technological infrastructure of the financial sector. The Telekurs AG which is owned by at present 350 Swiss banks provides its shareholders as well as outside customers with a wide range of services in the field of data processing and the collection and dissemination of market information. It also provides advisory services in the field of technology developments relating to payment services on the one hand and the securities business on the other. For example, the computerisation of the Zürich Stock Exchange was carried out by the Telekurs AG. Telekurs AG stressed in one of its brochures that in some areas of financial services competition is neither economically nor organisationally an adequate approach and may, in fact, produce disadvantages for the consumer (see Telekurs AG, "Know–how und Technik im Dienste der Banken und Börsen", Ein Unternehmensportraet, Zürich, no year).

Cedel S.A., a Luxembourg company, which, in competition with Euro–Clear, Brussels, offers clearing and settlement services as well as some other services relating to the eurobond market, is another example of a joint venture launched by a group of banks and is now owned by some 108 financial institutions from 18 countries. Cedel S.A. typically presented its Annual Report 1987 under the slogan "Founded by the market for the market".

34. See Annex III, Section IV, D.

35. See Members of the Bankers Clearing House, *Payment Clearing Systems*, Review of Organisation, Membership and Control, London, 1984.

36. See Annex III, Section XIII and Annex IV, which both deal with the treatment of the banking sector under restrictive practices legislation (competition rules).

37. See B. Ryder, D. Chaikin, Ch. Abrams, *Guide to the Financial Services Act 1986*, Bicester, Oxfordshire, United Kingdom, 1987, paragraph 319.

38. See Note 15.

39. See, for example, Chapter 3, Note 29, relating to two large mergers in Australia.

40. See section on Supervising Club Arrangements.

41. See, for example, Note 33 on Telekurs AG. The Stock Exchange in London also plays a role as a collector and vendor of market information and thus competes with other information vendors; see, for example, G. Hayter, "The Future for Trading Systems — Equity Worldwide", Financial Times Conference on *Technology in the Securities Markets — The Next Five Years*, London, 8th and 9th April 1987.

42. See Annex III, Section IV, A.

43. Several countries such as Austria, Spain, Turkey and the United Kingdom have had experiences with difficulties in the banking, or near–banking, sector which arose largely in an unregulated environment (United Kingdom) or in connection with deregulation measures which were not accompanied by a tightening of prudential regulation or supervision. In Austria, "destructive" competition between major banks or banking groups for market shares in retail banking following the interest rate deregulation measures of July 1980 eventually led to the reintroduction of interest rate agreements. Similarly, in Turkey, excessive bidding for deposits, "disguised" as repurchase agreements, threatened the stability of the system as a whole, which eventually led to the reintroduction of controls on deposit rates. See Annex III, Section I.

44. Japan and Spain may be seen as examples of countries which have pursued a policy of small steps as far as interest rate deregulation as well as product deregulation is concerned; see Annex III, Sections I, II, III and IV.

45. See, for example, Chapter 3, Note 28.

46. The question of foreign access to national markets for financial services, both on a cross–border or establishment basis, is the subject of several OECD publications on international trade in services; see Chapter 3, Note 25. See also: Stanley M. Beck, Chairman, Ontario Securities Commission, Toronto, Ontario, Canada, "Market Access and Barriers to Entry in the International Securities Arena: Some Reflections", paper given at the 12th Annual Conference of the International Organisation of Securities Commissions, Rio de Janeiro, 1st–4th September 1987; and Department of the Treasury, *National Treatment Study: Report to Congress on Foreign Government Treatment of United States Commercial Banking and Securities Organisations, 1986 Update*, 18th December 1986.

47. The idea of equality of competitive opportunity obtained by host–country national treatment can be illustrated by a hypothetical example. It is assumed that there are two countries, A and B. A has a universal banking system; B has strict separation between commercial banking and securities business. A bank from A sets up a securities firm in B and thus, on a consolidated basis, consists of a universal bank in A and a securities firm in B. At the

same time, a securities firm from B sets up a universal bank in A. On a consolidated basis the financial "conglomerate" from B also consists of a securities firm in B and a universal bank in A. Assuming equal sizes and management qualities, the two conglomerates, from A and from B, enjoy equality as far as opportunities for doing business in the two countries A and B together are concerned. If, for example, the universal bank from A were allowed to operate as a universal bank also in B — thus being granted "better than national treatment" — the opportunities for the two conglomerates to do business on a "consolidated basis" would be unequal. It is obvious that home-country national treatment — the EC approach — provides stronger pressure in the direction of harmonization of regulatory frameworks than host-country national treatment.

48. See Committee on Banking Regulations and Supervisory Practices, *International Convergence of Capital Measurement and Capital Standards*, Basle, July 1988.

49. Differences in the taxation of banks may be illustrated by the following table which is based on data published in OECD, *Bank Profitability — Financial Statements of Banks and Methodological Country Notes, 1980-1984*, and *Statistical Supplement 1982-1986*, Paris, 1987 and 1988, respectively:

INCOME TAX OF COMMERCIAL BANKS
Per cent of net income*

	Average 1980–1986	Trends 1980–1986	
	Over 30 per cent	1980	1986
Japan	49	50	50
Belgium	39	42	38
	Between 15 and 30 per cent		
Germany	29	32	32
Italy (1980–1985)	28	24	31
United Kingdom	24	22	24
Sweden (1981–1986)	19	15	37
Switzerland	18	20	16
Finland	17	23	11
France	17	17	14
Luxembourg	17	30	15
United States	15	21	12
	Below 15 per cent		
Canada (1982–1986)	14	3	14
Spain	12	13	14
Norway	9	9	8
Portugal	5	5	3

* Net income = gross income (net interest income plus non-interest income) minus operating expenses; the latter exclude provisions for income tax.

50. See for example, Commission of the European Communities, *Conference on Financial Conglomerates, Brussels, 14th–15th March 1988, Proceedings*, Brussels, 1988.

51. See Annex III, Section X.

52. See, for example, Bank of England, *Competition and Credit Control*, London, 1971.

53. See Reserve Bank of New Zealand, "Monetary Policy in New Zealand", in: *Reserve Bank Bulletin*, June 1985.

54. See Bank for International Settlements, *Changes in Money-market Instruments and Procedures: Objectives and Implications*, Basle, 1986.

55. There is a vast amount of literature on the question of how monetary policy has been influenced by structural changes in national financial systems and the financial deregulation and innovation process. The following references may be specifically mentioned: OECD (by T.R.G. Bingham), *Banking and Monetary Policy*, Paris, 1985; OECD, *Trends in Banking in OECD Countries*, Paris, 1985; Bank for International Settlements, *Recent Innovations in International Banking*, Basle, 1986, in particular Chapter 13 on "Consequences for the Conduct and Effectiveness of Monetary Policy"; Bank for International Settlements, *Changes in Money-market Instruments and Procedures: Objectives and Implications*, Basle, 1986.

It has not been intended to summarise, or discuss, the findings of these various reports. The purpose of the present section has essentially been to highlight very briefly to what extent policies towards efficient financial systems have received support from the monetary authorities as far as techniques of monetary policy are concerned, or to what extent the monetary authorities have found it necessary to adjust the techniques of monetary policy to the new environment.

56. Committee to Review the Functioning of Financial Institutions, *Report*, London, 1980, Cmnd. 7937, paragraphs 1111–1119.

57. *Australian Financial System*, Final Report of the Committee of Inquiry, Canberra, 1981, paragraph 2.74.

58. The Honourable Thomas Hockin, Minister of State for Finance, *New Directions for the Financial Sector*, tabled in the House of Commons, 18th December 1986, Ottawa, pages 6 and 9.

59. See *Report of the Presidential Task Force on Market Mechanisms*, Washington D.C., January 1988, page vii ("Conclusions").

60. See OECD, "Arrangements for the Regulation and Supervision of Securities Markets", Special Feature in *Financial Market Trends*, No. 41, Paris, 1988.

Annex I

CONCEPTS AND DEFINITIONS

1. Scope, Characteristics and Structural Features of the Markets for Financial Services

In the context of the present study, the term banking is used in a wide sense to comprise all financial services and related ancillary services that may be offered by financial institutions such as banks, savings banks, securities firms, brokers and other providers of financial services including non–financial enterprises. Only the business of insurance underwriting i.e. the management of the risks that are usually covered by life and non–life insurance companies, is excluded from the scope of the study. However, the selling of insurance contracts i.e. insurance brokerage business, is considered as a banking activity. Moreover, insurance companies are seen as competitors on the supply side of money and capital markets and in the markets for household savings. Thus, there is no clear–cut borderline between insurance companies and other providers of financial services.

Financial Services: A Multitude of Markets

The markets for financial services consist of a large number of sub–markets with different product characteristics, types of customers, institutional supply features and territorial boundaries. Accordingly, there are considerable differences between sub–markets of financial services as regards the demand and supply constellation, the competitive structure which is determined by the number of participants on either side of the market, and the degree of market visibility and related information that is readily available. The competitive situation in sub–markets for financial services is also affected by the choices regarding substitutes for specific services or financial instruments that are available to demanders for financial services. Finally, there are differences between sub–markets for financial services with regard to the types and combination of competitive weapons and strategies that providers of financial services are willing, or able, to use, depending, inter alia, on the regulatory frameworks within which they operate.

Various sub–markets for financial services are closely interrelated and may be grouped together to larger market areas which may be dominated by particular types of financial institutions depending, inter alia, on the institutional characteristics of a financial system. Examples of such larger groupings of sub–markets for financial services are the markets for retail banking services, the markets for corporate financial services, the markets for securities–related financial services etc. Other groupings are also possible as is shown in the classification below.

A distinction can also be made between the "production" side and the "distribution" side of the markets for financial services. While in many sub–markets the "production" of a financial instrument or service and its "distribution" occur simultaneously — the granting of a loan or the acceptance of a deposit are examples of this — there are other sub–markets in which financial institutions "distribute" products, instruments or services which they have not "produced" themselves. Credit cards, securities issued by others, various types of collective investment instruments such as mutual funds etc, foreign exchange, standardised loan, savings, or insurance contracts sold on behalf of other often specialised institutions are cases in point. Thus, the competitive situation in the markets for the "production" of financial instruments and services may be different from the one prevailing in the markets for the "distribution" of the same instruments and services.

Examples of Special Market Situations

Differences in the competitive structure of sub-markets for financial services may be illustrated by a few examples:

1. The international markets for loanable funds comprising money and credit markets and markets for new issues of fixed or variable interest rate or zero-coupon instruments are highly competitive. The market structure is, on the whole, well balanced as far as the bargaining power of market participants on either side of the market is concerned. Market visibility, the quality and quantity of information available to market participants and the speed at which information becomes available are high. Hence, price competition is intense while at the same time a single operator in the market has little power to influence market conditions. Competitors on the capital supply side of the market tend to moderate the impact of sharp price competition by considerable efforts towards product differentiation and innovation. Hence, innovative pressures in this market are strong. However, competitive advantages gained in this way are short-lived as new products in the financial markets can easily be imitated.

2. The competitive situation is different in the market for retail banking services that exists in a village or small town in which a local credit co-operative or a branch of a regionally operating commercial bank is the only provider of such services. The bank or bank branch has a local monopoly position with regard to the services it offers and the commissions and interest rates it may charge or the yields it may offer on savings instruments. Whether this will lead to monopolistic practices is another question as the bank or branch manager may refrain from abusing his monopoly position for ethical or social reasons. Moreover, more sophisticated demanders for financial services in local markets may escape the monopolistic situation through the use of modern communication techniques, mail order or home banking facilities which may be available in neighbouring towns where the competitive situation in the market for retail banking facilities may be different because of the presence of several competing providers of such services.

3. Nationwide or even worldwide markets for credit cards are dominated by a few large and financially powerful rival groups. Competition through advertising, canvassing new clients and, often, through efforts to gain support from major banking groupings or retailers in national markets is intense. Most credit card companies rely on banking networks for the distribution of their card services, and once bankers associations or other bank groupings in a particular country have decided to promote one or the other card system there remains reduced scope for competition through market access by newcomers. It is noteworthy, however, that large retailers such as department stores and petrol retailers are making increasing efforts to reduce their dependence on the large internationally operating credit card companies by issuing their own credit and payment cards. On the whole, the market structure appears to be in a state of flux, and local and regional issuers of credit cards compete increasingly with nationwide and worldwide credit card companies. As credit card systems form part of a country's payment system, the authorities insofar as they have an interest in an efficient and safe working of the payment system, may encourage co-operation in this field in order to see to it that different payment circuits are mutually compatible and effectively interlinked.

4. The market for new government bond issues is, in some countries, dominated by a single issuing consortium. In such a situation, issuing conditions, notably commissions, are subject to negotiation between the government debt manager and the lead manager(s) of the consortium. In order to increase the scope for more competition in the new-issuing market for government bonds, government debt managers of a number of countries have, in recent years, introduced auction techniques. Another alternative to the consortium technique is the tap issuing technique which provides considerable scope for flexibility in the issuing price. However, it is hardly avoidable that the government debt manager applies attractive uniform commissions to those financial institutions which are prepared to sell such tap issues on to the ultimate investor.

5. The markets for securities portfolio management have considerably grown in recent years. Competition for new customers has become very strong. But competition in quality of service or for highly qualified staff is more

important in this field than sharp price competition.

6. The markets for securities–related brokerage services have also shown an impressive expansion since the early eighties in connection with the expansion of securities markets generally and the trend towards securitisation. In this sub–market, price competition for large–order handling has become very strong in some countries in connection with the freeing of previously fixed commission rates. In addition, the introduction of modern order–handling technology providing scope for rationalisation gains and price reductions as well as time saving has become an important competitive weapon.

Thus, many sub–markets for financial services have special characteristics as regards their competitive structure. This has important implications for competition policies as the promotion of competition in particular sub–markets may require specific measures and cannot always be approached by deregulation measures of a more global nature.

Overview of the Markets for Financial Services

Providing an overview of the markets for financial services as a whole can be done in several ways depending on the kind and purpose of analysis that is to be carried out, on the criteria that are used for defining and classifying the numerous sub–markets and on the related detail that may be required in a particular context. Thus, markets for financial services may be classified according to functional criteria, by types of customers or demanders for financial services, institutional characteristics of providers of such services, according to territorial criteria, or by applying various combinations of any such criteria.

Analyses of national financial services markets are often based on institutional and organisational criteria and consist of a description of the activities and functions of different types of financial institutions such as commercial banks, savings banks, finance companies, securities firms, insurance companies, pension funds etc. and of a description of the functioning of organised markets such as money markets, bond markets, equity markets, foreign exchange markets etc. However, this approach does not easily lend itself to international comparisons and does not necessarily provide a suitable framework for describing particular sub–markets in which several types of financial institutions or non–financial providers of financial services compete with each other.

For international comparisons or analyses covering several countries, a functional approach towards classifying financial services markets is often preferable. The following is an attempt to classify sub–markets, or groupings of sub–markets, for financial services according to such functional criteria which in some cases are combined with type–of–customer or demand criteria.

**Functional classification
of financial service markets**

1. Payment services:
   1.1 Payment accounts;
   1.2 Payment instruments (cheques, transfers, credit cards, debit cards, travellers' cheques etc.);
   1.3 Payment circuits and clearing systems;
   1.4 Special services for foreign payments;
   1.5 Automated payments (electronic fund transfers).

2. Facilities and instruments for holding liquidity reserves and financial savings and investments:
   2.1 Sight deposits;
   2.2 Time deposits;
   2.3 Facilities and instruments for small savings;
   2.4 Money market instruments;
   2.5 Longer–term fixed and/or variable interest rate instruments (notes and bonds);
   2.6 Equities and equity–linked instruments;
   2.7 Special risk–hedging facilities and instruments such as interest rate or foreign currency swaps, options, futures and other forward market instruments.

3. Facilities and instruments for fund raising:
   3.1 Direct credit and loans from banks and other financial institutions for the financing of:
   — the household sector including housing;
   — enterprise sector (investment and trade finance);
   — public sector including local authorities;
   3.2 New issue markets for money market instruments;
   3.3 New issue markets for longer–term fixed and/or variable interest rate instruments (notes and bonds);
   3.4 New issue markets for equities and equity–linked instruments.

4. Secondary market (or trading) facilities for marketable instruments:
   4.1 Money markets;
   4.2 Note and bond markets;
   4.3 Markets for equities and equity–linked instruments;
   4.4 Foreign exchange markets;

4.5 Clearing and settlement facilities for the trading of financial instruments, notably securities.

5. Brokerage services for the buying and selling of financial instruments:

    5.1 Money market instruments;
    5.2 Notes and bonds;
    5.3 Equities and equity–linked instruments;
    5.4 Collective investment instruments (mutual funds etc.);
    5.5 Foreign exchange.

6. Investment services for private individuals and institutional investors:

    6.1 General wealth administration (trust business);
    6.2 Securities portfolio management:

    — Discretionary portfolio management;
    — Mutual fund management;
    — Pension fund management;

    6.3 Securities safe custody services (custodian business);
    6.4 Investment and financial market research services;
    6.5 Investment advisory services.

7. Special financial and finance–related services for industrial and commercial enterprises:

    7.1 Cash management facilities and services;
    7.2 Domestic and international trade financing;
    7.3 Leasing facilities;
    7.4 Factoring facilities;
    7.5 Venture capital facilities;
    7.6 Guarantee facilities;
    7.7 General and financial management and advisory services;
    7.8 Mergers, acquisitions and management buyouts;
    7.9 Enterprise pension system management and advisory services;
    7.10 Computer services for enterprises;
    7.11 Tax advisory services for enterprises;
    7.12 Transport brokerage services.

8. Miscellaneous finance–related services:

    8.1 Travel services including the selling of travel and holiday programmes;
    8.2 Insurance brokerage and advisory services;
    8.3 Real estate brokerage and advisory services;
    8.4 Real estate development;
    8.5 Commodity trading and brokerage services;
    8.6 Services related to the trading of gold and other precious metals and precious stones;
    8.7 Tax advisory services for private persons;
    8.8 General safe custody services.

For many of the financial services mentioned it would be possible to include further sub–items and thus identify further sub–markets. For example, under payment services a distinction could be made between payment services and facilities for private persons (credit cards, traveller cheques, home banking payment facilities), enterprises and financial institutions (the SWIFT system, clearing services etc.). Under the broad item of facilities and instruments for fund raising the sub–items of direct credit and loans, new issue markets for money market instruments and new issue markets for longer–term fixed and/or variable interest rate instruments could each be split up into a long list of further sub–items referring to different types of instruments or types of customers or territorial characteristics of sub–markets (domestic markets, international markets).

Financial Service Markets and Financial Systems

In this context, it is worth noting that in a given country context the markets for financial services taken as a whole are not identical with the country's financial system understood as the totality of financial institutions operating in the country concerned. The difference between the two is twofold. First, financial services may be offered by non–financial enterprises while financial institutions may also offer non–financial services. Second, financial services may be "imported" from other countries while, at the same time, providers of financial services in a given country may "export" such services to other countries. Thus, individual countries may be "net importers" or "net exporters" of financial services, or international "turntables" for such services.

An advantage of the functional classification of financial service markets is that it can be easily applied to cross–country studies because the services listed — to the extent that they correspond to basic needs that have to be satisfied in all countries — are being offered in any country through one type of institution or enterprise or another. This does not necessarily mean, however, that all the services that can be listed under the broad headings as sub–items are provided in all countries to the same extent or with the same degree of sophistication and efficiency; some sub–categories of services may not be available at all in some countries. Thus, the functional classification of financial services may, in fact, be used as a checklist for examining the availability of certain financial services in a particular country and may in this way help to assess one important aspect of the efficiency of national financial systems namely the availability aspect (see Section 2 of the present Annex).

The Impact of Regulation

The ways in which financial services are provided and the related institutional and organisational supply structure of the various sub–markets for financial services are different from country to country and depend largely on historical developments of national financial systems, their institutional characteristics, tradition, market practices and, last but not least, on the legal frameworks within which different types of financial institutions and other providers of financial services operate in each country. Government regulation of the activities of financial institutions which may be, and often is, different for different types of institutions, determines the kinds of financial services that such institutions are allowed to offer. Financial regulation also affects the extent to which certain financial services may be offered by non–financial enterprises or private persons. In most countries financial regulation imposes a certain degree of specialisation between different types of financial institutions. Even in countries with universal banking systems not all financial services can be offered by all types of financial institutions. In Germany, for example, building societies operate within a special legal framework which denies them the right to offer a wide range of ordinary banking and securities–related financial services; and ordinary commercial banks are not allowed to offer the same services as a building society except via capital participation in such a society. In countries in which stock exchange brokers have a monopoly position as members of the stock exchange, universal banks are not allowed to act as competitors of these brokers as far as order handling at the stock exchange is concerned. In most countries the post office system is allowed to operate only in a limited number of sub–markets for retail banking services.

Financial regulation also determines the scope available to non–financial enterprises to operate as providers of financial services. Thus, in a number of countries it is possible for department stores to offer consumer loans or credit card services to their clients without having to register as a bank; or manufacturing industries are allowed to grant supplier credits without special authorisation. In some countries such as Germany and Switzerland the management of private securities portfolios or of private wealth generally falls outside the scope of banking regulation, and these financial services

may, therefore, also be offered by non–financial enterprises or private persons.

These broad considerations relating to the question of the impact of financial regulation on the institutional structure of the supply side of financial service markets may suffice to indicate that regulation has a very important bearing on the competitive structure of many sub–markets for financial services and that legally imposed specialisation of financial institutions can represent important barriers to the entry of potentially strong competitors to some of these sub–markets. This applies, for example, to commercial banks in Japan and the United States which traditionally have not been allowed to operate domestically in the whole range of securities–related services that are provided by securities firms although the borderlines between these two broad financial services areas are becoming increasingly blurred in these countries as well. The role of government action supporting the despecialisation and integration process in the financial service markets is described in some detail in the main body of the present study.

A Pragmatic Approach

The present study which intentionally provides only a broad overview of trends in the financial service markets over the last two decades or so, has, for practical reasons, adopted a mixed approach to the classification of financial services markets by using partly type–of–customer and partly functional and territorial classification criteria. Thus, financial service markets have been grouped into five broad areas:

1. Markets for retail banking services;
2. Markets for corporate financial services;
3. Markets for securities–related services;
4. Markets for interbank financial services;
5. Markets for international financial services.

Although these market areas overlap in many instances, it was found most practical to discuss trends in the financial services markets in this way as these areas broadly correspond to organisational and operational approaches of individual banking institutions towards conducting their business. Banking strategies are, indeed, often discussed and developed with reference to these business areas, and those institutions which are active in several or all of these areas often operate in these areas through corresponding special departments inside the institution or through specialised subsidiaries.

The complex nature of the financial service markets taken as a whole has, as has already been indicated, important implications for competition policy in this field. Assessing the degree of concentration in the financial services markets simply by measuring concentration ratios on the basis of balance–sheet totals of commercial banks or other financial institutions makes little sense in situations in which the institutions in question operate at different degrees in a relatively large number of different sub–markets for financial services. Concentration ratios obtained in this way are no suitable indicator of the competitive situation in local or regional financial service markets. Thus, concentration in many local markets may have decreased as a result of the extension of branch networks of major commercial banks while at the same time global concentration ratios applying to a country as a whole may have risen. Furthermore, balance–sheet totals are in no way suitable for measuring concentration in markets for brokerage services or other services which are not reflected in the banks' asset or liability growth.

As financial service markets consist of a large number of sub–markets with different structural characteristics, government policies towards promoting competition in these markets need to take these characteristics into account and cannot exclusively rely on global measures such as deregulation of interest rates or the removal of barriers applying to the entry of new domestic or foreign banking institutions. Providing more scope for competition in some specific sub–markets may require specific measures which are only applicable to these particular situations. Thus, the intention to increase competition in the market for government bond issues may in a particular situation require a change in the issuing technique, for example, from the consortium technique to an auction technique. In other sub–markets for financial services in which financial institutions compete more through high quality of service rather than through fees and commissions, competition may be preferably promoted by attracting highly qualified foreign competitors with particular experience and highly specialised staff into these particular sub–markets. In some country cases, this may apply, for example, to the sub–markets for portfolio management, merger and acquisition activities, or foreign trade financing services. By contrast, other sub–markets for financial services which involve the intensive use of modern computer technology such as payment and clearing services or securities buy and sell order handling may require a good deal of co–operation amongst market participants or between market participants and the authorities in order to achieve the ultimate objective of an efficient functioning of these systems through developing an adequate technological infrastructure to which providers of financial services have equal access and on which they may compete on equal terms.

2. The Concept of Functional Efficiency

The complexity of the markets for financial services and of their institutional features described in Section 1 of the present Annex naturally has implications for adopting an appropriate efficiency concept that is suitable in the context of policies towards improving the efficiency of financial service markets and financial systems. Thus, the efficiency concept applicable to the markets for financial services as a whole or to any sub–market, or groupings of sub–markets, cannot be expected to be a simple one which can be easily assessed or measured. In fact, the concept of efficiency adopted in the present study on competition in banking is a rather broad and complex one. It relates to the role, the micro– and macro–economic functions and the functioning and operation of the markets for financial services and of financial systems and it is, therefore, referred to as "functional efficiency". This concept goes far beyond theoretical concepts of financial market efficiency developed in academic research in the field of securities markets, for example. It also goes beyond the macro–economic concept of the allocational efficiency of financial systems which relates to the allocation of financial resources to productive uses in an economy although this aspect is part of the functional efficiency concept adopted in the present study.

From the point of view of this concept, efficient financial service markets, or financial systems, are expected to perform adequately and satisfactorily their various micro– and macro–economic functions and to satisfy the manifold financial service needs that characterise modern industrialised economies and their participants. A detailed overview of these numerous needs is provided in Section 1 ("Functional Classification of Financial Service Markets") of the present Annex. As has been mentioned in the comments on the classification of financial service markets, there can be considerable country differences as regards the degree of sophistication of financial service needs and related quality and convenience standards. However, the basic demand for financial services that needs to be satisfied is broadly the same or similar in countries with similar standards of industrialisation and living although there may be considerable differences in the level of efficiency at which such basic needs are being satisfied.

Policy makers dealing with issues relating to the efficiency of financial systems often take a broader macro–economic view of the functions that a financial system should perform as efficiently and effectively as possible. These functions may be described as follows:

i) To develop and manage national payment systems and their linkages with payment systems of other countries, notably as regards large payments;

ii) To channel investible funds from surplus to deficit units in the economy in quantities and forms which correspond to the preferences of lenders, borrowers and financial intermediaries; this role includes functions which are sometimes referred to as maturity and/or liquidity transformation function and as risk transformation function;

iii) To administer and safeguard a national economy's financial wealth (macro–economic trust function).

While these broad functions are all related to the overall role of financial systems, namely to satisfy the micro– and macro–economic financial service needs of national economies, it needs to be stressed that in modern managed economies financial systems have a fourth function to perform, namely:

iv) To serve as a vehicle for the implementation of monetary policy; this function is inevitable insofar as monetary policy measures, in one way or another, have to be passed through the financial system.

However, the concept of functional efficiency does not normally relate to this latter role of a financial system although the issue of the relationship between efficient financial systems and an effective monetary policy receives considerable attention by policy makers.

In applying the concept of functional efficiency to analyses of financial systems or to policies towards improving the efficiency of financial systems as a whole, or in specific areas, it is useful to distinguish between the following efficiency aspects:

— The allocation aspect;
— The availability, quality and convenience aspect;
— The cost aspect;
— The aspect of competitiveness of financial institutions;
— The dynamic, or flexibility and adaptability, aspect.

The "allocation aspect" relates to the issue of generating and mobilising financial savings and allocating them through direct or indirect financing channels to productive or other uses such as the financing of government deficits and capital exports etc. Sometimes, this issue is referred to as the problem of optimal allocation of financial resources. The concept of allocational efficiency does not easily lend itself to designing broad policies towards improving the efficiency of financial systems insofar

as policy measures in this field usually are concerned with more concrete problems of improving particular aspects of the complex saving, financing and investment process in national economies such as, for example, mechanisms for housing finance, or the generation and allocation of risk capital to small– and medium–sized enterprises.

The "availability, quality and convenience aspect" of the functional efficiency concept relates, first of all, to the availability of financial services whether all the services for which there is a manifest, or underlying, demand are actually available in a given country. In order to assess this aspect of efficiency, the classification of financial service markets presented in Section 1 of the present Annex may serve as a check list. Many recent efforts in OECD Member countries towards improving financial systems have been aimed at this particular aspect of efficiency to the extent that services or financial instruments have been introduced that were previously not available. A closely related question is whether the financial services that are available actually meet the quality and convenience standards required by the demanders of such services. This aspect of efficiency has received particular attention in recent years both by market participants and the authorities, largely under the impact of increased domestic and international competitive pressures.

The "cost aspect" of the functional efficiency concept relates to the costs at which the financial service needs of an economy are satisfied and at which the function of channelling financial resources from surplus units to deficit units is performed. These latter costs, which are often referred to as cost of financial intermediation, are important indicators of the degree of cost efficiency of a financial system. However, other cost aspects play a role as well, some of which are implicit and not easy to assess. For example, in assessing the macro–economic cost of maintaining and operating the distribution network for financial services any convenience costs that may arise for the demanders of financial services in terms of travel, transport and delays of delivery (queuing at banking guichets) should be taken into account. This consideration is important in connection with a macro–economic cost/benefit analysis of branch networks in banking.

The "aspect of competitiveness of financial institutions" relates to the ability of financial institutions of similar or different types to compete efficiently and effectively in those sub–markets for financial services in which they operate at domestic and/or international level as the case may be. As governments have often made a strong effort in recent years towards strengthening the international competitiveness of their countries' financial centres, this aspect of efficiency — which is closely related with some of the other aspects mentioned —

receives increasing attention both by the authorities and the market participants themselves.

Finally, the "dynamic aspect" of the functional efficiency concept relates to the speed and flexibility with which a financial system is able to respond and adapt itself to changes and shifts in the demands and needs for financial services; it also relates to the innovative spirit and imaginative and creative powers of a country's financial community to identify and meet new demands and underlying needs for financial products and services, to respond to increasing competition from foreign providers of financial services resulting from the ever-intensifying internationalisation of financial systems, or to make productive use of new opportunities offered by technological progress. In their efforts directed towards the modernisation of their countries' financial systems, governments have often paid particular attention to this latter aspect of functional efficiency.

The concept of functional efficiency, although it does not easily lend itself to quantitative measurement, is useful for several reasons. First, it provides scope for dealing with different country situations. Thus, it may be applied to countries with a relatively high planning content in which banks are expected to make a major contribution to the achievement of specific macro-economic goals of a more structural nature, such as the promotion of export industries, the implementation of regional development plans, the promotion of residential construction or the development of small- and medium-sized enterprises. This means that functional efficiency may mean different things in different countries or, in one and the same country, at different times, depending on the role and functions that may have been assigned to the financial system. Efficiency would, in fact, have to be measured against broader objectives which financial or more general economic policy attempts to achieve.

Second, the concept of functional efficiency also makes it possible to differentiate between different types of financial service activities which may be conducted at different levels of efficiency. Thus, in some countries banks may be more efficient in the retail banking area than in corporate banking; in other countries there may be gaps in the supply of housing finance while facilities for the financing of exports and export industries may be well developed. Frazer and Vittas (1982) have made an attempt to assess the efficiency of retail banking institutions in ten countries by taking into account the following services and facilities, on the one hand:

— Deposit and lending facilities (chequing accounts, savings deposits overdrafts, consumer credit, housing finance);

— Infrastructure (branches, ATMs, other automation);

— Payment services (cheques, paper credits, automated payments, credit cards, wage payments);

and convenience, availability and costs/return features, on the other.

This practical example shows that, in principle, it should be possible to develop analytical tools and criteria for measuring and assessing the functional efficiency of financial systems and markets, or of segments and sub-markets of such systems, although this will be a difficult and complex task.

In general, it should be easier to assess the efficiency of particular sub-markets for financial services or particular institutional sectors of national financial systems than attempting to assess the efficiency of national financial systems as a whole. For sub-markets such as the markets and mechanisms for housing finance, or the secondary markets for government securities it seems, indeed, possible to carry out international comparisons and draw conclusions about the efficiency of these markets in different countries. In a similar way, the efficiency and competitiveness of particular types of financial institutions could be compared and assessed. As a matter of fact, in a number of countries, studies (largely of a confidential nature) have been carried out attempting to assess the international competitiveness of the respective national financial systems, partly by using the technique of comparing market shares in particular sectors of the international financial markets or by checking the availability and quality of particular financial services in which international competition is particularly strong.

The improvement of the functional efficiency of financial systems and financial service markets — in its various aspects — has become an important objective of financial policy in recent years in practically all OECD countries as can be documented by reference to numerous official publications such as government or parliamentary reports, government-assigned reports of commissions of inquiry or to related working papers prepared by public authorities or administrations. The following quotations from such reports are given as examples:

1. *1964 — Report of the Royal Commission on Banking and Finance, Ottawa, 1964 (sometimes referred to as the "Porter Commission Report")*

The Porter Commission which, inter alia, dealt with the question of the adequacy of the Canadian financial system "to meet the legitimate present and prospective needs of lenders and borrowers in an efficient, flexible, non-discriminatory and creative way", circumscribed the efficiency concept as follows: "An efficient financial system not only must encourage the transfer of funds from surplus to deficit units but must provide many other facilities essential to the progress of modern society, including a convenient and economical means of making payment for every kind of transaction and the provision of safekeeping, life insurance and trustee services. If the financial system fails to fulfil all these functions, or perform them only imperfectly, the result will be to deter some economic activity from taking place" ... "A financial mechanism which does not provide the wide variety of instruments, pools of special skills, and highly developed borrowing facilities needed in our complex economy, which fails to meet the needs of lenders for a broad range of outlets for their funds, or which does these things only at an excessive cost, will inevitably cause employment, production and growth to fall below their potential" ... "A creative financial system is one which does not just passively accommodate the usual — instead, it is one in which active and inventive efforts are constantly made to meet the sound requirements of lenders and borrowers, regardless of how untried and unusual such needs may be." (Page 8)

2. *The Report of the President's Commission on Financial Structure and Regulation, Washington, December 1971* (sometimes referred to as the "Hunt Commission Report")

The President's Mandate to the Commission includes a reference to the functioning of the private financial system. It reads as follows: "to review and study the structure, operation, and reregulation of the private financial institutions in the United States, for the purpose of formulating recommendations that would improve the functioning of the private financial system." (Page 1)

The broad reference to the improvement of the functioning of the private financial system can be read to mean the improvement of the functional efficiency of the private financial system.

3. *Australian Financial System, Final Report of the Committee of Inquiry, Canberra, September 1981* (sometimes referred to as the "Campbell Committee Report")

The Campbell Committee's Terms of Reference included a reference to efficiency and to a related improvement of the financial system as follows:

"The Terms of Reference are:

In view of the importance of the efficiency of the financial system for the Government's free

enterprise objectives and broad goals for national economic prosperity, the Committee is asked to:

... *(c)* To make recommendations:

i) For the improvement of the structure and operations of the financial system;" ...

In accordance with this part of the mandate the Committee gave efficiency considerations a high ranking in its work. The Committee's report refers in several instances to criteria or standards against which the efficiency of the financial system and its operations could be judged. The following is an example of such a reference:

"... an efficient system of financial intermediation must satisfy certain performance standards. The required standards are:

— Operational efficiency: are the operations of intermediaries being conducted at least costs (in terms of resource input for a given product output)?

— Allocative efficiency: are financial resources (which in turn are claims on real resources) being put to the most productive uses?

— Dynamic efficiency: is the system reasonably adaptable to changes in the economic climate, technology and market preferences?." (Page 522)

4. *Banca d"Italia, "Italian Credit Structures, Efficiency, Competition and Control", Euromoney Publications, 1984*

The Banca d'Italia published in this volume a number of staff papers amongst which a paper by Giulio Lanciotti on "Objectives and Instruments of Structural Supervision: Guidelines and Optimum Rules for Authorising Branch Openings" refers implicitly to functional efficiency by enumerating the following objectives:

a) The optimum allocation of credit;

b) Minimisation of the costs of producing services;

c) The orderly working of intermediation mechanisms and the payments system;

d) Speed and accuracy in transmitting monetary policy impulses;

e) Satisfaction of the demand for basic banking services throughout the country. (Page 250)

5. *Reserve Bank of New Zealand, Monetary Policy in New Zealand, Reserve Bank Bulletin, Vol. 48, No. 6, 1985*

The article reviewing monetary policy and related changes includes a section on "Efficiency Considerations" from which the following excerpt is reproduced:

"The financial sector performs a number of functions for the economy as a whole, including the provision of the payments mechanism, provision of a repository for people's savings, the mobilisation of those savings for investment, and the allocation of risks to those most able and willing to bear them. In general, the financial sector is likely to perform these services most efficiently, or at minimum cost to the rest of the community, if financial institutions have the flexibility to adjust their behaviour according to changing market conditions and are relatively free to compete with each other across the spectrum of financial services."

6. *Department of Trade and Industry, Financial Services in the United Kingdom, A New Framework for Investor Protection, presented to Parliament by the Secretary of State for Trade and Industry by Command of Her Majesty, January 1985, London, Her Majesty's Stationery Office, Cmnd. 9432* ("White Paper on Financial Services")

The White Paper on Financial Services in the United Kingdom states the following objectives in designing new legislation for investor protection:

"3.1 The Government's objectives in designing a new framework for investor protection are:

i) *Efficiency* — the financial services industry of the United Kingdom should be able to provide services to industry and commerce, private investors and Government in the most efficient and economic way.

ii) *Competitiveness* — the industry must be competitive both domestically and internationally. Regulation must stimulate competition and encourage innovation; it must be responsive to international developments and not a cover for protectionism.

iii) *Confidence* — the system of regulation must inspire confidence in issuers and investors by ensuring that the financial services sector is, and is seen to be, a 'clean' place to do business.

iv) *Flexibility* — the regulatory framework must be clear enough to guide but not cramp structural and other change in the industry. It must have the resilience not to be overrun by events." (Page 6)

Three of the stated objectives — efficiency, competitiveness and flexibility — fall within the scope of the concept of functional efficiency that has been adopted in the present study. The White Paper's reference to efficiency corresponds to the cost aspect of functional efficiency that has been explained in the present Section of this Annex.

7. *The Honorable Thomas Hockin, Minister of State for Finance, Executive Summary, New Directions for the Financial Sector, Canada, December 18, 1986*

The section on "Principles and Directions" begins with the following statement:

"The government is committed to maintaining a sound financial system that provides Canadians with innovative and competitive services, that broadens the range of choice for Canadian savers and investors, and that fosters safe and well supervised financial institutions that can compete effectively around the world." (Page 2)

The reference to innovative and competitive services, broadening the range of choice for savers and investors and to the ability of financial institutions to compete effectively around the world falls within the scope of the various aspects of the concept of functional efficiency that has been adopted in the present study, notably the availability, quality and convenience aspect, the aspect of competitiveness of financial institutions and the dynamic aspect.

3. Competition Policy

In the context of the present study, a distinction is made between competition policy in a narrow sense and competition policy in a wider sense. "Competition policy in a narrow sense" is seen as relating to restrictive business practices, concentration and dominant market positions, ownership linkages, mergers and acquisitions, and co-operation agreements in the financial service markets. The legal framework for competition policy in a narrow sense may be termed competition legislation, restrictive business practice legislation, fair trading legislation, or anti-trust legislation, depending on the country. The way in which the banking sector is treated under any such competition legislation in OECD countries is described in greater detail in Annex IV of the present study.

The concept of "competition policy in a wider sense" as used in the context of the present study, goes beyond the concept of competition policy in a narrow sense and is seen as relating also to the following categories of measures:

i) "Measures affecting competition in the financial service markets both at national and international level". Measures encouraging, or widening the scope for, competition or strengthening the working of market forces may be referred to as liberal competition policy or "deregulation" while measures restricting competition may be termed restrictive competition policy. Measures encouraging, or widening the scope

114

for, competition may include the following: abolition, or easing of, interest rate controls; abolition, or easing of, restrictions on market access i.e. on the setting up of new branches or new — domestic or foreign — institutions; abolition, or easing of, restrictions on particular types of activities or on the use of particular types of financing instruments. External "deregulation" measures such as the abolition, or easing of, capital movement controls or controls on other international financial service transactions, which fall also within this category of measures, are often referred to as "liberalisation" measures.

ii) "Measures designed to regulate the desirable intensity of competition or to ensure the proper working of market forces". This category of measures includes any action designed to implement the principle of competitive equality ("levelling the playing field"), and the implementation of "rules of the game" i.e. codes of conduct and market practices which are increasingly seen as being necessary conditions for an efficient functioning of markets.

Views may be divided as to the question whether any such "rules of the game" i.e. codes of conduct and market practices such as, for example, stock exchange regulations should be considered as falling within the scope of competition policy in a wider sense or whether they should be seen as investor protection measures. In the present study the line is taken that measures designed "to level the playing field" and "to set rules of the game" fall within the scope of competition policy in a wider sense although it is recognised that insofar as any such rules enhance the functioning of the financial service markets and thus help to improve the efficiency of these markets, they also "protect" the demanders of financial services against malpractices and bad quality services in general.

In this connection it needs to be stressed that in most countries in which the authorities pursue a liberal competition policy, competition is not seen as an end in itself. The ultimate objective is efficiency and not competition. Competition policy is used as one, perhaps the most, important instrument for achieving the efficiency objective. Thus, a liberal competition policy is by no means identical with a "laisser faire, laisser aller" policy. The authorities in many countries are, in fact, concerned with the problem of achieving an "adequate" or "reasonable" level of competition and of avoiding "excessive" or "destructive" — "cutthroat" — competition. In German–speaking countries a distinction is being made between "Leistungswettbewerb" ("performance competition") which is to be

encouraged and "Verdraengungswettbewerb" ("crowding–out competition") which has a negative connotation. Performance and quality competition is seen as enhancing the functional efficiency of financial service markets and financial systems while "crowding–out competition" is seen as having a negative impact on the working of the financial system.

The basic philosophy, which has, by now, been widely adopted in OECD countries, that the functional efficiency of financial service markets or of financial systems can be most powerfully promoted by encouraging, and widening the scope for, competition and by reliance on the working of market forces, can be documented with numerous references to official reports and studies such as government or parliamentary reports, government–assigned studies by commissions of inquiry, and working papers by public bodies or administrations. The following paragraphs are a selection of such references:

1. *1964 — Report of the Royal Commission on Banking and Finance, Ottawa, 1964. (Sometimes referred to as the "Porter Commission Report"*

"We have, in summary, favoured a more open and competitive banking system — carefully and equitably regulated under uniform legislation but not bound by restrictions which impede the response of the institutions to new situations, enforce a particular pattern of narrow specialisation or shelter some enterprises from competitive pressures. We believe that this framework will encourage creativity and efficiency and offer the public the widest possible range of choice of financial services, while reducing the danger of unregulated institutions springing up to serve real needs which others are prevented from meeting. Some institutions may attempt to offer a full range of services and others may choose to specialise in a variety of ways, but the legislation will allow all of them — and such new institutions as are qualified — to adapt to new opportunities and situations created by changing public preferences and needs". (Page 564)

2. *The Report of The President's Commission on Financial Structure and Regulation, Washington, December 1971* (sometimes referred to as the "Hunt Commission Report")

"The Commission's objective, then, is to move as far as possible towards freedom of financial markets and equip all institutions with the powers necessary to compete in such markets. Once these powers and services have been authorised, and a suitable time allowed for implementation, each institution will be free to determine its own course. The public will be better served by such competition. Markets will work more efficiently in the allocation of funds and total savings will expand to meet private and public needs." (Page 9)

3. *Australian Financial System, Final Report of the Committee of Inquiry, September 1981, Australian Government Publishing Service Canberra 1981* (sometimes referred to as "Campbell Committee Report")

"These performance standards (of an efficient system of financial intermediaries) are likely to be more fully met when the financial institutional structure is characterised by:

i)   High levels of competition — particularly price competition;...
ii) Competitive neutrality;...
iii) Diversity of choice;..."   (Page 522)

4. *Federal Reserve Bank of New Zealand, Monetary Policy in New Zealand, Reserve Bank Bulletin, Vol. 48, No. 6, 1985*

"In general, the financial sector is likely to perform these (financial) services most efficiently, or at minimum cost to the rest of the community, if financial institutions have the flexibility to adjust their behaviour according to changing market conditions and are relatively free to compete with each other across the spectrum of financial services".

5. *Department of Trade and Industry, Financial Services in the United Kingdom, A New Framework for Investor Protection, Presented to Parliament by the Secretary of State for Trade and Industry by Command of Her Majesty, January 1985, London, Her Majesty's Stationary Office Cmnd. 9432* ("White Paper on Financial Services")

"Market forces prove the best means of ensuring that an industry meets the needs of its customers. If market forces are to operate properly it is essential that:

... — the forces of competition are brought to bear on practitioners and their institutions." (Page 6)

While the five references just mentioned have all stressed the role of competition policy in a wider sense as an instrument for improving the efficiency of financial systems there is also relatively widespread recognition that some problems of improving the functioning of particular mechanisms within the financial system, for example, clearing and settlement systems for payment, or for the transfer of ownership of securities, should be better

approached by co-operation rather than by competition. The "Committee to Review the Functioning of Financial Institutions" in the United Kingdom (sometimes referred to as the "Wilson Committee"), although confirming the general principle that efficiency and innovation in the financial system can be promoted by competition, points to the limits of competition policy as a means of increasing the efficiency of the financial system:

Committee to Review the Functioning of Financial Institutions, Report, Presented to Parliament by the Prime Minister by Command of Her Majesty, June 1980, London, Her Majesty's Stationery Office, Cmnd. 7937 (sometimes referred to as "Wilson Committee Report")

"108. Competition between financial institutions should bring considerable benefits. In particular, it should provide a spur to efficiency and innovation. But at times it may result in apparently wasteful duplication of facilities, and there may be some types of activity which are more efficiently organised on a co-operative rather than a competitive basis. The clearing banks and certain other banks, for example, co-operate closely together in the clearing arrangements for money transmission."

"1335. Money transmission is an area where a significant degree of co-operation is needed because operating efficiency and the curtailment of costs require a high degree of standardization of procedures. The central clearing infrastructure has something of the characteristics of a natural monopoly and in many other countries is publicly owned, with the payment services being provided by private sector institutions. The central banks of other countries are also often more involved in cash distribution and clearing non-cash payments than in the United Kingdom."

"1336. The banks have argued that they have fully recognised the need for co-operation to avoid socially wasteful competition and to exploit fully the technological opportunities that are increasingly becoming available. They have pointed out that they, or their clients, are the major users of the clearing system, which gives them a powerful interest in its efficiency. Nor have we received any evidence to suggest that the banks have used their ownership of the system to impose unreasonable conditions on their competitors and so restrict competition from newcomers to retail banking. Any bank which is not a member of the Clearing House can still have access to it through an agency agreement with a bank that is. The agreement regulating the central clearing system is currently being examined by the Office of Fair Trading".

The importance of co-operation for promoting efficiency in certain areas of the financial service markets was confirmed at the *Symposium on Europe and the Future of Financial Services, Brussels, November 1986,*

"In the financial services area, the community has come together for mutual benefit to develop standards for CHAPS, SWIFT, magnetic stripe cards and a number of other areas. It is necessary for competitive instincts to be buried temporarily in order to ensure that a standard is meaningful and useful. This is not always easy for organisations who are competitors in the market place. The answer is to recognise the difference between co-operation in the creation of an infrastructure, and competition in the services which are provided on that infrastructure." (Commission of the European Communities, Symposium on Europe and the Future of Financial Services, Proceedings, Communications, Brussels, 5th, 6th and 7th November 1986, page 536).

4. Financial Regulation

The purpose of the present section is to clarify how terms such as financial regulation, deregulation, reregulation and liberalisation are used in the context of the present study.

Financial regulation i.e. the regulation of financial institutions and financial markets, serves essentially three basic purposes:

i) To ensure the solvency and financial soundness of financial institutions in order to maintain stability — and confidence in the stability — of the financial system as a whole;

ii) To protect investors, borrowers and other users of the financial system i.e. demanders of financial services, against undue risks of losses and other damage that may arise from failures, fraud, malpractices, manipulation and other bad conduct on the part of providers of financial services;

iii) To ensure a smooth, efficient, safe and effective functioning of financial institutions and markets and a proper working of competitive market forces (see Section 3 of the present Annex).

The first objective is to some extent linked with the second insofar as ensuring the solvency and financial soundness of financial institutions serves both purposes: maintaining the stability — and confidence in the stability — of the financial system as a whole, and protecting investors against losses

that may occur from failures of individual financial institutions.

The objective of ensuring the solvency and financial soundness of financial institutions may be, and in practice has been, approached by two types of regulation, first, by anti-competitive regulation which protects the banking or financial sector as a whole against competitive market pressures; and second, by prudent management regulation i.e. regulation which imposes specific prudential controls in the form of liquidity ratios, capital ratios and other balance-sheet ratios designed to cover different types of risks. Often, both types of regulation have been used side by side.

The objective of protecting investors, or demanders of financial services generally, against fraud, malpractices, manipulation and other bad conduct on the part of the providers of such services is often approached by several types of regulation such as licensing requirements aimed at ensuring that financial services are provided by qualified professionals, specific regulation applying to the activities of particular types of financial institutions, codes of conduct which also deal with conflict of interest situations, extensive disclosure and information requirements for specific types of services, notably in the securities business, and effective supervisory and enforcement procedures.

The third objective, setting a framework for a proper working of market forces and ensuring an adequate level of competition thereby ensuring an efficient and effective functioning of financial institutions and markets, is approached, inter alia, by applying restrictive business practices legislation to the financial sector, by an adequate regulation, or self-regulation, applying to financial markets in a narrow sense — money markets, securities markets, foreign exchange markets, markets for financial futures and options — and by codes-of-conduct types of regulation applying to the market participants, in particular the intermediaries. In addition, there is generally extensive regulation on information and disclosure requirements designed to increase the visibility and transparency of markets as regards the characteristics of financial instruments and the price determination process both in the primary and in the secondary markets.

It can be seen from the comments on regulatory approaches towards the second and third objective of financial regulation that certain types of regulation such as quality standards for the professional providers of financial services, disclosure requirements concerning the markets for financial instruments and the activities of providers of financial services and codes of conduct and market practices, often serve simultaneously two main purposes: adequate investor and consumer protection and an efficient and effective functioning of financial service markets. In a similar way, prudential regulation often serves simultaneously the two objectives of system stability and of investor protection. Thus, it is not always possible to make a clear-cut distinction between different types of regulation, or self-regulation, according to objectives.

Against this background of a broad overview of the objectives of financial regulation and the broad approaches applied, it can easily be understood that the widespread use of the term "financial deregulation" applies only to a small sector of financial regulation, namely that part of regulation that has been termed "anti-competitive" regulation and that has been designed to protect the financial sector as a whole against competitive pressures with a view to ensuring the solvency and financial soundness of financial institutions. While this category of financial regulation has been largely dismantled in most OECD countries in recent years, or earlier, regulatory activity in other areas of financial regulation concerning all three major ultimate objectives of such regulation: managing the systemic risk in the financial sector; protecting demanders for financial services against losses and malpractices; and ensuring the functioning of the financial service markets, has become quite intense in recent years in many countries. Prudential regulation and supervision has generally been tightened in the face of much increased risk exposure of banks and other financial institutions. Regulation designed to protect demanders for financial services against fraud and malpractices has also been intensified in a number of countries as increased competition at domestic and international level has also increased the risk that demanders of financial services are badly served or become victims of fraud and malpractices. Finally, with the general move towards a market-oriented approach in financial policy, regulation designed to provide an adequate framework for fair competition between market participants has also received increasing attention. This intensified regulatory activity has sometimes been referred to as "reregulation" although regulatory reform, or modernising financial regulation, may be a more appropriate description of recent regulatory activity.

With the increasing internationalisation of financial markets and national financial systems, pressures in the direction of convergence of financial regulation and of the underlying policy attitudes have increased in recent years. In this connection it seems important to note that there is increased recognition amongst financial regulators that with intensified competition amongst international financial centres, adequate financial regulation is increasingly gaining the importance of a "quality label". It can, indeed, be expected that international financial market activity will increasingly gravitate to those financial centres which are not only characterised by a high degree of functional efficiency but in which the market operators and market practices are well regulated and well supervised. The reputation of an international financial market place will largely rest on the quality and adequacy of its regulation and supervision. In this regard it may be said that the internationalisation of financial markets has added another dimension to the complex issue of financial regulation insofar as the strengthening of the international competitiveness of financial institutions and financial systems can be seen as a fourth basic objective of financial policy and, hence, of financial regulation. In practice it is no doubt difficult for regulators to set a country's regulatory and supervisory framework in such a way that the objective of efficiency and competition can be reconciled with the objective of safety, soundness and adequate investor protection and that the dangers of excessive and destabilising competition, on the one hand, and of regulatory overkill, on the other, are avoided.

5. Financial Policy and Financial System Management

The term "financial policy" is used in the context of the present study to mean policy towards the financial system comprising all policy measures that deal with the structure, the functioning, the regulation and the supervision of financial institutions and financial service markets which have been described in their complexity in Section 1 of the present Annex. Financial policy is to be distinguished from monetary policy which deals with monetary control measures designed to serve as an instrument of short-term demand management and conjunctural policy.

Insofar as financial policy manifests itself in regulatory changes affecting the structure and the operation of the markets for financial services there is a close relationship between financial regulation and financial policy in the sense that the existing regulatory framework within which a country's financial system operates reflects the sum of all financial policy measures that have been taken in the history of the country concerned. For assessing a country's financial policy during a given period it is necessary to examine the changes in financial regulation that have been implemented in that period.

Although the basic objectives of financial policy are broadly the same in all countries, as has been explained in Section 4 of the present Annex, there can be, and certainly are, considerable differences between countries and, within one and the same country, between different periods as regards the mode of conducting financial policy. Thus, financial policy may consist of a piecemeal approach to dealing with minor reforms and improvements in some specific sub–markets of the financial service markets or of a step–by–step adaptation of financial regulation to spontaneous changes in the financial system. At the other extreme, financial policy may take the form of a "grand–design" approach to far–reaching financial system reform. As countries increasingly develop a more coherent and integrated approach to financial policy and take a global view of the financial system and financial service markets, it seems appropriate to refer to any such comprehensive policy approach in terms of financial system management. It is understood, however, that some countries are more coherent and systematic in the management of their countries' financial systems than others. In fact, the authorities in some countries may go as far as denying that they are "managing" their countries' financial systems insofar as they may see their role confined to setting regulatory and supervisory frameworks within which financial institutions and markets may develop freely and spontaneously. Such a liberal and market–oriented approach to financial policy is, in the context of the present study, seen as falling within the scope of the concept of financial system management in a similar way as the term demand management is also applied to liberal and market–oriented approaches to conjunctural policy.

Annex II

STATISTICAL TABLES ON GROWTH OF FINANCIAL INSTITUTIONS AND MARKETS AND STRUCTURAL CHANGES IN FINANCIAL SYSTEMS

1. Introduction

The attached statistical tables are intended to illustrate and highlight main trends in the markets for financial services and structural changes in financial systems which have been briefly described in Chapter 2 of the present monograph. Due to lack of adequate statistics in many countries and financial service areas it has not been possible to illustrate statistically all features of developments in the financial services markets that have been described in Chapter 2. Thus, in many instances, the statistics shown in this Annex are more of an indicative rather than comprehensive nature; and not all developments highlighted in this way may be typical of all OECD countries. Nevertheless, it is believed that the statistics compiled do show main features of developments in the wide area of financial service markets covering the broadly defined banking area which includes securities–related activities.

While broad and longer–term structural changes in financial systems have been shown by statistics covering the period 1960 to 1984–85, an effort has been made towards bringing out the main features of more recent developments — the "explosion" of the securities business and its increasing internationalisation and the emergence of new markets — by providing statistics in these areas covering the period 1980–1986.

The statistical tables included in this Annex are grouped under broad headings which characterise major trends in the markets for financial services.

2. Increasing Importance of the Financial Service Sector

The tables in this section show the growing contribution of the financial service sector to Gross Domestic Product and Employment.

3. Growth of Financial Institutions and Banking Networks

The tables in this section are designed to illustrate the growth of banks and other financial institutions and the expansion of domestic banking networks including ATM (Automated Teller Machine) networks.

4. Expansion of Securities Markets

This section serves to illustrate the strong expansion in recent years of the markets for short–term securities, bonds, shares and derivative products (financial futures and options).

5. Growth of Financial Assets and Liabilities of Non–financial Sectors

In this section data on the accumulation of financial assets and liabilities of households, non–financial enterprises and the government sector are shown.

6. Internationalisation of Financial Markets

This final section is designed to illustrate the process of internationalisation in the markets for financial services; it includes data relating to national economies as a whole, banks and securities markets.

Table 2.1

GROWTH OF FINANCIAL SERVICE SECTOR 1960-1984

(Contribution of Financial Institutions to Gross Domestic Product) (1)

Country	Billion US$ (1980 Exchange Rates)				Compound Annual Rates of Change			Ratio to GDP			
	1960	1970	1980	1984	1960/1970	1970/1980	1980/1984	1960	1970	1980	1984
Austria	0.30	0.85	3.11	4.16	11.0	13.9	7.5	2.5	3.1	4.3	4.4
Belgium	0.50	1.43	5.10	7.35	11.1	13.6	9.6	2.8	3.6	4.7	5.3
Denmark	0.17	0.47	1.46	1.68	10.7	12.0	3.6	2.5	2.4	2.4	1.8
Finland	..	..	1.72	3.05	..	..	15.4	..	..	3.4	3.8
Germany	2.76	8.68	26.60	39.92	12.1	11.9	10.7	1.8	2.5	3.5	4.4
Italy	0.66	2.37	21.13	34.34	13.6	24.5	12.9	2.6	3.5	5.8	5.2
Netherlands	..	1.03	5.17	..	..	17.5	..	..	1.8	3.3	..
Norway	..	..	0.68	1.22	..	..	15.7	..	..	1.2	1.4
Spain	..	0.68	10.06	18.21	..	30.9	16.0	..	2.1	5.2	5.7
United States	10.50	23.90	66.70	109.60	8.6	10.8	13.2	2.0	2.4	2.5	3.0
Six OECD Countries (2)	14.89	37.70	124.10	197.05	9.7	12.7	12.3	2.0	2.5	3.1	3.5
Five European OECD Countries (3)	4.39	13.80	57.40	87.45	12.2	15.3	11.1	2.0	2.8	4.2	4.6
For comparison:	Gross Domestic Product										
Six OECD Countries (2)	730.06	1 510.09	4 054.35	5 599.49	7.5	10.4	8.4				
United States	513.60	1 009.20	2 688.50	3 713.00	7.0	10.3	8.4				
Five European OECD Countries (3)	216.46	500.89	1 365.85	1 886.49	8.8	10.6	8.4				

1. Excluding insurance companies.
2. Austria, Belgium, Denmark, Germany, Italy, United States.
3. Austria, Belgium, Denmark, Germany, Italy.

Source: OECD National Accounts and Country Submissions.

Table 2.2

GROWTH OF FINANCIAL SERVICE SECTOR 1960-1984

(Contribution of Financial Institutions to Employment) (1)

Country	Persons Employed by Financial Institutions — Thousands				Persons Employed by Financial Institutions — Compound Annual Rates of Growth			Ratio to Total Employed Persons			
	1960	1970	1980	1984	1960/1970	1970/1980	1980/1984	1960	1970	1980	1984
Austria	36.1	59.1	91.2	99.4 (2)	5.1	4.4	1.7 (2)	1.1	1.9	2.8	3.1 (2)
Belgium	22.6	39.3	48.4	48.0	5.7	2.1	-0.2	0.9	1.0	1.2	1.1
Canada (3)	65.0	92.0	151.0	163.0 (2)	3.5	5.1	1.5 (2)	1.5	1.7	2.7	2.8
Denmark	30.0	38.6	66.5	70.0	2.6	5.6	1.3	0.8	1.8	2.5	2.6
Finland	16.2	39.0	56.0	61.0	9.2	3.7	2.2	0.8	1.8	2.0	2.1
France	..	390.0 (4)	430.0	456.0	..	2.0 (4)	1.5	..	1.9 (4)	2.0	2.3
Germany	..	411.0	534.0	572.0	..	2.7	1.7	..	1.6	1.6	1.8
Italy	157.0	196.0	337.0	375.0	2.2	5.6	2.7	..	1.0	2.9	2.9
Japan (5)	788.0	1 254.0	1 711.0	1 808.0	5.3	2.6	1.1	1.7	2.3	2.8	2.7
Netherlands	43.5	72.0	109.0	100.0	5.2	4.2	-2.1	..	1.9	1.6	1.9
Norway	..	20.0	28.0	32.0	..	3.4	3.4	..	1.3	2.2	2.4
Spain	..	165.0 (6)	244.9	249.6	..	5.1 (6)	0.5	..	1.3 (6)	1.3	1.4
Sweden	..	43.4	53.0	58.6	..	2.0	2.5	..	1.1	1.9	1.9
United Kingdom	1 048.0	1 696.0	466.1	520.8 (2)	4.9	..	2.8 (2)	1.9	2.4	2.8	2.9 (2)
United States	1 353.4	2 140.0	2 482.0	2 978.0 (2)	4.7	3.9	3.7 (2)	1.6	2.0	2.5	3.1 (2)
7 OECD Countries (7)	1 353.4	2 140.0	3 190.1	3 623.4	4.7	4.1	3.2	1.6	2.0	2.5	2.7
of which: 6 European	(305.4)	(444.0)	(708.1)	(753.4)	(3.8)	(4.8)	(1.6)	(0.9)	(1.3)	(1.9)	(2.0)
12 OECD Countries (8)	..	..	4 480.0	4 991.5	..	..	2.7	..	..	2.3	2.5
of which: 11 European	..	..	(1 998.0)	(2 121.5)	..	..	(1.5)	..	..	(2.0)	(2.1)

Total Employed Persons

For comparison:

Country	1960	1970	1980	1984	1960/1970	1970/1980	1980/1984
7 OECD Countries (7)	87 233	105 825	126 935	133 290	2.0	1.8	1.2
of which: 6 European	(33 044)	(34 945)	(36 529)	(36 958)	(0.6)	(0.4)	(0.3)
12 OECD Countries (8)	..	..	192 144	196 376	..	..	0.6
of which: 11 European	..	..	(101 738)	(100 044)	..	..	(-0.4)

1. Excluding insurance.
2. 1985 and 1980-1985.
3. Data relate to domestic offices of chartered banks.
4. 1975 and 1975-1980.
5. Data relate to financial institutions (including government financial institutions) and insurance companies; and to the following years: 1960, 1969, 1981, 1986.
6. 1972 and 1972-1980.
7. Austria, Belgium, Denmark, Finland, Italy, Netherlands, United States.
8. Austria, Belgium, Denmark, Finland, France, Germany, Italy, Netherlands, Norway, Spain, Sweden, United States.

Sources: OECD National Accounts (Table 15), National Submissions.

Table 3.1

GROWTH OF FINANCIAL INSTITUTIONS 1960-1984

(Compound annual rates of growth of balance-sheet totals)

		Commercial Banks	Other Deposit Institutions	Special Credit Institutions	Finance Companies	Insurance Companies	Pension Funds	Investment Funds	Financial Institutions Total
Australia	1960-1970	7.2	10.3	17.5	...	11.3	11.6	4.1	9.7
	1970-1980	14.5	16.9	7.2	...	12.1	14.1	8.8	14.5
	1980-1984	22.6	13.5	31.6	4.7	13.7	20.8	12.0	15.7
Austria	1960-1970	14.2	13.9	...	...	14.7	...	20.9	14.2
	1970-1980	18.1	16.8	...	...	13.5	...	11.8	17.7
	1980-1984	7.5	11.6	...	...	...	...	20.1	8.6
Belgium	1960-1970	16.9	15.0	12.5	...	...	...	-0.2	...
	1970-1980	18.1	10.8	9.8	...	...	...	-5.6	...
	1980-1984	19.3	10.8	...	...	19.4	...	108.8	16.4
Canada	1960-1970	10.9	13.1	14.7	8.8	6.2	10.5	14.5	10.4
	1970-1980	17.9	19.1	15.2	9.9	9.8	16.5	5.5	16.1
	1980-1984	7.1	6.2	8.2	0.2	11.6	16.6	16.2	8.6
Denmark	1960-1970	11.2	...	...	...	9.1	11.6	...	10.8
	1970-1980	14.1	...	...	...	14.9	17.0	...	14.5
	1980-1984	16.3	...	...	...	18.6	25.7	57.5	...
Finland	1960-1970	14.5	10.9	17.9	...	15.9	17.8	–	13.7
	1970-1980	16.2	17.3	18.7	...	19.7	15.0	–	17.2
	1980-1984	22.7	17.3	16.5	57.0	16.4	18.8	–	20.0
Germany	1960-1970	12.4	13.0	9.7	...	13.6	9.2	13.0	12.5
	1970-1980	10.7	13.6	8.2	...	12.6	11.5	17.4	12.2
	1980-1984	5.3	7.0	8.9	...	11.1	13.7	13.2	7.6
Italy	1960-1970	16.0	16.9	17.1	...	...	...	...	16.4
	1970-1980	18.8	18.8	15.9	...	...	...	...	18.3
	1980-1984	15.2	15.7	16.2	...	...	...	...	15.5
Japan	1960-1970	17.0	22.0	18.5	...	23.8	...	17.0	18.7
	1970-1980	14.1	16.1	20.7	...	16.6	...	17.1	16.3
	1980-1984	10.4	8.2	11.6	...	12.3	...	18.6	10.9
Netherlands	1960-1970	15.3	13.3	11.6	...	8.8	14.9	12.9	13.3
	1970-1980	19.0	12.8	10.3	...	11.7	15.9	9.0	15.0
	1980-1984	8.2	6.6	8.6	...	9.9	11.9	11.2	8.9
Spain	1960-1970	18.4	22.9	16.2	...	19.9	...	4.9	...
	1970-1980	22.1	22.9	18.7	...	...	...	...	...
	1980-1984	18.3	21.1	22.1	...	10.1	...	20.1	...
Sweden	1960-1970	10.1	9.0	18.6	...	5.9	54.6	6.8	12.4
	1970-1980	14.8	12.1	14.3	26.2	12.7	15.1	12.6	14.3
	1980-1984	15.1	8.9	16.3	26.0	16.9	9.8	46.4	14.8
United States	1960-1970	8.3	8.7	14.9	8.8	5.9	11.4	10.7	8.4
	1970-1980	10.7	12.3	15.4	11.6	9.8	13.6	11.4	11.5
	1980-1984	9.8	10.9	11.2	10.3	10.0	12.4	28.1	11.3

Source: Country submissions.

Table 3.2

CHANGE IN RELATIVE IMPORTANCE OF FINANCIAL INSTITUTIONS 1960-1984
(Per cent of assets of all financial institutions; end-year)

		Commercial Banks	Other Deposit Institutions	Special Credit Institutions	Finance Companies	Insurance Companies	Pension Funds	Investment Funds	Financial Institutions Total
Australia	1960	37	27	1	..	23	10	2	100
	1970	29	29	2	..	27	12	1	100
	1980	25	30	1	16	18	10	0	100
	1984	31	28	1	11	17	11	1	100
Austria	1966	78	22	..	..	..	..	0	100
	1970	75	20	..	..	5	..	0	100
	1980	77	19	..	..	4	..	0	100
	1984	74	21	..	..	4	..	1	100
Belgium	1980	58	9	27	..	6	..	0	100
	1984	64	7	21	..	7	..	1	100
Canada	1960	39	12	6	6	24	11	2	100
	1970	40	16	9	5	16	11	3	100
	1980	47	20	9	3	9	11	1	100
	1984	44	19	9	2	10	15	1	100
Denmark	1961	71	..	..	..	24	5	0	100
	1970	74	..	..	..	20	6	0	100
	1980	71	..	..	..	21	7	1	100
Finland	1960	35	42	5	..	12	6	-	100
	1970	38	32	7	..	15	8	-	100
	1980	34	32	8	2	18	6	-	100
	1984	37	30	7	4	16	6	-	100
Germany	1960	31	40	13	..	12	2	2	100
	1970	30	42	10	..	14	2	2	100
	1980	26	48	7	..	14	2	3	100
	1984	25	47	7	..	16	2	3	100
Italy	1960	64	18	18	..	..	..	..	100
	1970	62	18	20	..	..	..	..	100
	1980	65	19	16	..	..	..	..	100
	1984	64	20	16	..	..	..	..	100
Japan	1960	52	19	17	..	5	..	7	100
	1970	45	25	17	..	7	..	6	100
	1980	38	24	24	..	7	..	7	100
	1984	37	22	25	..	7	..	9	100
Netherlands	1960	23	26	14	..	16	17	4	100
	1970	27	26	12	..	11	20	4	100
	1980	38	22	8	..	8	22	2	100
	1984	38	20	8	..	8	24	2	100
Spain	1980	63	26	8	..	2	..	1	100
	1984	61	28	9	..	2	..	0	100
Sweden	1960	39	22	13	-	23	1	2	100
	1970	32	16	22	1	13	15	1	100
	1980	34	13	22	3	11	16	1	100
	1984	34	11	23	4	12	14	2	100
United States	1960	38	19	2	5	23	10	3	100
	1970	37	20	3	5	19	13	3	100
	1980	35	21	5	5	16	15	3	100
	1984	33	21	5	4	15	16	6	100

Source: Country submissions.

125

Table 3.3

GROWTH OF BANKING SYSTEMS 1960-1985

| | Compound Annual Rates of Growth of Total Assets of Deposit Money Banks (1) | | | | | | Outstanding Amounts Billion Current US$ | |
| | Current US$ | | | Constant US$ (1) | | | | |
	1960/1970	1970/1980	1980/1985	1960/1970	1970/1980	1980/1985	End-1960	End-1985
North America	8.5	11.6	9.4	8.5	11.8	9.7	238	2 528
of which: United States	(8.3)	(11.2)	(9.8)	(8.3)	(11.2)	(9.8)	(226)	(2 314)
Europe	14.1	19.5	4.1	14.3	17.4	13.7	150	4 059
of which: Germany	(15.2)	(18.2)	(2.3)	(13.7)	(11.1)	(7.1)	(40)	(982)
United Kingdom	(11.8)	(21.2)	(8.7)	(13.6)	(21.2)	(20.3)	(27)	(849)
France	(14.8)	(21.8)	(1.8)	(16.2)	(19.3)	(12.8)	(16)	(500)
Italy	(24.5)	(15.1)	(2.0)	(15.6)	(19.8)	(14.7)	(19)	(364)
Switzerland	(13.2)	(15.9)	(6.5)	(13.2)	(6.0)	(10.0)	(13)	(262)
OECD - Asia (2)	16.7	21.2	9.2	16.7	14.9	9.6	42	2 078
of which: Japan	(18.3)	(21.7)	(9.5)	(18.3)	(15.0)	(9.3)	(33)	(1 996)
OECD Total	11.7	17.1	6.7	11.8	15.0	11.9	430	8 666
Memorandum Items:								
Nominal GDP Growth Rates (1980 exchange rates)								
OECD Total				8.8	11.8	9.0		
of which: United States				7.0	10.3	8.0		
Europe				9.1	12.6	10.5		
Japan				16.5	12.6	5.7		

1. US$ exchange rates at beginning of each period.
2. Includes Japan, Australia, New Zealand.

Source: IMF International Financial Statistics (Data on Commercial Banks or Deposit Money Banks).
OECD National Accounts (Data on GDP growth).

Table 3.4

EXPANSION OF BANKING NETWORKS 1960-1984

	Number of Bank Offices (1)				Compound Annual Rates of Growth			Density of Networks Number of Bank Offices per 100 000 Inhabitants			
	1960	1970	1980	1984	1960/1970	1970/1980	1980/1984	1960	1970	1980	1984
Australia	6 509	10 037	10 829	10 538	4.4	0.8	-0.7	63	80	80	68
Austria	2 829	3 261	4 971	5 331 (2)	1.4	4.3	1.4 (2)	40	44	66	71
Belgium	1 870	3 151	3 811	3 741 (2)	5.4	1.9	-0.4 (2)	20	33	39	38
Canada	5 060	6 184	7 437	7 331 (2)	2.0	1.9	-0.3 (2)	28	29	31	29
Denmark	2 368	3 465	3 707	3 581	3.9	0.7	-0.9	52	70	72	70
Finland	2 696	3 318	3 376	3 531	2.1	0.2	1.1	61	72	71	73
(3)	4 973	6 221	6 557	6 742	2.3	0.5	0.7	112	135	137	138
France	..	..	24 725 (4)	25 385 (4)	..	..	0.9 (4)	..	..	45	46
(3)	..	..	41 895 (4)	42 573 (4)	..	..	0.5 (4)	..	77	77	77
Germany	30 027	40 800	44 666	44 698	3.1	0.9	0.02	54	67	73	73
(3)	56 340	65 867	63 539	62 625	1.6	-0.4	-0.4	101	108	103	102
Italy	9 211	10 807	12 175	12 965	1.6	1.4	1.6	19	20	22	23
Japan (5)	31 943	35 597	40 697	44 078 (2)	1.1	1.3	1.6 (2)	34	34	35	37
(3)	47 721	56 148	62 984	67 050 (2)	1.6	1.2	1.3 (2)	51	54	54	56
Netherlands	3 459	5 177	7 399	6 529	4.1	3.6	-3.1	30	40	52	45
(3)	5 640	7 700	9 430	9 220	3.2	2.0	-0.6	49	59	67	64
Spain	..	12 642	24 566	31 117	..	6.9	4.8	..	37	66	81
(3)	..	14 105	26 165	32 867	..	6.4	4.7 (2)	..	42	70	85
Sweden	3 535	4 238	3 659	3 557	1.8	-1.5	-0.7	47	53	44	43
Switzerland	2 412	2 979	3 784	3 874	2.1	2.4	0.6	45	48	59	60
United Kingdom (6)	..	..	19 796	20 541 (2)	..	..	0.7 (2)	..	..	35	37
(3)	..	..	42 435	42 204 (2)	..	..	-0.1 (2)	..	..	76	75
United States	23 688	35 112	53 189	56 866	4.0	4.2	1.7	13	17	23	24

1. Head offices plus branches.
2. 1985 and 1980-85, respectively.
3. Including post offices offering retail banking services.
4. 1982, 1985; 1982-1985.
5. 1960 partly estimated.
6. Including building societies.

Sources: Country submissions (number of bank and post offices).
IMF International Financial Statistics (population).

Table 3.5
EXPANSION OF ATM NETWORKS 1978-1986 (1)
(Number of machines installed at the end of year)

	a) Absolute Number			b) Number per million Inhabitants		
	1978	1983	1986	1978	1983	1986
Belgium	..	517	655	..	52	66
Canada	250	1 960	3 241	11	79	127
France	1 000	4 500	9 500	19	82	172
Germany	..	790	4 053	..	13	66
Japan	12 800	37 900	60 000	111	318	494
United Kingdom	2 189	5 745	10 330	39	102	182
United States	9 750	48 118	69 161	44	205	286

1.   Cash dispensers (CDs) and Automated Teller Machines (ATMs).

Source: Country submissions and BIS; IFS (for population data).

Table 3.6

GROWTH OF INSTITUTIONS FOR COLLECTIVE INVESTMENT (ICIs) 1980-1986

	Number of Funds (end of period)		Total Assets (amounts outstanding at end-period in US$ billion)		For Comparison (Compound annual rate of growth of outstanding amounts)		
	1980	1986	1980	1986	ICIs	1980-1986 Shares	Bonds
France (1)	245	3 025	14.8	151.5	47.4	15.0	18.8
Germany (2)	496	1 065	24.0	67.3	18.8	11.2	23.8
Japan (3)	n.a.	n.a.	28.8	190.6	37.0	20.7	29.4
Luxembourg (4)	76	261	3.8	26.2	38.0	53.0	36.8
Switzerland (5)	120	165	8.6	17.4	12.5	14.1	20.2
United Kingdom (6)	655	1 120	32.4	78.0	15.8	13.0	14.9
United States (7)	n.a.	n.a.	138.1	715.9	31.6	19.2	10.2

1. Organismes de Placement Collectif en Valeurs Mobilières OPCVM (i.e. SICAV and FCP).
2. Including funds offered to the public and special funds (Kapitalanlagegesellschaften).
3. Investment trusts.
4. Organismes de Placement Collectif.
5. Fonds de placement (Anlagefonds).
6. Unit Trusts and Investment Trusts.
7. Mutual funds (incl. money market mutual funds).

Sources: France: Commission des Opérations de Bourse; Germany: Deutsche Bundesbank; Japan: Bank of Japan; Luxembourg: Institut Monétaire Luxembourgeois; United Kingdom: Central Statistical Office and Bank of England; United States: Federal Reserve Board.

Table 4.1

DEVELOPMENT OF MARKETS FOR SHORT-TERM SECURITIES 1980-1986

	Year of Introduction	Amounts outstanding (end-year; billion national currency)						
		1980	1981	1982	1983	1984	1985	1986
Negotiable Treasury Bills								
Australia (end-June)	1962	1.7	3.7	3.9	4.1	2.3	2.9	7.4
Canada	1976	20.5	20.5	25.4	38.6	49.3	59.1	69.5
Denmark	1976	21.4	33.3	36.2	40.7	37.8	28.8	27.5
France	1986	–	–	–	–	–	–	226.9
Italy (1 000 billion)	1975	73.8	107.5	140.1	151.2	160.5	173.7	183.4
Netherlands	before 1900	14.3	16.5	18.5	18.3	17.4	17.1	15.7
Norway	1985	–	–	–	–	–	8.6	8.4
Portugal	1985	–	–	–	–	–	350.0	500.0
Sweden	1982	–	–	38.0	58.0	71.0	100.0	93.0
United Kingdom	1982	3.9	2.2	1.8	1.8	1.9	2.0	2.0
United States	1929	216.1	245.0	311.8	343.8	374.4	399.9	426.7
Negotiable Certificates of Deposits								
Australia (end-June)	1969	3.4	2.6	3.4	3.6	4.1	5.9	5.3
France	1985	–	–	–	–	–	27.5	59.3
Italy (1 000 billion)	1983	–	–	–	3.3	7.5	13.3	21.4
Japan (1 000 billion)	1979	2.4	3.3	4.4	5.7	8.5	9.7	9.9
Netherlands	1986	–	–	–	–	–	–	1.9
Norway	1985	–	–	–	–	–	0.5	1.6
Sweden	1980	14.0	14.0	18.0	23.0	18.0	10.0	5.0
U.K. Sterling	1968	5.7	6.7	8.5	9.8	11.2	12.8	16.8
U.K. Foreign currency	1966	21.0	40.4	57.3	70.5	79.7	64.1	70.9
United States	1961	115.9	137.0	132.3	91.7	n.a.	n.a.	n.a.
Negotiable Bankers Acceptances								
Australia (end-June)	1965	5.3	7.1	9.9	13.2	17.3	19.0	28.3
Canada	1962	5.4	6.6	12.7	14.0	14.0	17.0	24.9
Italy (1 000 billion)	1978	2.5	3.6	2.7	1.6	0.6	0.4	0.3
Japan	1985	–	–	–	–	–	0.0	0.0
United Kingdom	1985	5.6	8.7	22.2	14.9	19.1	21.2	24.2
United States	1913	54.7	69.2	79.5	78.3	78.4	68.4	65.0
Commercial Paper								
Australia (end-June)	1973	n.a.	n.a.	2.1	3.3	3.6	3.9	6.1
Canada	1951	10.2	9.3	7.7	9.9	11.3	10.1	10.3
France	1985	–	–	–	–	–	3.3	24.0
Netherlands	1986	–	–	–	–	–	–	0.4
Norway	1985	–	–	–	–	–	2.5	5.2
Sweden	1983	–	–	–	1.0	10.0	17.0	30.0
United Kingdom	1986	–	–	–	–	–	–	0.7
United States	18th century	121.6	161.1	161.8	183.5	231.8	293.9	326.1
Finance Company Paper								
Australia (end-June)	1950s	n.a.	n.a.	n.a.	n.a.	11.9	13.5	15.1
Canada	1951	3.6	3.5	1.8	2.4	3.0	4.1	6.1
France	1986	–	–	–	–	–	–	0.2
Norway	1985	–	–	–	–	–	3.5	1.9
Sweden		26.0	26.0	34.0	49.0	55.0	67.0	93.0

Source: Country submissions and national financial statistics.

130

Table 4.2

GROWTH OF NEW ISSUE MARKETS FOR BONDS 1962-1986

(Billion Current US$)

	1962-1970 Cumulative		1971-1975 Cumulative		1976-1980 Cumulative		1981-1985 Cumulative		1986	
	Net	Gross	Net	Gross	Net	Gross	Net	Gross	Net	Gross
I. National Bond Markets (1)										
1. North America	176.2	436.1	314.8	560.2	702.0	1 167.2	1 413.6	2 333.6	511.7	750.5
Domestic issues	164.2	412.6	303.0	545.0	674.4	1 132.7	1 413.6(2)	2 296.9(2)	511.7(2)	744.6(2)
Foreign issues	12.0	23.5	11.8	15.9	27.6	34.5	.	36.7	.	5.9
of which: US	162.9	392.8	295.4	524.8	652.1	1 095.3	1 413.6	2 324.1	511.7	750.5
Domestic issues	150.9	369.4	283.6	509.0	624.6	1 061.6	1 413.6	2 296.9	511.7	744.6
Foreign issues	12.0	23.4	11.8	15.8	27.5	33.7	.	27.2	.	5.9
2. OECD Europe	134.3	221.0	264.7	416.8	543.1	958.8	780.2	1 418.4	216.9	430.8
Domestic issues	133.1(3)	218.0(3)	262.0	407.7	535.8(4)	922.2(4)	751.8(5)	1 346.4(6)	204.1(7)	402.9(8)
Foreign issues	1.2(9)	3.0	2.7(10)	9.1	7.3(10)	36.6	28.4(11)	72.0	12.8(11)	27.9
3. Japan	45.7	88.4	125.7	222.5	397.8	672.5	543.2	1 063.2	201.5	428.4
Domestic issues	45.7	88.7	125.7	220.2	397.8	659.7	543.2	1 042.1	201.5	423.6
Foreign issues	.	0.2	.	2.3	.	12.8	.	21.1	.	4.8
4. OECD Total	356.2	745.5	705.2	1 200.2	1 642.9	2 798.5	2 737.0	4 815.2	930.1	1 609.7
Domestic issues	343.0	718.8	620.7	1 172.9	1 608.0	2 714.6	2 708.6	4 685.4	917.3	1 571.1
Foreign issues	13.2	26.7	14.5	27.3	34.9	83.9	28.4	129.8	12.8	38.6
II. International Bond Market (12)	..	17.9(13)	..	33.5	..	98.6	..	359.0	..	187.0
Memorandum items:										
III. New Issues of shares										
OECD Total	..	101.5(14)	..	140.3	..	208.6(15)	..	360.6(16)	..	132.7(17)
of which: US		35.4		54.4		68.3		165.6		61.8
Japan		16.3		20.4		28.3		41.8		8.2

1. Excluding Australia, Ireland, New Zealand, Turkey. Figures for Denmark, France, Germany, Greece, Spain and Sweden do not include private placements; shares and net issues of bonds for Japan and Switzerland do not include private placements.
2. For Canada no figures for 1983 and 1986 available.
3. Austria since 1965, Portugal since 1963, excluding Luxembourg.
4. Portugal since 1978.
5. Excluding Portugal.
6. Excluding Portugal, Sweden.
7. Excluding Greece, Norway, Portugal and Sweden.
8. Excluding Norway, Portugal, Sweden.
9. Excluding Belgium, Luxembourg, Netherlands.
10. Excluding Belgium, Netherlands.
11. Excluding Austria, Belgium.
12. Including DM-foreign bonds.
13. Since 1963.
14. Austria since 1965, Portugal since 1963, Switzerland since 1965, excluding Luxembourg.
15. Excluding Denmark.
16. Excluding Denmark, Portugal. for Belgium no figures for 1985 and 1986 available, for Canada no figures for 1983 and 1986 available.
17. Excluding Belgium, Canada, Denmark, Finland, Norway, Portugal, Spain.

Source: OECD Financial Statistics.

131

Table 4.3

BOND ISSUES IN SELECTED OECD COUNTRIES 1980-1986

(Net Issues)

	1980	1981	1982	1983	1984	1985	1986
				US$ billion			
France	21.46	14.93	17.70	19.46	22.34	26.41	38.45
Germany	24.32	29.19	30.43	33.82	25.12	26.64	40.36
Japan	90.54	105.84	94.90	127.29	114.24	102.46	202.61
Netherlands	2.49	3.32	5.85	7.00	6.53	4.60	3.05
United Kingdom	25.79	15.39	11.33	14.01	13.29	13.24	12.86
United States	136.50	145.70	205.80	268.80	333.30	460.00	523.20
TOTAL	301.10	314.37	366.01	470.38	514.82	633.35	820.53

Memorandum Item:

Estimated net issues
of Eurobonds and
traditional foreign
bonds:

US$ billion	28.0	32.0	58.5	58.0	83.0	125.0	156.0
Ratio to "Total" (above)	9.3	10.2	16.0	12.3	16.1	19.7	19.0

Sources: Net bond issues on domestic markets: OECD Financial Statistics
Monthly; Estimated net issues of eurobonds and traditional foreign
bonds: BIS Annual Reports.

Table 4.4

GROWTH OF SECONDARY BOND MARKETS 1964-1985

| | Compound Annual Rates of Growth of Outstanding Amounts | | | | | | Outstanding Amounts | |
| | Current US$ | | | Constant US$ (1) | | | Current US$ | |
	1964/1970	1970/1980	1980/1985	1964/1970	1970/1980	1980/1985	End-1964	End-1985
North America	7.1	10.7	15.0	6.9	10.9	15.3	403	3 363
of which: United States	(6.7)	(10.9)	(15.4)	(6.7)	(10.9)	(15.4)	(367)	(3 106)
OECD - Europe (2)	10.1	17.3	7.4	10.8	14.8	16.8	123	1 551
of which: Germany	(13.1)	(20.0)	(7.8)	(11.5)	(12.8)	(12.8)	(23)	(425)
Italy	(17.5)	(13.7)	(10.7)	(17.5)	(18.4)	(24.5)	(17)	(276)
United Kingdom	(1.4)	(14.9)	(8.0)	(4.1)	(15.0)	(19.4)	(39)	(253)
France	(8.3)	(18.6)	(9.3)	(10.5)	(16.2)	(21.2)	(12)	(169)
Japan	18.2	29.4	13.2	18.2	22.3	12.9	20	1 362
OECD Total (14 countries)	8.3	14.7	12.5	8.6	13.6	15.1	546	6 276
For comparison:								
Growth of National Banking Systems								
North America	8.7	11.6	9.4	8.6	11.8	9.7	327	2 528
OECD - Europe (2)	13.9	19.2	4.2	14.5	17.3	13.7	219	3 394
Japan	16.5	21.7	9.5	16.5	15.0	9.3	71	1 996
OECD Total (14 countries)	11.6	16.8	7.0	11.8	14.7	11.7	617	7 919

1. 1980 US$ exchange rates.
2. Austria, Belgium, Denmark, Finland, France, Germany, Italy, Norway, Spain, Sweden, United Kingdom.

Sources: OECD Financial Statistics (Outstanding amounts of bonds issue on national bond markets).
IMF International Financial Statistics (Data on Deposit Money Banks or Commercial Banks).

Table 4.5

MARKET VALUE OF QUOTED SECURITIES END-1980 AND END-1986

	Amounts Outstanding at the End of Period in US$ Billion				Compound Annual Rates of Growth 1980-1986	
	Bonds		Shares			
	1980	1986	1980	1986	Bonds	Shares
Austria	14.18 (1)	43.48 (1)	1.96	6.65	20.5 (1)	22.6
Belgium	46.18	79.15	10.03	37.34	9.4	24.5
Canada (Toronto)	n.a.	n.a.	118.35	185.20	n.a.	7.8
Denmark	56.50 (1)	131.55 (1)	5.54	17.36	15.1 (1)	21.0
France	125.16	289.90	54.62	153.42	15.0	18.8
Germany	316.66 (1)	597.16 (1)	71.72	257.68	11.2 (1)	23.8
Italy	106.29 (1)	274.25 (1)	25.34	140.24	17.1 (1)	33.0
Japan (Tokyo)	248.37	767.48	379.21	1 783.64	20.7	23.4
Luxembourg	50.15 (1)	641.70 (1)	3.99	26.16	52.9	36.8
Netherlands	33.88	103.60	29.37	83.71	20.5	19.1
Norway	7.34	22.98	3.19	10.12	21.0	21.2
Spain (Madrid)	13.15	41.33	16.56	48.93	21.0	19.8
Switzerland (Zurich)	53.94	118.69	42.73	128.65	14.1	20.2
United Kingdom	215.38	447.45	205.18	472.90	13.0	14.9
United States (NYSE)	507.77	1 457.60	1 190.53	2 128.51	19.2	10.2
TOTAL	1 794.95	5 016.22	2 158.32	5 480.51	18.7	16.8

1. Nominal Value.

Source: International Federation of Stock Exchanges.

Table 4.6

DEVELOPMENT OF SECOND AND THIRD MARKET SEGMENTS FOR EQUITIES 1980-1986

Country Market (1)		Established in:	1980	1981	1982	1983	1984	1985	1986
ITALY									
Mercati Ristretti	A(2) Number	May 1978	..	..	36	35	37	35	..
	B(2) Bill Lira		..	..	138	89	75	155	..
	C(2) Bill Lira		..	..	8 753	8 044	6 292	7 885	..
UNITED KINGDOM									
Unlisted Securities Market	A Number	November 1980	23	86	135	204	268	337	368
(VMS)	B Mill £		52	282	620	1 226	1 469	1 705	2 757
	C Mill £		..	..	1 109	2 361	2 863	3 424	4 983
NETHERLANDS									
Parallel Market	A Number	Januay 1981		..	18	22	31	42	51
	B Mill GLD			..	56	354	624	1 889	5 228
	C Mill GLD			..	18	474	806	1 858	..
DENMARK									
Segment III	A Number	February 1982			1	8	24	23	34
	B Mill DKR				1	6	16	537	..
	C Mill DKR				4	173	859	1 384	..
FRANCE									
Second Marché	A Number	February 1983				42	72	127	181
	B Mill FF					2	3	10	30
	C Mill FF					9	20	52	112
BELGIUM									
Second Marché	A Number	January 1985						1	..
GERMANY									
"Geregelter Markt" (Regulated Market)		May 1987							
UNITED KINGDOM									
Third Market		May 1987							

1. Ordered according to year of establishment.
2. A = Number of listed companies; B = Transaction volume in billion or million national currency; C = Market value at end-period in billion or million national currency.

Source: Hartmut Schmidt, Freiverkehrsmaerkte an Europas Börsen, in "Die Bank", June 1987, and EEC Stock Exchanges Statistical Study.

Table 4.7

STOCK EXCHANGE VOLUME OF TRADING IN EQUITIES 1980-1986

	US$ Billion							Compound Average Annaul Rate of Growth 1980-1986
	1980	1981	1982	1983	1984	1985	1986	
Australia (1)	n.a.	7.94	5.11	9.33	10.80	15.26	22.63	24.3 (2)
Austria	0.11	0.08	0.07	0.13	0.11	0.80	1.20	48.9
Belgium	2.16	1.56	1.91	2.65	2.74	3.63	5.68	17.5
Canada (3)	28.54	23.71	16.57	28.63	25.99	39.25	48.60	9.3
Denmark	0.06	0.06	0.06	0.18	0.17	1.27	1.60	72.9
Finland	n.a.	n.a.	n.a.	0.25	0.42	0.50	1.60	85.7 (4)
France (Paris)	13.44	11.83	9.56	8.35	10.15	19.82	47.60	23.5
Germany (5)	18.09	15.57	16.61	32.95	35.46	94.21	130.33	39.0
Italy	8.57	10.85	12.79	3.87	4.05	15.35	38.35	28.4
Japan (6)	180.23	255.75	165.30	266.07	337.76	454.10	947.76	31.9
Luxembourg	n.a.	n.a.	n.a.	0.02	0.06	0.07	0.13	86.6 (4)
Netherlands	5.36	4.30	5.08	10.18	12.46	20.00	26.06	30.2
New Zealand	n.a.	n.a.	n.a.	n.a.	n.a.	0.91	2.15	136.3 (7)
Norway	0.08	0.10	0.10	0.91	1.34	2.11	1.45	62.1
Spain (Madrid)	0.78	1.28	1.14	0.96	1.78	3.16	10.71	54.7
Sweden	1.80	3.67	4.62	9.89	8.52	10.85	16.97	45.4
Switzerland (8)	(96.22)	(90.76)	(112.55)(#)	(218.71)	(229.99)	(354.98)	(425.12) (31.89) (9)	
United Kingdom (London)	35.82	32.84	32.74	42.58	48.28	76.36	113.89	21.8 (9)
United States (NYSE)	374.91	389.22	488.40	765.28	764.74	970.48	1 374.35	24.2
TOTAL	766.17(#)	849.52	862.61(#)	1 400.94	1 484.02(#)	2 083.11	3 215.29 (3 077.55) (10)	26.1 (10)

1. Australian Association of Stock Exchanges.
2. 1981-1986.
3. Toronto and Montreal.
4. German Federation of Stock Exchanges.
5. 1983-1986.
6. Tokyo and Osaka.
7. 1985-1986.
8. Including bonds: 1980-1982: Zürich and Basle; 1983-1986 Zürich, Basle, Geneva.
9. Excluding Geneva.
10. 1980-1986; excluding Australia, Finland, Luxembourg, New Zealand and Geneva.

#: Break in series.

Source: International Federation of Stock Exchanges.

Table 4.8

DEVELOPMENT OF FINANCIAL FUTURES MARKETS 1981-1986

Country	Number of Traded Contracts (1000)					
Type of Contract	1981	1982	1983	1984	1985	1986

I. UNITED STATES

1. Short-term interest rate futures

	1981	1982	1983	1984	1985	1986
US Treasury Bills (90 days) (1)	5 631	6 599	3 790	3 292	2 413	1 815
Domestic CDs (90 days) (1)	423	1 556	1 079	929	84	3
Euro-$ deposits (3 months)	15	324	891	4 193	8 901	10 825
TOTAL	6 069	8 479	5 760	8 414	11 398	12 643
[Number of types of contracts] (3)	[8]	[6]	[4]	[4]	[4]	[4]

2. Long-term interest rate futures

	1981	1982	1983	1984	1985	1986
US Treasury Notes (6.5-10 years) (1)	0	881	815	1 662	2 860	4 426
US Treasury Bonds (2)	14 017	17 159	19 817	30 214	40 745	53 067
GNMA Mortgages	2 293	2 056	1 692	862	84	24
TOTAL	16 310	18 040	22 324	32 738	43 689	57 517
[Number of types of contracts] (3)	[7]	[5]	[6]	[5]	[4]	[5]

3. Foreign exchange futures

	1981	1982	1983	1984	1985	1986
	6 123	6 689	11 872	13 789	16 912	19 032
[Number of types of contracts] (3)	[12]	[7]	[12]	[12]	[12]	[13]

4. Stock index futures

	1981	1982	1983	1984	1985	1986
	0	4 912	12 753	18 532	21 834	25 390
[Number of types of contracts] (3)	0	[6]	[6]	[6]	[10]	[10]

5. GRAND TOTAL

	1981	1982	1983	1984	1985	1986
	28 502	38 120	52 709	73 473	93 833	114 582

II. UNITED KINGDOM (LIFFE only)

1. Short-term interest rate futures

	1981	1982	1983	1984	1985	1986
Three Month Sterling		40	201	341	493	959
Three Month Eurodollar		122	459	1 024	1 282	1 107
TOTAL		163	660	1 365	1 775	2 065

2. Long-term interest rate futures

	1981	1982	1983	1984	1985	1986
Long Gilt		29	527	775	685	2 618
Short Gilt					43	61
US T-Bond				167	627	1 546
Japanese Government Bond (introduced in 1987)						
TOTAL		29	527	942	1 355	4 225

Table 4.8 (contd.)

DEVELOPMENT OF FINANCIAL FUTURES MARKETS 1981-1986

Country Type of Contract	1981	1982	1983	1984	1985	1986
3. Currency futures						
Sterling		42	122	145	117	41
Deutschemark		7	26	28	20	16
Dollar Mark						1
Swiss Franc		1	12	13	7	6
Japanese Yen		1	19	12	10	8
TOTAL		51	179	198	154	71
4. Stock index futures						
FT-SE 100				73	89	122
5. GRAND TOTAL		243	1 365	2 578	3 372	6 485
III. AUSTRALIA						
1. Interest rate futures						
90 Day Bank Bills	28	145	161	172	594	1 074
Ten Year Treasury Bonds				2	242	1 431
Two Year Treasury Bonds (delisted March 1986)				107		
Three Year Treasury Bonds (commenced trading 17/5/88)						
2. Currency futures						
US Dollar (delisted 16/9/88)	32	43	43	60	59	44
Australian Dollar (commenced trading 23/2/88)						
3. Stock index futures						
All Ordinaries Share Price Index Futures			180	237	282	466
4. Linked contracts						
US Treasury Bonds (linked with LIFFE)						7
Euro-dollars (linked with LIFFE)						1
Comex Gold (linked with Comex)						4
5. GRAND TOTAL	60	188	384	578	1 177	3 027

Number of Traded Contracts (1000)

Table 4.8 (contd.)

DEVELOPMENT OF FINANCIAL FUTURES MARKETS 1981-1986

Country	Number of Traded Contracts (1000)					
Type of Contract	1981	1982	1983	1984	1985	1986
IV. FRANCE						
Long-term interest rate futures						
Treasury bonds (10 years)						1 600 (4)
V. JAPAN						
Long-term interest rate futures						
Treasury bonds					45 (5)	937 (5)

1. Chicago Mercantile Exchange only.
2. Chicago Board of Trade and Midamerican Commodity Exchange.
3. Contracts in the same or similar instruments traded on different exchanges are counted separately.
4. Operations started in March 1986.
5. Yen 1 000 billion; Trading started on 19th October 1985.

Sources: United States: Futures Industry Association; France: The Paris Financial Futures Exchange (MATIF); Japan: The Bond Underwriters' Association of Japan ("Bond Review"); United Kingdom: The London International Financial Futures Exchange (LIFFE); Australia: Sydney Future Exchange Ltd.

Table 4.9

DEVELOPMENT OF FINANCIAL OPTIONS MARKETS 1981-1986 (1)

Country Type of Contract	Number of Traded Contracts (1000)					
	1981	1982	1983	1984	1985	1986
I. UNITED STATES						
1. Options on short-term interest rate futures						
US Treasury bills						64
Euro-dollar deposits					743	1 757
2. Options on long-term interest rate futures						
US Treasury notes					177	1 001
US Treasury bonds	..	19	1 664	6 636	11 901	17 314
3. Foreign exchange options				726	2 216	4 412
4. Stock index options			588	919	1 286	2 182
5. Grand Total	119	2 252	8 281	16 323	26 730	
II. UNITED KINGDOM (LIFFE only)						
1. Options on short-term interest rate futures						
Three month sterling						
Three month euro-dollar					31	39
Total					31	39
2. Options on long-term interest rate futures						
Long Gilt						279
US T-Bond						52
Total						331

Table 4.9 (contd.)

DEVELOPMENT OF FINANCIAL OPTIONS MARKETS 1981-1986 (1)

Country Type of Contract	Number of Traded Contracts (1000)					
	1981	1982	1983	1984	1985	1986
3. Currency Options						
Sterling					140	105
Dollar Mark						9
Total					140	114
4. Stock index options						
FT-SE 100						3
5. Grand Total					<u>171</u>	<u>487</u>
III. AUSTRALIA						
1. Options on Interest Rate Futures						
90 Day Bank Bills					12	31
Ten Year Treasury Bond					6	183
Three year Treasury Bonds (commenced trading 16/6/88)						
2. Options on Currency Futures						
US Dollar						2
Australian Dollar (commenced trading 15/3/88)						
3. Options on Stock Index Futures						
All Ordinaries Share Price Index futures					3	27
4. Grand Total					<u>21</u>	<u>243</u>

1.   Excluding options on individual shares or bonds.

Sources: See Table 4.8.

Table 5.1

GROWTH OF HOUSEHOLDS' FINANCIAL ASSETS AND LIABILITIES 1960-1984

	Compound Annual Growth Rates			Growth Rate Differential vis-à-vis All Domestic Non-financial Sectors' Financial Assets/Liabilities (1)			Ratio to All Domestic Non-financial Sectors' Financial Assets/Liabilities			
	1960/1970	1970/1980	1980/1984	1960/1970	1970/1980	1980/1984	1960	1970	1980	1984
Financial Assets										
Australia	9.8	14.5	12.0	1.1	1.1	0.5	66.9	67.8	74.8	76.1
Canada	8.6 (2)	13.8	9.9	-0.4 (2)	0.6	0.4	60.8 (2)	58.9	61.7	62.6
Germany	13.5	11.5	7.5	2.4	1.3	-	44.8	55.6	62.8	62.9
Italy	11.5 (3)	19.2	19.1	1.3 (3)	-0.8	1.4	57.3 (3)	62.3	58.3	61.1
Japan	18.4	17.0	10.6	-0.6	1.9	1.5	45.8	43.6	51.1	54.0
Sweden	..	9.6	13.7	..	-2.3	-0.7	..	52.3	42.5	41.5
United States	7.1	8.9	10.0	0.2	-0.2	0.7	78.6	79.4	77.6	79.6
Liabilities										
Australia	9.1	14.5	13.5	2.0	2.5	-1.2	22.3	26.8	33.4	32.1
Canada	11.7 (2)	14.5	5.4	2.8 (2)	1.1	-4.2	14.3 (2)	17.9	19.6	16.8
Germany	13.6	15.9	5.9	2.7	5.3	-1.8	3.0	3.8	6.1	5.7
Italy	13.7 (3)	16.9	15.9	4.2 (3)	-4.1	-4.6	4.2 (3)	5.5	3.9	3.3
Japan	21.3	16.5	8.8	2.1	1.8	0.3	15.9	19.0	22.3	22.5
Sweden	..	13.6	11.0	..	-0.3	-3.8	..	26.3	25.7	22.5
United States	8.2	11.6	9.6	1.2	0.9	-1.3	29.1	32.6	35.2	33.7

1. Annual rate of growth of households' financial assets/liabilities minus annual rate of growth of all domestic non-financial sectors' financial assets/liabilities.

2. 1961-70 and 1961, respectively.

3. 1963-70 and 1963, respectively.

Source: Country submissions.

Table 5.2

GROWTH OF ENTERPRISES' FINANCIAL ASSETS AND LIABILITIES 1960-1984

	Compound Annual Growth Rates			Growth Rate Differential vis-à-vis All Domestic Non-financial Sectors' Financial Assets/Liabilities (1)			Ratio to All Domestic Non-financial Sectors' Financial Assets/Liabilities			
	1960/1970	1970/1980	1980/1984	1960/1970	1970/1980	1980/1984	1960	1970	1980	1984
Financial Assets										
Australia	8.4	15.1	12.4	-0.3	1.7	0.9	12.4	12.1	14.0	14.5
Canada	10.1 (2)	13.8	8.8	1.1 (2)	0.6	-0.7	21.2 (2)	23.1	24.2	23.6
Germany	11.3	10.7	8.9	0.2	0.5	1.4	23.1	23.6	24.6	26.0
Italy	8.0 (3)	21.4	17.1	-2.2 (3)	1.4	-0.6	34.9 (3)	30.3	34.1	33.4
Japan	20.0	12.9	6.9	1.0	-2.2	-2.2	47.0	51.2	42.0	38.7
Sweden	..	15.3	17.0	..	3.4	2.6	..	29.9	40.2	43.9
United States	6.9	10.1	6.6	-	1.0	-2.7	17.0	16.9	18.5	16.7
Liabilities										
Australia	8.9	11.8	16.9	1.8	-0.2	2.2	28.7	33.9	33.6	36.2
Canada	8.9 (2)	13.4	8.6	- (2)	-	-1.0	60.3 (2)	60.2	60.1	58.0
Germany	11.2	9.4	6.8	0.3	-1.2	-0.9	79.4	81.6	73.2	70.9
Italy	7.7 (3)	20.1	17.7	-1.8 (3)	-0.9	-2.8	73.1 (3)	65.3	60.6	55.1
Japan	18.7	12.2	6.9	-0.5	-2.5	-1.6	79.5	76.6	61.7	58.3
Sweden	..	12.4	12.2	..	-1.5	-2.6	..	62.2	54.3	49.5
United States	9.0	10.7	9.2	2.0	-	-1.7	37.2	44.9	44.6	42.1

1. Annual rate of growth of enterprises' financial assets/liabilities minus annual rate of growth of all domestic non-financial sectors' financial assets/liabilities.

2. 1961-70 and 1961, respectively.

3. 1963-70 and 1963, respectively.

Source: Country submissions.

143

Table 5.3

GROWTH OF GOVERNMENT SECTOR'S FINANCIAL ASSETS AND LIABILITIES 1960-1984

	Compound Annual Growth Rates			Growth Rate Differential vis-à-vis All Domestic Non-financial Sectors' Financial Assets/Liabilities (1)			Ratio to All Domestic Non-financial Sectors' Financial Assets/Liabilities			
	1960/1970	1970/1980	1980/1984	1960/1970	1970/1980	1980/1984	1960	1970	1980	1984
Financial Assets										
Australia	8.3	6.9	7.1	-0.4	-6.5	-4.4	20.7	20.1	11.2	9.4
Canada	8.9 (2)	10.6	8.9	- (2)	-2.6	-0.6	18.0 (2)	18.0	14.1	13.8
Germany	6.4	4.8	4.2	-4.7	-5.4	-3.3	32.1	20.8	12.6	11.1
Italy	9.4 (3)	20.2	9.0	-0.8 (3)	0.2	-8.7	7.9 (3)	7.5	7.6	5.5
Japan	15.3	18.2	10.8	-3.7	3.1	1.7	7.2	5.2	6.9	7.3
Sweden	..	11.6	9.7	..	-0.3	-4.7	..	17.8	17.3	14.6
United States	5.0	9.7	8.0	-1.9	0.6	-0.7	4.4	3.7	3.9	3.7
Liabilities										
Australia	4.7	10.0	13.5	-2.4	-2.0	-1.2	49.0	39.3	33.0	31.7
Canada	7.1 (2)	12.5	15.9	-1.8 (2)	-0.9	6.3	25.4 (2)	21.9	20.2	25.2
Germany	8.8	14.5	11.1	-2.1	3.9	3.4	17.6	14.6	20.7	23.4
Italy	13.5 (3)	23.4	25.4	4.0 (3)	2.4	4.9	22.7 (3)	29.2	35.5	41.6
Japan	18.6	30.6	13.4	-0.6	15.9	4.9	4.6	4.4	16.0	19.2
Sweden	..	20.4	24.8	..	6.5	10.0	..	11.5	20.0	28.0
United States	2.8	9.5	16.1	-4.2	-1.2	5.2	33.7	22.5	20.2	24.2

1. Annual rate of growth of government sector's financial assets/liabilities minus annual rate of growth of all domestic non-financial sectors' financial assets/liabilities.

2. 1961-70 and 1961, respectively.

3. 1963-70 and 1963, respectively.

Source: Country submissions.

Table 6.1

GROWTH OF EXTERNAL FINANCIAL ASSETS AND LIABILITIES OF SELECTED OECD COUNTRIES 1960-1984

	Amounts Outstanding at end-period Billion US$ at 1980 exchange rates				Compound Annual Rates of Growth			Growth Rate Differential vis-à-vis all Domestic Non-financial Sectors' Financial Assets/Liabilities (1)		
	1960	1970	1980	1984	1960/1970	1970/1980	1980/1984	1960/1970	1970/1980	1980/1984
External Financial Assets (2)										
Australia	0.71	1.89	7.79	17.12	10.3	15.2	21.8	1.6	1.8	10.3
Belgium	2.79 (3)	12.11	85.38	211.59	15.8	21.6	25.5	7.6	10.3	16.5
Canada	6.86 (3)	21.51	88.39	138.36	12.1	15.2	11.9	4.0	2.0	2.4
Denmark	1.20	2.84	15.88	34.08	9.0	18.8	21.0	..	..	..
Finland	0.63	1.72	10.10	24.84	10.6	19.4	25.2	0.4	-0.1	2.5
Germany	32.26	95.61	249.36	364.57	11.5	10.1	10.0	..	4.1	11.8
Japan	..	27.50 (4)	159.60	341.20	..	19.2	20.9	..	1.8	3.6
Spain	..	4.63 (5)	32.99	74.83	..	21.7	22.7	..	4.2	4.5
Sweden	..	5.03	22.41	44.82	..	16.1	18.9	..	..	..
United Kingdom	103.30	183.20 (6)	543.50	1 486.10	..	19.9 (6)	28.6	..	0.1	-3.8
United States	147.75	204.10	491.00	608.70	7.1	9.2	5.5	0.2	0.1	..
Seven OECD countries (7)	..	339.78	947.90	1 399.26	8.7	10.8	10.2	..	0.7	2.8
Eight OECD countries (8)	..	372.38	1 136.92	1 801.19	..	11.8	12.2	..	..	..
External Liabilities (2)										
Australia	3.42	9.80	26.80	71.90	11.1	10.6	28.0	2.2	-2.8	18.4
Belgium	4.43 (3)	14.41	77.22	165.36	12.5	18.3	21.1	4.3	5.7	9.1
Canada	20.10 (3)	46.71	177.70	270.78	8.8	14.3	11.1	-0.1	0.9	1.5
Denmark	1.26	5.32	32.45	71.49	15.5	19.8	21.8	..	..	..
Finland	0.68	2.71	17.53	39.24	14.8	20.5	22.3	..	..	..
Germany	20.78	69.47	220.57	320.67	12.9	12.3	9.8	2.0	1.7	2.1
Japan	..	18.70 (4)	148.00	266.90	..	23.0	15.9	..	8.3	7.4
Spain	..	4.81 (5)	49.64	117.47	..	26.3	24.0	..	5.5	4.1
Sweden	..	3.89	34.07	92.16	..	24.2	28.3	..	10.3	13.5
United Kingdom	40.60	177.70 (6)	504.90	1 292.20	..	19.0 (6)	26.5	..	4.3	0.7
United States	91.27	99.00	399.60	620.80	9.3	15.0	11.6	2.3	..	..
Seven OECD countries (7)	..	247.42	951.87	1 560.24	10.5	14.4	13.2	..	3.4	4.0
Eight OECD countries (8)	..	266.79	1 133.60	1 926.04	..	15.6	14.2	..	..	..
Memorandum Items:										
Eight OECD countries (8)										
Domestic non-financial sectors										
a) Financial assets	..	4 041.67	11 542.68	16 530.25	..	11.1	9.4			
b) Liabilities	..	3 128.00	9 898.40	14 577.84	..	12.2	10.2			

1. Annual rates of growth of external financial assets/liabilities minus annual rates of growth of financial assets/liabilities of all domestic non-financial sectors.
2. External financial assets and liabilities of all domestic sectors.
3. Scaled down from 1961 data.
4. Scaled down from 1971 data.
5. Scaled down from 1972 data.
6. 1974 and 1974-1980, respectively.
7. Australia, Belgium, Canada, Denmark, Finland, Germany, United States i.e. countries for which data for 1960 to 1984 are available.
8. Australia, Belgium, Canada, Germany, Japan, Spain, Sweden, United States i.e. countries for which data on financial assets and liabilities of all domestic non-financial sectors are available.

Source: Country Submissions.

Table 6.2

GROWTH OF FOREIGN ASSETS OF BANKS 1960-1985

| | Compound Annual Rates of Growth of External Assets of Deposit Money Banks | | | | | | Outstanding Amounts Billion Current US$ | |
| | Current US$ | | | Constant US$ (1) | | | | |
	1960/1970	1970/1980	1980/1985	1960/1970	1970/1980	1980/1985	End-1960	End-1985
North America	10.6	26.2	0.5	10.6	26.6	1.1	8	232
of which: United States	10.8	29.5	-0.2	10.8	29.5	-0.2	5	190
OECD - Europe	27.7	24.6	7.3	27.1	23.0	17.6	9	1 394
of which: Germany	29.1	19.5	5.8	28.1	12.3	10.7	1	113
United Kingdom	36.5	25.5	10.2	38.7	27.5	27.8	2	585
France	27.7	30.8	2.4	29.2	28.1	14.1	1	167
Italy	27.3	11.9	8.2	27.3	16.2	21.8	1	46
Switzerland	24.6	15.0	5.1	24.6	5.2	8.6	2	85
OECD - Asia (2)	22.1	23.1	18.4	22.1	16.5	18.2	1	127
of which: Japan	22.7	23.3	18.6	22.8	16.5	18.3	1	126
OECD Total	21.3	24.8	6.8	21.7	23.4	15.3	18	1 753

Memorandum items:

Total Assets of Deposit Money Banks

| | Compound Annual Rates of Growth | | | | | | Outstanding Amounts | |
	1960/1970	1970/1980	1980/1985	1960/1970	1970/1980	1980/1985	End-1960	End-1985
OECD Total	11.7	17.1	6.7	11.8	15.0	11.9	430	8 666
of which: United States	8.3	11.2	9.8	8.3	11.2	9.8	226	2 314
Europe	14.1	19.5	4.1	14.3	17.4	13.7	150	4 049
Japan	18.3	21.7	9.5	18.3	15.0	11.9	33	1 996

1. US$ exchange rate at beginning of each period.
2. Includes Japan, Australia and New Zealand.

Source: IMF International Financial Statistics.

Table 6.3

EXPANSION OF INTERNATIONAL BANKING NETWORKS 1960-1986
(at end-period)

1. Foreign Banking Presence in OECD Countries (1)

Host country	1960	1970	1980	1984	1985	1986
Australia	3	3	2	2	10	18 (2)
Austria	..	..	17	22	22	22
Belgium	14 (3)	26	51	56	57 (4)	..
Canada	0	0	0	..	57 (4)	..
Denmark	0	0	5	..	8	8
Finland	0	0	0	3	..	..
France	33	58	122	147	148	152
Germany	24	77	213	..	283 (4)	..
Greece	2	3	18	..	19	..
Italy	1	4	25	34	36	36
Japan: banks	34	38	85	108	114	115
Japan: securities firms	..	..	5	11	22	38
Luxembourg	3	23	99	103	106	110
Netherlands	1	23	39	42	41	42
New Zealand	3	3	3	3	3	3 (5)
Norway	-	-	-	-	7	7
Spain	4	4	25	45	47	49
Sweden	0	0	0	0	0	12
Switzerland	8	97	99	119	120	125
United Kingdom	51 (6)	95	214	..	293 (4)	..
United States (7)	..	79 (8)	153	233	234	243

147

Table 6.3 (contd.)

EXPANSION OF INTERNATIONAL BANKING NETWORKS 1960-1986
(at end-period)

2. Presence of Domestic Banks Abroad (1)

Home Country	1960	1970	1980	1984	1985	1986
Australia	..	..	..	..	..	85
Austria (9)	0	0	1	3	5	5
Belgium (10)	5	6	14	27	..	..
Denmark	0	0	18	41	50	56
France	..	..	..	351	385	455
Germany	3	8	126	..	164	..
Ireland	60	84	224	..	276	..
Italy (9)	17	22	44	69	74	75
Japan: banks	37	67	213	294	346	380
Japan: securities firms	..	..	39	56	62	82
Netherlands	3	55	145	171	171	170
New Zealand	1	1	1	1	1	1
Norway	1	6	16	18	23	27
Spain (9)	5	25	82	135	133	136
Sweden	0	0	7	21	19	17
Switzerland	..	..	71	76	79	79
United States (11)	8	79	159	163	162	151
	(131)	(532)	(787)	(917)	(916)	(899)

1. Number of branches and subsidiaries if not otherwise indicated; subsidiaries and branches of overseas subsidiaries are generally excluded.
2. End-June 1988; does not include savings bank subsidiaries.
3. End-1958.
4. End-June 1985.
5. 1987: 12.
6. End-1962.
7. United States branches and agencies of foreign banks.
8. 1975
9. Branches only.
10. Three large banks.
11. Number of Federal Reserve member banks with foreign branches; figures in brackets: number of foreign branches of these banks.

Sources: Country submissions; BIS, Recent Innovations in International Banking, April 1986; Japan 1980-1986: Bank of Tokyo.

148

Table 6.4

NUMBER OF FOREIGN COMPANIES WITH SHARES LISTED ON
STOCK EXCHANGES 1976, 1980, 1986, 1987

	1976	1980	1986	1987
Australia	23	n.a.	31	40
Austria	29	35	39	43
Belgium	150	152	140	145
Canada (Toronto)	72	68	51	61
Canada (Montreal)	26	24	20	22
Denmark	4	4	7	8
France (Paris)	160	162	195	202
Germany	135	175	181	212
Italy (Milan)	1	0	0	0
Japan (Tokyo)	17	15	52	88
Japan (Osaka)	0	0	0	0
Luxembourg (1)	69	94	168	171
Netherlands	318	294	239	227
Norway	n.a.	n.a.	7	8
Spain (Madrid)	3	2	-	-
Spain (Barcelona)	0	1	-	-
Sweden	0	0	7	7
Switzerland (Zurich)	127	156	194	213
Switzerland (Geneva)	144	175	207	225
Switzerland (Basel)	135	159	192	209
United Kingdom (London)	370	482	584	597
United States (New York S.E.)	35	37	59	70
United States (American S.E.)	65	55	49	51
United States NASDAQ	n.a.	n.a.	244	272
TOTAL	1 883 (2)	2 090 (3)	2 666	2 871

1.   Data include investment funds (32 in 1986).
2.   Excluding Norway and the NASDAQ market in the U.S.
3.   Excluding Australia, Norway and the NASDAQ market in the U.S.

Sources: International Federation of Stock Exchanges and NASDAQ Fact Books.

Table 6.5

CROSS-BORDER TRANSACTIONS IN SECURITIES 1980-1986 (1)

(Net Flows)

(US$ billion) (2)

	1980	1981	1982	1983	1984	1985	1986	For Comparison: Ratio of cross-border transactions in securities to net issues on domestic securities markets	
								1980	1986
1. Net purchases of foreign securities by residents of:									
France	2.08	2.18	-0.26	1.68	0.46	2.45	6.00	7.9	10.3
Germany	4.24	2.67	4.69	4.06	5.53	10.71	9.48	15.1	19.8
Japan	3.75	8.78	9.74	16.02	30.80	59.77	101.98	3.9	48.4
Netherlands	-0.17	0.09	1.05	1.03	0.93	2.11	6.74	-6.3	161.2
United Kingdom	7.51	8.72	11.76	9.89	12.76	23.72	29.94	26.8	124.3
United States	3.57	5.70	7.98	6.76	4.76	7.48	3.30	2.2	0.6
TOTAL	20.98	28.14	34.96	39.44	55.24	106.24	157.44	6.1	16.9
2. Non-resident net purchases of domestic securities issued in:									
France	2.40	1.81	6.98	7.26	7.56	8.87	7.81	9.1	13.4
Germany	0.48	0.45	1.14	5.32	6.13	14.30	34.05	1.7	71.1
Japan	13.11	13.22	11.86	14.15	7.19	16.74	0.55	13.5	0.3
Netherlands	2.99	1.18	1.08	1.39	0.76	2.59	1.73	111.6	41.4
United Kingdom	3.49	0.66	0.39	2.86	1.90	9.16	11.78	12.5	48.9
United States (3)	8.10	9.83	13.11	16.85	35.57	71.40	79.08	5.1	13.5
TOTAL	30.57	27.15	34.56	47.83	59.11	123.06	135.00	8.9	14.5

1. Data include new issues and redemptions as well as secondary market transactions.
2. Conversion at average annual exchange-rates (Source: IFS).
3. Excluding net purchases of US securities by foreign official institutions i.e. central banks etc.

Sources: Data on cross-border transactions in securities: National balance-of payments statistics; data on net issues on domestic securities markets: OECD Financial Statistics Monthly.

Table 6.6

CROSS-BORDER TRANSACTIONS IN SECURITIES 1980-1986
(Gross Flows)

| | Gross Purchases and Sales in US$ Billion (1) | | | | | | | Compound Average Annual Rate of Growth |
	1980	1981	1982	1983	1984	1985	1986	1980-1986
1. Resident transactions in foreign securities								
France	33.00	34.60	42.88	66.04	68.32	99.29	153.77	29.2
Germany	45.31	38.21	63.00	73.47	85.52	118.79	183.41	26.2
Japan	28.44	14.63	29.99	36.86	89.01	539.17	2 635.74	112.7
United States	53.12	59.49	76.64	106.23	146.70	212.09	438.53	42.2
TOTAL	159.87	146.93	212.51	282.60	389.55	969.34	3 411.45	66.5
2. Non-resident transactions in domestic securities								
France	11.67	13.00	22.00	26.34	28.28	53.03	100.63	43.2
Germany	15.16	14.95	18.86	30.91	41.84	90.39	219.50	56.1
Japan	46.34	91.82	89.45	137.20	205.18	279.18	591.40	52.9
United States	198.03	226.98	296.36	435.16	639.52	1 285.27	2 554.55	53.1
TOTAL	271.20	346.75	426.67	629.61	914.82	1 707.87	3 466.08	52.9
For Comparison:								
Secondary market transaction volume								
France	25.04	23.81	30.05	37.41	54.56	94.53	293.08	50.7
Germany	45.76	38.39	53.07	72.68	82.35	148.10	277.48	35.0
Japan (2)	1 362.79	1 531.69	1 460.57	1 852.13	3 201.84	9 404.71	16 494.78	51.5
United States (2)	1 872.90	2 514.90	6 319.20	5 141.10	6 515.20	10 140.40	14 765.50	41.1
TOTAL	3 306.49	4 108.79	7 862.89	7 103.32	9 853.95	19 787.74	31 830.84	45.9

1. Conversion at average annual exchange rates (Source: IFS).
2. Including government bond transactions on the OTC (Over-the-Counter) market.

Sources: France: Ministère de l'Economie, des Finances et de la Privatisation and Banque de France, "La Balance des Paiements de la France", Rapports Annuels.

Germany: Deutsche Bundesbank, Statistical Supplements to the Monthly Reports, Series 3, Balance of Payments Statistics.

Japan: Foreign Department and Bank of Japan, Balance of Payments Monthly.

United States: U.S. Treasury Bulletin, Federal Reserve Bulletin, NASDAQ Fact Books.

Annex III

DOCUMENTATION ON MEASURES AFFECTING COMPETITION IN BANKING AND ON DIVERSIFICATION OF FINANCIAL SERVICE ACTIVITIES

The present Annex has been prepared with a view to providing factual material in support of the description of policies towards efficient financial systems given in Chapter 3 of the present study. It contains detailed documentation on regulatory changes affecting competition in banking and on diversification of financial services activities which has resulted from, and at the same time contributed to, greater competition in the vast area of financial service markets. Although it has not been possible to provide an exhaustive record of all deregulation measures taken by the authorities in OECD countries in the field of banking and finance in the period covered by the study — 1960–1985/86 — an effort has been made to extend the coverage of the survey as much as possible. It would not have been possible to compile this factual information without assistance from the Members of the Expert Group on Banking.

I. INTEREST–RATE DEREGULATION

The present note provides a country–by–country list of measures designed to widen the scope for interest rate competition in the financial system. The measures comprise both the abolition, or easing of, official interest rate controls and the prohibition or abolition of interest rate agreements amongst banks or other financial institutions. Measures designed to increase the market element in the financial system by the introduction of new marketable or negotiable instruments, notably money market instruments, are listed in Section II. Each country section starts with information on interest rate controls or cartels existing at the beginning of the sixties and ends with information on remaining interest rate controls and cartels (if any) that were in force at the end of 1986/1987.

AUSTRALIA

Interest Rate Restrictions at the End of 1960

Prohibition of interest payments on cheque accounts.

Maximum interest rates on:

— Time deposits (4.5 per cent p.a.);
— Overdrafts (7 per cent p.a. provided the average rate did not exceed 6 per cent p.a.);
— Housing loans (as for overdrafts).

Changes in Restrictions on Interest Rates 1961–1986

July 1967 and May 1968	Exemptions from the long–standing interest rate maximum and applying to overdrafts and housing loans granted to short–term mortgage and bridging loans (July 1967) and leasing (May 1968).
Feb. 1972 and Feb. 1976	The maximum interest rate on overdrafts and housing loans and applies only to amounts under A$50 000 (February 1972). This limit was increased to under A$100 000 in February 1976.
Dec. 1980	Official interest rate ceilings on all bank deposits removed. (However, banks were prohibited from paying interest on deposits with short maturities until August 1984.)
Aug. 1984	Banks permitted to pay interest on all cheque accounts. Maturity controls on bank deposits were abolished.
April 1985	The maximum interest rate on overdrafts (applying to amounts of under A$100 000 since February 1976) abolished.
April 1986	The maximum interest rate on loans for owner–occupied housing (applying to amounts under A$100 000 since February 1976) abolished.

Remaining Restrictions on Interest Rates (end–1986)

None.

AUSTRIA

Interest Rate Restrictions at the End of 1960

Official agreement on bank deposit rates (so–called "Habenzinsabkommen").

Changes in Restrictions on Interest Rates 1961–1986

July 1980	Abolition of deposit rate agreement ("Habenzinsabkommen") Agreement on interest rate payable on standard (i.e. 3 months) savings accounts remains in force.

March 1985	Reintroduction of interest rate controls through the Interbank Regulatory Policy Agreement on bank lending and deposit rates ("Ordnungspolitische Vereinbarungen") designed to limit interest rate competition and competition through advertising.

Remaining Restrictions on Interest Rates (end–1986)

Interbank agreement on bank lending and deposit rates (introduced in March 1985).

BELGIUM

Interest Rate Restrictions at the End of 1960

All bank lending and deposit rates tied to the interest rates applied by the Belgian National Bank; interest rates on current accounts subject to interbank agreements.

Changes in Restrictions on Interest Rates 1961–1986

1962	Creation by the Belgian Bankers Association of a Creditor Rate Committee fixing deposit rates for all banks in agreement with the Belgian National Bank.
1964	Interest rates on large deposits (BF 30 million and over) exempted from the interbank agreement.
1966	Interest rates on savings books (carnets de dépôts) also fixed by the Creditor Rate Committee; certain banks — List B — not covered by the agreement.
1970	Creation of a Committee for Concerted Action on the Harmonization of Creditor Rates comprising representatives from banks, public–sector financial institutions and private savings banks. The Committee operates under the control of the monetary authorities (Belgian National Bank and Ministry of Finance).
1974	Creation by the Belgian Bankers Association of a Committee on Concerted Action on Debitor Rates (however, banks remain free to fix debitor rates at their discretion); the Belgian Na-

tional Bank encourages banks to untie their lending rates from the central bank's rates.

1979   Certain banks no longer adhere to the interbank agreement on deposit rates.

1980   Interest rates on deposits of BF 1 to 5 million fixed in line with market conditions.

1984   Introduction of rules on the remuneration of savings books (carnets de dépôts) with a view to moderate price competition in this area.

1986   Maximum interest rates on savings accounts (passbook savings) are fixed by law.

Remaining Restrictions on Interest Rates (end–1986)

Maximum interest rates on savings accounts (passbook savings) fixed by law.

The interest rate on current accounts fixed by interbank agreement (0.5 per cent per annum).

CANADA

Interest Rate Restrictions at the end of 1960

Maximum interest rate on bank loans of 6 per cent per annum.

Interbank agreement on bank lending and deposit rates.

Changes in Restrictions on Interest Rates 1961–1986

1967   Abolition of the maximum interest rate on bank loans; prohibition of the interbank agreement on bank lending and deposit rates.

Remaining Restrictions on Interest Rates (end–1986)

None.

DENMARK

Interest Rate Restrictions at the End of 1960

Interbank agreement on maximum rates on deposits. Bank lending and deposit rates usually changed with the official discount rate.

Changes in Restrictions on Interest Rates 1961–1986

1973   Abolition of interbank agreement on maximum rates on deposits.

Spring 1975 to March 1979   Indirect interest rate regulation by way of ceilings on commercial banks' and savings banks' interest rate margins ("Interest Rate Margins Act").

Jan. 1978 to Dec. 1982   Cartel agreement between the seven largest banks and savings to banks on interest rate ceiling on large deposits (special term deposits).

March 1978 to March 1979   Temporary interbank agreement on a maximum for average deposit rates.

March 1979   Interest rates on bank deposits in principle subject to control under general price and antitrust laws ("The Prices and Profits Act").

March 1978 to July 1981   Agreement between Denmark's National Bank and individual banks regulating the banks' average lending rates (movements of average lending rates linked to official discount rate changes). The motivation for the agreement was an attempt to reduce the impact of worldwide interest rate increases on the domestic economy in a period of recession.

July 1981   Expiry of the agreement between Denmark's National Bank and the banks on average lending rates (introduced in March 1979).

Dec. 1982   Expiry of the cartel agreement between the seven largest banks and savings banks on interest rate ceilings on large deposits (special term deposits) concluded in January 1978.

Remaining Restrictions on Interest Rates (end–1986)

Bank lending and deposit rates only subject to supervision under general price and antitrust laws ("The Prices and Profits Act" of March 1979 aimed at encouraging competition).

FINLAND

Interest Rate Restrictions at the End of 1960

Official ceilings on bank lending rates.

Changes in Restrictions on Interest Rates 1961–1986

1971	Abolition of ceilings on banks' average lending rates.
1979	Central bank sets ceilings on banks' average lending rates.
1984	Restrictions on interest rates on short-term business loans abolished.
1986	All restrictions on interest rates on new credits and average lending rates abolished.

Remaining Restrictions on Interest Rates (end–1986)

None.

FRANCE

Interest Rate Restrictions at the End of 1960

Direct control on bank lending and deposit rates.

Changes in Restrictions on Interest Rates 1961–1986

April 1966	Deregulation of bank lending rates.
Dec. 1966	Law on usury interest rates (setting maximum interest rates on loans at twice the primary bond market yield).
June 1967	New regulation on interest rates on bank deposits and other bank liabilities: *i)* prohibition from paying interest on current accounts; *ii)* controlled interest rates on time deposits and cash bonds (bons de caisse) below specified (relatively large)

amounts with maturities of less than a specified number of months; and controlled interest rates on savings books and the savings–for–housing scheme; unregulated interest rates on all other deposits and similar deposit instruments.

1967–86	Several changes in the minimum amounts and maturities applying to time deposits and similar instruments with unregulated interest rates.

Remaining Restrictions on Interest Rates (end–1986)

The regulation on interest rates introduced in June 1967 still in force: i.e. interest payments on current accounts prohibited and interest rates on time deposits below specified (relatively large) amounts with maturities of a specified number of months and on savings accounts controlled.

GERMANY

Interest Rate Restrictions at the End of 1960

Official agreement on bank lending and deposit rates ("Soll– und Haben-zinsabkommen")

Changes in Restrictions on Interest Rates 1961–1986

March 1965	Official agreement on bank lending and deposit rates replaced by Interest Rate Decree ("Zinsabkommen") deregulating interest rates on long–term bank loans (with maturities of 4 years and over) and longer–term deposits (with maturities of 2 1/2 years and over).
April 1967	Abolition of Interest Rate Decree i.e. full deregulation of bank lending and deposit rates.

Remaining Restrictions on Interest Rates (end–1986)

None.

GREECE

Interest Rate Restrictions at the End of 1960

Statutory ceilings on bank lending and deposit rates.

Changes in Restrictions on Interest Rates 1961–1981

June 1978	Interest rates in the interbank market freely determined.
June 1981 to May 1983	Banks free to determine interest rates on special time deposits, subject to an upper limit.
Sept. 1984	Creation of a forward market in convertible drachmas (implying freely determined interest rates on convertible drachma balances).
March 1985	Commercial banks permitted to offer housing loans at freely negotiable interest rates (exceeding 21.5 per cent per annum). Loans falling into this category cannot exceed 2 per cent of the previous year's deposit liabilities.
Nov. 1985	A minimum interest rate for working capital loans set at one percentage point above the rate applicable to savings deposits with commercial banks.
June 1986	A minimum interest rate set for medium- and long-term loans equal to the rate applicable to savings deposits with commercial banks. Abolition of housing loans extended at subsidised interest rates.
July 1987	A minimum interest rate of 21 per cent set on all working capital loans to which maximum interest rates of 20 per cent to 21.5 per cent previously applied. The minimum interest rates on short-term and long-term loans raised by one percentage point to 17 per cent and 16 per cent respectively.
Nov. 1987	Interest rates on time deposits and savings deposits on notice freely determined by the banks. Coupon rates and other conditions applying to new issues of bank bonds deregulated.
Dec. 1987	Financial institutions authorised to extend loans for fixed investment at freely negotiable interest rates.

Remaining Restrictions on Interest Rates (end–1987)

Only interest rates on loans to small-scale industry and on some categories of loans related to social housing schemes as well as the rate on savings deposits are administratively determined.

IRELAND

Interest Rate Restrictions at the End of 1960

Agreement between clearing banks on lending and deposit rates; rates set in consultation with the Central Bank.

Changes in Restrictions on Interest Rates 1961–1986

1985	Abolition of agreement between clearing banks on lending and deposit rates.

Remaining Restrictions on Interest Rates (end–1986)

None.

ITALY

Interest Rate Restrictions at the End of 1960

Interbank agreement on bank lending and deposit rates.

Changes in Restrictions on Interest Rates 1961–1986

1969	Expiry of the interbank agreement on interest rates.

Remaining Restrictions on Interest Rates (end–1986)

Direct control on interest rates on liabilities of special credit institutions.

JAPAN

Interest Rate Restriction at the End of 1960

Direct control on interest rates on all bank deposits and post office savings accounts.

Changes in Restrictions on Interest Rates
1961–1986

Oct. 1985 to April 1987   Ceiling on interest rates on large time deposits removed. Minimum amounts of large time deposits lowered in several steps from 1 million (October 1985) to Yen 100 million (April 1987).

Remaining Restrictions on Interest Rates
(end–1986)

Direct control on interest rates on bank deposits other than large time deposits i.e. smaller than Y 300 million and on post office savings accounts. Interest rates on negotiable deposit instruments such as certificates of deposit (CDs) and Money Market Certificates (MMCs) free.

NETHERLANDS

Interest Rate Restrictions at the End of 1960

No official control on bank lending and deposit rates: however, as a matter of practice bank lending rates tied to the official discount rate on promissory notes.

Changes in Restrictions on Interest Rates
1961–1986

None.

Remaining Restrictions on Interest Rates
(end–1986)

Although there is no official control on interest rates and there are no interbank agreements on bank lending and deposit rates, banks as a matter of practice change their lending rates in line with changes of the official discount rate on promissory notes. The differential between bank lending rates and the official discount rate may differ from bank to bank.

NEW ZEALAND

Interest Rate Restrictions at the End of 1960

Savings bank deposit rates were fixed and trading bank, building and investment society deposit rates were subject to maximum limits. The average rate on bank advances was regulated (at the time advances or overdrafts were almost the sole form of bank lending). Interest rates on contributory mortgages, debentures and preference shares were also controlled.

Changes in Restrictions on Interest Rates
1961–1986

1962   Interest rate controls on contributory mortgages, debentures and preference shares removed.
Ceilings on building and investment society deposit interest rates removed.

1969   Ceilings on trading bank interest rates for fixed deposits of more than $25 000 or for terms of more than two years removed.

1972   Regulations laying down maximum interest rates which financial institutions could pay reintroduced.

1974   Financial institutions secured deposits of more than five years exempt from 1972 regulations.

1975   Financial institutions secured deposits of between 3–5 years also exempt from 1972 regulations.

1976   Interest on Deposit Regulations of 1972 revoked, interest rate controls on trading bank deposits of more than $12 000 or terms of more than three years abolished, and restrictions on the average rate charged on bank advances abolished.

1977   Savings banks were given the freedom to set the structure and rates on their term deposits. This move effectively freed all trading bank term deposits still subject to restriction.

1981   Banks had to give the Reserve Bank fourteen days notice before increasing their interest rate charges on lending. If the increase was considered inappropriate (as it generally was) it could be disallowed.

1982   All deposit interest rates were frozen as part of a wage price freeze under an Interest on Deposit Order.

1983 The Minister of Finance on announcing reductions in government security interest rates indicated that government institution borrowing and lending rates would also be reduced and that he expected the private sector to follow suit.

Later in the year the Interest on Deposit Regulations were revoked.

Ceilings on mortgage interest rates introduced.

1984 Regulations placing maximum ceilings on mortgage rates extended to include all non-mortgage lending and Interest on Deposit Regulations reintroduced. Following a change of government in July all standing lending and deposit interest rate controls were removed including rules limiting savings banks to paying 3 per cent on their call savings accounts and rules restricting trading banks from paying interest on cheque accounts.

Remaining Restrictions on Interest Rates (end-1986)

None.

NORWAY

Interest Rate Restrictions at the End of 1960

Official control on all bank lending and deposit rates.

Changes in Restrictions on Interest Rates 1961-1986

1977 Official control on bank lending rates discontinued.

1978-80 General price freeze, also applicable to lending rates.

1980 Lending rates charged by banks (and life insurance companies) regulated by Interest Rate Declaration of the Minister of Finance. The Interest Rate Declaration set an upper limit on the average interest rate level for long-term loans (exceeding one year) and another limit on the average interest level for short-term loans (less than one year).

1985 Regulation of bank lending and deposit rates by the Interest Rate Declaration of the Minister of Finance discontinued.

Remaining Restrictions on Interest Rates (end-1986)

None.

PORTUGAL

Interest Rate Restrictions at the End of 1960

Official ceilings on all bank lending and deposit rates.

Changes in Restrictions on Interest Rates 1961-1987

June 1984 Deregulation of interest rates on deposits except time deposits with maturities of over 180 days up to one year.

Jan. 1985 Official fixing of a minimum interest rate on time deposits with maturities of over 180 days up to one year.

Aug. 1985 Deregulation of interest rates on loans with maturities of up to 90 days and over 180 days up to two years (official ceilings on rates were abolished).

Jan. 1987 Deregulation of interest rates on sight deposits.

Official fixing of *two* maximum interest rates on loans.

March 1987 Official fixing of just *one* maximum interest rate on loans.

Remaining Restrictions on Interest Rates (end-1987)

Maximum rate on bank lending, regardless of maturity.

Minimum rate on time deposits with maturities of over 180 days to one year.

SPAIN

Interest Rate Restrictions at the End of 1960

Direct control on all bank lending and deposit rates.

Changes in Restrictions on Interest Rates 1961–1987

July 1969   Bank of Spain discount rate created and most interest rates set in relation to it.
Deregulation of interest rates on:
— Loans with maturities of over 3 years;
— Deposits with maturities of over 2 years (applicable to
— industrial banks);
— Deposits in foreign currencies.

Aug. 1974   Deregulation of interest rates on:
— Loans with maturities of over 2 years;
— Deposits with maturities of over 2 years generalised (i.e. applicable to all banks);
— Loans with maturities of over 2 years;
— Deposits with maturities of over 2 years generalised (i.e. applicable to all banks).

July 1977   Deregulation of interest rates on loans with maturities of one year and over; and of interest rates on deposits with maturities of one year and over.

Jan. 1981   Deregulation of interest rates on all loans and other lending instruments not covered by legal investment requirements; and of interest rates on time deposits with maturities of 6 months and over and minimum amounts of Ptas 1 million.

March 1987   Deregulation of interest rates on all demand deposits, savings deposits and time deposits.

Remaining Restrictions on Interest Rates (end–1987)

None; except for interest rates on assets eligible for legal investment requirements.

SWEDEN

Interest Rate Restrictions at the End of 1960

Officially sanctioned interbank agreement on all bank lending and deposit rates and linkage of all interest rates with the official discount rate, as a matter of practice.

Changes in Restrictions on Interest Rates 1961–1986

1978   Banks formally authorised by Central Bank to set interest rates on deposit account at their discretion; however, interbank agreements continue to play a role.

1985   Average ceiling on bank lending rates abolished.

Remaining Restrictions on Interest Rates (end–1986)

None.

SWITZERLAND

Interest Rate Restrictions at the End of 1960

No official interest rate controls; however, there are a great number of local or regional interbank agreements, mainly on bank lending rates.

Changes in Restrictions on Interest Rates 1961–1986

None.

Remaining Restrictions on Interest Rates (end–1986)

No official interest–rate controls; however, a great number of interbank agreements, mainly on bank lending rates, continue to remain in force.

TURKEY

Interest Rate Restrictions at the End of 1960

Direct control on all bank lending and deposit rates.

Changes in Restrictions on Interest Rates 1961–1988

July 1980   Deregulation of all bank lending and deposit rates.

Dec. 1983   Central Bank was authorised to regulate interest rate on deposits.

July 1987   Interest rates on 1 year deposits and on Certificate of Deposits with denominations over TL 10 million were deregulated.

Feb. 1988   Central Bank set ceilings on deposit rates.

Oct. 1988   Deregulation of deposit rates.

Remaining Restrictions on Interest Rates (end–1988)

None.

UNITED KINGDOM

Interest Rate Restrictions at the End of 1960

London clearing banks' and Scottish banks' cartel agreement on bank lending and deposit rates and linkage of all rates with the official discount rate; Recommended Interest Rate System (of 1939) applied by building societies; Government control on National Savings interest rates.

Changes in Restrictions on Interest Rates 1961–1986

Sept. 1971   "Competition and Credit Control"; the interest rate cartel of London clearing banks and Scottish banks dismantled at official request; (Recommended Interest Rate System of building societies continued).

Since Autumn 1980   More active sale of National Savings instruments at competitive

1984   Recommended Interest Rate System of building societies discontinued.

Remaining Restrictions on Interest Rates (end–1986)

None.

UNITED STATES

Interest Rate Restrictions at the End of 1960

Statutory ceilings on interest rates on all deposits of banks and thrift institutions ("Regulation Q"); prohibition of interest payment on sight deposits and time deposits of up to 31 days. Some state limitations on interest rates allowed (on first mortgages, business, and agricultural loans).

Changes in Restrictions on Interest Rates 1961–1986

1978   Six month money market certificate (MMC) authorised for banks and thrifts. Permissible rate payable indexed to the 6 month Treasury bill rate.

1979   Small saver certificate (SSC) (4 year denomination) authorised for banks and thrifts. Ceiling rate based on 4–year yield of Treasury securities.

1980   Minimum maturity on SSCs reduced to $2^1/_2$ years.
The Depository Institutions Deregulation and Monetary Control Act permits banks, savings banks, savings and loan associations and credit unions to offer interest–bearing equivalents of checking accounts to non–business customers. A six–year phase out (until March 1986) of ceilings on interest rates on deposits ("Regulation Q") was adopted.
State laws limiting interest rates on first mortgages and business and agricultural loans pre–empted.
Negotiable order of withdrawal (NOW) accounts authorised for banks and thrifts to offer to individuals at a maximum rate of $5^1/_4$ per cent.

1981   All savers certificate (ASC) authorised. Ceiling rate set at 70 per cent of latest 52 week Treasury bill auction.
Ceiling free $1^1/_2$ year and over IRA/ Keogh account authorised.

1982   7–31 and 91 day indexed accounts authorised.
$2^1/_2$ to $3^1/_2$ year account indexed to $2^1/_2$ year treasury yields and $3^1/_2$ year and over ceiling free accounts authorised.
Money market deposit account (MMDA), a ceiling free account with limited transactions features, authorised.

1983   Super–Nows, an interest bearing transaction account without a rate ceiling for individuals authorised.

	Rate ceilings on all time deposits removed.
1984	Passbook (savings accounts) ceilings equalised at 5.5 per cent for banks and thrifts.
1985	Minimum balance requirements on MMDAs, 7–31 day and Super–Nows reduced to $1 000.
1986	All remaining minimum balances and interest rate ceilings removed (interest on demand deposits still prohibited).

Remaining Restrictions on Interest Rates (end–1986)

Prohibition of interest payments on demand deposits and time deposits with maturities of up to 7 days still in force although interest bearing equivalents of checking accounts continue to be available to non–business customers.

II. CREATION AND DEVELOPMENT OF MONEY MARKETS

In an effort to encourage competition and to strengthen the market element in the financial system, the authorities in Member countries often have not only deregulated interest rates on bank loans and deposits but have also created, or encouraged the creation or development of, money markets i.e. markets for bank deposits earning free market rates or for negotiable/marketable instruments such as certificates of deposit, bankers acceptances, commercial paper, Treasury bills etc. In fact, in a number of countries the interest rate deregulation process has started with the creation of such negotiable debt instruments rather than with the immediate deregulation of bank loan and deposit rates. The present note is intended to provide an overview of the creation and development of money markets and money market instruments in selected OECD countries in the period 1960 to 1986. The overview is not comprehensive and exhaustive although an effort has been made to cover as many countries and instruments as possible. Quantitative information on the growth of money markets is given in Table 4.1 of Annex II.

AUSTRALIA

July 1962	First issue of marketable Treasury bills ("Treasury Notes").
March 1965	Authorisation of trading in bankers acceptances.
March 1969	Authorisation of issue of certificates of deposit (CDs) subject to interest and maturity control.
1973	Development of commercial paper market.
Sep. 1973	Interest rate ceilings on CDs abolished.
Aug. 1984	Maturity control on CDs abolished.

CANADA

| 1962 | Introduction of bankers acceptances. |
| Note: | Markets for negotiable Treasury bills, certificates of deposit and commercial paper already existed before 1960. |

DENMARK

| 1970 | Establishment of an interbank money market. |
| April 1976 | Reintroduction (after 20 years) of negotiable Treasury bills (with maturities of 1 year 80 days and 2 year 80 days). |

FINLAND

Sept. 1975	Creation of an official call money market.
1975–1980	Development of an unregulated wholesale money market.
1982	Banks authorised to issue certificates of deposit.
1983	Call money loans only source of central bank finance for banks.
1985	Introduction of auction technique for treasury bills/notes.
1986	Introduction of commercial paper.
1987	Restrictions on issues of certificates of deposit relaxed. Certificates of deposit (with maturity less than one year) exempted from cash reserve requirement. Commencement of Bank of Finland open market operations in the market for certificates of deposit.

Introduction of forward contracts on interest rates and interest rate futures. Introduction of investment funds.

FRANCE

1981	Introduction of money market mutual funds (Sicav dites de trésorerie ; fonds communs de placement monétaires).
March 1985	Authorisation to issue negotiable certificates of deposit denominated in francs or foreign currencies (US$ and ECU).
Sept. 1985	Reform of the money market structure: creation of markets for negotiable claims (certificates of deposit, commercial paper etc.); modification of the functioning of, and the conditions of access to, the interbank market.
Dec. 1985	Creation of a market for commercial paper.
Jan. 1986	Introduction of negotiable Treasury bills, and notes issued by specialised financial institutions and finance companies.

GERMANY

May 1986	No further objection to domestic issues of DM certificates of deposit after extending the coverage of minimum reserve requirements to CD issues and other bond issues with an original maturity of less than two years.

GREECE

1975	Authorisation of the issue of negotiable certificates of deposit.
July 1985	First issue of negotiable Treasury bills.
Nov. 1986	First issue of government bonds with an ECU clause.
March 1987	Authorisation of banks to accept 7 to 90 days term deposits at freely negotiable interest rates.

July 1987	Authorisation of the issue of certificates of deposit with maturities ranging from 3 to 18 months, at freely negotiable interest rates.

IRELAND

1970	Central bank assists in early development of money markets.

ITALY

1975	Introduction of negotiable Treasury bills.
1978	Introduction of bankers' acceptances.
1983	Introduction of negotiable certificates of deposit.

JAPAN

May 1971	Establishment of a bill discount market.
April 1972	Establishment of a US dollar call money market.
March 1976	Official recognition of Gensaki market (market for repurchase agreements).
April 1979	Deregulation of the interbank call money market.
May 1979	Introduction of negotiable certificates of deposit.
1979–1986	Gradual widening of the scope for the issue of negotiable CDs by reducing minimum amounts and minimum maturities and increasing maximum amounts (defined as multiples of banks' capital) that individual banks can issue.
April 1984	Authorisation of domestic sales of foreign–currency certificates of deposit and commercial paper.
Nov. 1984	Authorisation of the issue of Euro–yen certificates of deposit.
March 1985	Introduction of money market certificates (deposits earning money–market related interest rates).
June 1985	Introduction of bankers' acceptances.
July 1985	Introduction of call money market without collateral.

NETHERLANDS

1986   Authorisation of the issue of certificates of deposit and commercial paper.

NEW ZEALAND

1962   Short–term money market given official recognition.
Capital issues controls over finance companies removed.

1971   Trading banks given permission to accept time deposits secured by transferable certificates of deposit.

1977   Trading banks given approval to introduce negotiable certificates of deposit.

1978   Trading banks permitted to operate fully in the commercial bill market.
Rules governing operations of official money market dealers relaxed to give dealers greater flexibility to invest in government stock and commercial bills.
As part of the Government's plan to encourage a more active market in government securities the Reserve Bank released a list of firms it would recognise as "specialised dealers" in government securities, and would trade government securities with, in return for a commitment to provide statistics and develop the market.

1984   The Reserve Bank's approval of the four dealing companies operating in the official short–term money market was withdrawn. Coupled with this measure, the "lender of last resort" facility available to the official market was also withdrawn.

NORWAY

1985   Authorisation of the issue of short–term negotiable instruments with maturities of up to one year:
- Treasury bills (issued by the Government);
- Certificates of deposit (issued by banks);
- Commercial paper (issued by non–financial enterprises);
- Finance company paper (issued by finance companies).

PORTUGAL

July 1976   Creation of the Interbank Money Market (IMM).

Feb. 1978   Creation of the Interbank Securities Market (ISM).

Sept. 1980   Creation of Treasury bills only negotiable among the institutions operating on the ISM.
Savings banks and investment companies admitted to the ISM.

Aug. 1985   Introduction of negotiable Treasury bills.
Companies managing investment trusts admitted to the ISM.

Feb. 1987   Introduction of negotiable certificates of deposit, issued by deposit–taking institutions, with maturities between 181 days and 5 years.

June 1987   Introduction in the ISM of Central Bank's monetary certificates with maturities ranging from one day to one year.
Introduction in the ISM of Central Bank's intervention bills with a maturity of 26 weeks.
The deposit–taking institutions were authorised to constitute interest–earning deposits of 182 days at the Central Bank.

Feb. 1988   The maturity of the above deposits was extended to 364 days.

SPAIN

Dec. 1964   Deregulation of the interbank money market.

April 1969   Industrial banks authorised to issue negotiable certificates of deposit with maturities between one and five years.

Dec. 1973   Savings banks admitted to the interbank money market.

Aug. 1974   All banks and savings banks authorised to issue negotiable certificates of deposit with maturities between one and five years.

Jan. 1976   Co–operative banks admitted to the interbank money market.

1980   Development of market for bankers' acceptances.

Jan. 1981	Reduction of minimum maturity of certificates of deposit to six months.
Sept. 1981	Introduction of negotiable Treasury bills ("Pagarés del Tesoro") with a favourable fiscal treatment.
1982	Development of markets for repurchase agreements and commercial Paper.
1983	Introduction of bank's promissory notes issued by banks and saving banks.
1985	Treasury bills became the only financial instruments with favourable tax treatment, which affected their interest rates and placed them below market rates.
1987	Introduction of negotiable Treasury bills (Letras del Tesoro) issued at market interest rates and without advantages from a fiscal point of view. Creation of a book entry system for public debt instruments, including all kinds of Treasury bills.

SWEDEN

1968	Introduction of special term (wholesale) time deposits.
1980	Banks authorised to issue negotiable certificates of deposit.
1982	Creation of a Treasury bill market open to banks and non–banks.
1983	Local authorities and industrial and commercial enterprises authorised to issue short–term marketable promissory notes (commercial bills).

SWITZERLAND

July 1979	Introduction of three–month money market debt register claims on the Federal Government.
Feb. 1981	Introduction of six–month money market debt register claims on the Federal Government.

TURKEY

1980	Introduction of certificate of deposit.
May 1985	First issue of marketable Treasury bills and Government bonds.
April 1986	Establishment of interbank money market.
Feb. 1987	Open market operations were started.
March 1987	Introduction of commercial papers (Dec. 1986 – regulation of commercial paper were completed).
July 1987	Introduction of mutual funds (1982 – Deregulation of mutual funds started).
Sept. 1988	Establishment of interbank foreign exchange market.

UNITED KINGDOM

1966	First issues of US$ certificates of deposit.
1968	Authorisation to issue sterling certificates of deposit.
1965–1971	Development of wholesale sterling money market, notably interbank market; first appearance of money market funds.
1986	Authorisation to issue sterling commercial paper.
1988	Draft proposals for the extension of the Bank of England's dealing relationships in the sterling money markets.

UNITED STATES

1961	First issue of negotiable certificates of deposit by Citicorp.
1964	First National Bank of Boston initiated sales of short–term promissory notes.
1969	Introduction of repurchase agreements, loan sales, small capital notes, and bank holding company and related commercial paper as additional non–deposit sources of funds.
1970	Interest rate ceilings on large CDs (denominations of $100 000 and above) with maturities of less than three months removed.
1973	Interest rate ceilings on other large CDs removed.

1974   Introduction of money market mutual funds to compete with depository institutions.

Note on situation before 1960:

Federal funds call money market

The federal funds rate always has been market determined.

Treasury bill market

Beginning in April 1942, the Federal Reserve attempted to peg interest rates on Treasury securities. There was some relaxation in this policy in the late 1940s. Under the Federal Reserve/Treasury accord in March 1951, the Federal Reserve discontinued pegging rates on treasury securities.

Commercial paper market

This market has been an uncontrolled market since its inception in the 1800s. The 1933 Securities and Exchange Act exempted commercial paper issuers from filing a prospectus.

III. INTRODUCTION OF AUCTION TECHNIQUES FOR SELLING GOVERNMENT DEBT INSTRUMENTS

Governments in their function as borrowers in financial markets have also contributed in recent years to a strengthening of market elements in the financial system by introducing auction techniques for selling their own debt instruments. Auction techniques may, in fact, be seen as the most competitive way of selling debt instruments in financial markets as compared with other selling techniques such as the consortium technique and the tap sale technique. Amongst various auction techniques the following two broad categories may be distinguished:

— The uniform price (yield) auction: the price (yield) of the last accepted bid is applied to all bids;
— The competitive price (yield) auction: each bidder pays the price he bids, or earns the yield he asks for.

The competitive price auction is usually applied in sophisticated professional markets in which all bidders have the professional knowledge and expertise to engage in sharp bidding. The uniform auction technique is used in less sophisticated markets in which less experienced bidders are seen as needing a certain degree of protection against bidding "mistakes".

Chronology of Introduction or Broadened Use of Auction Techniques in the Selling of Government Debt Instruments

YEAR	COUNTRY	TYPE OF DEBT INSTRUMENT
1967	Germany	Medium–term Government notes ("Kassenobligationen")
	Netherlands	Government bonds
1978	Japan	Medium–term interest–bearing (coupon) government notes
1979	Australia	Treasury bills ("Treasury Notes")
	Switzerland	Treasury bills
	United Kingdom	Government stock[1]
1980	New Zealand	Government bonds

YEAR	COUNTRY	TYPE OF DEBT INSTRUMENT
	Switzerland	Government bonds
1981	Spain	Treasury bills (Pagarés del Tesoro)
1982	Australia	Government bonds
1983	Canada	2–year Government notes
	New Zealand	Government bonds
1984	Sweden	Treasury notes
1985	Finland	Treasury notes
	France	Government bonds
	Italy	Variable–rate Treasury certificates
	New Zealand	Treasury bills
	Portugal	Treasury bills
	Turkey	Government bonds (coupon securities)
		Treasury bills
1986	France	Negotiable Treasury bills
1987	Austria	Government securities
	Japan	20–year Government bonds
	Spain	Treasury bills (Letras del Tesoro)
	United Kingdom	Government stock[1]
1988	Portugal	Medium–term Government bonds

1. In 1979, a minimum price tender technique combined with tap sales was introduced, while in 1987 a first experiment was made with a competitive price auction at which bidders pay the price they bid.

IV. DEREGULATION AND DIVERSIFICATION OF FINANCIAL SERVICE ACTIVITIES

The authorities in OECD countries have often attempted to encourage or to increase the scope for competition amongst financial institutions and in financial markets by enlarging the range of permissible activities of different categories of financial institutions — commercial banks, investment banks, savings banks, credit co–operatives, postal services, securities firms etc. — or by tolerating the diversification of financial services activities of these institutions within existing legal frameworks. In most countries, such different types of financial institutions have traditionally been subject to specific and separate regulation imposing on financial institutions a certain degree of specialisation and separation of functions. Such regulatory differences have, in fact, often constituted barriers for financial institutions to enter each others' territories of doing business. By removing such entry barriers, the authorities have actively supported a more general trend towards diversification and despecialisation that resulted from the strategy of banks and other financial institutions to exploit opportunities for extending their activities to new areas of business thereby responding actively to changes in the demand for a wide range of financial services. Although it is not always possible to identify clearly whether and to what extent the authorities, or the financial institutions themselves, have taken the lead in the diversification and despecialisation process, it seems clear that in many instances the deregulation of previously prohibited financial service activities has been a public policy response to pressures from particular types of financial institutions. In a number of countries with less restrictive regulation on permissible activities of different types of financial institutions, the authorities have often tol-

167

erated or otherwise encouraged the despecialisation process without having recourse to specific regulatory action. The present note provides an overview of the deregulation and diversification of financial service activities of typical categories of financial institutions: commercial banks, savings banks, postal services and securities firms in selected OECD countries. The listing of new activities relates to both activities requiring regulatory changes and activities that financial institutions were able to carry out within existing legal frameworks.

Developments in the countries covered in the present overview may be considered as indicative of similar developments taking place in other countries not especially mentioned, in particular as regards the diversification of financial service activities of commercial banks.

The present note consists of four sections as follows:

a) Deregulation and Diversification of Financial Service Activities of Commercial Banks in Selected OECD Countries;

b) Deregulation and Diversification of Financial Service Activities of Savings Institutions in Selected OECD Countries;

c) Deregulation and Diversification of Financial Service Activities of Post Office Systems in Selected OECD Countries;

d) Deregulation of Separation of Functions between Banks and Securities Firms and Access by Banks to Stock Exchange Membership in Selected OECD Countries:

1. Reduction of Demarcation Lines between Banks and Securities Firms;
2. Bank Access to Stock Exchange Membership.

A. DEREGULATION AND DIVERSIFICATION OF FINANCIAL SERVICE ACTIVITIES OF COMMERCIAL BANKS

FRANCE

1966	Important amendments to the Banking Act which widen the scope of activities of deposit banks (banques de dépôts) and investment banks (banques d'affaires) and reduce the demarcation lines between the two types of institutions.
	Deposit banks may accept deposits from the general public with maturities of over two years (previously up to two years) and may grant credit with maturities of over one year including personal loans and mortgage loans (previously up to one year).
	Investment banks may accept deposits from the general public (previously prohibited) with maturities of up to two years and may merge with deposit banks.
	Establishment of a mortgage market (marché hypothécaire) (permitting banks and other deposit–taking institutions to engage directly in mortgage lending or through the acquisition of mortgage loan mobilisation paper).
Since 1966–1967	Following the banking reforms of 1966–1967 deposit banks developed the following business activities:

— Issue of non–marketable cash bonds;
— Personal loans;
— Mortgage loans;
— Active promotion of the sale of investment certificates (SICAV shares);
— Securities business (buying and selling securities for customers, trust business, safe custody).

1967	Introduction of credit card: Carte Bleue (initially only used domestically).
Since early 1970s	Strong development of automated payments services and cash dispensers.
1973	Carte Bleue linked with Visa.
Since 1980	Banks become important issuers of bonds both on the domestic and international bond markets as loans financed with proceeds from bond issues are exempted from credit ceilings.
	Introduction of a number of newly authorised savings and investment instruments:

— Variable rate bonds and bonds with other special features (zero-coupon bonds, extendable bonds etc.);

— Money market investment funds (SICAVs and FCPs) (1981);

— Index–linked savings book ("Livret Rose") (1982);

— Equity–linked savings instruments (certificats d'investissement, obligations à bons de subscription d'action, actions à dividende prioritaire sans droit de vote, titres participatifs) (1983);

— Special savings account for promoting industrial development (including small and medium–sized enterprises) (compte pour le developpement industriel — CODEVI) (1983);

— Special savings account for investment in equities (compte d'épargne en actions) (1983);

— Negotiable certificates of deposit (1985);

— Commercial paper (1985);

— Finance company paper (1986);

— Interest rate futures (1986).

In addition, banks have developed or modernised the following activities and services:

— Home video banking;

— Discretionary portfolio management and general wealth and estate administration;

— Advisory and administrative services for investment clubs;

— Safe custody services;

— Tax advisory services;

— Management–consultancy services and computer services, notably for small and medium–sized enterprises;

— Acquisitions, mergers, management buyouts;

— Venture capital funds.

1985 Banks (and other financial intermediaries) are authorised to set up, together with brokerage firms (agents de change), incorporated jobber firms (sociétés de contrepartie).

1987 Banks are authorised to take participations in brokerage firms ("sociétés de bourse", formerly "agents de change") up to 100 per cent and thus have access to stock exchange membership.

During the 1960s Private commercial banks, notably the "big three", begin to engage actively in retail banking business through various lines of action:

a) Competing strongly for wage and salary accounts (partly by convincing their large industrial customers of the usefulness of such accounts);

b) Launching standardised credit schemes for private persons:

   i) Small credits (up to DM 2 000 initially);

   ii) Purchase credits (up to DM 6 000 initially);

   iii) Personal mortgage loans (which may or may not be used for housing finance purposes);

c) Competing actively in the small savings market (mainly after the liberalisation of interest rates of 1967).

Introduction of non–marketable savings bonds by some banks and savings banks.

Since early 1970s Introduction of "Eurocheque" (guaranteed cheque). Strong expansion of lending to the government sector (Federal Government, Federal Railways, Federal Post Office Authorities, Laender) against promissory notes ("Schuldscheindarlehen").

Strong expansion of mortgage lending. Fixed–interest medium–term lending to enterprises.

Diversification of savings instruments (saving with premium, savings plans, savings accounts with bond–market related interest rates etc.).

Strong promotion of sale of investment fund certificates and related fund management.

Introduction of common credit card (Eurocard) (1977).

Since early 1980s Gradual introduction of automated payment facilities (ATMs, EFT methods).

Further development or introduction of the following activities/instruments:

— Leasing;

— Factoring;

- Venture capital;
- Cash management programmes;
- Management consultancy business;
- Savings plans with life insurance;
- Issue of new types of DM bonds for domestic and foreign issuers (zero–coupon bonds, floating rate notes, dual currency bonds, and bonds linked to interest rate and foreign currency swaps on own or customer account (authorised in 1985);
- The outstanding volume of negotiable DM certificates of deposit, though authorised since May 1986, is practically nil due to the incidence of the securities turnover tax.

GREECE

1971	Introduction of interest–bearing cheque accounts for private persons and unincorporated businesses. Commencement of direct crediting.
1972	Introduction of credit cards.
1973	Authorisation of investment fund management.
1979	Introduction of guaranteed cheques on private accounts.
1981	Introduction of automated teller machines (ATMs) and pre–authorised direct debiting.
1984	Introduction of overdraft facilities on private accounts.
1986	Introduction of leasing.
1987	Introduction of factoring and forfeiting. Authorisation of the issue of certificates of deposit, at freely negotiable interest rates. Extension of bank loans on collateral of government bonds.

IRELAND

From 1970 onwards Newly introduced activities/products:

- Leasing;
- Factoring;
- Housing finance;

- Equity participation through subsidiaries;
- Computer services;
- Credit cards;
- Investment fund management;
- Participation in general insurance and life assurance through associated companies.

JAPAN

1981	New Banking Law provides more scope for securities–related activities of commercial banks [see Section (iv) *d)* below] and authorises the following new activities:

- Factoring;
- Issuing credit cards;
- Mortgage lending.

1982	Banks begin to offer gold (coins, bullion) for client investment purposes. Introduction of instalment saving schemes.
1983	Commencement of over–the–counter selling of newly issued government bonds (authorised under the New Banking Law of 1981).
1984	Commencement of market–making in commercial paper and negotiable certificates of deposit issued in foreign countries. Commencement of secondary market trading in government bonds (authorised under the New Bank Law of 1981).

NETHERLANDS

Newly introduced activities/products:

1962	— Insurance brokerage;
1968	— Salary accounts; significant increcrease in non–cash payments;
1971	— Computer services;
1973	— Selling of special coins;
1980	— Participation in venture capital for non–bank enterprises.

NEW ZEALAND

1963	Detailed instructions for selective advance control were withdrawn. Re-

strictions on low priority (personal, speculative, etc.) and the quantity of advances remained in place.
Permission given to finance export industries.

1964   Trading banks empowered to form savings bank subsidiaries on a fully guaranteed basis.

1965   The trading banks were encouraged to acquire interests in finance companies where they did not already have an interest.

1967   Databank (a computerised cheque clearing facility) was established by the trading banks. Previously cheques had been cleared manually between the banks.

1971   All but one trading bank took up an interest in merchant banks transferable certificates of deposit were introduced.

1977   Negotiable certificates of deposit were introduced and permission to invest in local authority stock was given.

1978   Permission was given for trading banks to operate fully in the commercial bill market.

1979   Permission was given to issue credit cards.
First insurance services offered by a trading bank.

1982   First automatic teller machine introduced by trading banks.

1984   Interest rate regulations removed. Trading banks had previously been required to hold a set proportion of their deposits in Government Stock.

1985   Introduction of the "new banks" policy allowing financial institutions to become registered as banks. This policy opened up what had been a statutory restricted capacity for financial institutions to trade under the name "bank". The new policy framework enables financial institutions to call themselves banks, provided they meet the (generally qualitative) criteria laid down by the Reserve Bank. Removal of ratios applying to trading banks.

Apr. 1969   Commercial banks may grant credits with maturities of over one year up to 5 years.

May 1973   Introduction of credit cards for domestic use only.

Aug. 1977   Commercial Banks may grant credits with maturities up to 10 years.

Dec. 1977   Investment banks may accept sight deposits, under certain conditions.

Feb. 1983   Introduction of cash certificates issued by investment banks.

May 1983   Investment banks may grant short term credits, under certain conditions.

May 1985   Commercial and investment banks may trade participation units insecurities investment trusts.

June   Creation of the spot exchange market.

July   Commercial and investment banks may trade participation units in real estate investment trusts.

Aug.   Introduction of debit cards for domestic use only.
Commercial and investment banks may issue participation bonds.
Commercial and investment banks may trade Treasury bills.

March 1986   Housing finance by commercial banks.
Commercial banks may accept time deposits with maturities of over 1 year.
Introduction of housing saving accounts.

May   Use of credit cards abroad.

June   Introduction of retirement saving accounts.

Dec.   Use of debit cards abroad.

Feb. 1987   Introduction of certificates of deposit issued by commercial and investment banks.
Creation of the forward exchange market.

Apr.   Introduction of youth savings accounts.

May   Commercial and investment banks may trade "Tesouro Familiar" (Government bonds) on the secondary market.

Oct.   Further liberalisation of operating in the spot exchange market.

March 1988 Further liberalisation of operating in the forward exchange market (operation up to 1 year).

SPAIN

1962   Commercial banks authorised to set up industrial banks that can issue bonds but cannot engage in specified commercial banking operations.

1968   Authorisation of foreign currency asset operations.

1969   Authorisation to grant longer–term loans (with maturities of over 18 months) within the limit of 25 per cent of total deposits.
Authorisation of mortgage lending.
Industrial banks are allowed to issue CDs.

1974   Abolition of limitation on longer–term loans (with maturities of over 18 months) applying to commercial banks.
Commercial banks authorised to issue CDs.
Some enlargement of authorised activities of industrial banks.

1979   Liberalisation of foreign currency operations of authorised banks.
Introduction of variable rate loans in pesetas.

1980–81   Introduction of syndicated peseta loans and bankers' acceptances.
Authorisation of the issue of some types of mortgage bonds.

1982   Strong expansion of repurchase agreements between banks.
Introduction of commercial paper programmes and related back–up facilities.

1983   Introduction of repurchase agreements with non–financial institutions and the general public.

1985   Abolition of limits on fixed assets and securities portfolio investments and risk concentration, which from that time on are subject to higher weights in the new capital ratio. Former limits to some off–balance sheet operations were also abolished.

1986   Foreign banks' permissible operations will be the same as those of the domestic banks. A calendar starting 1st January 1988 was established so that full homogeneisation will be achieved by 31st December 1992.

1987   Further liberalisation of foreign currency loans and deposits.
Possibility of holding short foreign currency positions and substantial increase in authorised long positions.
Authorisation to act as agents in the treasury bills book entry system on own account or on third party account. A requirement of own funds of over Ptas. 1 000 millions is established for these agents.
A Bill under discussion will allow banks to carry out leasing operations.

SWEDEN

1960–86   Newly introduced activities/products:

— Brokerage and new issue business in equities;

— Trading and market–making in short–term promissory notes issued by commercial enterprises and local authorities;

— Formalised co–operation with insurance companies;

— Bank giro (i.e. fund transfer) services;

— Introduction of negotiable certificates of deposit and special term deposits.

TURKEY

During the 1960s   Introduction of direct controls on bank credits (1961).
Introduction of preferential credit facilities (1964).
Various schemes have been developed during the 1964–1980 period to widen the scope of preferential credits.
Banks were allowed to accept foreign exchange deposits from non–residents (1967) (convertible TL deposits).

During the 1970s   Commercial bank began to grant medium–term credits (1972)
Authorised banks were allowed to hold foreign exchange position (1974).

Since early 1980s   Major reforms in legal and institutional framework of the financial system which widen the scope of activities of the commercial banks:

financial system which widen the scope of activities of the commercial banks:

Following the enactment of the Capital Market Law (1981) banks have introduced or developed the following activities and services:

— Buying and selling securities for customers;
— Advisory services;
— Management of mutual funds;
— Underwriting agreements.

After the major liberalisation of foreign exchange controls (1983–1984):

— Commercial banks' operations in foreign currency have grown substantially;
— Banks began to participate in international markets.

The following developments have been instrumental in the further diversification of activities of commercial banks:

— Introduction of auctioning of Government Securities (1985);
— Establishment of the interbank money market (1986);
— Introduction of open market operations;
— Establishment of foreign exchange and currency markets.

Further development or introduction of the following activities/products:

— Certificates of deposit;
— Credit cards;
— Housing finance;
— Expansion of wholesale business;
— Leasing;
— Consumer credits.

UNITED KINGDOM

From 1957 Foreign banks in London and merchant banks develop the London euro–currency market and domestic sterling lending business (sterling interbank wholesale market and wholesale business in short–term sterling loans to industry and commerce) at competitively–determined interest rates.

Late 1950s Clearing banks begin setting up their own subsidiaries for hire purchase and instalment credit finance; in 1957 Barclays acquired Mercantile Credit.

1965 First bank cheque guarantee card introduced.

1966 First bank credit card introduced (Barclaycard).

1966 Dollar CDs first issued in London.

1965–71 Development of foreign currency business with non–residents. Credit ceilings reinforce the development and growth of the wholesale sterling market, in particular the sterling interbank market. First sterling CD issued October 1968.
Expansion of industrial leasing.
First appearance of money market funds.

1968 First bank cash dispenser introduced (Barclays).

1969 Standard cheque guarantee card introduced by all the major banks except Barclays (which extends its Barclaycard to guarantee cheques in 1974). Banks cease to open on Saturdays.

Since 1971 Further developments of the innovations first introduced in the 1950s and 1960s:

Personal customers:

Credit cards, cheque guarantee cards, cash dispensers and automated teller machines (ATMs) more readily available (automated credit transfers and direct debit facilities).
Easier access to a complete array of instalment loan facilities.
Access credit card introduced (linked with Mastercard and Eurocard) (1973).

Corporate customers:

Access on a growing scale to the wholesale sterling markets by companies whether as lenders or borrowers. Widespread use of medium–term lending by the banks at variable interest rates linked to the interbank rate in sterling interbank market, in response to high and volatile rates of inflation and interest rates.
Clearing banks for the first time enter the mortgage loan market at very competitive conditions (end 1980).

Banks

Early 1980s — Expansion of BACS input media to include cassette, diskette and telecommunications. Cash management services introduced. ATM sharing arrangements among groups of banks. Interest bearing current/chequing accounts introduced (often as part of financial services packages).

1982 — Acquisition by a large clearing bank of a nationwide chain of estate agents.

1983 — Nationwide announcement that the clearing banks intend to develop a national system for Electronic Fund Transfer at the Point of Sale.

1983–84 — As part of moves towards dual capacity on the Stock Exchange (i.e. securities firms being allowed to act as both brokers and jobbers), larger banks form shareholding links with Stock Exchange firms.

UNITED STATES[1] [2]

Newly Authorised Activities

1971 — Mortgage finance.
Consumer finance.
Credit card lending.
Factoring.
Industrial bank or industrial loan company.
Servicing loans.
Trust and fiduciary activities.
Investment or financial advice (some restrictions apply).
Leasing.
Investment in community welfare or rehabilitation corporations.
Data processing (some restrictions apply).
Insurance related to extension of credit.
Insurance agency (in limited geographic areas).

1973 — Underwriting credit–related insurance.
Courier services for time–critical or financially–related documents.

1974 — Management consulting to non–affiliated banks and other depository institutions.

1976 — Underwriting and dealing in United States government obligations and obligations of states and political subdivisions and money market instruments.

1977 — Issuance and sale of money orders and United States Savings bonds.
Acting as futures commission merchant for various futures contracts.

1979 — Issuance and sale of travellers' cheques.

1980 — Performing real estate appraisals.

1982 — Arranging equity financing of commercial and industrial real estate.

1983 — Securities brokerage and margin lending.
Advising on foreign exchange operations and arranging for execution of transactions.

B. DEREGULATION AND DIVERSIFICATION OF FINANCIAL SERVICE ACTIVITIES OF SAVINGS INSTITUTIONS

The measures listed in the present section show that in practically all countries covered by the overview, efforts have been made to integrate savings banks and other savings institutions such as building societies fully, or to a large extent, with the commercial banking sector, thereby creating, or moving towards, a "level playing field" for competition between these two categories of financial institutions.

AUSTRALIA

1963–78 — Regulations governing savings banks altered five times reducing the minimum required proportion of deposits to be placed in government paper from 70 to 40 per cent thereby widening the scope for other asset activities.

Aug. 1982   Easing of regulation of savings banks. The 40 per cent ratio of mandatory government securities investments replaced with a 15 per cent liquidity ratio. 6 per cent of total deposits can be freely employed. Deposits of up to A$100 000 may be accepted from profit–making bodies.

Aug. 1984   Permission to offer cheque accounts and removal of maturity and size restrictions on deposits.

Aug. 1988   Announcement of removal of distinction between trading banks and savings banks.

AUSTRIA

1979   The new Austrian Banking Law ("Kreditwesengesetz 1979") unifies the legal frameworks of different kinds of banking institutions and confirms the universal banking system: each bank is authorised to conduct those banking activities that are defined in its licence.

BELGIUM

1967   First extension of list of authorised activities.

1975   Further steps towards bringing the legal framework for savings banks into line with banking regulation.

1979   Abolition of most restrictions on, or special conditions for, authorised asset holdings.

1981   Authorisation to conduct foreign exchange operations.

1984   Authorisation to place euro–bonds.

1985   The EEC directive of 12th December 1977 is translated into Belgian law and thus becomes also applicable to savings institutions.

DENMARK

1975   "The Commercial Banks and Savings Banks Act 1975" forms a common legal framework for commercial banks and savings banks.

FINLAND

1969   A new set of banking laws places different types of banking institutions on a more similar footing. Co–operative financial institutions and savings institutions transformed into co–operative banks and savings banks.

FRANCE

1969   Ordinary savings banks and the National Savings Bank authorised to offer specified money transfer facilities in connection with passbook savings accounts (automated credit transfers of pensions and other social security benefits, automated debit transfers of pre–authorised payments of public utility bills).

1970   Establishment of Groupements Régionaux d'Epargne et de Prévoyance (GREP) which enable ordinary savings banks to issue non–marketable savings bonds (bons de caisse) in competition with commercial banks etc.

1983   Law on new organisation of savings banks designed to strengthen the competitiveness of savings banks.

1984   The new Banking Act applies also to savings banks.

GERMANY

[See Germany under sub–section IV. A. as far as applicable.]

IRELAND

From 1975 onwards   Provision of current account facilities, bridging finance and retail foreigne exchange services.

| 1976 | Legislation introduced to regulate the establishment and activities of building societies. |

ITALY

| 1960s and 1970s | Savings banks are authorised in successive steps to carry out all banking operations. |
| 1980s | Bank of Italy takes action to adapt special regulation applying to different categories of banks and savings banks etc. to changed operating conditions. In particular, the detailed listing of permitted operations specified in different banking statutes is replaced by a common reference to the activities indicated in Article 1 of the Banking Law. The banks most heavily involved in this revision are savings banks and rural and artisans' banks which most strongly felt a need for adopting more flexible statutes. Determined efforts by the Bank of Italy to introduce, or reinforce, the entrepreneurial management of savings banks and public–law banks. Further reforms involving internal reorganisation, the acquisition of capital from third parties and the creation of new fund–raising instruments (savings certificates, certificates of deposit, advances from the bodies participating in the capital). |

JAPAN

1981	Shimkin banks were authorised:
	— To sell newly issued government bonds over the counter;
	— To start foreign exchange business.
1982	To trade public–sector bonds in the secondary market.

NETHERLANDS

| 1963 | Savings banks start granting personal loans. |

1969	Savings banks start offering chequing account facilities.
1972	Savings banks start insurance brokerage business.
1976	Savings banks may opt for full application of solvency requirements for commercial credit.
1981	Introduction of a transitional regime for savings banks wishing to enter the field of commercial credit (limited to institutions with balance sheet totals of over Gld 1 million). Savings banks start offering business loans.
1984	Large savings banks (accounting for 80 per cent of the savings market) opt for transition to commercial lending.

NEW ZEALAND

1964	Private savings banks introduced. These institutions were empowered to provide general savings and lending facilities at a retail level, and are wholly guaranteed by parent trading banks.
1973	Home ownership accounts permitted. Personal loan facilities introduced.
1977	Fishing vessel accounts were permitted. Trustee banks introduce housing bonds. Second mortgage finance introduced.
1980	Private savings banks permitted to introduce farm and fishing vessel accounts. Trustee banks introduce a credit card facility. Limits on personal lending by Trustee banks abolished.
1981	Trustee banks introduce automatic teller machines.
1982	Private savings bank allowed to introduce home ownership accounts.
1984	Interest rate controls removed.
1985	Removal of ratios applying to savings banks. They had previously been required to hold a set proportion of their deposits in Government Stock.
1986	General liberalisation of trustee banks' operating powers.
1988	Trustee banks converted to companies and all constraints on their operating powers removed.

NORWAY

1976	Full tax exemption for savings banks.
1977	New banking laws reduce the difference between commercial banks and savings banks.
1983	Tax liability partly reintroduced for savings banks (about 16 per cent).

PORTUGAL

May 1979	Redefinition and enlargement of the operational scope of savings banks.
Aug. 1986	Savings banks may hold participations in companies on the same terms as commercial banks.
Feb. 1987	Savings banks may trade in certificates of deposit.
Nov. 1988	Savings banks may trade in medium-term government bonds.

SPAIN

1962	New Banking Law extends range of permissible activities of savings banks.
1966–69	Further extension of permissible asset and liability operations of savings banks.
1974	Savings banks authorised to issue certificates of deposit.
1976	Savings banks authorised to participate in the newly created interbank telephone service.
1977	Savings banks are subject to the same regulations as commercial banks.

SWEDEN

1969	Banking legislation is co-ordinated in order to create similar legal frameworks for commercial banks, savings banks and co-operative banks. (The explicit purpose is to make the competitive situation equal and thereby stimulate competition.)

UNITED KINGDOM

Building Societies

Early 1960	Amendment to the Building Societies Act limiting the scope for lending to companies following the collapse of a building society engaged in commercial lending.
1962	New Building Societies Act (largely consolidating existing law).
1983	Building societies given the right to pay interest rates gross on (and thereby making it worth raising funds via) Sterling CDs (May 1983) and large time deposits (October 1983).
Oct. 1985	First building society eurobond issue.
Jan. 1987	The 1986 Building Society Act came into effect, widening the scope for commercial lending, allowing societies to provide other services relating to house purchase and finance, and allowing societies (from 1988) to operate in the EEC. The Act also made provision for societies to convert from mutual to corporate status (also from 1988), and created the Building Societies Commission to supervise the societies.
June 1987	Two of the largest societies join BACS.
Feb. 1988	Review of Section 8 of the 1986 Building Societies Act completed, resulting in a widening of the range of financial services that societies can provide. Building societies able to issue subordinated debt to count towards their capital base (previously, building society capital was confined to their reserves, so that increases in capital could only be achieved via their operating surpluses).
March 1988	First announcement by a large building society of plans to convert from mutual to corporate status.

Trustee Savings Banks

1976 to 1987	The Trustee Savings Bank Act starts the reorganisation of the trustee savings bank movement (which culminates in the 1987 privatisation of the Trustee Savings Bank in 1987 and thus in the institution's full integration with the banking sector).

UNITED STATES

Federally Chartered Thrift Institutions

1966   Interest rate ceilings applied to time and savings deposits at Federally insured thrifts. Interest rate ceilings for thrift institutions set slightly higher than those for commercial banks.

1970   Interest rate ceilings on large CDs (denominations of $100 000 and above) with maturities of less than three months removed.
Ceilings on savings and time deposits raised.
Savings and loans and mutual savings banks defined by the Federal Reserve Board for the purpose of lending in the federal funds market.
Federal Home Loan Bank Board expands use of advances to support mortgage lending.

1973   Interest rate ceilings on other large CDs removed.

1978   Six month money market certificate authorised. Permissible rate indexed to the 6–month Treasury bill rate.

1979   Small saver certificate (SSC) (4–year denomination) authorised. Ceiling rate based on 4–year yield of Treasury securities.
Federal S&Ls receive approval to grant variable rate mortgage loans.

1980   The Depository Institutions Deregulation Committee established, charged with phasing–out interest rate ceilings by March 1986.
The following changes in ceilings and activities were authorised under this authority unless otherwise noted:

- Minimum maturity on SSCs reduced to $2^1/_2$ years;
- Negotiable order of withdrawal (NOW) accounts authorised for thrifts to offer to individuals. Maximum rate of interest $5^1/_4$ per cent;
- Federal Savings and Loan Associations (S&Ls) authorised to hold commercial paper, corporate debt securities and consumer loans; also authorised to issue credit cards and to exercise fiduciary powers; service corporation investment expanded to 3 per cent

of assets; geographic restrictions on mortgage lending removed;
- Federal savings banks authorised to make commercial and industrial loans;
- State laws limiting interest rates on first mortgages and business and agricultural loans pre–empted.

1982   Major expansion of asset powers of Federally chartered thrifts via the Garn–St. Germain Act.:

- Thrifts allowed to hold up to 10 per cent of their assets in commercial and industrial loans. The 10 per cent limit was phased in by 1984; thrifts also authorised to issue corporate demand deposits in conjunction with those loans;
- Consumer lending constraints increased from 20 to 30 per cent of assets;
- Restrictions on educational lending eased;
- Thrifts authorised to invest up to 10 per cent of assets in personal property leases;
- Constraints on investing in state and local government securities removed;
- State laws prohibiting the enforcement of due–on–sale clauses in mortgage contracts pre–empted;
- Federal S&Ls given the power to grant unconstrained adjustable-rate mortgage loans;
- 7–31 and 91 day indexed accounts authorised;
- S&Ls authorised to convert to federal savings banks;
- $2^1/_2$ to $3^1/_2$ year account indexed to $2^1/_2$ year treasury yields and $3^1/_2$ year (and over) interest rate ceiling–free accounts authorised;
- Money market deposit account (MMDA), a ceiling–free account with limited transactions features authorised; minimum balance of $2 500 required;
- Super–Nows, an interest–bearing transaction account without a rate ceiling for individuals authorised; minimum balance of $2 500 required;
- Interest rate ceilings on all time deposits removed.

| 1984 | Federal S&Ls and savings banks authorised to establish finance subsidiaries to raise funds. | | FSLIC–insured thrift institutions tied to growth rate of liabilities and to levels of certain types of investments. |
| 1985 | Minimum balance requirements on MMDAs, 7–31 day time deposits, and Super–Nows reduced to $1 000. Minimum capital requirements for | 1986 | All remaining minimum balances and interest rate ceilings removed. (Prohibition of paying interest on demand deposits maintained.) |

C. DEREGULATION AND DIVERSIFICATION OF FINANCIAL SERVICE ACTIVITIES OF POST OFFICE SYSTEMS

In a number of OECD countries post office systems have been authorised to become important competitors in retail banking. Some countries have gone as far as transforming the financial services of the post office system into full–service commercial banks (Finland, Netherlands, Sweden, United Kingdom) while in Austria the Postal Savings Bank has been authorised to set up a wholly–owned subsidiary operating as a commercial bank.

AUSTRIA

1969	The Postal Savings Bank ("Oesterreichische Postsparkasse", PSK) (established in 1927 as an independent legal entity to operate postal chequing and savings accounts) introduces salary accounts.
1970	The Postal Savings Bank Act of 1969 becomes effective. The Postal Savings Bank operates on commercial principles and is authorised to conduct all ordinary banking activities other than granting loans to the business sector and private households without government or state guarantee.
1973	Introduction of bonus–savings scheme and savings certificates.
1976	Introduction of anonymous (bearer) savings passbook.
1978	Establishment of a fully–owned banking subsidiary ("Bank der Oesterreichischen Postsparkasse AG"). Commencement of brokerage business in bonds.
1979	Commencement of brokerage business in consumer loans granted by the "Bank of the Postal Savings Bank". Buying (but not selling) of retail foreign exchange authorised.

| 1981 | Authorisation to issue own bonds and to engage in guarantee business within certain limits. |

BELGIUM

| Early 1980s | Introduction of cheque payment facilities and limited overdraft facilities on postal chequing accounts; creation of a network of automated cash dispensers (in the period 1960–1986 the Postal Chequing Office lost much of its earlier attraction amongst the general public). |

FINLAND

| 1988 | Legal status of Post Office Banks changed into commercial bank. |

GERMANY

1975	Introduction of limited overdraft facilities on postal chequing accounts.
1976	Authorisation of issue of eurocheques.
1986	Authorisation to operate special saving schemes.

JAPAN

1960	Authorisation of deposit taking.
1972	Introduction of postal savings plans for house purchase.
1973	Introduction of loan facilities for holders of savings accounts.
1977	Introduction of direct crediting of payrolls (salary accounts).

| 1982 | Introduction of pre–authorised direct debits. |

NETHERLANDS

1968	Introduction of interest–bearing accounts.
1973	Introduction of first mortgage lending.
1977	Introduction of consumer credit and personal loans.
1980	Introduction of overdraft facilities, second mortgage lending and personal time deposits.
1981	Introduction of travellers' cheques, travel insurance, interest–bearing business accounts and prefinancing of state–aided residential construction.
Jan. 1986	Merger of the Postal Giro Service and Postal Savings Bank into the Postbank, a commercial bank, which is at present not allowed to offer securities–related services to the public.

NEW ZEALAND

1973	Home ownership accounts authorised.
1974	Farm ownership accounts authorised.
1977	Fishing vessel accounts authorised. Second mortgage finance permitted. Housing bonds introduced.
1979	Overdrafts on cheque accounts permitted.
1983	Automatic teller machines were introduced.
1987	Post Office Savings Bank corporatised with commercial objectives; banking activities separated from other Post Office functions.
1988	Government guarantees of (new) Post Office Bank deposits removed.

PORTUGAL

| Dec. 1960 | Post Offices may trade saving certificates. |

| Nov. 1969 | Authorisation to receive salaries and retirement pensions through postal cheques. |

SPAIN

1960	Authorised activities: demand and savings accounts; securities brokerage business; investment in domestic public–sector securities; loans with maximum maturities of 2 years within the limit of 25 per cent of securities holdings.
1972	Introduction of salary and cashless payments accounts; harmonization of interest rates and other conditions with those applied by savings banks.
1978	Authorisation to carry out the same activities as savings banks.
1981	End of the process of harmonization of legal frameworks applying to the Post Office Savings Bank and savings banks.

UNITED KINGDOM

1968	National Giro launched as a money transfer service using the Post Office branch network.
1976	The Post Office (Banking Services) Act gives authority for National Giro to provide a comprehensive range of banking services through post offices.
1978	National Giro adopts name of National Girobank.
1982	National Girobank opens first regional office in Birmingham.
1983–84	National Girobank becomes settlement member in the London–based clearing system for paper and electronic payments.
1985	Girobank PLC incorporated as a wholly owned subsidiary of the Post Office (though it continues to trade under the name of National Girobank) and recognised under the Banking Act (previously exempt). National Girobank introduces its own credit card in the VISA group, and its own debt card. As a member of the Link ATM–sharing Consortium it has installed some 180 ATM machines.

| 1987 | National Girobank revises its corporate identity and trades under the new company tital "Girobank". The government also examines the possibility of privatising Girobank. | 1988 | Official announcement that Girobank will be sold to a financial services company. No decision yet taken, though the TSB has publicly expressed its interest. |

D. DEREGULATION OF SEPARATION OF FUNCTIONS BETWEEN BANKS AND SECURITIES FIRMS AND ACCESS BY BANKS TO STOCK EXCHANGE MEMBERSHIP

In a limited number of OECD countries there has traditionally been a certain separation of functions between commercial banks and securities firms. This has notably been the case in Canada, Japan and the United States while in a number of other countries such as Belgium, Denmark, France, Italy, Spain and the United Kingdom commercial banks have been excluded from stock exchange membership and related trading activity although they were quite active in other types of securities-related activities such as the new issuing business, brokerage business with clients, fund management, investment advisory business etc. This separation of functions has gradually been reduced, or eliminated altogether, under the impact of both competitive strategies of commercial banks and securities firms and deregulation measures taken by the authorities or self-regulatory bodies i.e. stock exchanges themselves. The present note provides a brief overview of deregulation measures affecting securities-related activities of commercial banks on the one hand and the scope for diversification of the financial service activities of securities firms on the other. The diversification of activities not requiring legal changes are in some cases listed as well.

1. REDUCTION OF DEMARCATION LINES BETWEEN BANKS AND SECURITIES FIRMS

CANADA

Commercial Banks

| 1980 | Until the 1980 Bank Act revision, chartered banks were permitted to deal in securities, but their involvement was almost wholly in activities related to Canadian government securities, with little activity in corporate securities. The 1980 Bank Act prohibited banks from underwriting corporate securities, although they could be members of a selling group distributing corporate securities. Banks were also prohibited from soliciting orders for securities or executing trades, although they were permitted to take orders on a passive basis and pass those orders to brokers for execution. |
| Dec. 1986 | In the policy paper "New Directions for the Financial Sector", it was announced that banks, and other financial institutions, would be permitted to own securities dealers. |

| June 1987 | Legislation was passed allowing federally chartered financial institutions, which includes banks, to own securities dealers. |

Securities Firms

| 1980s | Canadian securities firms have kept pace with innovation in financial markets in the 1980s, and have been in a position to offer the latest financial services to their clients. |

Permissible Activities Abroad

Under Canadian legislation, Canadian banks and securities firms are permitted to participate in foreign financial markets.

FRANCE

| 1984 | For banks, portfolio management is a "bank-related" (connexe) activity (in |

181

the sense of Article 5 of the Banking Act) in the same way as the underwriting and placement of securities. Securities-related activities of banks are not subject to any restrictions with the exception of securities trading on the stock exchange, which is the domain of the stock exchange companies (sociétés de bourse). Securities firms (maisons de titres) are dealt with in Article 99 of the Banking Act and are like banks and other credit institutions subject to supervision by the Banking Commission (Commission bancaire).

JAPAN

Banks

1983   Banks start selling newly issued government bonds over-the-counter (authorised under the Bank Act of 1981).

1984   Banks start trading government bonds in the secondary market. (Authorised under the Bank Act of 1981.)

1985   Banks authorised to participate in bond futures markets.
        Banks start offering integrated bond-deposit accounts.
        Banks authorised to trade public-sector foreign currency bonds.

Securities firms

1980   Securities houses authorised to offer medium-term government bond funds (a kind of money market mutual fund).

1984   Securities houses authorised:
        — To offer sweep accounts;
        — To sell foreign-currency CDs and commercial paper in the domestic market.

1986   Securities houses authorised:
        — To trade negotiable certificates of deposit in the secondary market;
        — To offer loans against the collateral of government bonds.

1986   Securities houses authorised to trade yen-denominated bankers acceptances in the secondary markets.

Permissible Activities Abroad

The separation of functions between commercial banks and securities houses applies only to institutions operating on Japanese territory. In foreign countries, notably in the international financial market centres outside Japan, Japanese banks can carry out all securities-related activities and Japanese securities houses can carry out all banking operations.

NEW ZEALAND

Commercial Banks

1970s   Investment advisory services introduced.

1980s   Trading banks participate in unit trust and other investment schemes.

Savings Banks

1988   Trustee banks authorised to offer unit trust investment facilities.

PORTUGAL

Jan. 1974   Credit institutions may act as brokers in transactions outside the stock exchange.

May/July and Aug. 1985   Credit institutions may trade participation units in securities real estate investment trusts and Treasury bills.

TURKEY

1981   According to the Capital Market Law, commercial banks are permitted to engage in all types of securities operations including the activities which securities firms are allowed to conduct.

UNITED STATES

Commercial Banks

Under the Banking Act of 1933 (Glass Steagall Act) which provides the legal basis for the separation of functions between commercial banks and investment banks and/or securities firms, banks were authorised to carry out a wide range of securities–related activities such as dealing in government obligations on own account, private placements (but not underwriting) of corporate securities, act as agents for customers in buying and selling securities, operate common trust funds and collective funds for pension plans, act as trustees and custodians for individuals, manage dividend investment plans, employee stock purchase plans and offer general investment advice.

Newly authorised securities–related activities

1982   The Comptroller of the Currency approved the application by Security Pacific National Bank to establish a subsidiary, Discount Brokerage, to act as a broker–dealer under the Securities Exchange Act (investment advice not permitted).

1983   The Federal Reserve Board approved the application of Bank America Corp. (bank holding company) to acquire Charles Schwab Corp., the nation's largest discount brokerage firm. Discount brokerage services include the purchase and sale of securities for customers, paying interest on customer balances and providing margin loans and related services such as customer–directed Individual Retirement Accounts. However, giving individual investment advice is not included. Later on, discount brokerage was added to the list of authorised activities in which bank holding companies may engage ("Regulation Y").

1985   The Federal Reserve Board approved the application by Bankers Trust to engage in the placement of commercial paper. Since then a significant number of banks and bank holding companies have engaged in discount brokerage services, and the Comptroller and the Federal Reserve Board have permitted investment advice (under certain conditions).

1987   The Federal Reserve Board approved the application by Citicorp, J.P. Morgan and Co. Incorporated, and Bankers Trust to underwrite and deal in certain debt securities to a limited extent (up to 5 per cent of revenues) through a bank holding company subsidiary.

Securities firms

As securities firms (or investment banks) were generally less strictly regulated than commercial banks as regards permissible activities these firms could move into "bank–like" activities and other activities without specific deregulatory measures. The pressure on commission income resulting from the deregulation of stock brokerage commissions in May 1975 encouraged the diversification of financial service and related activities by these firms such as real estate, insurance business, "non–bank" banking operations and other "bank–like" activities. Amongst the latter the most noteworthy innovations were the following:

— Money market mutual funds (MMMFs) (combining savings and transactions characteristics); and
— Cash management accounts (CMAs) combining a margin account for the purchase and sale of securities, investment in one or several money market mutual funds, credit card services and a checking account maintained with a bank.

Permissible Activities Abroad

The separation of functions between commercial banks and securities firms applies only to institutions operating in the United States. As far as operations abroad are concerned, notably in the international financial markets, securities firms are free to set up full–service banking subsidiaries and commercial banks have specifically been authorised under Regulation K to underwrite, distribute and deal in debt and equity securities outside the United States (under certain conditions).

2. BANK ACCESS TO STOCK EXCHANGE MEMBERSHIP

CANADA

See under item 1., of the present section.

DENMARK

May 1986   The new Securities Market Law taking effect in 1987 deregulates access to Copenhagen Stock Exchange membership and authorises banks to acquire participations in brokerage companies or to set up new brokerage companies.

FRANCE

1985   Banks (and other financial intermediaries) are authorised to set up, together with brokerage firms (agents de change), incorporated jobber firms (sociétés de contrepartie).

1987   Banks are authorised to take participations in brokerage firms ("sociétés de bourse", formerly "agents de change") up to 100 per cent and thus have access to stock exchange membership. Moreover, as from 1992 the number of stock exchange members will no longer be restricted.

ITALY

1987   Proposals to authorise bank participation in brokerage firms (stock exchange members) under discussion.

SPAIN

1987   Proposals to authorise bank participation in brokerage firms (stock exchange members) under discussion.

TURKEY

1986   Establishment of Istanbul Stock Exchange. Banks have direct access to the Stock Exchange.

UNITED KINGDOM

April 1982   The limit on capital participation in stock exchange member firms by non–member firms (including banks) was raised from 10 per cent to 29.9 per cent.

March 1986   The limit on capital participation in stock exchange member firms by non–member firms (including banks) was abolished and banks — as well as other firms — were allowed to acquire a 100 per cent participation in member firms or to set up new member firms.

V. CREATION AND DIVERSIFICATION OF MARKETABLE FINANCIAL INSTRUMENTS

Competition in banking and finance often takes the form of the creation of new financial instruments through which innovators can gain a competitive edge over other market operators. Although any such new instruments in banking and finance can generally be easily and quickly imitated so that initial gains in market shares may be lost subsequently, it is generally believed that a wide range of financial instruments with different characteristics opening up corresponding choices for borrowers and lenders tends to enhance the competitive climate and strengthen market elements in the financial system. Thus, the authorities in many countries have often made an effort to strengthen market forces in banking and finance by encouraging the creation and diversification of financial instruments.

The present listing of new financial instruments is confined to marketable debt and equity, or equity–linked instruments. No distinction has been made between instruments the introduction of which required special authorisation by the authorities and instruments which could be introduced by banks and other issuers within existing legal frameworks. The listing is not exhaustive although an effort has been made to extend its coverage as much as possible. The information on the introduction of money market instruments contained in Section II has been taken into account for convenience.

AUSTRALIA

Money market and bond market instruments

1962	Marketable Treasury bills ("Treasury Notes").
1965	Bankers' acceptances.
1973	Marketable certificates of deposit. Commercial paper.
1985	Index–linked Treasury bonds.

Financial futures and options

1979	90–day bank bill futures.
1983	Share price index futures.
1984	2–year government bond futures (suspended in March 1986). 10–year government bond futures.
1985	Options on 10–year government bond futures.
1988	3–year government bond futures.

AUSTRIA

1980s	Zero–coupon bonds (1985). Adjustable interest rate bonds. Participation certificates ("Partizipationskapital") (1986). Warrant issues (with warrants for bank participation certificates or certificates of investment funds investing in equities). Profit participation certificates (without voting rights).

CANADA

1962	Bankers' acceptances.
1980s	Stripped bonds (bearer bonds from which coupons have been detached to create zero–coupon instruments).

Floating–rate notes.
Mortgage–backed securities.

DENMARK

1976	Treasury bills (reintroduced after twenty years).
1982	Index–linked mortgage bonds.
1984	Variable–rate government bonds.

FINLAND

1982	Certificates of deposit.
1985	Treasury bills/notes. Commercial paper. Bonds with warrants.
1987	Taxable government bonds. Interest–rate futures.
1988	Index options.

FRANCE

Money market instruments

1985	Negotiable certificates of deposit. Commercial paper.
1986	Negotiable Treasury bills. Finance company paper.

Longer–term debt securities

1970s and 1980s	Variable or adjustable interest rate reference rates such as money market rates or a bond yield index etc.) (1974). Extendible bonds (i.e. bond with option for investor to extend final maturity). Convertible bonds (convertible into other bonds including variable–rate bonds at predetermined conditions). Retractable bonds (i.e. bonds with option for issuer and investor for reimbursement before final maturity). Renewable government bonds (with final maturity of 6 years and option for holder to exchange after 3 years against bonds of another series). Single–coupon bonds (coupon payable at final maturity). Zero–coupon bonds and stripped bonds.

Bonds with warrants (for subscription to another category of bonds).
Bonds with reinvestible coupon (reinvestible into bonds with the same characteristics).
"Bull and Bear" bonds (i.e. bonds with a "bull" and a "bear" tranche the redemption of which is positively or negatively correlated to the performance of a reference stock exchange index).

Equity–linked securities or securities with both bond and equity features

Investment certificates (shares without voting rights essentially issued by nationalised companies) (1983).
Preference non–voting shares (1983).
Shares with warrants (warrants to subscribe to new shares issued in future).
Participating certificates (issued by public–sector enterprises such as EDF and SNCF and credit co–operatives).
Bonds with warrants (right to buy shares at a predetermined price).
Bonds redeemable in shares or investment certificates.

Financial futures

1986	90–day Treasury bill futures. 10–year government bond futures.
1988	Options on government bond futures 3–months PIBOR futures.
1989	Stock exchange index ("CAC 40") futures.

GERMANY

1979	5–year marketable government bonds for personal savers.
1985	Zero–coupon bonds. Variable–rate bonds/notes. Dual currency bonds. Bonds linked to interest rate and currency swaps.

GREECE

1975	Negotiable certificates of deposit.
1985	Negotiable Treasury bills.

1986	Government bonds with an ECU clause.

IRELAND

1978	Variable interest rate government bonds.

ITALY

1975	Negotiable Treasury bills.
1977	Variable interest rate Treasury certificates.
1978	Bankers acceptances.
1983	Negotiable certificates of deposit. Investment fund certificates. Index–linked Treasury certificates.
1987	Deep–discount Treasury certificates.

JAPAN

1977	5–year discount Government bonds.
1978	3–year interest–bearing Government bonds.
1979	Negotiable certificates of deposit.
1980	4–year interest–bearing Government bonds.
1983	15– and 20–year Government bonds.
1986	Bankers' acceptances.

NETHERLANDS

1980	Extendible government bond (with option for investor to extend final maturity).
1986	Negotiable certificates of deposit. Commercial paper. Variable interest rate bonds/notes.
1987	Zero–coupon bonds. Deep–discount bonds. In fact, all financial instruments are allowed, with the exception of index–linked loans. Moreover, an options exchange and a futures market are in operation.
1988	Medium–term rates.

NORWAY

1985	Treasury bills. Negotiable certificates of deposit.

Commercial paper.
Finance company paper.

PORTUGAL

May 1985	Participation units in securities investment trusts.
July 1985	Participation units in real estate investment trusts.
Aug. 1985	Negotiable Treasury bills. Participation bonds.
July 1986	Accrued–interest Treasury bonds.
Oct. 1986	Zero–coupon Treasury bonds. Fixed–rate accrued Treasury bonds.
Dec. 1986	Earmarked certificates.
Feb. 1987	Certificates of deposit.
May 1987	"Tesouro Familiar" (Government bonds).
Nov. 1987	Medium–term Government bonds.

SPAIN

1969	Negotiable certificates of deposit.
1977	Negotiable 3–5 year Treasury notes.
1981	Negotiable Treasury bills (Pagarés del Tesoro).
1983	8–year marketable government bonds.
1986	Forward rate agreement can be subscribed both with clients and deposit–taking institutions under certain assumptions.
1987	Negotiable treasury bills (Letras del Tesoro).

SWEDEN

1978	Stepped–interest rate government bonds (interest rate increasing at specified optional redemption dates).
1979	Variable interest rate and adjustable interest rate government bonds.
1980	Negotiable certificates of deposit.
1982	Negotiable Treasury bills.
1983	Negotiable Treasury notes. Commercial paper.

TURKEY

1980	Introduction of certificates of deposit.
1984	Income–sharing certificates.
1985	Profit–and–loss–sharing certificates.
1987	Mutual funds. Commercial papers. Indexed bonds and income–sharing certificates.

UNITED KINGDOM

1966	Negotiable US$ certificates of deposit.
1968	Negotiable Sterling certificates of deposit.
1973	Convertible government bonds (with option for investors to convert on maturity into a longer–dated bond). Deep–discount government bonds.
1977	Short–term variable–rate government bonds.
1981	Convertible government bonds (with several options for investors to convert into longer–date bonds on pre–determined dates and conditions).
1981–82	Index–linked government bonds (the 1981 issue was only available to pension funds and insurance companies in respect of pension business).
1983	Index–linked convertible government bonds (with several options for investors to convert into conventional high–coupon government bonds on pre–determined dates and conditions).
1986	Sterling commercial paper.

UNITED STATES

Money market instruments

1961	Negotiable certificates of deposit.
1964	Short–term promissory notes.
1974	Treasury cash management bills (no standard maturities).
1980s	Performance–Indexed Paper (PIPs) (i.e. commercial paper with yield indexed on exchange rates, stock price indices, gold price, silver price, crude oil price etc.). Short–term asset–backed securities (i.e. securities backed by receivables

such as credit card receivables (CARDs), automobile loans (CARs) and leases.

Master notes (i.e. unsecured demand notes issued by a variety of non–financial and financial corporations).

Longer–term debt securities

1970s and 1980s

US Treasury zero–coupon bonds (i.e. US Treasury bonds with coupons stripped by market participants to create zero–coupon marketable instruments) (1980s).

Continuously offered medium–term corporate notes (i.e. medium–term notes — known as shelf paper — with maturities of one to ten years sold by corporations in relatively small amounts within the framework of commercial paper–type programmes).

Medium–term certificates of deposit notes (issued by banks).

Dual coupon bonds (with step–up, step–down or zero–to–full coupon).

Progressive rate bonds.

Index–linked bonds (yields linked to inflation rates, stock indices, or commodity prices).

Participation bonds (interest payments vary with company profits).

Income bonds (interest payment depends on adequate earnings).

Deep–discount bonds.

Variable interest rate or adjustable interest rate bonds.

Home mortgage–backed securities.

Commercial mortgage–backed securities.

Securities with equity features

Fixed rate preferred stocks (stocks with fixed–rate dividend).

Adjustable rate preferred stocks (stocks with variable rate dividend tied to a specified interest rate or bond yield indicator).

Financial futures and options

1970s and 1980s

Interest rate futures

Government National Mortgage Association (GNMA) mortgage futures

(1975) 90–day US Treasury bill futures (1976).

15–year US Treasury bond futures (1977).

90–day commercial paper futures (1977).

1–year US Treasury note futures (1978).

4–6 year US Treasury note futures (1979).

90–day certificates of deposit futures (1981).

3–month Eurodollar deposit futures (1981).

Foreign currency futures and options

Options on interest rate futures

Stock exchange index futures and options

INTERNATIONAL MONEY AND SECURITIES MARKETS

Since 1960s

Money market instruments

Negotiable Eurodollar certificates of deposit (London: 1966).

Eurocommercial paper.

Eurodollar bankers' acceptances.

Euronotes (1–6 month paper issued by non–banks).

RUF (Revolving Underwriting Facility) (i.e. combination of Euronote issues and back–up lines).

NIF (Note Issuance Facility) (i.e. combination of Euronote issues and commitment of banks to assist in the placing of the notes under certain conditions).

Longer–term debt securities

Floating rate notes (FRNs).

Variants of floating rate notes:

— Drop–lock FRNs (combination of features of floating rate and fixed rate notes);

— Mismatch FRNs (interest rate adjustment periods are different from the reference period of the underlying interest rate);

— Mini–max FRNs (with a minimum and maximum interest rate);

— Capped FRNs (with a maximum interest rate);

— Flip–flop FRNs (combination of very long maturity and option to convert into shorter maturity FRNs);

— Convertible rate FRNs (option to convert from floating rate into fixed rate note or vice versa).

Deep discount bonds.
Zero—coupon bonds.
Bull and bear bonds (i.e. bonds with a bull and bear tranche the redemption amounts of which are positively or negatively correlated with a stock exchange index).
Bonds with call options (issuer may redeem before final maturity).
Bonds with put options (investor may request redemption before final maturity).
Retractable bond (investor and issuer may request redemption before final maturity).
Extendible bond (investor may request extension of final maturity).
Perpetual bonds (without specified maturity, usually with call option feature).

Equity—linked issues

Euro—convertible bonds (eurobonds convertible into the shares of the issuer).
Euro—warrant issues (eurobonds with warrants attached entitling the holder to purchase shares of the issuer).

Debt securities with warrant for other debt securities

VI. REMAINING RESTRICTIONS ON FINANCIAL SERVICE AND RELATED ACTIVITIES OF COMMERCIAL BANKS
(excluding activities that may be carried out via subsidiaries)

The present section provides an overview of financial service activities which commercial banks in the countries concerned are not (yet) allowed to carry out. The list is not exhaustive as far as country coverage is concerned; it is thus more of an illustrative rather than a comprehensive nature.

CANADA

— Underwriting of corporate debt and equity securities;
— Insurance underwriting and brokerage business;
— Portfolio management in Canada;
— Fiduciary business in Canada;
— Management of mutual funds and selling of mutual fund shares;
— Full—service brokerage activities (including individual investment advice).

DENMARK

— Insurance underwriting and brokerage business.

FINLAND

— Insurance underwriting and brokerage business.

FRANCE

— Insurance underwriting;
— Securities trading on the stock exchange.

GERMANY

— Insurance underwriting business (insurance brokerage business is allowed);
— Own issues of mortgage bonds and communal bonds (subject to special law);
— Building society ("Bausparkassen") business (subject to special law);
— Issues of foreign—currency bonds on own account (restrictive authorisation practice of the Bundesbank); however, there are no restrictions for those foreign—currency issues which are offered by a syndicate composed of non—resident banks only.

189

GREECE

— Insurance underwriting and brokerage business;
— Portfolio management;
— Leasing (only via subsidiaries);
— Real estate development.

ITALY

All financial service and related activities that are not specifically authorised by the banking law, in particular:

— Investment in non–financial corporate securities;
— Limitations on medium–term deposits and loans (with maturities between 18 months and 5 years).

JAPAN

— Buying and selling of real estate on own account (except for own use);
— Brokerage business (for client account) in real estate, commodity futures, insurance contracts, travel packages;
— New issuing and underwriting of domestic equities and equity–related instruments on behalf of corporate customers;
— Securities brokerage services and investment advice;
— Tax advisory services;
— Venture capital management and advisory services.

NETHERLANDS

— Insurance underwriting business (brokerage allowed).

NORWAY

— Insurance underwriting and brokerage business.

PORTUGAL

— Brokerage business on the Stock Exchanges;
— Leasing;
— Insurance business;
— Factoring;
— Buying and selling of real estate on own account (except for own use);
— Investment trusts management;
— Pension funds management.

SPAIN

Banks are prohibited from carrying out the following activities directly; but they may offer some of these services via subsidiaries:

— Bullion dealing;
— Collective investment fund management;
— Credit reference services;
— Real estate agency services;
— Insurance underwriting and brokerage services;
— Leasing.

SWEDEN

— Leasing;
— Factoring;
— Brokerage business in equities beyond certain amount limitations;
— Equity holdings in connection with the new issuing business beyond certain time limitations.

TURKEY

— Buying and selling of real estate;
— Buying and selling of commodities (with the exception of gold bullion).

UNITED STATES

(Activities denied to Bank Holding Companies by Federal Reserve Board):

- Insurance premium (equity) funding (combined sale of mutual funds and insurance;
- Underwriting life insurance not sold in connection with an extension of credit;
- Real estate brokerage;
- Land investment and development;
- Real estate syndication;
- Management consulting;
- Property management services;
- Underwriting mortgage guaranty insurance;
- Operating a travel agency;
- Operating a savings and loan association, except financially troubled thrifts;
- Underwriting home loan life mortgage insurance;
- Contract key entry services (data entry for computer processing);
- Underwriting property and casualty insurance, claims adjustment, and appraisals;

- Dealing in platinum, palladium and other commodities;
- Issuance of market rate intrastate notes;
- Underwriting group mortgage life insurance;
- Pit arbitrage;
- Issuance and sale of large denomination money orders;
- Publication and sale of personnel tests and related materials;
- Providing public credit ratings on securities;
- Providing independent actuarial services.

(Restrictions imposed by Glass–Steagall Act of 1933):
- Underwriting and distribution of corporate securities (private placement allowed);
- Full–service brokerage activities (including individual investment advice);
- Selling mutual fund shares and management of mutual funds.

VII. RESTRICTIONS ON BANK OWNERSHIP

AUSTRALIA

1972	The Banks (Shareholdings) Act requires government approval for the acquisition of 10 per cent or more of a bank's equity capital.
1984	The Government called for applications from both domestic and foreign interests wishing to operate as banks in Australia.
1985	The limit on individual shareholdings in banks raised from 10 to 15 per cent; exemptions from this higher limit may be granted. The measure was taken to facilitate new bank entry.

AUSTRIA

No restrictions.

BELGIUM

In accordance with an agreement between the banks and the Banking Commission ("Commission bancaire") any important change in bank ownership requires the approval by the Banking Commission.

CANADA

Under present legislation, an important distinction is made between Schedule A banks, which are widely held; and Schedule B banks, which are closely held.

For Schedule A banks, no single person/firm can own more than 10 per cent of a bank's share capital; and non–residents in total cannot hold more than 25 per cent of a bank's share capital.

A domestically owned Schedule B bank created de novo which is closely held must become widely held within ten years.

According to the new regulation announced in "New Directions for the Financial Sector" (December 1986), banks with capital under C$750 million will be allowed to be closely held by domestic investors with no commercial interests. However, once a bank attains a capital base above C$750 million, it will be subject to ownership rules which would gradually restrict individual holdings to a maximum of 10 per cent of the banks share capital, and require at least 35 per cent of voting shares of the bank to be publicly traded and widely-held within five years. Banks with capital above C$750 million will be subject to the existing 10/25 per cent restrictions mentioned above for Schedule A banks.

DENMARK

There are generally no restrictions on bank ownership except that insurance companies may not hold direct participations in a bank. However, insurance companies may set up a new bank through the establishment of a holding company.

FINLAND

There are generally no restrictions on bank ownership, except that insurance companies are not allowed to hold participations in a bank exceeding 20 per cent of the bank's share capital. Industrial and commercial (non-financial enterprises) may, partially or wholly, own banks or other financial institutions.

FRANCE

No formal restrictions; but changes in ownership require prior authorisation by the Credit Institutions Committee of a certain importance ("Comité des établissements de crédit"). However, if a transaction results in the acquisi-

tion of more than 5 per cent and less than 10 per cent of the voting rights prior notification is sufficient.

GERMANY

No restrictions other than those implied by general antitrust laws: mergers and participations of 25 per cent or over involving banks are subject to the merger control of the Federal Cartel Office, as applicable to all sectors of the economy. Mergers leading to dominant market positions are prohibited by antitrust laws; mergers and acquisitions of 25 per cent or over require notification to the Federal Cartel Office.

GREECE

The acquisition of a participation in a bank or the setting up of a new bank requires prior authorisation by the Bank of Greece.

IRELAND

In 1971, legislation was introduced which allows the Central Bank to specify ownership criteria. In 1974, the previous emphasis on banks having a major Irish shareholding interest was relaxed to accommodate membership from within the European Community. In 1981, the emphasis on non-EC owned banks having an appreciable Irish shareholding was abolished.

ITALY

The formation of new banks is affected by controls regarding bank ownership in the sense that the "fit and proper person" criterion refers, besides managers and controlling of officers, to shareholders owning 2 per cent or more of a bank's capital. Moreover, the Bank of Italy examines each case with a view to avoiding dominant market positions in terms of capital if bank owners from the non-financial side are involved.

JAPAN

The acquisition of participations in banks, or the setting up of a new bank, is subject to controls under the Anti-Monopoly Law, which requires that no holding company shall be formed and that acquisitions and mergers shall not result in dominating market positions or shall not result from unfair business practices.

LUXEMBOURG

Holders of participations in banks who are in a position to influence the conduct of the bank's business must be of honourable standing, and changes in major shareholdings in banks are subject to prior authorisation.

NETHERLANDS

The exercise of more than 5 per cent of the voting rights in banks or the exercise of a comparable degree of control over banks require prior authorisation by the Minister of Finance or by the Netherlands Bank on the former's behalf. Insurance companies and mortgage banks in which insurance companies have the exercise of more than 5 per cent of the voting rights are not permitted to establish a bank.

NEW ZEALAND

There are generally no restrictions on bank ownership in New Zealand. In terms of the criteria used by the Reserve Bank in assessing applications for bank registration there are no limits placed on individual shareholdings and both bank and non-bank shareholdings are permitted. Where there are material non-bank share-holders, the bank's exposure to those connected parties is restricted. Acquisition of dominance in respect of market share is a factor the Commerce Commission has regard to when assessing any application from a bank to merge with or acquire a shareholding in another bank.

NORWAY

Individual participations in banks above the limit of 10 per cent of a bank's capital or voting rights are prohibited.

PORTUGAL

Feb. 1984   Participations exceeding 20 per cent of the bank's share capital were not allowed.

June 1986   That restriction was abolished but participation exceeding 15 per cent shall be notified to the Banco de Portugal. However, special laws concerning venture capital companies, investment companies, leasing companies, regional development companies and insurance companies prohibit the participation of these categories of financial institutions in banks.

SPAIN

Only individuals can be shareholders of a bank at the moment of establishment and during the first five years thereafter. The establishment of a bank is subject to a discretionary authorisation by the Ministry of Finance. Starting in 1993 this authorisation will no longer be discretionary.

1987   A bill is under consideration to subject the purchase of bank shares that could enable a single holder to own shares of 15 per cent (or over) of the corporation's equity to prior authorisation by the Bank of Spain. Significant (5 per cent) participations in a bank must be notified both to the bank and to the Bank of Spain.

SWEDEN

The establishment of a new bank requires a special licence from the Government.

SWITZERLAND

No restrictions. Exceptions are the authorisation requirements regarding reciprocity in cases of foreign-controlled banks.

TURKEY

No restrictions, but any transfer of shares that represent 10 per cent or more of the capital or any transfer of shares that results in one person controlling that amount of capital, requires the approval by the Under-

secretariat of Treasury and Foreign Trade (UTFT).

UNITED KINGDOM

For participations of 15 per cent or over the Bank of England requires a letter of comfort confirming full and ultimate support by the holder of the participation.

UNITED STATES

Changes in bank ownership involving more than 5 per cent of the voting stock of a bank require prior authorisation by the competent control agencies. A major consideration for approval is whether or not the proposed owners would be a source of financial and managerial strength to the bank.

VIII. DEREGULATION OF BRANCH BANKING

a) Situation at the End of 1960

At the end of 1960 the following countries already applied a liberal policy towards branch banking:

> Australia
> Belgium
> Canada
> Denmark
> Finland
> Germany (since 1958)
> Luxembourg
> Netherlands
> Switzerland
> United Kingdom

b) Deregulation of Branch Banking 1960-1986

AUSTRIA

1979   New Bank Act ("Kreditwesengesetz") deregulates the setting up of new branches.

GREECE

Branching requires authorisation on a case-by-case basis.

FRANCE

Jan. 1967   Abolition of restrictive controls on the setting up of new bank branches (authorisation procedure replaced by simple notification procedure).

1982   Reintroduction of restrictive controls (prior authorisation) on branch banking.

1986   Restrictive control on branching by banks, finance companies, securities firms etc. abolished.

IRELAND

Branching requires authorisation on a case-by-case basis.

ITALY

Jan. 1987   New guidelines for the authorisation of new branches. The objectives are:
- To encourage a supplementary presence of banking institutions in poorly served areas, in accordance with present and prospective development needs;
- To seek to implement more even competition within the various geographical areas, taking into account the number and types of banks already established.

NORWAY

1983   Widening of the scope for banks to set up new branches.

PORTUGAL

The request by banks to open new branches on Portuguese territory is subject to prior authorisation by the Minister of Finance and to annual planning. The criterion for examining those requests will take particularly into account:
- The financial standing of the applicant institution, by attributing a certain capital value (equity or own capital) to each type of branch;
- The number of branches already existing in the locality or zone in question.

March 1988   Under discussion a proposal to deregulate the setting up of new branches (authorisation procedure replaced by simple notification procedure).

SPAIN

1971   Industrial banks authorised to set up more branches.

Aug. 1974   Important relaxation of regulations concerning the setting up of new banks and bank branches.

1985   Branch banking is liberalised and subject only to capital ratio requirements except for a few cases.

SWEDEN

1981   Control on establishment of domestic branch offices abolished.

TURKEY

Branching requires authorisation on a case-by-case basis.

UNITED STATES

Between end-1960 and end-1985, the number of "unit banking states", in which branching is not allowed, was reduced from 18 to 8; the number of states in which state-wide branching is allowed increased from 17 to 24; the number of states in which branching is allowed although not on a state-wide basis increased from 16 to 19.

IX. DEREGULATION OF FOREIGN BANK ENTRY

a) Situation at the End of 1960

At the end of 1960, the following countries, in principle, already applied a liberal policy towards foreign bank entry although related entry conditions varied from country to country:

Austria
Belgium
France
Germany
Ireland
Italy
Japan
Luxembourg
Netherlands
Switzerland
United Kingdom
United States

b) Deregulation of Foreign Bank Entry 1960–1986

AUSTRALIA

Jan. 1983 The Treasurer announced the Government's decision to permit the entry of about ten foreign banks.

Jan. 1984 The Treasurer called for the issue of a further four to six banking licences for both domestic and foreign–owned institutions.

Sept. 1984 The Treasurer announced that the Government was calling for applications from domestic and foreign interests wishing to operate as banks in Australia. To facilitate the entry of new banks the Banks (Shareholdings) Act of 1972 would be amended to lift the individual shareholding limit to 15 per cent, and to allow for exemptions from this new higher limit (amendments passed by Parliament on 22nd May 1985).

Feb. 1985 The Treasurer announced that 16 overseas banks had been invited to establish banking subsidiaries in Australia.

DENMARK

Since Jan. 1975 Foreign banks are free to establish branches in Denmark.

FINLAND

Jan. 1979 Entry into force of a law enabling foreign financial institutions to acquire domestic financial institutions or to establish subsidiaries in Finland.

1982 Based on the above law, the first foreign–owned banks are given permission to be established.

NEW ZEALAND

1987 Under the "new bank" provisions of the Reserve Bank Amendment Act, which came into effect on 1st April 1987, the Reserve Bank is able to register additional banks both foreign and domestic. Any suitably qualified institution whose business substantially comprises the borrowing and lending of money, or the provision of other financial services, or both, is eligible to apply to become a "registered bank". The Act requires the Reserve Bank to have regard to a number of broad factors when considering applicants. These include the applicant's capital, its ability to carry on banking business and its standing in the financial market. In addition where the applicant is a foreign–owned entity the Reserve Bank is required to have regard for the degree of reciprocal entry rights for New Zealand banks in the applicant's home country. In practice this has not precluded foreign ownership and almost all banks operating in New Zealand are foreign owned. While a foreign–owned bank also requires (as for any foreign–owned business starting up in New Zealand) Overseas Investment Commission consent, this is automatic if Reserve Bank consent has been granted.

NORWAY

1974 Foreign banks allowed to set up representative offices.

1984 Bank Act amended to permit foreign banks to set up subsidiaries.

1985 Seven foreign banks granted permission to set up subsidiaries.

PORTUGAL

Oct. 1979 Issuance of regulations governing the establishment and operations of representative offices of foreign banks (subject to prior authorisation by the Finance Ministry).

Feb. 1984 Private banks (both national and foreign) are allowed to set up in Portugal, subject to some limitation.
Since the reopening of the Portuguese banking system to private capital, six foreign private banks have been established in Portugal.

Jan. 1986 The banking law was harmonized with the EEC regulation.

SPAIN

June 1978   Foreign banks are allowed to set up in Spain, subject to some limitations.

Jan. 1987   Minimum capital required at incorporation was adjusted to equal that of domestic banks. Limits on operating conditions are being gradually eased over time until full equality with domestic banks on 1st January 1993 is achieved.

SWEDEN

1970   Foreign banks are allowed to establish representative offices.

1985   Foreign banks are allowed by law to establish subsidiaries in Sweden.

1986   First entry of foreign banks setting up subsidiaries.

TURKEY

Until 1980   Foreign bank entry was not prohibited; however, restrictive foreign exchange regulations were not encouraging foreign banks to establish branches in Turkey. An amendment to the Foreign Investment Law in 1980 and the gradual liberalisation of regulations governing foreign exchange operations since the early 1980s attracted foreign banks to set up branches in Turkey.
According to the Bank Act, establishment of representative offices by foreign banks is subject to the permission of the Ministry to which UTFT is attached.
The permission of the Council of Ministers is also required to establish a bank or to open a branch in Turkey by a foreign bank, in accordance with the Bank Act.

1981   Foreign banks are allowed to establish two branches in Istanbul and one at most in other cities, not exceeding five branches totally in Turkey.

X. ABOLITION OF CREDIT CEILINGS AND DEREGULATION OF MANDATORY INVESTMENT REQUIREMENTS

In implementing policies towards increasing the scope for competition and for the working of market forces in financial resource allocation, the authorities in OECD countries have often abandoned the application of credit ceilings as an instrument of monetary policy and have abolished, or eased, mandatory investment requirements applying to financial institutions such as banks, savings banks and institutional investors.

a) Abolition of Credit Ceilings

AUSTRALIA

1974   Quantitative guidance on bank lending discontinued.

AUSTRIA

1981   Ceilings on total bank lending discontinued.

DENMARK

1985   A market–oriented system of marginal reserve requirements relating to bank deposits replaces various forms of regulation of bank lending applied since 1970.

FRANCE

1986   Abolition of credit ceiling system (i.e. minimum reserves on credit expansion). However, minimum reserves on deposits are maintained.

GREECE

1987   Commercial banks are no longer required to earmark 15 per cent of their deposits for financing fixed investment by private enterprises.

IRELAND

1985   No ceilings on credit expansion in force for the first time since 1965.

ITALY

1983   Direct control on bank lending abolished.

NETHERLANDS

1981   Credit ceilings on bank lending no longer applied.

1986–87   Informal credit ceilings applied to the banking sector in 1986 and 1987.

NEW ZEALAND

1984   Credit growth guidelines removed.

NORWAY

1984   Direct regulation of bank lending abolished.

SWEDEN

1985   Bank lending regulation abolished.

TURKEY

1961   Ceilings on total bank lending abolished. Reserve requirement system replaced credit ceiling system.

UNITED KINGDOM

1971   Competition and credit control: abolition of direct credit controls applying to banks. However, lending guidance continued to be practised through the 1970s and into the early 1980s, and was not formally withdrawn until January 1987.

1973–80   Restrictions on interest–bearing eligible liabilities of banks working as indirect restrictions on credit expansion ("corset"): first introduced in December 1973, suspended in February 1975, reintroduced in November 1976, suspended in August 1977, reintroduced in June 1978 and finally abolished in June 1980.

b) Deregulation of Mandatory Investment Requirements in Selected OECD Countries

AUSTRALIA

1963–78   Savings banks: the minimum proportion of deposits to be invested in government paper was reduced in five steps from 70 to 40 per cent.

Aug. 1982   Savings banks: the minimum proportion of deposits to be invested in government paper was reduced from 40 per cent to 15 per cent.

Sept. 1984   The Treasurer announced the abolition of the 30/20 rule which required insurance companies and pension funds (superannuation funds) to hold at least 30 per cent of assets in public securities and at least 20 per cent in Commonwealth securities.

BELGIUM

1962   Mandatory investment requirements concerning minimum holdings of government paper applying to banks abolished.

FRANCE

1985   Abolition of mandatory holdings of medium–term mobilisation paper.

NEW ZEALAND

1985   Removal of mandatory minimum investment requirements in Government paper and, for some institutions, in local authority paper and in the housing and farming sectors.

NORWAY

1984   Bond purchase requirements applying to banks and insurance companies (introduced in 1969) abolished.

PORTUGAL

April 1982   Insurance companies must hold at least 20 per cent of assets in public securities, 10 per cent in private bonds and 10 per cent in shares.

Jan. 1986   Securities investment trusts must hold at least 80 per cent of assets in national quoted securities, of which 50 per cent must be bonds and/or participation bonds.

Nov. 1986   Pension funds must hold at least 5 per cent of assets in shares (in the first year) and 10 per cent (in the fifth year) of functioning.

March 1987   Insurance companies must hold at least 20 per cent of assets in public securities (Treasury bills excluded) 10 per cent in bonds, and 7.5 per cent in shares and participation bonds.

Feb. 1988   Securities investment trusts must hold at least 75 per cent of assets in domestic quoted securities, of which at least 25 per cent in Government bonds.

SPAIN

1977   Important reduction in the level of legal investment requirements applying to banks and savings banks.

Feb. 1985   Further reduction of legal investment requirements of banks (from 21.5 per cent to 16.5 per cent) and savings banks (from 35.25 per cent to 26.5 per cent).

Dec.   Legal investment requirements of banks, savings banks and co-operative banks are all reduced to 13 per cent of borrowed funds over a period of 5 years.

1987   Legal investment requirements are reduced to 11 per cent of borrowed funds. Ten points must be fulfilled with Treasury bills (Pagarés del Tesoro).

SWEDEN

1983   Investment regulations applying to banks abolished (investment regulations applying to insurance companies and pension funds remain in force).

TURKEY

Banks are subject to invest specified proportion of total TL deposits in government bonds or treasury bills, in accordance with the liquidity requirement system.

XI. CONCENTRATION IN BANKING

An assessment of the competitive situation in a particular market often takes the concentration ratio as an indicator of the market structure. Thus, concentration ratios in banking are sometimes used as indicators for the competitive structure of the banking market. However, as has been pointed out in Annex 1 of the present study, on "Concepts and Definitons", as far as the complex markets for financial services are concerned it is difficult to use concentration ratios based on balance-sheet totals in banking as indicators of the competitive structure in particular sub-markets for financial services. Nevertheless, concentration ratios in banking meet with interest of policy makers insofar as these ratios are sometimes taken as indicators of the concentration of financial power in a given country context. For this reason the following figures are included in the present report.

Share of Five Largest Banks in Total Assets (T) and Domestic Assets (D) of All Banks (in per cent)

		end–1960	end–1984				end–1960	end–1984
Australia[1]	(D)	60	64[3]	Italy	(T)		38[8]	36
Austria	(T)	27	36		(D)		36[8]	32
	(D)	16	30	Japan	(T)		33	33
Belgium[1]	(T)	69	45		(D)		33	28
	(D)	70	60	Netherlands	(T)		79	97
Denmark	(T)	46	57		(D)		78	97
Finland	(T)	..	97[4]	Portugal[6]	(T)		52	55
	(D)	..	59[4]		(D)		54	56
France	(T)	..	52[5]	Spain[7]	(T)		42	43
	(D)	..	48[5]		(D)		42	42
Germany	(T)	18[2]	26	Sweden	(T)		79	89
Greece	(T)	96	83		(D)		82	86
	(D)	95	84	Turkey	(T)		..	63
Ireland	(T)	81	69	United States	(D)		15	13

1. Three largest banks.
2. End–1961.
3. End–1985.
4. End 1987: savings banks and co–operative banks count as one institution each.

5. End 1987.
6. Four largest banks.
7. End–1987: (T) 40; (D) 43.
8. End–1965.

XII. ENTRY AND EXIT OF BANKS
a) Number of Domestic and Foreign Banks End–1960 and End–1985

Country		Number of Institutions Operating on National Territory (D = Domestic; F = Foreign)		Change 1960–1985
		End–1960	End–1985	
Australia	D	21	22	1
	F	3	12	9
		24	34	10
Austria	D	..	1 235	..
	F	..	22	..
		2 169	1 257	–912
Belgium	D	68	27	–41
	F	15	58	43
		83	85	2
Denmark	D	643	219	–426
	F	0	6	6
		643	225	–420
Finland	D	933	631	–302
	F	0	3	3
		933	634	–299
Germany	D	..	4 675	..
	F	..	64	..
		13 979	4 739	–9 240

Country		Number of Institutions Operating on National Territory (D = Domestic; F = Foreign)		
		End–1960	End–1985	Change 1960–1985
Greece	D	8	14	6
	F	2	18	16
		10	32	22
Ireland	D	9	11	2
	F	13	27	14
		22	38	16
Italy	D	1 262	1 065	−197
	F	1	36	35
		1 263	1 101	−162
Japan	D	87	90	3
	F	14	77	63
		101	167	66
Netherlands	D	478	179	−299
	F	2	41	39
		480	220	−260
New Zealand	D	1	1	0
	F	3	14[1]	11[1]
		4	15	11
Portugal	D	23	16	−7
	F	2	9	7
		25	25	0
Spain	D	105	97	−8
	F	4	38	34
		109	135	26
Switzerland	D	..	..	..
	F	50	191	141
		..	..	..
Turkey	D	51	31	−20
	F	6	15	9
		57	46	−11
United States	D	13 464	14 662	1 198
	F	8	393	385
		13 472	15 055	1 583

Source: Country submissions.
1. Mid–1988; and end–1960–mid–1988.

b) Gross Changes in the Number of Domestic and Foreign Banks Operating on National Territory

		1961–1970			1971–1980			1981–1985		
		Entry	Exit	Net Change	Entry	Exit	Net Change	Entry	Exit	Net Change
Australia	D	5	2	3	1	2	−1	4	5	−1
	F	0	0	0	1	1	0	9	0	9
		5	2	3	2	3	−1	13	5	8
Austria		..	..	−145	..	..	−429	..	..	−338
Belgium	D	9	25	−16	1	22	−21	0	4	−4
	F	10	1	9	39	9	30	11	7	4
		19	26	−7	40	31	9	11	11	0
Denmark	D	18	237	−219	19	204	−185	4	26	−22
	F	0	0	0	4	0	4	2	0	2
		18	237	−219	23	204	−181	6	26	−20
Finland	D	..	..	−153	..	..	−125	..	..	−24
	F	..	..	−	..	..	−	..	..	3
		..	..	−153	..	..	−125	..	..	−21
Germany	D + F	..	..	−4 710	..	...	−3 914	..	..	−616
Greece	D	1	1	0	5	0	5	1	0	1
	F	1	0	1	15	0	15	3	3	0
		2	1	1	20	0	20	4	3	1
Ireland	D	10	3	7	1	2	−1	0	4	−4
	F	8	1	7	7	0	7	2	2	0
		18	4	14	8	2	6	2	6	−4
Italy	D	88	175	−87	86	217	−131	71	50	21
	F	4	1	3	21	0	21	12	1	11
		92	176	−84	107	217	−110	83	51	32
Japan	D	2	3	−1	2	2	0	4	0	4
	F	5	1	4	46	0	46	17	4	13
		7	4	3	48	2	46	21	4	17
Netherlands	D	..	..	−176	..	..	−102	..	..	−21
	F	..	..	7	..	..	30	..	..	2
		..	..	−169	..	..	−72	..	..	−19
Portugal	D	0	8	−8	3	6	−3	4	0	4
	F	0	0	0	1	0	1	6	0	6
		0	8	−8	4	6	−2	10	0	10
Spain	D	22	20	2	12	17	−5	0	5	−5
	F	0	0	0	19	0	9	15	0	15
		22	20	2	31	17	14	15	5	10
Switzerland	F	..	..	54	..	..	42	48	3	45
Turkey	D	0	14	−14	1	4	−3	1	5	−4
	F	0	1	−1	0	1	−1	11	0	11
		0	15	−15	1	5	−4	12	5	7
United States	D	1 701	1 537	164	2 401	1 408	993	1 520	1 479	41
	F	52	0	52	162	7	155	189	11	178
		1 753	1 537	216	2 563	1 415	1 148	1 709	1 490	219

Source: Country submissions.

XIII. THE TREATMENT OF THE BANKING SECTOR UNDER COMPETITION LAWS WITH REGARD TO INTERBANK AGREEMENTS ON INTEREST RATES, FEES AND COMMISSIONS

(Situation end–1986)

AUSTRALIA

Interbank agreements on interest rates, fees and commissions prohibited.

AUSTRIA

Bank lending and deposit rates are subject to an interbank agreement [on the basis of the Interbank Regulatory Policy Agreement of 1985 ("Ordnungspolitische Verein-barungen")].
No special regulation for fees and commissions.

BELGIUM

Freedom of setting interest rates on bank credits and loans and on large deposits (in amounts of over 20 million Belgian francs).
Gentlemen's agreement between financial institutions, the Belgian National Bank and the Ministry of Finance on interest rates on time deposits.
Interbank agreement on interest rates on current accounts (0.5 per cent).
Interbank agreement on fees and commissions.

DENMARK

Interbank agreements on interest rates, fees and commissions generally allowed; but since December 1982, no interbank agreement nor any other interbank arrangement limiting competition on bank lending or deposit rates in force.

FRANCE

Bank lending rates are free since 1966 (subject to usury limits). Banks are held to inform their clientele and the general public of the conditions they apply.

GERMANY

Non–binding recommendations by bankers' associations on interest rates, fees and commissions allowed. (Recommendations have to be filed with the Federal Cartel Office and the Banking Supervisory Office. Any abuse of these recommendations is prohibited.)

GREECE

Interbank agreements on fees and commissions are prohibited. Until end–1976, fees and commissions were determined by the Bank of Greece. In the period January 1977 to April 1983, the Bankers Association made binding recommendations on fees and commissions. Since then, banks are free to set fees and commissions.

IRELAND

Banks are excluded from restrictive practices legislation, but the Central Bank has a role to ensure that the banks do not engage in restrictive practices. Up to 1985, the main clearing banks had an agreement to quote similar rates of interest on loans and deposits, and prior to 1984, to charge identical fees and commissions for services.

JAPAN

Interest rate ceilings on bank deposits have existed since 1948 (Temporary Interest Rates Adjustment Law); but interest rates on large deposits have been gradually deregulated from October 1985 onwards.

Interbank agreements on fees and commissions are prohibited under the Anti–Trust Law.

NETHERLANDS

There are no agreements, or recommendations, on bank lending and deposit rates although, as a matter of practice, all bank lending rates are tied to the central bank discount rate on promissory notes.

Minimum fees and commissions are generally subject to interbank agreements.

NEW ZEALAND

1986   Commerce Act passed which prohibits contracts, arrangements or understandings substantially lessening competition. The Commerce Commission, who administer the Commerce Act, can authorise an agreement between businesses if the public benefit outweighs the lessening of competition. However, banks are not treated any differently from other businesses.

SPAIN

Interbank agreements on interest rates, fees and commissions are permitted.

Before July 1964, *minimum* fees and commissions were subject to direct control. Between July 1964 and February 1972, *maximum* fees and commissions were subject to control.

Between February 1972 and January 1981, *maximum* fees on asset operations and *minimum* fees and commissions on services were subject to control.

Since January 1981, only fees on credit operations in pesetas were legally set; all other fees and commissions were deregulated; but interbank agreements were not prohibited.

Since March 1987, all commissions and fees are liberalised.

SWITZERLAND

Interbank agreements on interest rates, fees and commissions are permitted.

TURKEY

There are ceilings on interest rates paid on deposits. However, there are no regulations about interbank agreements on fees and commissions.

UNITED STATES

Interbank agreements on interest rates, fees and commissions are prohibited under Anti–Trust legislation.

NOTES AND REFERENCES

1. Most diversification of activities has taken place through the bank holding company under the provisions of the 1970 Amendments to the Bank Holding Company Act of 1956. The Act provides that proposed activities be both closely related to banking and provide net public benefits when performed by the bank holding company.

Because of the provision that activities be closely related to banking, banks are also permitted to perform most of these activities.

2. Dates refer to the first approval; authorised activities may be subject to restrictions in individual cases.

Annex IV

THE APPLICATION OF COMPETITION LAWS
AND POLICIES TO THE BANKING SECTOR

The present annex contains information on how competition laws in OECD countries apply to the banking sector and is based on information received from Members of the Committee on Competition Law and Policy. It generally reflects the situation as of June 1987. Since the note was written, new legislation has been adopted in Finland as from 1st October 1988 and Ireland as from 25th January 1988 which has removed the exemption for banking from the competition legislation.

The Application of Competition Laws and Policies to the Banking Sector

a) *Introduction*

The scope and nature of the application of national competition laws to the banking sector vary considerably from country to country. In three countries — Austria, Finland and Ireland — the banking sector is totally exempt from the principal competition legislation. In Belgium, public establishments subject to permanent authority or control of a Minister are also exempt from the competition legislation and, to the extent that many financial institutions come within this definition, they are also exempt. In six others — Australia, France, Germany, Netherlands, Norway and Portugal — partial exemptions exist for particular activities. In all countries, financial institutions are also subject to other special regulations which may sometimes supplant or override the competition legislation. In eight other countries — Canada, Denmark, Japan, New Zealand, Sweden, Switzerland, United Kingdom, United States — as well as in the European Communities, the competition provisions are generally fully applicable to the banking sector.

Broadly speaking, it would seem that, where the law does apply, it is a relatively recent development. Historically, a number of countries adopted legislation to control services later than goods but the increasing importance of the banking sector has led to increased interest on the part of governments in the operations of banks. This has led not only to amendments to legislation but also to increased enforcement of existing legislation against the activities of the banks.

In addition, as noted in the Committee of Experts on Restrictive Business Practices' report on competition policy and deregulation (OECD, 1986), the banking sector has been the object of a large number of measures and proposals in recent years to liberalise the regulatory system and to open up the sector to competition subject to control under general competition legislation.

In several Member countries such measures have included allowing foreign banks to establish themselves in what was formerly a protected market in these countries. The countries involved here are Australia, Canada, Finland, New Zealand, Norway and Sweden. In Australia, the number of banks more than doubled from 1985 to 1986, rising from 12 to 28 as a result of liberalising entry.

Moreover, in France an amendment to the banking legislation in July 1985 makes agreements and abuses of dominant positions in the banking sector, hitherto subject to the banking legislation, now subject to the general prohibition of Articles 7 and 8 of the new 1986 Ordinance on Freedom of Prices and Competition. In Canada, the recently adopted Competition Act 1986 brings bank mergers and interbank agreements within the scope of the general rules of the new Act, subject to a right of authorisation of mergers by the Minister of Finance if he considers a merger desirable in the interest of the financial system. In Finland and Ireland, consideration is also being given to extending the respective competition legislation to the banking sector. In the United Kingdom, on the other hand, the new legislation on the financial services sector largely exempts the sector as regards investment business from the competition legislation. However, building societies, under new legislation, are permitted to carry on a wide range of additional activities traditionally reserved for banks, and the former exemption from the Restrictive Trade Practices Act of agreements between building societies to agree on interest rates is abolished.

b) Agreements between Banks

At present certain horizontal agreements between banks are exempt in three countries — Germany, Norway and the United Kingdom – from the full force of the competition legislation. This exemption is however only partial. Thus, in Germany, restrictive agreements between banks and recommendations of associations of banks are exempted from the general prohibition of the Act but banks are subject to abuse supervision and to the merger control provisions of the Act. In practice, a few non–binding recommendations with regard to interest rates still exist in Germany as well as recommendations and agreements in connection with certain payment methods and technologies such as eurocheques, cash dispensers and electronic fund transfer systems. In Norway, six agreements between banks on interest rates, fees and commissions have been granted special exemption from the Royal Decree of 1960 but otherwise banking practices remain subject to the Act on Control of Prices, Profits and Restraints of Competition of 1953. In the United Kingdom, certain agreements in the financial sector are exempt from the registration requirement under the Restrictive Trade Practices Act (RTPA). However, agreements between banks on for example, interest rates, will generally be subject to registration under the RTPA and banks are subject to the general provisions of the Competition Act 1980 and the Fair Trading Act 1973. The Fair Trading Act has been employed in relation to the supply of credit card franchise services.

In all other countries, interbank agreements fall within the general provisions of the competition legislation and in several countries enforcement action has been taken against them, with the general effect of eliminating or reducing their tenor to that of recommendations rather than agreements.

c) Mergers

In most countries with merger control provisions mergers and acquisitions involving banks enjoy no special treatment under competition legislation. Indeed there may be additional requirements imposed on their banking regulations over and above the provisions of the competition legislation. Thus in Australia, the prior consent of the Treasurer is required for mergers between authorised banks and individual shareholdings are generally limited to 15 per cent. In Denmark, although there are no special provisions to control mergers under the Monopolies Supervision Act under Section 48 of the Bank Act, mergers between banks must be notified to the Banking Supervisory Authority and approved by the Minister of Industry. Other than this qualification, bank mergers are fully subject to control under general merger control laws in all countries except Finland and Ireland (Austria has no merger control). There have been several cases of enforcement of this provision, especially in the United Kingdom and the United States, while in other countries the generally small size of the mergers that have taken place in the banking sector has not given cause for intervention.

d) Abuses of dominant positions

The general rule is that abuses of dominant position by banks are fully subject to the relevant provisions of the competition legislation, except in the countries which have exempted the sector entirely. It would appear however that in most countries few banks are large enough to qualify for control under this provision and there have been relatively few cases of it having been applied.

Statistical Data on Mergers and Concentration in the Banking Sector

Some data were available from 14 countries on merger and concentration trends over the period 1960–1984/5. The figures show a clearly rising trend in concentration during the period 1960–1984 (when measured by the share of the largest four or five banks of total banking assets) in seven countries — Australia, Austria, Denmark, Germany, Netherlands, Sweden and Switzerland. The largest increase was in Switzerland where the share of total assets held by the five largest banks almost doubled from 37.3 per cent in 1960 to 66.7 per cent in 1984. In Finland, the number of savings banks and co–operative banks declined between 1960 and 1985 but the number of commercial banks doubled (from five to ten). In six other countries — Belgium, Canada, Greece, Ireland, Japan and the United States — the five–firm concentration ratio declined over the same period. However, the ratio in Japan and the United States declined only slightly.

In most countries it would appear that there remains a considerable number of banks despite evidence of widespread merger activity especially among the smaller banking institutions. There would seem however to have been relatively few "large" bank mergers, perhaps due to the existence of merger control in many countries, whether operated by the banking or competition authorities. For example, in the United States there have been no mergers either permitted or prohibited involving two banks ranking within the top ten.

Country Notes on the Treatment of the Banking Sector under Restrictive Business Practices Legislation

The following country notes are structured as follows:

1. How do the national competition laws apply to banking? Notably to:

   a) Agreements between banks (e.g., on interest rates, fees and commissions);
   b) Mergers, acquisitions and joint ventures involving banks;
   c) Abuses of dominant positions by banks.

Significant cases in application of the laws are covered as well.

2. Statistical data on mergers and concentration in the banking sector.

AUSTRALIA

1. Anti-competitive practices in Australia are generally subject to the provisions of the Trade Practices Act 1974. Nevertheless, statutory exemption is provided for activities specifically authorised by Commonwealth, State or Territory legislation. This exemption is of particular relevance to the banking sector, as it is subject to various forms of banking legislation, principally the Banking Act 1959. Moreover, the universal application of the Trade Practices Act may be affected by constitutional limitations.

This situation should be borne in mind in reading the following paragraphs a) – c), which describe sections of the Trade Practices Act which would most likely apply to anti-competitive practices in the banking sector.

   a) Under the Act, agreements which have the purpose, effect or likely effect of substantially lessening competition are prohibited. Agreements which are aimed at fixing, controlling or maintaining prices are deemed to be anti-competitive *per se*. Except for most price agreements on goods and certain other agreements, authorisation is available if the public benefit outweighs any anti-competitive detriment.

   b) The Act covers mergers and incorporated joint ventures that result in, or strengthen, a position of market dominance. Authorisation is available if the public benefit outweighs any anti-competitive detriment. The application of these provisions to the banking sector is reinforced by provisions of the Banking Act 1959, which requires that an authorised bank may not dispose of its business by merger, sale or otherwise without the prior consent of the Treasurer. Also the Banks (Shareholdings) Act 1972 requires a general limit of 15 per cent on the beneficial interest of any one shareholder in a bank, but allows for exemptions from this limit in the national interest.

   c) Under the Act, corporations that have a substantial degree of power in a market are prohibited from taking advantage of that power if it has a requisite predatory purpose, such as to eliminate or substantially damage a competitor.

2. There has been an historically high and generally rising level of concentration in the Australian banking sector. However, this trend has changed somewhat with the decision in September 1984 to allow a limited number of foreign banks to operate in Australia.

Prior to this decision, mergers reduced the number of major nationally operating trading banks in Australia from eight in 1960 to four in 1985. In addition to these four national banks and the fifteen foreign banks which have commenced operations in Australia, there are four State banks, three other minor national trading banks, the Bank of China, and two other long-standing foreign banks with limited branch representation.

A variety of factors appear to have motivated the bank mergers. These include the potential for rationalisation of operations and exploitation of economies of scale; the provision of more geographically balanced networks of branches; a desire of the larger merging bank to increase international competitiveness associated with being a larger bank; and a reaction to increased competition in Australian banking from overseas sources.

The following table presents trading bank concentration levels since 1960 as expressed by the percentage share of assets controlled by the four largest banks.

The table relates only to trading banks. Trading banks comprise the largest institutional group in the Australian financial system, but their importance has declined over recent decades, reflecting principally the emergence of more specialised finance companies, money–market corporations, building societies and co–operative credit unions. Trading banks, however, retain their special position in the financial system due to their dominant role in both the domestic and international payments systems and their operations across all business sectors and most classes of business finance.

In addition to trading banks, savings banks have been an important institutional group in the Australian financial system. Apart from the four major trading banks which conduct savings bank operations, there are several State savings banks and eight other savings banks, two of which are subsidiaries of new foreign banks. The role of savings banks is more specialised than trading banks in that they are principally directed towards household savings and the provision of housing finance.

	Share of assets held by largest four banks	Total number of banks	Total assets A$M
June 1960	64	15	3 872
June 1965	64	15	5 297
June 1970	66	15	7 960
June 1975	73	13	17 973
June 1980	71	13	34 074
June 1985	83	12	76 706
June 1986	76	28	103 319

AUSTRIA

1. Financial institutions are totally exempted from the Cartels Act 1972 (Section 5). This exemption also applies to market dominating banks (Section 40).

a) According to Section 20 of the Banking Act 1979, as amended in 1986, the setting of interest rates on deposits is generally unrestricted, but the banking associations, as well as the Postal Savings Bank, may enter into agreements concerning interest rates for all kinds of savings deposits.

While an agreement on bank deposit rates was abolished 1st July 1980, an agreement on interest rates on three months savings deposits was concluded in February 1979 and is still in force.

In March 1985, a gentlemen's agreement was reached amongst banks, whereby they agreed on certain guidelines for lending and deposit rates. There are no special regulations for fees and commissions.

According to Section 21 of the Banking Act, the banking associations and the Austrian Postal Bank shall, in order to regulate competition and advertising, conclude an agreement regarding competition and create a committee on competition. For this agreement a permit from the Federal Minister of Finance shall be required, in order to make sure that the agreement does not contradict the principles of creditor protection, or impair the effectiveness of the banking system. The competition agreement was concluded January 1985 and permitted March 1985.

b) According to Section 8 of the Austrian Banking Act, as amended in 1986, a special authorisation by the Federal Minister of Finance is required for the acquisition by a bank, whether direct, indirect or in trust for another party, of holdings in other banks, or by means of partnerships under the Commercial Code or by means of legal entities which conduct no banking business but in which banks have holdings, and for the increase or reduction of such holdings as well; excepted are holdings of banks in their central institutions and vice versa. Holdings are shares in other enterprises which are intended to benefit their own business operations by creating a permanent connection with the other enterprise. In this connection it is irrelevant whether or not share certificates are issued.

Shares of a corporation or of a co–operative society, the par value of which exceeds 25 per cent of the stated capital or of all the shares, shall always be deemed holdings; the same shall apply by analogy to holdings in limited partnerships. Memberships in a partnership which entail unlimited liability shall always be deemed a holding.

c) The provisions of the Cartel Act which cover market dominating enterprises do not apply to banks.

2. Concentration in the banking sector: the balance sheet total of the ten largest institutions amounted to 50.6 per cent of the balance sheet total of all Austrian banks together (as of 31st December 1984).

The concentration ratio, defined as total (domestic) assets of the five largest banks as a ratio of total (domestic) assets of all banks, was 27 per cent at end–1960 and 36 per cent at end 1984.

BELGIUM

1. The Act of 27th May 1960 on protection against the abuse of economic power applies in principle to the banking sector. However, under Section 27 of the Act, public financial institutions do not fall under the Act when they are subject to the authority or permanent control of a Minister. Section 27 states that "Sections 1 to 26 of this Act shall not apply to the State, provinces, municipal authorities or public establishments or to public bodies under the permanent authority or control of the Minister responsible for them unless, on the advice of the Ministers assembled in Council, the King has supplemented and amended the Act to that effect. Such Royal Decree shall be issued within five years from the date of coming into force of this Act." However, no such Royal Decree has been issued within the prescribed period.

The new Competition Bill proposes that the banking sector, like the insurance sector, will be exempted.

a) Banks are free to fix interest rates, but financial institutions, the national banks and the Minister of Finance have concluded a Convention concerning the fixing of interest rates on loans. In addition, there are interbank agreements on interest on deposits as well as tariffs and commissions. it should also be mentioned that in the fiscal context, Royal Decrees have been issued concerning income from savings deposits.

The legal regime instituted by these Royal Decrees consists in fixing the level of remuneration from savings deposits – a uniform rate for all participants in the market as well as a margin for savers beyond which they would forfeit their fiscal privileges for ordinary savings deposits.

These Royal Decrees fixing the level of remuneration on savings are currently the object of legal proceedings for their annulment in Belgium and proceedings before the European Court of Justice.

b) Mergers are not restricted in Belgium. However, Article 4 of the Royal Decree of 9th July 1935 on the control of banks subjects all mergers to the authorisation of the Banking Commission which must ascertain whether the merger is compatible with the regulations.

c) There have been no cases of application of the Act of 27th May 1960 to the banking sector.

2. Statistical data on mergers and concentration.

a) During the period 1960–1985, 35 banks established in Belgium have participated in mergers or have been acquired by other banks. Moreover, a foreign bank, the Banque de Paris et des Pays–Bas (France) merged with the Banque de Financement to create the Banque de Paris et des Pays–Bas Belgique established under Belgian law in 1968.

b) Concentration ratios, three largest banks:

Year	In relation to total assets	In relation to domestic assets
1960	69.2	69.5
1984	44.6	59.4

CANADA

1. Chartered banks, which are the largest financial group in the country, are subject to competition policy legislation, but only to the extent that no parallel legislation is provided for in the Bank Act. In 1976 chartered banks became subject to the Combines Investigation Act with respect to offences of monopoly, predatory pricing, price maintenance, and offences relating to consumer protection. With the passage of the new Competition Act in June 1986, competition policy provisions were extended to further cover banks.

Prior to the new Competition Act interbank agreements and mergers involving banks were exempted from competition law and remained subject to the Bank Act. Agreements regarding the rate of interest on deposits or loans, the amount of service charges, or the amount or kind of loan or service provided to the customer were prohibited *per se* under section 309 of the Bank Act.

Mergers involving a chartered bank, according to section 261.4 of the Bank Act, require the agreement of the Minister of Finance before being submitted to shareholders for approval. The Bank Act statutes do not describe any test or guidelines to be used in approving the merger, thus giving the Minister substantial discretionary authority.

To date, there have been no formal inquiries or prosecutions of banks under the provisions of either the Combines Investigation Act or the Bank Act.

The new Competition Act grants the Director of Investigation and Research responsibility concerning bank mergers and anti–competitive horizontal agreements. Section 309 of the Bank Act, which contains prohibitions on interbank agreements, was replaced and enacted in similar form (along with existing exemptions) in the Competition Act. Also, the merger section of the Competition Act will apply to bank amalgamations. However, in recognition of the special role played by the banks, the provision will not apply if the Minister of Finance certifies to the Director that the merger is desirable in the interest of the financial system.

2. Concentration in Canadian banking has declined steadily since the 1960s. In 1966, the four largest banks accounted for 82 per cent of Canadian banking sector assets. Their share of banking sector assets has declined gradually to 77 per cent in 1979 and 73 per cent in 1986.

There are currently eight domestically–owned banks and fifty–five foreign bank subsidiaries in Canada. Foreign banks have been allowed to establish subsidiaries to accept deposits and make loans in Canada since 1980. Throughout the early 1960s, there were eight chartered banks in the country: however, in 1967 the Bank of British Columbia received a charter bringing the total number of banks up to nine. A tenth bank, La Banque Populaire, commenced operations in 1969. In 1970, it merged with La Banque Provinciale du Canada, bringing the total number of banks in the country down to nine. In 1979, La Banque Provinciale du Canada merged with the Banque Canadienne Nationale to become the National Bank of Canada. More recently, in 1986, the National Bank acquired the Mercantile Bank of Canada, and three small domestically–owned banks were acquired by foreign (Schedule B) banks: Security Pacific Bank Canada acquired the Morguard Bank, Lloyds Bank International Canada acquired the Continental Bank of Canada, and Hong Kong Bank of Canada acquired the Bank of British Co-

lumbia. A number of new domestically–owned banks commenced operations during this period. These include: the Northland Bank (1976), Canadian Commercial Bank (1976), Continental Bank of Canada (1979), Western and Pacific Bank of Canada (1983), and the Bank of Alberta (1984). The last bank failure to occur in Canada prior to 1985 was the failure of the Home Bank in 1923. However, in 1985, two small regional banks, the Canadian Commercial Bank and the Northland Bank, failed and ceased operations. Together, these two banks accounted for approximately 1 per cent of Canadian banking sector assets.

DENMARK

1. The banking sector is subject to the Monopolies Supervision Act 1955. According to a Regulation issued in 1955 by the Minister of Commerce, supervision of the banking sector was transferred to the Supervision of Banks, which also controls these financial institutions as provided by the Bank Act.

However, in 1979 the ministerial regulation of 1955 was repealed by an amendment to the Monopolies Supervision Act.

In a new provision of the Act [Section 3(3)] it was established that, as far as commercial banks, savings banks and co–operative banks were concerned, the powers of the Monopolies Control Authority (MCA) under this Act should be exercised by the Supervision of Banks.

According to this, the provisions of the Monopolies Supervision Act on notification and registration of agreements and dominant individual enterprises, intervention against terms of business, prices etc., and on release of investigations fully apply to the banking sector, with the only exception that decisions cannot be brought before the Monopolies Appeal Tribunal.

In pursuance of Section 3(4) of the Act, the decisions of the Supervision of Banks can be appealed to the Minister of Industry.

Before decisions are made on measures which might influence the monetary policy, the Supervision of Banks must consult Danmarks Nationalbank (the Danish National Bank), cf. Section 3(5), and if it is found that considerations of competition policy should be weighed against considerations of monetary policy, the decision rests with the Minister of Industry, thus opening up the possibility that the Government can take a position on the monetary problems.

a) In pursuance of Section 6(1) of the Monopolies Supervision Act 21 agreements are registered with the Supervision of Banks, including an information agreement, according to which the five largest banks brief one another when one of them decides any change in a number of rates, i.e., interest rates, fees and commissions, rental of safe–deposit boxes, cheques, information, inquiries and interest coupons.

b) While the Monopolies Supervision Act does not contain special rules on merger control, it is provided in Section 48 of the Banks Act that a commercial bank or savings bank may not, without the permission of the Minister of Commerce (now the Minister of Industry), take over another commercial bank or savings bank, or any branch or department of such. The same applies if a commercial bank or savings bank is merged with another commercial bank or savings bank.
In 1983 Sjaellandske Bank and Frederiksborg Bank obtained the permission of the Minister of Industry to merge under the name of Kronebanken, and in 1985 the Minister of Industry permitted Den Danske Provinsbank to take over Kronebanken.

c) As to the present situation of the banking sector, competition between Danish banks is more keen today than ever. The main reason is the rather large number of banks. At the end of 1985 there were 80 commercial banks and 150 savings banks, and none of these holds a dominant position.

2. Concentration ratios, five largest banks:

Year	In relation to total assets	In relation to domestic assets
1960	46.0	not
1984	57.0	available

FINLAND

1. While Finnish banking institutions are not governed by general competition laws, they are controlled by a special authority — the Banks Inspectorate — by virtue of the Inspection of Banks Act. According to Section 3 of the Act on the Promotion of Economic Competition and Section 7 of the Bank Inspection Act, the Bank Inspectorate shall in particular follow the circumstances prevailing in banking and make suggestions for measures to be taken on the basis of economic development, especially for the promotion, from the general point of view, of acceptable economic competition in banking.

a) Finnish banking institutions have had different kinds of mutual interest rate agreements. The present agreement applies exclusively to deposits governed by the Act on Tax Privileges for Deposits. The interest rate agreement was concluded in the 1930s at the instigation of the Bank of Finland. The tax privilege systems concerning deposits have been in force as temporary acts since the beginning of the 1940s. In principle the interest rate agreement in force is a cartel agreement stipulating the rights of withdrawal and the conditions of notice, whereas the interest rate depends upon the decisions of the Bank of Finland concerning the basic rate of interest, and is therefore variable but always bound to the basic rate of interest fixed by the Bank of Finland.
Finnish banking institutions have had different kinds of tariff agreements establishing the minimum rates for certain charges and commissions. Since the beginning of 1985 no such agreement has been in force.

b) Permission for a merger of one bank with another or for merger of banks for the purpose of establishing a new banking institution is granted by the Ministry of Finance. The Ministry has the right to give in each case detailed orders of how the merger shall be carried out. A commercial bank can be merged only with another commercial bank (Section 89a of the Act on Commercial Banks), a savings bank with another savings bank (Section 112 of the Act on Savings Banks), a co–operative bank only with another co–operative bank (Section 90a of the Act on Co–operative Banks), a mortgage bank only with another mortgage bank (Section 76a of the Act on Mortgage Banks) and a mortgage society only with another mortgage society (Section 4 of the Act on Mortgage Societies).

c) Not available.

The degree of concentration varies according to the item of the balance sheet to be compared, and is highest in foreign exchange transactions. This is due to the fact that only commercial banks and the Post Office Bank are authorised foreign exchange banks.

2. Number of banking institutions in Finland:

	Commercial Banks	Savings Banks	Co-operative Banks	Mortgage Banks	Mortgage Societies
1960	5	390	537	4	2
1985	10	254	370	6	1

FRANCE

1. In January 1984, bank activities became subject to a specific regulation under a law relating to the activities and control of banks. The Act defines three different kinds of activities: *a)* "banking operations" such as deposit taking, credit granting, and payment transactions; *b)* "related operations", as for instance, exchange operations and trade in securities; *c)* "acquisitions" as defined by the Bank Regulatory Committee; and *d)* "different operations", such as product selling, travel agencies, and insurance.

Banking operations are subject to Articles 7 to 10 of the Ordinance of 1st December 1986 on Freedom of Pricing and Competition which concern cartels, abuses of a dominant positions or the abuse of a situation of economic dependence. Contraventions are sanctioned by the Competition Commission. In addition, the Ordinance applies to banking operations carried out under legislation or regulatory provisions relating to the Exchequer, the Bank of France, financial services of the Post Office, Issuing Authority for Overseas Departments, and the Deposit and Consigment Bank (Caisse des Dépôts et Consignations).

As regards *related operations and acquisitions*, illegal cartels and abuses of dominant positions are under the jurisdiction of the Banking Commission even if the offences are found to occur outside banking activities proper.

Other operations remain subject to the common law provisions, in their entirety, of the Ordinance of 1st December 1986 and to the jurisdiction of the Competition Council.

A particular procedure has been laid down for restrictive business practice cases concerning the banking sector under the Decree of 29th December 1986. When a case is referred to the Competition Council, the Council must inform the Banking Commission which has two months to comment upon the case. These comments are added to the file.

2. Not available.

GERMANY

1. In general, banks are subject to the Act Against Restraints of Competition. The only exemption refers to restrictive agreements between banks and recommendations of associations of banks. The need for maintaining confidence in the banking business and for protecting in particular the vast number of private customers, as well as the importance of this industry as a medium and a partner of the Government's currency, credit and cyclical policies are seen as justifying grounds for the cartel–law exemption of the banking industry.

a) According to Section 1 of the Act, restrictive horizontal agreements are prohibited. The same applies to recommendations of associations of enterprises (Section 38). However, under Section 102 the banking sector is exempted from these regulations, although the conduct exempted is subject to abuse supervision by both the cartel authority and the banking supervisory authority. Moreover, if it is intended to make use of the exemption, the applicant has to state reasons for the intended restriction of competition. In particular, the party making the notification must state what the restriction of competition consists of and why it is considered to be necessary. The restriction cannot take effect immediately but only after a period of three months from the receipt of the notification by the competent regulatory authority. In individual cases, this period can be shortened or dispensed with, for example if the underlying provisions and recommendations are in the interest of the bank's customers or if they are necessary for reasons of supervisory, currency, monetary or capital market policy. Within this waiting period the cartel authority must give the economic circles involved an opportunity to present their views. This is not necessary in cases of minor importance and in cases where the restrictive agreement merely relates to banking methods and procedure.

In practice, there are only non–binding interest recommendations made by the central associations of the banking industry. During the last few years, no fixed rates have been recommended, but only the directions which interest rates were to take were indicated. More recently, the central associations have been considering dropping even such recommendations.

Recommendations and agreements by the central associations regarding prices and conditions are often made among the financial institutions and addressed to the bank customers in connection with the use of certain payment methods and technologies (eurocheque, cash dispensers, POS systems). In general, the new communication and information technologies, which are widely used in the banking industry, increasingly tend to result in agreements and recommendations that are not least designed to allow a smooth and low–cost handling of mass payments and to grant bank customers a minimum of transparency.

b) Banks are subject to merger control under Section 23 and 24a of the Act Against Restrictions of Competition, but to date there has been no need to apply these rules. The concentration process, which in the past mainly affected the area of co–operative banks and the savings banks sector, has in recent years taken place mostly in the sector of small private banks by way of acquisition of equity holdings. The main reasons for this development are that the banks involved are smaller specialised institutions offering services (such as asset counselling) which do not appear on their balance sheets, and that such specialised services are also offered by the large universal banks together with the full range of banking services. In addition, the trend towards concentration among small private banks is due to their limited amount of own resources, the lack of possibilities of geographical expansion and, due to the low level of customers' deposits, their strong dependence on expensive refinancing in the interbank market.

c) Under Section 22 of the Act against Restraints of Competition, banks are subject to abuse supervision of market dominating enterprises. In practice there have been no indications of such abuse by individual banks.

2. Concentration ratios, five largest banks:

Year	In relation to total assets	In relation to domestic assets
1961	18	not
1984	26.4	available

GREECE

1. a)–c) Not available.
2. Concentration ratios, five largest banks:

Year	In relation to total assets	In relation to domestic assets
1960	95.9	94.8
1984	83.3	84.9

IRELAND

1. The present position is that banks remain outside the scope of the Restrictive Practices Act 1972 and are also excluded from the scope of the Mergers, Takeovers and Monopolies (Control) Act 1978. In November 1986, the Minister for Industry and Commerce published the Restrictive Practices (Amendment) Bill, 1986. This provided, *inter alia*, that banks would be brought within the scope of the Restrictive Practices Act, 1972. However, banks would continue to be excluded from the scope of the Mergers, Take–overs and Monopolies (Control) Act, 1978. In the event, the Bill was not dealt with when the term of office of the Government ended, and the Bill will have to be re–introduced to the next Dail (Irish Parliament).

a) Cartel arrangements operated by the four associated banks have recently been gradually dismantled. The first change occurred in late 1984, when variable charges for banking services were introduced by the banks on an individual basis. Then, in mid–1985, the ending of the cartel on interest rates previously operated by the four associated banks in association with the Central Bank was announced. The new arrangements introduced by the Central Bank provide that there will be one maximum permissible prime lending rate with each bank free to set its own prime lending rate at or below the permitted maximum. The banks are now also free to individually decide upon lending and deposit rates subject to conformity with parameters — which reflect the current structure of interest rates — set by the Central Bank. The Central Bank reserves the right to suspend the operation of the system, should this be necessary in the public interest. It is proposed to review the operation of the interest rate arrangements within a period of six months. The normal arrangements governing associated bank interest charges were suspended on 4th February 1986 in the light of exceptional and temporary pressures on interest rates deriving from speculative flows. This action lasted until 10th April 1986, when normal arrangements were resumed.

b) Not available.
c) Not available.

2. a) List of major bank mergers/acquisitions:

Year	Name and balance sheet total of institutions involved	(Ir £ mil)
1966	Munster and Leinster Bank	152
	Provincial Bank of Ireland	79
	Royal Bank of Ireland	39
1965	Bank of Ireland	137
	National Bank	76

b) Concentration ratios, five largest banks:

Year	In relation to total assets	In relation to domestic assets
1960	81	82
1984	69	85

JAPAN

1. Banks are not specifically exempted from the Antimonopoly Act. A special regulation, however, exists under the Banking Act and the Act for Temporary Adjustment of Interest Rates in order to control competition in banking. There have been no significant cases in application of competition laws in the banking sector since 1979.

a) Any agreement which substantially restrains competition in any particular field of trade is prohibited as "unreasonable restraint of trade" under the Antimonopoly Act.
b) Under the Antimonopoly Act, mergers and acquisitions are prohibited when the effect of such action may be to substantially restrain competition in any particular field of trade and/or when unfair trade practices have been employed. Prior notification to the Fair Trade Commission is required with respect to the following activities:

i) Mergers;
ii) Acquisitions or leasing of the whole or a substantial part of a business;
iii) Acquisition of the whole or a substantial part of fixed assets;
iv) Undertaking of the management of the whole or a substantial part of a business;
v) Entering into a contract which provides for a joint profit and loss account for a business.

Moreover, under the Banking Act, no merger or acquisition involving banks can be put into effect without the approval of the Finance Minister.

c) Under the Antimonopoly Act, any activity through which an entrepreneur substantially restrains competition in any particular field by means of excluding or controlling the business of others is prohibited as "private monopolisation". Also, the following practices are prohibited as "abuse of dominant bargaining positions" — one of the unfair trade practices designated by the FTC:

i) Trading with other parties on unjustly disadvantageous conditions by making use of dominant bargaining positions;
ii) Causing transaction partners to follow the dominant party's direction or to require its approval regarding the appointment of officers.

2. Statistical data on mergers in the banking sector: 1960-1985

Fiscal Year	Number of bank mergers if not 0
1967	1
1968	1
1969	2
1970	5
1971	5
1972	4
1973	3
1976	2
1983	1

Note:

1. 1960–1966: mergers between banks, the capital of one of which exceeds Y 500 million.
2. 1967–1980: mergers after which the capital exceeds Y 1 billion.
3. 1981–1985: mergers after which the total assets exceed Y 30 billion.

b) Concentration ratios, five largest banks:

Year	In relation to total assets	In relation to domestic assets
1960	33.4	33.1
1984	32.6	28.2

NETHERLANDS

1. The regulation of the banking system is elaborated in the Act of Supervision of the Credit System 1978.

a) The authorities exercise no control on interest rates on bank deposits and other savings instruments.

The Netherlands Bankers' Association has established agreed minimum tariffs for a wide range of banking services.

The authorities exercise no control over bank lending rates and rates on lending by other financial institutions. Banks and other financial institutions as a rule follow the central bank discount rate. They are not obliged to do so and the degree of linkage may differ.

Lending rates are not subject to cartel agreements or recommendations by associations within the financial sector.

b) Any merger which is defined as any participation of more than 5 per cent is subject to prior approval by the Minister of Finance after consultation with the Central Bank. Approval is not given when the merger leads to an undesirable development of the credit system (Section 25). Some categories of financial institutions are exempted from this supervision. Till end of 1985, the most important one was the postal cheque and transfer service, which has now been privatised and takes the same position as all other banks with respect to the control of mergers.

c) Not available.

2. *a)* List of major bank mergers:

Note: The following table is designed to provide information on "large" mergers. "Large" means here that the respective institutions belong to the ten largest ones.

Fiscal Year	Number of Bank Mergers if not 0
1964	2
1966	1
1967	2
1968	1
1970	1
1975	2

b) Concentration ratios, five largest banks:

Year	In relation to total assets	In relation to domestic assets
1960	70	78
1984	97	97

NEW ZEALAND

1. In New Zealand all businesses including those in the finance and banking sector are subject to the general competition law provided for in the Commerce Act 1986.

The Commerce Act has as its aim the promotion of competition in markets within New Zealand. To meet this objective the Act provides mechanisms to prevent restrictive trade practices, scrutinise the competition consequences of mergers and takeovers and to impose price controls where effective competition is absent.

a) In relation to restrictive trade practices the act provides a general standard for competitive commercial behaviour. More specifically:

i) The entering into or giving effect to contracts, arrangements or understandings which substantially lessen competition in a market is prohibited. Convenants running with land having a similar effect are also prohibited;

ii) Exclusionary provisions in contracts, arrangements and understandings are also prohibited. Exclusionary provisions generally relate to collective boycotts by traders or suppliers directed at other particular traders or groups of traders;

iii) Collective price fixing arrangements are deemed to substantially lessen competition. All such arrangements are therefore prohibited. All the above practices can be authorised by the Commerce Commission, where it can be shown that the practices have a benefit to the public which outweighs the anti–competitive effects of the practice.

iv) Resale price maintenance, whereby suppliers specify and enforce resale prices, is prohibited and cannot be authorised by the Commerce Commission. However, the recommendation of prices is not held to constitute resale price maintenance. The Act does provide an exemption from its restrictive trade practices provisions for acts, matters or things which are specifically authorised by any other enactments of Parliament or Orders–in–Council. The legislation and regulation governing the banking sector does not apparently specifically authorise any anti–competitive activities which would otherwise contravene the Commerce Act.

b) The Commerce Act 1986 also mentions a pre–notification scheme for mergers and takeovers which requires the Commerce Commission to examine the competitive effect of these transactions. All mergers and takeover proposals involving participants with combined assets of $500 million must be notified and receive the approval of the Commission. The Commission may act to prevent a merger where it would result on the acquisition of strengthening of a dominant position in a market and would have no offsetting public benefits. With the opening up of the banking sector to increased entry of new firms it is most unlikely that a merger in this sector would be of significant concern.

c) The Act also prohibits a company having a dominant position in a market from using that position for the purposes of restricting entry, preventing or deferring competitive conduct or eliminating persons from a market. The price control provisions of the Commerce Act are not applied to the banking or finance sectors.

2. There has been only one merger in banking affecting New Zealand in the last twenty years. The bank of New South Wales and the Commercial Bank of Australia merged to form the Westpac Banking Corporation. Both these banks were subsidiaries of Australian Banks. Entry into the field of banking has been restricted with the availability of banking licences granted to the existing banks. The Government has removed this restriction on the number of banks able to operate in New Zealand.

Market share statistics (per cent of total trading bank deposits 12 months to June 1986) (U/L):

Tradings banks (U/L)	
Australia NZ banking group	23.0
Bank of New Zealand	40.7
National Bank	16.7
Westpac	19.6

There are two other banking organisations in New Zealand. They are the Post Office Savings Bank and the Trustee Savings Bank. The operations of these organisations are limited by statute and they mainly operate in the household savings and home mortgage markets.

NORWAY

1. Banking is subject to the Act on Control of Prices, Profits and Restraints of Competition 1953. In addition there are, however, special laws affecting the functioning of the sector. When the aforementionad laws are in conflict, the antitrust laws normally give way. Thus, the special laws limit the scope of the antitrust laws.

a) According to the Royal Decree of 1st July 1960 on horizontal price–fixing agreements, agreements between banks on interest rates, fees and commissions are, to be legal, subject to special authorisation. As of December 4th, 1986 there were in banking six such authorisations.

b) The Norwegian antitrust laws do not prohibit mergers and acquisitions, but according to special laws on banks of May 24th 1961, mergers and acquisitions between banks must have the approval of the Government.

As to joint ventures, the Norwegian antitrust authorities deem such arrangements illegal, according to the Royal Decree of 1st July 1960 on horizontal price–fixing agreements. The antitrust authorities do, however, regard some kinds of joint venture to be pro–competitive, and have given general exemption for some types.

c) As mentioned below in Section 2, the market structure does not imply any abuse of dominant positions. No cases of abuse have been noted. Being the case, the special laws and the antitrust laws allow the authorities to intervene.

2. Since 1960 the number of banks in Norway has been decreasing. The table below shows the development in the number of banks in recent years.

Year	Saving banks	Commercial banks
1968	518	48
1982	270	22
1984	227	21
1985	198	27

From 1960 to 1985 the three largest commercial banks have increased their share of their sector's total assets. In 1960 they accounted for 49.6 per cent of total assets of the commercial banks. In 1985 their share was 72.6 per cent.

In 1968 the ten largest saving banks' share of their sector's total assets was 23.6 percent. In 1985 their share was 53.5 per cent.

In the years 1976–1985 the number of merging commercial and savings banks fluctuated between seven and 38. In the same period nine commercial banks and 192 saving banks merged.

The number of merging banks in proportion to the total number of banks seems to have been increasing. In the years 1976–80 on average 3.9 per cent of the total number of banks were merging within a one year period. In the period 1981–85 the share averaged 9.7 per cent.

The increase in the number of commercial banks from 1984 to 1985 is due to the establishment of subsidiaries of foreign banks. This trend continued in 1986, when two new foreign owned commercial banks were granted permission to operate in Norway.

The recent development might be an omen of a change in the tendency to the ever increasing concentration that has occurred in previous years.

Recent Developments in Competition Policy

Recent years have been dominated by a roll–back of business agreements on restraint of trade between banks and other financial institutions. Among other things, many regulations that are supposed to prevent banks from competing on commissions, interest rates and fees have been abolished. Consequently it has become easier for banks to adjust their prices to their costs and to adjust their services to the demand of the customers.

An important first move in this respect was made in 1977 when the authorities did away with the interest rate–agreement. This was an agreement of great importance made between the authorities and the most important groups of banks and other financial institutions. The agreement's effect was to regulate the interest rates both on loans and deposits. The abolition of the agreement resulted in several new offers of deposits and competition in the deposit market increased. On the loan side of the market, however, the agreement was succeeded by a new kind of regulation of interest rates, the so-called declarations of interest rates issued by the Minister of Finance. In the period following the abolition of the declaration of interest rates in the autumn of 1985, an increase of competition on interest rates on the loan market has been made possible.

In the wake of the abolition of the interest rate-agreement in 1977, a great number of restrictive business agreements in the banking sector ceased.

In 1983 the authorities decided to abolish the banks' general exemption from the prohibition of 1960 to make horizontal price agreements. The abolition was effective as from January 1st, 1984 and subsequently some agreements on restraints of competition were formally abolished. Some of those had already come to an end because the banks and their organisations themselves wanted to increase competition.

This cessation of agreements on restrictive business practices — along with changes in the credit policy — is thought to have laid the basic conditions for, and made it possible for, banks to develop new services that to a greater extent are adapted to the needs of consumers, and to charge prices that to a greater extent reflect production costs.

Prior to, and simultaneous with, this cessation of agreements on restraints of competition, there has been a further concentration towards fewer and bigger units both in banking and insurance. The greater units that have been created have expanded their activities to greater geographical areas and to new kinds of services.

In 1982 the Ministry of Finance established a working party to appraise the banking structure. The report was discussed by the Government in the Revised National Budget in 1983 and by the Storting in January 1984. The discussion was based on the need to have a banking sector that secured the presence of alternative banking services and an effective competition on local markets. After the discussion in the Storting, guidelines to attain these goals were enacted. Among other things, it was permitted to establish foreign banks in Norway, and the policy was made more liberal as to establishing branches and new banks. At the same time new rules were made that are very restrictive as to mergers that might involve any of the three largest commercial banks.

By a Royal Decree of January 25th 1985 seven foreign owned subsidiaries were allowed to establish themselves in Norway. The authorisations were given on special terms. Among other things, the banks were not allowed to establish branches in Norway or to acquire ownership in other financial institutions, including insurance companies and broker's businesses, without the consent of the Ministry of Finance. The background to these restrictions was that the authorities wanted to proceed gradually with the establishment of foreign banks.

In 1986 two more banks were allowed to establish in Norway. The conditions were the same as for the other foreign banks.

PORTUGAL

1. The banking sector, which was opened broadly to private initiative in 1983, is generally subject to the Competition on National Market Law, December 1983. "However, this law does not apply to situations, where competition is restricted as a result of legal or regulatory provisions, older or younger than this document" (Section 36, 1 c). It is the task of the Directorate General of Competition and Prices to propose measures which seem to be adequate in order to re-establish competition if there are any distortions.

The banking sector is rather regulated, especially with respect to its activities. Most regulations are provided for by the Central Bank. The recent trend in favour of liberalisation and deregulation measures also covers the scope of application of competition rules. To date there has been no case with respect to anti-competitive practices in the banking sector.

a) Under Section 13 of the Competition on National Market Law, agreements between enterprises, decisions of associations of enterprises or practices of all kinds are prohibited, which are aimed at, or result in, impeding, perverting or restricting competition on the whole market or in a special sector.

It is the responsibility of the Competition Council — an authority which has to decide on cases relating to restrictive practices in competition — to justify such agreements or practices, if they lead to a "balanced economic result".

b) The competition legislation does not provide for the control of concentration and mergers. As far as joint ventures are concerned, they can be justified by the Competition Council.

c) Abuses of dominant positions on the national market, held by one or more enterprises, are prohibited (Section 14). There is the same possibility of justification as described under a) and b).

2. Statistical data on mergers in the banking sector: 1964–85 (if not 0):

Year	Number
1964	1
1965	3
1966	1
1967	2
1969	1
1971	1
1976	2
1977	3
1978	2

SWEDEN

1. Although the commercial bank sector is still regulated by the Commercial Bank Act 1955, the Competition Act is fully applicable to banks. This means that agreements between banks, mergers and abuses of dominant positions by banks can be dealt with in the same way as in the rest of the trade and industry.

a) The commercial banks within The Swedish Bankers' Association formerly had fixed fees for many services to the public. After the Competition Ombudsman had criticised the binding character of the fees the Association made them recommended. After two years the Ombudsman reviewed the application of that recommendation and found out that it was followed by the banks almost 100 per cent. After the Competition Ombudsman had stated that the recommendation had harmful effects according to the Competition Act and that he was prepared to bring the case before the Market Court, the Bankers' Association abolished the recommendation. In May 1985 the Riksbank raised the official discount rate and at the same time dropped its recommendations to banks on the rates of interest to be charged for loans. On the day after this decision the banks inserted a joint advertisement in the newspapers, from which it emerged that they were raising their lending rates even more than the higher discount rate warranted. To determine whether the banks had been collaborating in their rate setting in restraint of trade, the Competition Ombudsman made various inquiries of, among others, the Swedish Bankers' Association. It was learned that informal talks had been held between the bank representatives who were present when the Riksbank announced its decision. Among other things, views were expressed as to which across-the-board increases over and above discount rate would be appropriate. The banks that did not attend the Riksbank's meeting were informed of these discussions. The case was closed after the banks explained that henceforth every bank in a situation of free interest-rate-setting would decide its rates independently and not inform other banks or banking organisations before a decision was taken. Nor will the banks advertise jointly in the press.

b) According to the banking legislation, mergers and acquisitions are subject to approval by the Government or in certain cases by the Bank Inspection Board. Thus there exists a dual system of merger control for banks, under the Competition Act and under banking legislation. A Government investigation is looking into this question as well as into the question of limitation of ownership in banks.

c) Not available.

2. The number of commercial banks has on the whole been unchanged during the period 1960–1985. At 1st January 1986 there were 14 commercial banks. During the period there has been 4 mergers or acquisitions in this group and 1 new establishment. However, during 1986 12 foreign-owned banks were established and more foreign establishments are expected. In the savings banks group there has during the period been a continuous trend towards concentration. 1960

there were 434 savings banks and at 1st January 1986 the number had diminished to 139.

b) Concentration ratios, five largest banks:

Year	In relation to total assets	In relation to domestic assets
1960	79	82
1984	89	86

SWITZERLAND

1. A new cartel law came into force on 1st July 1986.

a) In 1968, the Swiss Cartels Commission published a report on the state of competition in the Swiss banking sector. This publication dealt with associations in the banking sector and with cartel agreements. At present, a new report is under preparation which will probably deal with these questions as well. Following the 1968 report, there is a complicated network of cartel agreements, some of them among the large banks, while others are limited to certain regions or specific banking groups. They cover a wide range of activities, including setting of prices, fees and commissions. Under Section 23 of the Banking Law, the Swiss Banking Commission is not responsible for dealing with these agreements. They are considered to be internal matters of the banking sector. From the Swiss point of view, they do not restrain competition seriously, which could be described as "friendly competition". It is supposed that in the long run, these agreements will lead to results which are not far away from free market results. Moreover, they are supposed to retard the concentration process.

b) In 1979, the Cartels Commission published a report on "Concentration in the Swiss Banking Sector". This publication dealt with questions of mergers. The Act on cartels and similar organisations does not provide for measures against the establishment of economic power. Nevertheless, competition policy is influenced by structural changes stemming from the concentration trend of enterprises. Resulting distortions of competition can lead to detrimental economic and social effects. In order to prevent such developments and to provide political and economic circles with material necessary for examining the usefulness of legal interventions, the concentration process must be known and watched. Moreover, the Cartels Commission states openly what it would like the banks to do (or to refrain from doing) with respect to mergers and acquisitions.

c) Abuse of economic power is prohibited. Investigations of the Commission of Cartels did not lead to any indications that there could be monopolistic situations on single relevant markets.

2. a) Takeovers of banks:

Year	Number	Total assets (million Swiss Francs)
1956–1960	1	19.6
1961–1965	4	115.3
1966–1970	14	1 577.7
1971–1975	30	776.0

b) Concentration ratios, 5 largest banks:

Year	In relation to total assets percentage	In relation to domestic assets percentage
1965	39.9	35.6
1970	51.7	40.5
1975	51.4	39.3
1976	52.2	40.3
1984	66.7	42.7

UNITED KINGDOM

1. In general, competition law applies to banking. Banks are therefore subject to the Restrictive Trade Practices Act 1976, the Fair Trading Act 1973 and the Competition Act 1980, with the few exemptions mentioned below. However, two significant legislative changes have been introduced which will substantially amend the scope of application of competition law to the financial services sector in general.

The Financial Services Act, which received Royal Assent on 7th November 1986, establishes a new regulatory regime for the provision of financial services in the United Kingdom aimed to improve investor protection. The Act provides that, subject to certain exemptions, no one may engage in investment business unless specifically authorised to do so, either by direct authorisation by the Secretary of State for Trade and Industry (who may delegate his powers to an agency, namely the Securities and Investments Board) or by membership of a self–regulating organisation whose rules have been approved by the Secretary of State or his agent, or a corresponding body. It also provides that the Secretary of State may not delegate to an agency nor allow the recognition of a self–regulating organisation until he has considered the effect on competition of the agency's or the organisation's rules and come to the conclusion that any restrictions are no greater than are necessary for the protection of investors. In taking a view on competition he is bound to seek, and to take account of, the views of the Director General of Fair Trading. The Director General will at any time after recognition be able to consider the effect on competition of any self–regulating organisation's rules and report his findings to the Secretary of State as appropriate: this could ultimately lead to the withdrawal of the organisation's recognition. Once the Act is fully in force, the financial services sector, in respect of their investment business, will be largely exempt from the Restrictive Trade Practices Act and other existing competition legislation.

The Building Societies Act, which received Royal Assent on 25th July 1986, came into effect on 1st January 1987. Building societies in the United Kingdom have traditionally fulfilled two main functions: to provide finance for house purchase; and to provide a secure means of small scale saving. They have therefore been exempt from many of the provisions of existing competition legislation. The Act enables them, subject to various limits and safeguards, to engage in a wide range of additional activities traditionally reserved for banks and other institutions, including money transmission, foreign exchange services, insurance, estate and other house buying services etc.; and at the same time removes their immunity from existing competition legislation. This removal includes the current exemption from the Restrictive Trade Practices Act of agreements between building societies to adhere to agreed or recommended interest rates for investors and borrowers. In addition, since building societies will be allowed for the first time to arrange for the provision of credit, and to provide services in connection with loan agreements, they will be required to comply generally with the Consumer Credit Act of 1974 and to obtain a consumer credit licence. More significantly, as they begin to engage in the wider range of activities permitted by the Act they will, in practice, increasingly be subject to existing competition legislation.

a) Under the Restrictive Trade Practices Act 1976 (RTPA) details of certain kinds of restrictive agreements must be supplied to the Director General of Fair Trading and entered into a Register, most of which is open to public inspection. In relation to services including banking, the relevant restrictions are those relating to: charges; the terms or conditions on which services are supplied; the extent and scale to or on which services are made available or supplied; the form or manner of supplying; and the persons to or the areas in which services are supplied.

Thus agreements between banks on, for example, interest rates will generally be subject to registration under the RTPA. Certain agreements are, however, exempt from the legislation, including: those between trustees or managers of unit trust schemes in which the restrictions relate to the management of or the sale or purchase of authorised unit trust schemes; those which relate exclusively to the exercise of control by the monetary authorities over financial institutions, or over the monetary system generally, or to the conduct of markets in money, in public sector debt instruments or in foreign currencies. The exemption previously granted to banking services in Northern Ireland has recently been withdrawn by the Restrictive Trade Practices (Services)(Amendment) Order 1985 which came into operation on 21st December 1985.

Once agreements have been registered the Director General has a duty to refer them to the Restrictive Practices Court for a judgment on whether the restrictions can be justified on certain specified public interest grounds. If the restrictions are not defended, or if the defence is unsuccesful, the Court is bound to declare the restrictions contrary to the public interest and can order the parties to refrain from giving effect to or enforcing them. The Director General need not refer an agreement to the Court, however, if he concludes, and the Secretary of State for Trade and Industry agrees, that the restrictions are not significant. The Director General will normally tell the parties to an agreement when he considers that restrictions are significant, and allow them the opportunity to amend them to remove their anti-competitive effects. In practice this is the course normally followed and few agreements are referred to the Court. Furthermore, the Director General need not refer to the Court if he thinks it appropriate having regard to EC provisions. In addition to the general requirement to register restrictive agreements, banks are also subject to the general provisions of the Competition Act 1980 and the Fair Trading Act 1973. The Competition Act 1980 empowers the Director General to carry out a preliminary investigation to establish whether a particular course of business conduct amounts to an anti-competitive practice. If the Director General identifies an anti-competitive practice he must state, in a published report of his investigation, whether he considers it appropriate to make a reference to the Monopolies and Mergers Commission (MMC). Alternatively, he may decide to accept an undertaking from the persons who have been pursuing the practice to remedy their behaviour.

When a reference is made, the MMC are required, within a limited period, to establish whether the anti-competitive practice is, or was, being operated and, if so, whether it is, or was, against the public interest. If their report contains an adverse finding the Secretary of State may ask the Director General to seek an undertaking to remedy the behaviour of those concerned. If they are unwilling to give an acceptable undertaking, the Secretary of State can make an order to prohibit the practice or to remedy or prevent its adverse effect. If he sees fit, the Secretary of State can make an order directly, without first asking the Director General to seek an undertaking.

Under Section 2 of the Fair Trading Act 1973 the Director General is required to make himself aware of "monopoly situations" or anti-competitive practices. The Office of Fair Trading carries out reviews of monopoly situations in two ways: by monitoring the economic performance of industries to identify areas where there may be monopolies and monopoly abuse; and by taking note of complaints and other representations it receives from industry and the public. Where a monopoly situation is believed to exist the Director General can, at his discretion, refer it to the MMC for investigation. There is no presumption that a monopoly as such is against the public interest, or that possible monopoly situations, when found, should always be referred. It is for the MMC to determine whether a monopoly situation does exist and, if so, whether it operates or is expected to operate against the public interest.

b) Mergers between banks are subject to the merger provisions of the Fair Trading Act 1973. Under the Act it is the duty of the Director General to advise the Secretary of State for Trade and Industry whether a merger or proposed merger should be referred to the MMC for investigation. The Secretary of State may make a reference to the MMC if:

i) Two or more enterprises, at least one of which is carried on in the United Kingdom or by or under the control of a body corporate incorporated in the United Kingdom, have ceased or will cease to be distinct enterprises; and

ii) Either one or both the following conditions are satisfied:

— In consequence at least 25 per cent of the services of any description supplied in the United Kingdom are supplied by or to the merged enterprises, or by or to an individual and persons associated with him, or by or to a body corporate and other corporations which it controls;

— The value of the assets acquired in the merger exceeds £30 million.

If the MMC conclude that the merger will operate against the public interest the Secretary of State may prohibit the merger or (if it has been effected) require it to be undone or impose conditions or requirements with regard to it. Alternatively, the Director General may negotiate an undertaking.

In recent years there has been only one report on mergers in the banking sector. In January 1982 the MMC reported on the proposed mergers between the Hongkong and Shanghai Banking Corporation (HSBC) and the Royal Bank of Scotland Group Limited (Royal Bank Group) and between Standard Chartered Bank Limited (Standard Chartered) and Royal Bank Group. The MMC concluded in the case of the Standard Chartered bid that its effects would be damaging to the public interest of the United Kingdom as a whole. In the case of HSBC bid they found the same adverse effects, and also that transfer of control of Royal Bank Group outside the United Kingdom would raise possibilities of divergence of interest which would not otherwise arise. In each case they concluded that the adverse effects outweighed any benefits that could be foreseen, and therefore found that either proposed merger might be expected to operate against the public interest. They were unable to suggest any action which could be taken to remedy or prevent the adverse effects foreseen other than prohibition of the merger. They added that it was not their intention to imply that leading Scottish financial institutions in general, or clearing banks in particular, should

in no circumstances be taken over by companies based outside Scotland. Their recommendation was that neither merger should be permitted and this was accepted by the Secretary of State.

Although there have been few mergers among the United Kingdom clearing banks, the structure of which is already highly concentrated, mergers have become more common in other parts of the financial sector, notably among building societies. These have led to some increase in concentration but so far have not caused sufficient concern for the Secretary of State to make any references to the MMC.

c) Any abuse of a dominant position in the banking sector will be handled under the provisions of either the Fair Trading Act or the Competition Act. Neither Act, however, has been used to date specifically in relation to banks or banking, although the provisions of the Fair Trading Act have been used in relation to the supply of credit card franchise services. On 23rd June 1977 the Director General referred to the MMC the matter of the existence or possible existence of a monopoly situation in relation to the supply in the United Kingdom of such services. The reference included "travel and entertainment" or charge cards, such as those issued by American Express and Diners Club, and cards issued by banks which offer revolving extended credit, but excluded "in house" cards issued by department stores etc., which can be used only at outlets of the business concerned. The report, published in September 1980, concluded that scale monopolies existed in favour of Barclays Bank, in respect of the Barclaycard credit operation, and in respect of the joint service company, the Joint Credit Card Company Limited (JCCC) and the five banks which are shareholders in it, in respect of the Access credit card operation. It found that these scale monopolies did not operate against the public interest, but that the complex monopoly situation that existed in favour of Barclays, JCCC, the five Access banks, American Express, Diners Club, and other credit card companies who operated a "no discrimination" clause (whereby traders who accepted the cards were forbidden to charge different prices to credit card customers than those charged to cash or cheque customers) operated against the public interest. It recommended that the practice be prohibited. The MMC also found that the practice of the JCCC and Barclays of holding discussions with each other on matters that might materially affect competition between them was a step taken for the purpose of maintaining or exploiting their status as monopolies, and they recommended that this practice should be permanently abandoned.

Lastly, they suggested that the Director General should keep the credit card business as a whole under review, since there were features in the market which could possibly become detrimental to the public interest in the future including, for example, the level of charges made by the credit card companies to small traders, the levels of interest rates, the growth of "in house" credit card schemes, and the levels of indebtedness resulting from credit card use.

The MMC's recommendation on the "no discrimination" clause was rejected by Ministers and continues to be applied by the JCCC and Barclaycard in contracts with traders. Both the JCCC and Barclays have, however, given assurances to the Director General that they have abandoned the practice of holding discussions on common policies. The Director General has continued to monitor the credit card market as a whole, and the JCCC and Barclays, and certain other suppliers of credit card services, have provided him with regular information on an annual basis in relation to their credit card operations.

2. Statistical data on bank mergers (1977 to 1986):

Year	Number
1977	0
1978	3
1979	2
1980	0
1981	0
1982	1
1983	1
1984	0
1985	0
1986	2

UNITED STATES

1. Competition in banking is subject to various forms of regulation in addition to the antitrust laws. This regulation encompasses statutes and rules on capital, insurance and other supervisory requirements, statutory limits on the powers and locations of commercial banks and other depository institutions at both the State and Federal levels and agency rules interpreting such limits, and statutes and rules on mergers and acquisitions. The antitrust laws are the primary but not sole constraint on banks' conduct in offering permitted services and in setting interest rates, service charges and fees.

a) Previously, interest rates on deposits at federally supervised bank and thrift institutions (except credit unions) were regulated by federal law. As of 1st April 1986, pursuant to the Depository Institutions Deregulation Act of 1980 ("DIDA"), all interest rate regulation was removed. The only remaining restriction is that interest may not be paid on demand deposits for business customers.

Under the antitrust laws price–fixing has been the most frequently prosecuted violation.

Uniform interchange fees could also raise antitrust concerns depending on whether they are "reasonably necessary" under the circumstances.

b) Under Section 18(c) of the Bank Merger Act of 1966, the Comptroller of the Currency (OCC) for national banks, the Federal Deposit Insurance Corporation (FDIC) for federally–insured state–chartered banks that are not members of the Federal Reserve System, and the Board of Governors of the Federal Reserve System (FRB) for state–chartered banks that are System members, must conduct their own competitive analysis of bank mergers, and obtain competitive factors reports from each other and from the Antitrust Division of the Department of Justice, before approving a bank merger. In approving a merger, the agency is required to apply the competitive standard in Section 1828 (c) that reiterates the criteria of Section 7 of the Clayton Act, and Sections 1 and 2 of the Sherman Act. There is a 30–day waiting period (except in instances of emergencies or probable failures) after agency approval, during which the Antitrust Division may sue to enjoin the merger on competitive grounds and obtain an automatic stay of the transaction. After that time, the transaction is immune from antitrust challenge except under Section 2 of the Sherman Act. A similar procedure applies to FRB approval of bank holding company acquisitions of banks. Non–bank acquisitions, including investments in joint ventures, must be approved by the FRB under Section 4 of the Bank Holding Company Act (BHCA). Approvals of thrift mergers or acquisitions follow less rigid procedures but are also reviewed by the Antitrust Division of the Department of Justice. The Antitrust Division screens each merger or acquisition under the Department of Justice Merger Guidelines as applied to depository institutions. Analysis under the Guidelines centres on three factors: the product market, the geographic market, and the likely anti–competitive effects of the transaction within those markets, and thus applies the legal elements of Section 7 of the Clayton Act, which bars a merger or acquisition "where in any line of commerce or in any activity affecting commerce in any section of the country, the effect of such acquisition may be substantially to lessen competition, or to tend to create a monopoly". The standard is that, unless other factors indicate an anticompetitive effect, the Antitrust Division will not oppose a bank or thrift merger unless the post–merger Herfindahl–Hirschman Index ("HHI") is 1 800 points or greater and the HHI increase is at least 200 points. Factors such as evidence of a competitive market, recent or expected entry, efficiencies, and a bank's failing condition when no less anti–competitive alternative exists are considered as mitigation. Divestitures of branches and associated deposits and assets are often negotiated to eliminate competition concerns.

Joint ventures to provide electronic funds transfer services have been a recent focus of emerging antitrust policy. Most recently, the Antitrust Division declined to challenge admission into an ATM joint venture of an institution already participating in a competing ATM joint venture. The current approach permits the formation of EFT joint ventures, including voluntary ATM sharing, because of the economic efficiency of such arrangements.

c) Not available.

2. a) Bank Mergers: There have been no mergers either permitted or prohibited involving two banks ranking within the top ten banks in the country.

b) Concentration ratios, five largest banks:

Year	In relation to total assets	In relation to domestic assets
1960	Not available	14.36
1984	19.35	13.00

EUROPEAN COMMUNITIES

1. With respect to the banking sector, the Community Law does not provide for any exemption or modification of the competition rules, which are laid down in Article 85 and 86 of the Treaty. Under Article 85(1), all agreements between undertakings, decisions by associations of undertakings and concerted practices which may affect trade between Member States and which have as their object or effect the prevention, restriction or distortion of competition within the Common Market, are prohibited. Under Article 86 any abuse by one or more undertakings of a dominant position within the Common Market or in a substantial part of it shall be prohibited in so far as it may affect trade between Member States. However, the provisions of Article 85(1) may be declared inapplicable, if an agreement, a decision or a practice contributes to improving the production or distribution of goods or to promoting technical or economic progress, while allowing consumers a fair share of the resulting benefit. As far as the banking sector is concerned, the first decision of the Commission was adopted December 1984. It was decided to exempt the agreements on the international use and clearing of uniform eurocheques under Article 85 (3). In this context the Commission underlined that future decisions in the banking sector would not be limited to exemptions but might also include prohibitions.

a) Agreements on interest rates, fees and commissions are prohibited under Article 85 (a) 1, which covers fixing of purchase or selling prices or of any other trading conditions. Although the Community competition rules are in general applicable to banking, the Commission has endeavoured to determine whether, and if so to what extent, monetary policy reasons might require to delimit the scope of Articles 85 and 86. The question as to whether, and if so, how far, certain banking agreements should be treated as "monetary policy instruments" of the Member States arises in respect of agreements on interest rates, authorised or approved by the national monetary authorities and also perhaps in respect of other banking agreements which could be considered as being an essential aspect of interest rate arrangements. The question does not arise for interbank agreements, whose relevance to monetary policy can be almost definitely ruled out.

b) Mergers are not explicitly prohibited under the competition rules of the Treaty, but the Commission desires to establish a Community merger control instrument. The draft regulation was submitted to the Council in

1973 and has sometimes been amended to date. Meetings in the Council's "Economics Questions Group" have indicated that although the majority of the Member States have expressed their approval of the principle of establishing a Community instrument for merger control, their views on points of detail and on certain essential points are quite divergent.

c) See a).

2. Mergers[1], acquisitions[2] and joint ventures in the banking sector 1984/1985:

	National[3]	Community[4]	International[5]	Total
Mergers	10	6	2	18
Acquisitions	10	6	5	21
Joint Ventures	9	2	2	13
Total	29	14	9	52

1. Including acquisitions of majority holdings.
2. Of minority holdings.
3. Cases where only firms from the same Member State are involved.
4. Cases where firms from different Member States are involved.
5. Cases where at least one firm from outside the Community is involved.

CONFLICTS OF INTEREST IN BANKING AND FINANCE
AND THEIR CONTROL AND MANAGEMENT

I. INTRODUCTION

Conflict of interest considerations play an important role in the context of policies towards the structural organisation of countries' financial systems, notably as regards the desirability of legally separating certain areas of financial service activities such as, for example, commercial banking and securities–related activities. In this sense, policies designed to handle conflict of interest problems in banking and finance have an important bearing on competition policies in this field as a separation of functions introduced on conflict of interest grounds may represent limitations on market access and hence on the scope for the working of competitive market forces. There is another relationship between the conflict of interest issue and competition policies insofar as reliance on adequate competition and market discipline is often seen as an acceptable approach towards dealing with certain broader conflict of interest situations such as may arise for universal banks, for example, as regards the respective promotion of deposit–taking business on the one hand and selling securities to small investors on the other.

In recent years, the discussion on conflict of interest problems in banking and finance, which has a long history, notably in the United States, has seen a considerable revival in a number of countries such as Canada, France, Germany, the United Kingdom and the United States. In Canada and the United States the conflict of interest issue receives particular attention in connection with policies towards, or discussions on, structural and regulatory reforms of the financial system which are strongly influenced by the general trend towards the blurring of demarcation lines between formerly separated sectors of the financial system.

In the United States the ongoing debate in this field includes a critical review of the Glass–Steagall Act of 1933, which, largely on conflict of interest grounds, introduced a separation of commercial banking and a large number of securities–related activities. In France, efforts are being made in connection with comprehensive securities market reforms to deal with conflict of interest problems, inter alia, by the introduction of a legally binding code of conduct applying to market operators. In Germany, questions of conflicts of interest were discussed in considerable detail by the Gessler–Commission whose report on "Basic Questions of the Credit System" was published in 1979. The Gessler Commission looked into this question mainly in the context of a critical review of the universal banking system and reached the conclusion that the latter system had functioned satisfactorily and should, therefore, be maintained. Any necessary reforms dealing with conflicts of interest could be taken care of by the banks themselves within the framework of the universal banking system. In the United Kingdom, where important securities market reforms, often referred to as the "Big Bang" of 27th October 1986, paved the way for the formation of large capital market groups operating in a wide range of securities–related activities, the question of an appropriate management of conflicts of interest received particular attention in connection with the implementation of the Financial Services Act 1986. The importance of this question is highlighted by the following paragraph of the White Paper on "Financial Services in the United Kingdom" issued by the Department of Trade and Industry, London, in January 1985:

"*Conflicts of Interest*

The rapid increase in the number of firms engaging in more than one type of investment business and the blurring of demarcation lines (for example, between brokers and jobbers) have made it more important than ever that investors are adequately protected against abuses arising from conflicts of interest within investment business."

II. DEFINITION AND PRACTICAL EXAMPLES

Definition

Stated in an abstract way, a conflict of interest situation arises for a bank — or any other enterprise — dealing with a client if it has a choice between two solutions for a deal, one of which is preferable from its own interest point of view while the other represents a better deal for the client. A conflict of interest situation arises also for a bank or another financial institution if it carries out activities involving two different groups of customers and if it has to strike a balance between the respective interests of the two customer groups. A practical example of the latter case is the new–issuing, or underwriting, business which always requires a compromise between the interests of the issuer and those of the buyers of the securities. As soon as a financial institution — or any other enterprise — offers two or more technically or functionally unrelated services leaving scope for certain choices, it is faced with the problem of how much effort to put into the promotion of each of these different services.

As financial institutions often operate in a wide range of different financial services they are bound to be confronted with a relatively large number of conflict of interest situations. This explains why the issue of conflicts of interest generally receives more attention in banking and finance than in other sectors of the economy.

Practical examples and related concerns

The practical examples of conflict of interest situations listed below are, apart from the general conflict between banking and non–banking activities, grouped under two headings: first, conflicts of interest considered as typical of universal banks; second, conflicts of interest between different types of securities–related activities. The list is not exhaustive; nor is it intended to discuss in any detail the pros and cons of the arguments put forward.

The principle of separation of "banking and commerce" which is applied in most countries to varying degrees in the sense that bank participations in industrial and commercial enterprises are either prohibited or severely restricted, is essentially based on conflict of interest considerations. A typical concern in this regard was expressed by the US Congress in a House Committee Report of 1955 on the extension of the Bank Holding Company Act:

"If banks were permitted to own non–banking businesses they would be compelled in many instances to extend credit to such businesses to the detriment of other competitive businesses in the community and possibly also to a degree which would be unsound from a banking point of view." (US Congress, House Report 609, 84th Congress, 1st Session 1955.)

Conflict of Interest Situations Considered as Typical of Universal Banks Combining both Banking and Securities–Related Activities

a) *Deposit business versus securities brokerage and related investment advisory business*

It is sometimes feared that banks might promote deposit taking for balance–sheet growth reasons to the detriment of promoting household investments in securities. The argument may, however, be reversed if banks were particularly interested in promoting their securities underwriting business.

b) *Deposit business and fund management (trust business i.e. the management of mutual funds, pension funds, and private securities portfolios on a discretionary basis)*

Banks should not be allowed to use managed funds for strengthening their own deposit base.

c) *Combination of corporate credit business and securities brokerage and investment advisory services and security trading on own acount*

Banks should not be allowed to influence their securities business with clients (brokerage and investment advice) or their securities trading business (on own account) through company information obtained in connection with lending activities.

d) *Corporate credit business versus new–issuing (underwriting) business*

Critics of this combination of activities fear that universal banks would unduly favour their credit business with corporate clients for profit and balance–sheet growth considerations to the detriment of the development of an efficient corporate bond and equity market.

e) *Combination of credit business with private customers and securities brokerage and investment advisory services, security trading on own account and underwriting business*

Banks should not unduly encourage private securities purchases via imprudent lending to private customers to finance such purchases.

f) *Conflict between the banks' involvement in industrial and commercial enterprises via participations, proxy voting rights and mutual interlocking membership on supervisory boards and their securities business with private customers*

Banks should not abuse their relationships with industrial and commercial enterprises against the interests of small and minority shareholders.

Conflicts of Interest Between Different Types of Securities–Related Activities

a) *Combination of securities brokerage (agency) business and dealing on own account (jobbing, market making)*

Securities firms or securities departments of universal banks should not unduly benefit from serving client orders from their own books.

b) *Combination of security dealing on own account (jobbing, market making) and trust business (fund management for pension funds, mutual funds and discretionary portfolio management for private persons)*

The market making function should not be based on security holdings managed under trust business. Undesirable own holdings of securities should not be dumped into funds under management.

c) *Combination of new–issuing (underwriting) business and trust business (fund management for pension funds, mutual funds and discretionary portfolio management for private persons)*

The new–issuing departments of securities firms or universal banks should not be allowed to demonstrate their placing power by dumping low–quality issues or inadequately priced issues into funds under management. Conversely, funds under management should not unduly benefit from the pricing of new issues to the detriment of issuers. -

d) *Combination of investment research and securities trading on own account (jobbing, market making)*

Securities trading on own account should not benefit in an unfair manner from early information on purchase recommendations to be released by investment research departments.

e) *Combination of investment advisory services and securities brokerage business*

Investment advice should not be biased in favour of overtrading ("churning") i.e. unnecessarily high turnover of the securities portfolio of private clients intended to generate high fee income.

III. OVERVIEW OF BASIC CONCERNS

Public policy concerns about conflicts of interest are essentially motivated by three types of basic considerations: efficiency considerations, investor protection considerations and prudential, i.e. stability and soundness, considerations. In addition, it should be mentioned that, in practice, discussions about conflicts of interest have often been closely related to fears about concentration of power in banking and finance, or in the economy as a whole, and measures intended to deal with conflicts of interest by a separation of functions have often been motivated by such fears.

As far as the "efficiency aspect" of conflicts of interest is concerned it has been argued that a financial institution operating in different broad areas of financial services such as retail banking, corporate financial services, securities–related activities etc. cannot be expected to be equally efficient and competitive in all these services at the same time and will, hence, tend to offer less than lowest cost and highest quality services in areas of activity which are less profitable or in which the institution in question has less experience or less qualified staff. In other words, according to this argument the financial service needs of particular customer groups or of the economy as a whole will be better satisfied if more specialised institutions were responsible for offering particular types of services or for dealing with particular customer groups instead of allowing multi–function institutions to operate in all these areas at the same time. Policy makers can deal with this problem either by imposing a certain degree of specialisation between financial institutions, or setting up special institutions dealing with particular financing problems; or they can take appropriate measures designed to improve the efficiency of less developed sub–markets for financial services by increasing the scope for competition and, in particular, facilitating market access from inside or outside the country. This latter approach has generally become the preferred way of dealing with this aspect of conflicts of interest as the authorities have accepted, and often supported, the general trend towards despecialisation and diversification of activities in banking and finance. It is increasingly realised that universal banks tend to be more flexible to adjust to new needs of market participants and structural changes in the financial services markets than specialised institutions that are legally prevented from moving into new areas of business.

The second type of concern about conflicts of interest which is motivated by "investor protection considerations" goes a step further than the efficiency concern. It is argued that in certain conflict of interest situations the quality of service offered may suffer to such an extent that investors need special protection against intentionally bad service and malpractices. This applies mainly to securities–related activities in which a securities firm, or the securities department of a universal bank, has a fiduciary function vis–à–vis clients who moreover, may have little experience with investment in securities. It is feared that professionals which may have various choices for doing securities business with clients may unduly weigh their own interests against those of their clients. In some of these cases the authorities go beyond reliance on market forces and market discipline and handle conflict of interest situations by codes of conduct, rules of practice or conditions for doing business, the supervision and control of compliance with which may be left to self–regulatory bodies.

The third type of concern about conflicts of interest is motivated by "stability and soundness considerations". It is argued that in extreme situations a conflict of interest can lead to mismanagement and unacceptable risk–taking in business areas in which a given financial institution has little experience and for which it is not "fit and proper", and that in order to protect the general public against undesirable failures and losses appropriate precautionary measures need to be taken. This concern played, for example, a major role in the United States in the debate leading to the introduction of the Glass–Steagall Act of 1933 which approached the underlying conflict of interest problem by a separation of commercial banking and a wide range of securities–related activities. Today, the prudential aspect of conflicts of interest, like other risk aspects of banking and securities–related activities, is generally dealt with by prudential regulation and supervision rather than by a separation of functions.

IV. CONTROL AND MANAGEMENT OF CONFLICTS OF INTEREST

Conflicts of interest in banking and finance can be handled in many ways depending on their nature and the severity of concern that the authorities attach to them. In principle, the following approaches are available:

— Separation of functions by separating the institutions which operate in conflicting types of financial services;
— "Chinese Wall" arrangements inside financial institutions designed to separate departments carrying out conflicting types of operations;
— Disclosure of information necessary for recognising and judging conflict of interest situations;
— Codes of conduct, rules of practice and conditions for doing business prescribing how professionals should deal with conflict of interest situations;
— Ensuring effective competition by providing sufficient choice as regards the institutions with which consumers may wish to do business;
— Arrangements for in–house and external monitoring of the handling of conflict of interest situations;
— Effective complaints procedures for consumers who have become victims of abuses of conflict of interest situations.

An extreme solution for dealing with conflicts of interest is to seek their avoidance by a strict separation of institutions operating in conflicting financial service activities. This approach could even go so far as requiring also separate ownership of such institutions which would prevent a financial institution from operating in conflicting business areas via separately capitalised subsidiaries. Examples of this approach are: the separation of "banking and commerce" which applies to varying degrees in most OECD countries; a full or partial separation of commercial banking from securities–related operations applying in Japan and the United States and until recently also in Canada; and the separation of the jobber and broker functions which until the 1986 "Big Bang" applied to members of the London Stock Exchange. As it is now widely accepted that financial institutions often see an entrepreneurial advantage in combining a wide range of financial services for the benefit of the general public, it is also increasingly recognised that conflicts of interest are bound to occur in banking and finance more frequently than in other sectors of the economy and that public policy should mainly focus on the avoidance of abuses of conflicts of interest rather than on the avoidance of their occurrence.

One widely accepted broader approach towards protecting investors and consumers against abuses of conflicts of interest by providers of financial services is based on the principles of adequate disclosure requirements and effective competition. According to this approach the clients of financial institutions should be fully informed about all aspects of the business they are doing with financial institutions (nature of the transaction, capacity in which the institution is acting — as agent or principal, risks, return and costs involved etc.); any such information should be readily available in understandable form. In addition, there should be an adequate level of competition providing sufficient choice for consumers as regards financial institutions with which they wish to do business. This approach generally applies to broader conflict of interest situations in which a given financial institution may promote one line of business, for example, deposit taking, to the detriment of another line of business, for example, securities brokerage and investment advisory services with private savers.In a number of more specific conflict of interest situations the authorities attempt to avoid their abuse by requiring that multi-function institutions apply "Chinese Wall" arrangements by which different departments are functionally separated in the sense that information giving rise to conflicts of interest cannot be exchanged between them either on a personal contact basis or via in-house information flow arrangements or access to files. Such separations of functions often apply in multi-function institutions to the corporate finance department, the trust, i.e., fund management department, securities brokerage, trading and investment advisory services, and the investment research department.

Chinese Wall arrangements are, however, often seen as requiring complementary codes of behaviour, rules of practice and conditions for doing business which need to be respected by providers of financial services with a view to providing adequate investor and consumer protection against abuses of conflicts of interest. This applies in particular to the profession of securities dealers. In the London market, for example, securities dealers acting as principals i.e. on own account, have to respect three principles:

— The principle of fair dealing which implies that unfair practices are avoided and that deals are executed in accordance with the rules governing the London market;
— The duty of skill, care and diligence when investment advice is given which should correspond to the needs and the level of experience of the client; or when orders are executed;
— The duty of disclosure of information on the capacity in which the dealer is acting, the interest he may have in a particular transaction and the fees he is earning.

Securities firms acting as agents of clients for buying and selling securities have to respect the principles of "best execution" and "subordination of interests", which requires that client orders must be given priority over the execution of own transactions and that orders must be executed in the client's best interest.

Furthermore, public policy dealing effectively with abuses of conflict of interest situations needs to provide a basis for effective monitoring arrangements at three levels: first, at the in-house level of the institutions themselves so that the management can control how any conflict of interest situation is actually handled; second, at the level of any self-regulatory organisations responsible for setting rules and procedures applying to their members; and, third, at the level of the authorities.

Finally, there need to be effective complaints procedures for clients who have become victims of abuses of conflicts of interest. The importance of this latter point is highlighted by the fact that in Canada, the Technical Supplement to the Green Paper on "The Regulation of Financial Institutions: Proposals for Discussion", published in June 1985, contains a proposal for a new public body dealing with conflicts of interest in banking and finance: the Financial Conflicts of Interest Office. It may be noted in this context that some countries go so far as to provide bank customers with legal rights against the supervisory authority itself whereas other countries implicitly refer them to their banks as legal counterparts.

V. SELECTED BIBLIOGRAPHY

Canada

Department of Finance, Canada, Capital Markets Division, *Potential Conflicts of Interest in the Financial System*, Ottawa, February 1984.

Department of Finance, Canada, *The Regulation of Canadian Financial Institutions: Proposals for Discussion*, ("Green Paper"), Ottawa, April 1985.

Department of Finance, Canada, *The Regulation of Canadian Financial* Institutions: Proposals for Discussion (Technical Supplement), *Ottawa*, June 1985.

House of Commons, Canada, *Canadian Financial Institutions*, Report of the Standing Committee on Finance, Trade and Economic Affairs, Ottawa, November 1985.

Senate of Canada, Towards a More Competitive Financial Environment, Sixteenth Report, Standing Senate Committee on Banking, Trade and Commerce, Ottawa, May 1986.

Hockin, Thomas, Minister of State for Finance, Canada, *New Directions for the Financial Sector*, Ottawa, December 1986.

France

Commission des Opérations de Bourse, *Rapport d'étape du groupe de déontologie des activités financières*, Supplément au *Bulletin Mensuel*, No. 206, August–September 1987.

Germany

Bundesministerium der Finanzen, *Grundsatzfragen der Kreditwirtschaft*, Bericht der Studienkommission, ("Gessler–Commission Report"), Schriftenreihe Bunderministeriums der Finanzen, Heft 28, Bonn 1979.

Pohl, Manfred, *Entstehung und Entwicklung des Universalbankensystems: Konzentration und Krise als wichtige Faktoren*, Schriftenreihe des Instituts für Bankhistorische Forschung e.V., Band 7, Frankfurt am Main, 1986.

United Kingdom

Berrill, Sir Kenneth, KCB, Chairman of the Securities and Investment Board (SIB), *Conflicts of Interest: The SIB's Approach*. Lecture at a Seminar of the Society of Investment Analysts, London, May 1985.

Knight, J.R., *The Management of Conflicts of Interest in a Multi–Function Securities Market*, The Stock Exchange, London, May 1986.

United States

US Department of the Treasury, *Public Policy Aspects of Bank Securities Activities*, An Issues Paper, Washington, November 1975.

J-P. Morgan & Co., *Rethinking Glass–Steagall*, New York, December 1984.

US Congress, House, *Restructuring Financial Markets: The Major Policy Issues*, A Report from the Chairman of the Sub–committee on Telecommunications, Consumer Protection, and Finance of the Committee on Energy and Commerce, Washington, July 1986.

BIBLIOGRAPHY

Administrator of National Banks, *Studies in Banking Competition and the Banking Structure*, articles reprinted from *The National Banking Review*, Office of the Comptroller of the Currency, Washington D.C.: United States Treasury Department, 1966.

Akhtar, M.A., Financial Innovations and their Implications for Monetary Policy: An International Perspective, *BIS Economic Papers No. 9*, Basle: BIS, December 1983.

Andreas, Kurt, "A Central Bank View of Financial Innovation on the Capital Markets", Deutsche Bundesbank, *Auszüge aus Presseartikeln*, No. 90, 30th September 1985.

Andriessen, Frans, *Banking in the EEC — The Balance between Co-operation and Competition*, Paper presented to the Banking Conference at the Royal Lancaster Hotel, London, 30th November–1st December 1981.

Association Française des Banques, *La concurrence bancaire en France et en Europe*, Paris, 1987.

Australian Financial System, Final Report of the Committee of Inquiry, ("Campbell Report"), Canberra, 1981.

Australian Financial System, Report of the Review Group, ("Martin Report"), Canberra, 1983.

Australian Payments System Council, *First Report of the Australian Payments System Council*, Canberra, 1985.

Banca d'Italia, *White Paper on the Payments System in Italy*, Rome, 1988.

Banca d'Italia, Italian Credit Structures — Efficiency, Competition and Controls, *London: Euromoney Publications, 1984*.

Baltensperger, E. and Dermine, J., *Banking Deregulation and Financial Stability, A European Regulatory Perspective*, 4th Panel of Economic Policy, London, 16th–17th October 1986.

Bankers Clearing House Members, *Payment Clearing Systems*, London, 1984.

Baxter, William F., Assistant Attorney General, Antitrust Division, Department of Justice, *Competition in the Financial Services Industry*, Testimony before the Committee on Banking, Housing and Urban Affairs, United States Senate, 8th June 1983.

Bank for International Settlements, *Changes in Money-market Instruments and Procedures: Objectives and Implications*, Basle, 1986.

Bank for International Settlements, *Recent Innovations in International Banking*, Basle, 1986.

Bank for International Settlements, *Payments System in Eleven Developed Countries*, Basle, 1985.

Bank for International Settlements, *Financial Innovation and Monetary Policy*, Basle, 1984.

Bank of England, The Regulation of the Wholesale Markets in Sterling, Foreign Exchange and Bullion, *London, 1987*.

Bank of England, "Change in the Stock Exchange and Regulation of the City", *Quarterly Bulletin*, London, February 1987.

Bank of England, "Changing Boundaries in Financial Services", *Quarterly Bulletin*, London, March 1984.

Bank of England, *Monetary Policy in EEC Countries, United Kingdom Institutions and Instruments,* London, February 1974.

Bank of England, *Competition and Credit Control,* London, 1971.

Bartling, Hartwig, *Leitbilder der Wettbewerbspolitik,* München: Verlag Vahlen, 1980.

Batchelor, R.A. & Griffiths, B., *Monetary Restraint through Credit Controls — The Lessons of Current Practice in the United Kingdom,* Paper presented to the Colloquium on Financial Markets: Structure, Conduct, Performance and Regulation, Katholieke Universiteit Leuven, Belgium, 13th September 1979.

Beck, Stanley, *Market Access and Barriers to Entry in the International Securities Arena: Some Reflections,* Paper given at the 12th Annual Conference of the International Organisation of Securities Commissions, Rio de Janeiro, 1st–4th September 1987.

Becker, Wolf–Dieter, *Wettbewerb im Bankensystem,* Diskussionsbeitraege zur monetaeren Makroökonomie, Fachbereich Wirtschaftswissenschaften, Universitaet Gesamthochschule Siegen, 1983.

Bellinger, Dieter, "Die Hypothekenbanken in dem sich entwickelnden EG–Bankrecht", *Die Bank,* 7/81, pp. 318–325, 1981.

Berliner Handels– und Frankfurter Bank, "Finanzplatz Bundesrepublik und Wettbewerbsfaehigkeit des Kreditgewerbes", *Wirtschaftsdienst,* Nr. 1445, Frankfurt: BHF–Bank, 1st March 1986.

Berliner Handels– und Frankfurter Bank, "Banken im Wettbewerb", *Wirtschaftsdienst,* Nr. 1374, Frankfurt: BHF–Bank, 17th March 1984.

Berrill, Sir Kenneth, KCB, Chairman of the Securities and Investment Board (SIB), *Conflicts of Interest: The SIB's Approach,* Lecture at a Seminar of the Society of Investment Analysts, London, 1985.

Binhammer, H.H. & Williams, Jane, *Deposit–Taking Institutions: Innovation and the Process of Change,* Economic Council of Canada, Ottawa: Printing and Publishing Supply and Services, 1976.

Blenkarn Report, *Canadian Financial Institutions,* Report of the Standing Committee on Finance, Trade and Economic Affairs, Ottawa: Canadian Government Publications Centre, Supply and Services, 1985.

Bond, David E., Chant, John F. & Shearer, Ronald A., *The Economics of the Canadian Financial System: Theory, Policy and Institutions,* Second Edition, Scarborough, Ontario: Prentice Hall of Canada, 1984.

Bröker, Günther, "Strukturwandlungen im Bankwesen — ein internationaler Ueberblick", in *Oesterreichisches Bank–Archiv,* Heft 3, March 1986.

Bueschgen, Hans E., "Banken im sich veraendernden Umfeld", *Zeitschrift für Betriebswirtschaft,* Vol. 52, Nr. 1, pp. 3–26, 1982.

Bundesministerium der Finanzen, *Grundsatzfragen der Kreditwirtschaft,* Bericht der Studienkommission, ("Gessler Commission Report"), Schriftenreihe des Bundesministeriums der Finanzen, Heft 28, Bonn, 1979.

Bundesminister für Wirtschaft, *Wettbewerbsverschiebungen im Kreditgewerbe und Einlagensicherung,* Bericht der Bundesregierung, Drucksache des Deutschen Bundestages V/3500, Bonn, 1969.

Bundesministerium für Wirtschaft, *Competition Policy in a Social Market Economy,* Bonn: BMWI, undated.

Campbell Report, *Australian Financial System,* Final Report of the Committee of Inquiry, Canberra: Australian Government Publication Service, 1981.

Campbell Report, *Australian Financial System,* Interim Report of the Committee of Inquiry, Canberra: Australian Government Publication Service, 1980.

Cesarini, Francesco, Monti, Mario & Scognamiglio, Carlo, *Report on the Italian Credit and Financial System,* Special Issue of the *Banca Nazionale del Lavoro Quarterly Review,* Rome, June 1983.

Commissariat Général du Plan, *Quels Intermédiaires Financiers pour Demain,* Annexes 1 et 2 au Rapport de la Commission, La Documentation française, Paris, 1985.

Commissariat Général du Plan, *Quels Intermédiaires Financiers Pour Demain,* La Documentation française, Paris, 1984.

Commissione Nazionale per le Società e la Borsa (CONSOB), *Linee de Progretto per Una Reforma del Mercato Borsistico* ("Blueprint for the Reform of the Securities Markets"), Milan, 1987.

Commission of the European Communities, *Conference on Financial Conglomerates, Proceedings,* Brussels, 1988.

Commission of the European Communities, *Symposium on Europe and the Future of Financial Services, Proceedings,* Brussels, 1986.

Commission of the European Communities, *Completing the Internal Market,* White Paper from the Commission to the European Council, Luxembourg, June 1985.

Commission of the European Communities, *Participation by Banks in Other Branches of the Economy*, Report prepared by Professor Dr. U. Immenga, Studies, Competition — Approximation of Legislation Series No. 25, Brussels, February 1975.

Commission des Opérations de Bourse, *Rapport d'étape du groupe de déontologie des activités financières*, Supplément au *Bulletin Mensuel*, No. 206, August–September 1987.

Committee on Banking Regulations and Supervisory Practices, *International Convergence of Capital Measurement and Capital Standards*, Basle, 1988.

Committee to Review the Functioning of Financial Institutions, *Report, Appendices*, ("Wilson Report"), Cmnd. 7937, London, 1980.

Conseil National du Crédit, *L'Incidence des technologies nouvelles sur l'activité des intermédiaires financiers*, Paris, 1987.

Corrigan, E. Gerald, *Financial Market Structure: A Longer View*, Federal Reserve Bank of New York, New York, 1987.

Corrigan, E. Gerald, "United States Bank Deregulation: The Longer-term Consequences", *The Banker*, pp. 21–27, August 1984.

Crane, Dwight B., Gregor, William T. & Kimball, Ralph T., *The Effects of Banking Deregulation*, Study prepared for the Trustees of the Banking Research Fund, Association of Reserve City Bankers, July 1983.

Credit Market Committee, *The Establishment of Foreign Banks in Sweden*, Stockholm, September 1984.

Davis, K.T. and Lewis, M.K., *Economies of Scale in Financial Institutions*, Technical Paper No. 24, Australian Financial System Inquiry, Economics Department, University of Adelaide, Adelaide, 1981.

Department of Finance, Canada, *The Regulation of Canadian Financial Institutions: Proposals for Discussion* ("Green Paper"), Ottawa, April 1985.

Department of Finance, Canada, Technical Supplement to *The Regulation of Financial Institutions: Proposals for Discussion*, June 1985.

Department of Finance, Canada, Capital Markets Division, *Potential Conflicts of Interest in the Financial System*, Ottawa, February 1984.

Department of the Treasury, *National Treatment Study, Report to Congress on Foreign Government Treatment of United States Commercial Banking and Securities Organisations, 1986 Update*, Washington D.C., 1986.

Department of the Treasury, *Public Policy Aspects of Bank Securities Activities — An Issues Paper*, Washington D.C.: Department of the Treasury, 1975.

Department of the Treasury, *Public Policy for American Capital Markets*, Washington D.C.: Department of the Treasury, 1974.

Department of Trade and Industry, *Financial Services in the United Kingdom — A New Framework for Investors Protection*, London: Her Majesty's Stationery Office, 1985.

Deumer, Robert, "Die Gesetzgebung des Auslandes auf dem Gebiet der Kreditbanken", in *Untersuchungsausschuss für das Bankwesen 1933*, Berlin, 1933.

Dormanns, Albert, "Der Universalbankcharakter der Banken des Auslandes", *Die Bank*, 9/78, pp. 424–431, 1978.

Economic Council of Canada, *A Framework for Financial Regulation*, Canadian Government Publishing Centre, Ottawa, 1987.

Economic Council of Canada, *Reforming Regulation*, Ottawa: Canadian Government Publishing Centre, Supply and Services, 1981.

Economic Council of Canada, *Responsible Regulation, An Interim Report*, Ottawa: Canadian Government Publishing Centre, Supply and Services, 1979.

Economic Council of Canada, *Efficiency and Regulation — A Study on Deposit Institutions*, Ottawa: Printing and Publishing Supply and Services, 1976.

Economic Council of Canada, *Interim Report on Competition Policy*, Ottawa: Queen's Printer, July 1969.

Edwards, Franklin R., *Financial Institutions and Regulation in the 21st Century: After the Crash?*, Paper presented at the Colloquium on Financial Markets: Structure, Conduct, Performance and Regulation, Katholieke Universiteit Leuven, Belgium, 13th September 1979.

Engelkern, Gerhard, "Neuere Tendenzen auf dem Gebiete des Investitionskredits", *Bank–Betrieb*, 2/1970, pp. 46–51, 1970.

Federal Reserve Bank of Atlanta, *Interstate Banking*, Special Issue of *Economic Review*, May 1983.

Federal Reserve Bank of Boston, *Policies for a More Competitive Financial System, A Review of the Hunt Report*, Proceedings of a Conference, Boston, 1972.

Federal Reserve Bank of Chicago, *Bank Structure and Competition*, Proceedings of a Conference, Chicago, Illinois, 1983.

Federal Reserve Bank of Chicago, *Bank Structure and Competition*, Proceedings of a Conference, Chicago, Illinois, 1980.

Federal Reserve Bank of Kansas City, *Restructuring the Financial System*, Kansas City, 1987.

Federal Reserve System, *The Bank Holding Company Movement to 1978: A Compendium*, A Study by the Staff of the Board of Governors of the Federal Reserve System, Washington D.C.: Board of Governors of the Federal Reserve System, 1978.

Federation of Bankers Association of Japan, *Banking System in Japan*, Tokyo: Federation of Bankers Associations of Japan, 1984.

Financial Times Conferences, *Technology in the Securities Markets — The Next Five Years*, London, 1987.

Floitgraf, Hans, "Die deutsche Banken- und Sparkassenkrise 1931", *Bank-Betrieb*, 12/1967, Cologne, 1967.

Frazer, Patrick & Vittas, Dimitri, "Privatkundengeschaft im internationalen Vergleich", *Die Bank*, 3/83, pp. 111–116, 1983.

Frazer, Patrick & Vittas, Dimitri, *The Retail Banking Revolution — An International Perspective*, London: Michael Lafferty Publications, 1982.

Fforde, J.A., "Competition, Innovation and Regulation in British Banking", Bank of England, *Quarterly Bulletin*, September 1983.

Gardener, E.P.M., "Securitisation and the Banking Firm", *Revue de la Banque/Bank- en Financiewezen*, Brussels, January 1987.

Germany, David J. & Morton, John E., "Financial Innovation and Deregulation in Foreign Industrial Countries", *Federal Reserve Bulletin*, pp. 743–753, October 1985.

Ginsburg, Douglas H., Statement before the Committee on Banking, Housing and Urban Affairs, United States Senate, concerning the "Financial Services Competitive Equity Act" and the "Depository Institutions Holding Company Act Amendments of 1984", on 21st March 1984, Washington D.C.: United States Department of Justice.

Goedecke, Wolfgang, "Hypothekenbanken im Vergleich", *Die Bank*, 12/79, pp. 579–587, 1979.

Government of Canada, *White Paper on the Revision of Canadian Banking Legislation*, Canada, 1976.

Gower Report, *Review of Investor Protection*, Report: Part 1 by Gower, L.C.B., London: Her Majesty's Stationery Office, 1984.

Gronn, Audun, "Towards Market-Oriented Monetary and Credit Policy", *Economic Bulletin*, Vol. 56, No. 3, Norges Bank, pp. 220–229, September 1985.

Gurwitz, A.S. and Rappaport, J.N, "Structural Change and Slower Employment Growth in the Financial Services Sector", *Federal Reserve Bank of New York Quarterly Review*, New York, Winter 1984–85.

Hanson, D.G., *Service Banking — The Arrival of the All-Purpose Bank,* Second Edition, London: The Institute of Bankers, 1982.

Heffernan, Shelagh A., *The Impact of Regulatory Changes and New Technology on the Competitive Structure of United Kingdom Financial Markets: Analysis and Methodology,* The City University Business School Centre for the Study of Financial Institutions, Working Paper No. 85, 1987.

Hockin, Thomas, Minister of State for Finance, Canada, *New Directions for the Financial Sector*, Ottawa, December, 1986.

House of Commons, Canada, *Canadian Financial Institutions*, Report of the Standing Committee on Finance, Trade and Economic Affairs, Ottawa, November 1985.

Hunt Report, *The Report of the President's Commission on Financial Structure and Regulation,* Washington D.C.: United States Government Printing Office, 1971.

Interbank Research Organisation, *Banking Systems Abroad — The Role of Large Deposit Banks in the Financial Systems of Germany, France, Italy, the Netherlands, Switzerland, Sweden, Japan and the United States*, London: Interbank Research Organisation, 1978.

International Savings Banks Institute, *The ISBI Guide to Savings Banking*, Geneva: International Savings Banks Institute, 1975.

Institute of Bankers, "The Banks and the Public", Cambridge Seminar, London: The Institute of Bankers, 1981.

Jones, David, "Gearing Up for the Corporate Customer", *Banking World*, pp. 11–14, February 1984.

Kantzenbach, Erhard, *Die Funktionsfaehigkeit des Wettbewerbs*, Wirtschaftspolitische Studien aus dem Institut für Europaeische Wirtschaftspolitik der Universitaet, Hamburg, Göttingen, 1966.

Karsten, Erich, "Grossbanken forcieren den Wettbewerb", *Die Bank*, 10/77, pp. 4–7, 1988.

Kaufmann, George G., Mote, Larry R. & Rosenblum, Harvey, "Consequences of Deregulation for Commercial Banking", *Journal* of Finance, Vol. 39, No. 3, pp. 789–805, July 1984.

Kinoshita, Masatoshi, "Bank Management and Financial Order in the Phase of Liberalisation and Internationalisation of Financial Markets", *Bank of Japan Monetary and Economic Studies*, Vol. 3, No. 2, pp. 31–75, September 1985.

Kleffel, Andreas, "Künftige Wettbewerbsprobleme der Banken", *Bank-Betrieb*, 12/1971, pp. 438–442, 1971.

Klinner, Bernhard, "Zehnjahresvergleich der Ertraege im Kreditgewerbe", *Die Bank*, 6/79, pp. 283–294, 1979.

Knight, J.R., *The Management of Conflicts of Interest in a Multi-Function Securities Market*, The Stock Exchange, London, May 1986.

Llewellyn, David T., "The Changing Structure of the United Kingdom Financial System", *The Three Banks Review*, No. 145, pp. 19–34, March 1985.

Lusser, Markus, *A Central Banker's View on the Role and the Impact of Financial Innovations*, English Translation of a Presentation at the 1985 Forex Conference in Luxembourg, 19th November 1985.

Macmillan Report, *Report by the Macmillan Committee on Finance and Industry*, Cmnd. 3897, London, 1931.

Maier, Gerhard, "USA: Monetaere Innovationen — ihre Ursachen und Konsequenzen für die Geldpolitik", *Die Bank*, 11/81, pp. 544–546, 1981.

Martin Report, *Australian Financial System*, Report of the Review Group, Canberra: Australian Government Publishing Service, 1983.

McIver, Colin & Naylor, Geoffrey, *Marketing Financial Services*, London: The Institute of Bankers, 1980.

Mertin, Klaus, "Wandel in der Ertragsstruktur des Kreditgewerbes", *Die Bank*, 1/80, pp. 7–11, 1980.

Mertin, Klaus, "Ergebnisstrukturen des Kreditgewerbes", *Die Bank*, 2/77, pp. 4–11, 1977.

Métais, Joel, & Szymczak, Philippe, *Les mutations du système français (innovations et déreglementation)*, La Documentation française, Notes et études documentaires, No. 4820, 1986.

Miller, Merton, H., "Financial Innovation: The Last Twenty Years and the Next", in *La Revue Banque/Bank- en Financiewezen*, 7/1986, 1986.

Ministère de l'Economie, des Finances et de la Privatisation, *Les Valeurs du Trésor en 1988*, Paris, 1988.

Ministère de l'Economie, des Finances et du Budget, *Livre Blanc sur la Réforme du Financement de l'Economie*, La Documentation française, Paris, 1986.

Mitchell, Jeremy, *Electronic Banking and the Consumer — The European Dimension*, Policy Studies Institute, London, 1988.

Morgan, J.P. & Co. Incorporated, *Rethinking Glass-Steagall*, New York: J.P. Morgan & Co. Inc., 1984.

Moussu, Auguste, "Les Nouveaux Moyens de Paiement", *Banque*, No. 438, pp. 463–468, April 1984, and *Banque*, No. 439, pp. 564–580, May 1984.

Muehlhaupt, Ludwig & Wielens, Hans, "Zum Streit um die Ausgliederung des Effektengeschaefts aus dem Aufgabenbereich der Universalbank; offprint from Bueschgen, Hans E. (ed.) Geld, Kredit und Kapital, Stuttgart: Peeschel Verlag, 1968.

National Association of Securities Dealers (NASD), *An Introduction to NASD*, Washington D.C., 1985.

National Board for Prices and Incomes, *Bank Charges*, Report No. 34, Cmnd. 3292, London, May 1967.

New Zealand Bankers' Association, *Electronic Fund Transfer at Point of Sale — A Summary of the New Zealand Trading Banks' EFT-POS System*, Wellington, New Zealand: New Zealand Bankers' Association, 1985.

Nomura Research Institute, *The World Economic and Financial Markets in 1995 — Japan's Role and Challenges*, Kanagawa, Japan, 1986.

Organisation for Economic Co-operation and Development, "Arrangements for the Regulation and Supervision of Securities Markets", in *Financial Market Trends*, No. 41, Paris, November 1988.

Organisation for Economic Co-operation and Development, *Bank Profitability — Financial Statements of Banks, Statistical Supplement, 1982-86*, Paris, 1988.

Organisation for Economic Co-operation and Development, Pecchioli, R.M., *Prudential Supervision in Banking*, Paris, 1987.

Organisation for Economic Co-operation and Development, Harrington, R., *Asset and Liability Management in Banking*, Paris, 1987.

Organisation for Economic Co-operation and Development, *International Trade in Services: Securities*, Paris, 1987.

Organisation for Economic Co-operation and Development, "Bank Profitability 1980-85: Recent Trends and Structural Features", in

Financial Market Trends, No. 38, Paris, November 1987.

Organisation for Economic Co-operation and Development, *Bank Profitability — Financial Statements of Banks with Methodological Country Notes, 1980–84*, Paris, 1987.

Organisation for Economic Co-operation and Development, *Trends in Banking in OECD Countries*, Paris, 1985.

Organisation for Economic Co-operation and Development, Bingham, T.R.G., *Banking and Monetary Policy*, Paris, 1985.

Organisation for Economic Co-operation and Development, *International Trade in Services: Banking*, Paris, 1984.

Organisation for Economic Co-operation and Development, Revell, J.R.S., *Banking and Electronic Fund Transfers*, Paris, 1983.

Organisation for Economic Co-operation and Development, Pecchioli, R.M., *The Internationalisation of Banking*, Paris, 1983.

Organisation for Economic Co-operation and Development, *Government Debt Management, Volume I: Objectives and Techniques; Volume II: Instruments and Selling Techniques*, Paris, 1983.

Organisation for Economic Co-operation and Development, *Annual Reports on Competition Policy in OECD Member Countries*, 1982/No. 2 — 1983/No. 1, Paris, 1983.

Organisation for Economic Co-operation and Development, *Competition Policy in Regulated Sectors*, Report of the Committee of Experts on Restrictive Business Practices, Paris, 1979.

Organisation for Economic Co-operation and Development, Revell, J.R.S., *Flexibility in Housing Finance*, Paris, 1975.

Organisation for Economic Co-operation and Development, *Housing Finance — Present Problems*, Paris, 1974.

Ortner, Reinhart, "Wettbewerb und Synergien zwischen Banken und Versicherungen", in *Die Bank*, 5/87, Cologne, 1987.

Padoa-Schioppa, T., "The Blurring of Financial Frontiers: In Search of an Order", in Commission of European Communities, *Conference on Financial Conglomerates, Proceedings*, Brussels, 14th–15th March 1988.

Paersch, Fritz, "Massnahmen des Staates hinsichtlich einer Beaufsichtigung und Reglementierung des Bankwesens", in *Untersuchungsausschuss für das Bankwesen 1933*, Berlin, 1933.

Page Report, *Report of the Committee to Review National Savings*, London: Her Majesty's Stationery Office, Cmnd. 5273, 1973.

Pastré, Olivier, *La modernisation des banques françaises*, Rapport au Ministre de l'Economie, des Finances et du Budget, La Documentation française, November 1985.

Phillips, Almarin, "Competitive Policy for Depository Financial Institutions", in Phillips, Almarin (ed.), *Promoting Competition in Regulated Markets*, pp. 329–367, Washington D.C.: Brookings Institution, 1975.

Pöhl, Karl Otto, "Finanzinnovationen — Ein Handikap für die Geldpolitik, Börsenzeitung", Frankfurt am Main, 12th October 1985.

Pohl, Manfred, *Entstehung und Entwicklung des Universalbankensystems. Konzentration und Krise als wichtige Faktoren*, Schriftenreihe des Instituts für Bankhistorische Forschung e. V., Band 7, Frankfurt am Main, 1986.

Porter Commission, *Report of the Royal Commission on Banking and Finance*, Ottawa: Queen's Printer, 1964.

Porter, Michael E., *Competitive Strategy Techniques for Analysing Industries and Competitors*, New York: The Free Press, 1980.

Prechtl, Manfred, "Beobachtungen zum Firmengeschaft", *Die Bank*, 11/84, pp. 508–511, 1984.

Price Commission, *Banks: Charges of Money Transmission Services*, No. 377, London, 1978.

Pünder, Barthel, *Analyse des nationalen und internationalen Wettbewerb der Banken in der Bundesrepublik Deutschland*, Diplomarbeit, Hochschule St. Gallen für Wirtschafts- und Sozialwissenschaften, 1985.

Rapport-de Voghel, *Rapport de la Commission gouvernementale pour l'Etude de Propositions de Réforme des Lois relatives à la Banque et à l'Epargne*, Brussels: Banque Nationale de Belgique, 1970.

Remsperger, Hermann, "Finanzdienstleistungen: Kontrollierte Freiheit", in *Der Langfristige Kredit*, Heft 2, 1987.

Remsperger, Hermann, "Geldpolitik und Bankenwettbewerb", *Die Bank*, No. 12/1984, Cologne, 1984.

Remsperger, Hermann, "Geldmengen- und Zinssteuerung: Bankeninteressen und Verhalten", *Die Bank*, 1/83, pp. 4–9, 1983.

Report of the Presidential Task Force on Market Mechanisms, ("Brady Report"), Washington D.C., 1988.

Reserve Bank of New Zealand, "Monetary Policy in New Zealand", in *Reserve Bank Bulletin*, June 1985, Wellington, New Zealand.

Revell, Jack, "International Comparisons of Bank Costs and Profits", *The Banker*, pp. 25–29, January 1985.

Revell, Jack, *The Complementary Nature of Competition and Regulation in the Financial Sector,* Paper presented to the Coloquium on Financial Markets; Structure, Conduct and Performance, Katholieke Universiteit Leuven, Belgium, 13th September 1979.

Revell, Jack, "Competition and Regulation of Banks", in: Revell, Jack (ed.), *Competition and Regulation of Banks*, Bangor Occasional Papers in Economics, No. 14, Bangor: University of Wales Press, 1978.

Ryder, B., Chaikin, D., Abrams, Ch., *Guide to the Financial Services Act 1986*, Bicester, Oxfordshire, United Kingdom, 1987.

Schlesinger, Helmut, *Kapitalmarkt, Kapitalbildung und Kapitalallokation,* Vortrag auf der Jahrestagung 1986 der Gesellschaft für Wirtschafts- und Sozialwissenschaften — Verein für Socialpolitik, Munich, 15th September 1986.

Schneider, Manfred, "Der Wettbewerb der Kreditinstitute in Spannungsfeld von Bankenaufsicht und Notenbankpolitik", *Bank-Betrieb*, 4/1973, pp. 122–126, 1973.

Schroeder-Hohenwarth, Hanns C., "Zur Problematik insolvenzgefaehrdeter Kredit-institute", *Die Bank*, No. 5/84, Cologne, 1984.

Securities and Exchange Commission, *The Effect of the Absence of Fixed Rates of Commissions*, Fifth Report to Congress, Washington D.C., 1977.

Senate of Canada, *Towards a More Competitive Financial Environment*, Sixteenth Report, Standing Senate Committee on Banking, Trade and Commerce, Ottawa, May 1986.

Stein, Jürgen, "Beeintraechtigen Konzentrations-tendenzen den Bankenwettbewerb?", *Die Bank*, 2/77, pp. 13–15, 1977.

Stützel, Wolfgang, *Bankpolitik heute und morgen*, Frankfurt am Main, 1964.

Suzuki, Yoshio, "A Comparative Study of Financial Innovation, Deregulation and Reform in Japan and the United States", in *Bank of Japan Monetary and Economic Studies*, Vol. 4, No. 2, October 1986.

The Administrator of National Banks, United States Treasury, *Studies in Banking Competition and The Banking Structure*, articles reprinted in *The National Banking Review*, Washington D.C., 1966.

The Institute of Bankers, *The Banks and their Competitors*, Cambridge Seminar 1980, London, 1980.

Tobin, James, "Financial Innovation and Deregulation in Perspective" *Bank of Japan Monetary and Economic Studies*, Vol. 3, No. 2, pp. 19–30, September 1985.

Tobin, James, "On the Efficiency of the Financial System", *Lloyds Bank Review*, No. 153, pp. 1–15, July 1984.

Troberg, Peter, *The Regulation of Credit Institutions — Recent Developments in the United States Compared with Possible Evolutions in the European Community*, Washington D.C., July 1982.

US Congress, House, *Restructuring Financial Markets: The Major Policy Issues,* A Report from the Chairman of the Sub-committee on Telecommunications, Consumer Protection, and Finance of the Committee on Energy and Commerce, Washington D.C., July 1986.

US Department of the Treasury, *Public Policy Aspects of Bank Securities Activities*, An Issues Paper, Washington, November 1975.

Untersuchungsausschuss für das Bankwesen 1933, contributions by several authors, Berlin, 1983.

Van Hoven, Eckart, "20 Jahre persönlicher Kredit", *Die Bank*, 5/79, pp. 202–213, 1979.

Vittas, Dimitri, "Bank's Relations with Industry (An International Survey)", *National Westminster Bank Quarterly Review*, pp. 2–14, February 1986.

Weiss, Ulrich, "Sparmarketing in der Inflation — 1. Teil", *Bank-Betrieb*, 12/1974, Köln; "Sparmarketing in der Inflation — 2. Teil", *Bank-Betrieb*, 1/1975, Cologne, 1974.

Wielens, Hans, *Fragen der Bankorganisation — Führt die verstaerkte Marktorganisation der Universalbanken zur Divisionalisierung?,* Frankfurt am Main: Fritz Knapp Verlag, 1977.

Wilson Report, *Report and Appendices to the Report of the Committee to Review the Functioning of Financial Institutions,* London: Her Majesty's Stationery Office, Cmnd. 7937, 1980.

Zavvos, Giorgios, "EC Strategy for the Banking Sector: The Perspective of 1992", *European Affairs*, No. 1/88, Elsevier, 1988.

WHERE TO OBTAIN OECD PUBLICATIONS
OÙ OBTENIR LES PUBLICATIONS DE L'OCDE

ARGENTINA - ARGENTINE
Carlos Hirsch S.R.L.,
Florida 165, 4º Piso,
(Galeria Guemes) 1333 Buenos Aires
Tel. 33.1787.2391 y 30.7122

AUSTRALIA - AUSTRALIE
D.A. Book (Aust.) Pty. Ltd.
11-13 Station Street (P.O. Box 163)
Mitcham, Vic. 3132   Tel. (03) 873 4411

AUSTRIA - AUTRICHE
OECD Publications and Information Centre,
4 Simrockstrasse,
5300 Bonn (Germany)   Tel. (0228) 21.60.45
Gerold & Co., Graben 31, Wien 1 Tel. 52.22.35

BELGIUM - BELGIQUE
Jean de Lannoy,
Avenue du Roi 202
B-1060 Bruxelles   Tel. (02) 538.51.69

CANADA
Renouf Publishing Company Ltd
1294 Algoma Road, Ottawa, Ont. K1B 3W8
Tel: (613) 741-4333
Stores:
61 rue Sparks St., Ottawa, Ont. K1P 5R1
Tel: (613) 238-8985
211 rue Yonge St., Toronto, Ont. M5B 1M4
Tel: (416) 363-3171
Federal Publications Inc.,
301-303 King St. W.,
Toronto, Ont. M5V 1J5   Tel. (416)581-1552
Les Éditions la Liberté inc.,
3020 Chemin Sainte-Foy,
Sainte-Foy, P.Q. GIX 3V6,   Tel. (418)658-3763

DENMARK - DANEMARK
Munksgaard Export and Subscription Service
35, Nørre Søgade, DK-1370 København K
Tel. +45.1.12.85.70

FINLAND - FINLANDE
Akateeminen Kirjakauppa,
Keskuskatu 1, 00100 Helsinki 10   Tel. 0.12141

FRANCE
OCDE/OECD
Mail Orders/Commandes par correspondance :
2, rue André-Pascal,
75775 Paris Cedex 16   Tel. (1) 45.24.82.00
Bookshop/Librairie : 33, rue Octave-Feuillet
75016 Paris
Tel. (1) 45.24.81.67 or/ou (1) 45.24.81.81
Librairie de l'Université,
12a, rue Nazareth,
13602 Aix-en-Provence   Tel. 42.26.18.08

GERMANY - ALLEMAGNE
OECD Publications and Information Centre,
4 Simrockstrasse,
5300 Bonn   Tel. (0228) 21.60.45

GREECE - GRÈCE
Librairie Kauffmann,
28, rue du Stade, 105 64 Athens Tel. 322.21.60

HONG KONG
Government Information Services,
Publications (Sales) Office,
Information Services Department
No. 1, Battery Path, Central

ICELAND - ISLANDE
Snæbjörn Jónsson & Co., h.f.,
Hafnarstræti 4 & 9,
P.O.B. 1131 – Reykjavik
Tel. 13133/14281/11936

INDIA - INDE
Oxford Book and Stationery Co.,
Scindia House, New Delhi 110001
Tel. 331.5896/5308
17 Park St., Calcutta 700016   Tel. 240832

INDONESIA - INDONÉSIE
Pdii-Lipi, P.O. Box 3065/JKT.Jakarta
Tel. 583467

IRELAND - IRLANDE
TDC Publishers - Library Suppliers,
12 North Frederick Street, Dublin 1
Tel. 744835-749677

ITALY - ITALIE
Libreria Commissionaria Sansoni,
Via Benedetto Fortini 120/10,
Casella Post. 552
50125 Firenze   Tel. 055/645415
Via Bartolini 29, 20155 Milano   Tel. 365083
La diffusione delle pubblicazioni OCSE viene
assicurata dalle principali librerie ed anche da :
Editrice e Libreria Herder,
Piazza Montecitorio 120, 00186 Roma
Tel. 6794628
Libreria Hœpli,
Via Hœpli 5, 20121 Milano   Tel. 865446
Libreria Scientifica
Dott. Lucio de Biasio "Aeiou"
Via Meravigli 16, 20123 Milano   Tel. 807679

JAPAN - JAPON
OECD Publications and Information Centre,
Landic Akasaka Bldg., 2-3-4 Akasaka,
Minato-ku, Tokyo 107   Tel. 586.2016

KOREA - CORÉE
Kyobo Book Centre Co. Ltd.
P.O.Box: Kwang Hwa Moon 1658,
Seoul   Tel. (REP) 730.78.91

LEBANON - LIBAN
Documenta Scientifica/Redico,
Edison Building, Bliss St.,
P.O.B. 5641, Beirut   Tel. 354429-344425

MALAYSIA/SINGAPORE -
MALAISIE/SINGAPOUR
University of Malaya Co-operative Bookshop
Ltd.,
7 Lrg 51A/227A, Petaling Jaya
Malaysia   Tel. 7565000/7565425
Information Publications Pte Ltd
Pei-Fu Industrial Building,
24 New Industrial Road No. 02-06
Singapore 1953   Tel. 2831786, 2831798

NETHERLANDS - PAYS-BAS
SDU Uitgeverij
Christoffel Plantijnstraat 2
Postbus 20014
2500 EA's-Gravenhage   Tel. 070-789911
Voor bestellingen: Tel. 070-789880

NEW ZEALAND - NOUVELLE-ZÉLANDE
Government Printing Office Bookshops:
Auckland: Retail Bookshop, 25 Rutland Stseet,
Mail Orders, 85 Beach Road
Private Bag C.P.O.
Hamilton: Retail: Ward Street,
Mail Orders, P.O. Box 857
Wellington: Retail, Mulgrave Street, (Head
Office)
Cubacade World Trade Centre,
Mail Orders, Private Bag
Christchurch: Retail, 159 Hereford Street,
Mail Orders, Private Bag
Dunedin: Retail, Princes Street,
Mail Orders, P.O. Box 1104

NORWAY - NORVÈGE
Narvesen Info Center – NIC,
Bertrand Narvesens vei 2,
P.O.B. 6125 Etterstad, 0602 Oslo 6
Tel. (02) 67.83.10, (02) 68.40.20

PAKISTAN
Mirza Book Agency
65 Shahrah Quaid-E-Azam, Lahore 3 Tel. 66839

PHILIPPINES
I.J. Sagun Enterprises, Inc.
P.O. Box 4322 CPO Manila
Tel. 695-1946, 922-9495

PORTUGAL
Livraria Portugal, Rua do Carmo 70-74,
1117 Lisboa Codex   Tel. 360582/3

SINGAPORE/MALAYSIA -
SINGAPOUR/MALAISIE
See "Malaysia/Singapor". Voir
«Malaisie/Singapour»

SPAIN - ESPAGNE
Mundi-Prensa Libros, S.A.,
Castelló 37, Apartado 1223, Madrid-28001
Tel. 431.33.99
Libreria Bosch, Ronda Universidad 11,
Barcelona 7   Tel. 317.53.08/317.53.58

SWEDEN - SUÈDE
AB CE Fritzes Kungl. Hovbokhandel,
Box 16356, S 103 27 STH,
Regeringsgatan 12,
DS Stockholm   Tel. (08) 23.89.00
Subscription Agency/Abonnements:
Wennergren-Williams AB,
Box 30004, S104 25 Stockholm Tel. (08)54.12.00

SWITZERLAND - SUISSE
OECD Publications and Information Centre,
4 Simrockstrasse,
5300 Bonn (Germany)   Tel. (0228) 21.60.45
Librairie Payot,
6 rue Grenus, 1211 Genève 11
Tel. (022) 31.89.50
Maditec S.A.
Ch. des Palettes 4
1020 – Renens/Lausanne   Tel. (021) 635.08.65
United Nations Bookshop/Librairie des Nations-
Unies
Palais des Nations, 1211 – Geneva 10
Tel. 022-34-60-11 (ext. 48 72)

TAIWAN - FORMOSE
Good Faith Worldwide Int'l Co., Ltd.
9th floor, No. 118, Sec.2, Chung Hsiao E. Road
Taipei   Tel. 391.7396/391.7397

THAILAND - THAILANDE
Suksit Siam Co., Ltd., 1715 Rama IV Rd.,
Samyam Bangkok 5   Tel. 2511630
INDEX Book Promotion & Service Ltd.
59/6 Soi Lang Suan, Ploenchit Road
Patjumamwan, Bangkok 10500
Tel. 250-1919, 252-1066

TURKEY - TURQUIE
Kültur Yayinlari Is-Türk Ltd. Sti.
Atatürk Bulvari No: 191/Kat. 21
Kavaklidere/Ankara   Tel. 25.07.60
Dolmabahce Cad. No: 29
Besiktas/Istanbul   Tel. 160.71.88

UNITED KINGDOM - ROYAUME-UNI
H.M. Stationery Office,
Postal orders only: (01)873-8483
P.O.B. 276, London SW8 5DT
Telephone orders: (01) 873-9090, or
Personal callers:
49 High Holborn, London WC1V 6HB
Branches at: Belfast, Birmingham,
Bristol, Edinburgh, Manchester

UNITED STATES - ÉTATS-UNIS
OECD Publications and Information Centre,
2001 L Street, N.W., Suite 700,
Washington, D.C. 20036 - 4095
Tel. (202) 785.6323

VENEZUELA
Libreria del Este,
Avda F. Miranda 52, Aptdo. 60337,
Edificio Galipan, Caracas 106
Tel. 951.17.05/951.23.07/951.12.97

YUGOSLAVIA - YOUGOSLAVIE
Jugoslovenska Knjiga, Knez Mihajlova 2,
P.O.B. 36, Beograd   Tel. 621.992

Orders and inquiries from countries where
Distributors have not yet been appointed should be
sent to:
OECD, Publications Service, 2, rue André-Pascal,
75775 PARIS CEDEX 16.

Les commandes provenant de pays où l'OCDE n'a
pas encore désigné de distributeur doivent être
adressées à :
OCDE, Service des Publications. 2, rue André-
Pascal, 75775 PARIS CEDEX 16.

72380-1-1989

OECD PUBLICATIONS, 2, rue André-Pascal, 75775 PARIS CEDEX 16 - No. 44607 1989
PRINTED IN FRANCE
(21 89 01 1) ISBN 92-64-13197-3